THE
Enjoyment of
MUSIC

Picasso, *Three Musicians*.

SHORTER EDITION

THE
Enjoyment of
MUSIC

AN INTRODUCTION
TO PERCEPTIVE LISTENING

By JOSEPH MACHLIS

Associate Professor of Music, Queens College of the City of New York

W · W · NORTON & COMPANY · INC · New York

FOR

EARLE FENTON PALMER

Library of Congress Catalog Card No.: 57-6038

PRINTED IN THE UNITED STATES OF AMERICA
FOR THE PUBLISHERS BY THE VAIL-BALLOU PRESS

CONTENTS

PART TWO

NINETEENTH-CENTURY ROMANTICISM

SONG AND PIANO PIECE

PROGRAM MUSIC

SYMPHONY AND CONCERTO

OPERA

Part Three   MORE MATERIALS OF MUSIC

Part Four   EIGHTEENTH-CENTURY CLASSICISM

Contents

PART FIVE   THE OLDER MUSIC

PART SIX   THE TWENTIETH CENTURY

PART SEVEN   THE AMERICAN SCENE

Contents

PREFACE

THIS SHORTER VERSION of *The Enjoyment of Music* aims to retain the basic principles incorporated in the original edition—the presentation of an introductory course which will arouse the student's interest in music and teach him to respond intelligently to the great works which constitute our musical heritage.

As in the original edition, care has been taken to explain, in terms understandable to the layman, how music is put together; the art is presented against its social background, as part of the history of culture, and in relation to parallel developments in the sister arts; the great composers have been considered both as artists and men; forms and styles have been analyzed; and this combination of knowledge has been applied to an understanding of characteristic works. By beginning with pieces either familiar to the student or easily accessible to him, we have striven to build up his confidence in his ability to enjoy music; and by proceeding gradually from the simplest level to the more advanced, to expand his horizons and develop his taste.

By compressing the treatment of certain areas, such as the music of the pre-Bach era, and cutting down on the space allotted to certain figures, it has been possible to design this shorter version so that it will serve a course which is more limited in time and scope than that envisaged for the original. However, this version follows completely the methodology and approach of the longer book. Also, care has been taken to retain at full strength many useful features of the original: the biographical and analysis sections, the general discussions of each period and style, the rather detailed treatment of twentieth century music, and the appendices.

This book, like its predecessor, has grown out of the introductory course in music at Queens College of the City of New York. As the project in music appreciation at Queens College embraces a thousand students a year, those of us who are engaged in this work have as extensive a laboratory as could be desired in which to test both our

xiii

theory and our practice. It has, consequently, been possible to shape the material so as to adapt it to the exigencies of different teaching situations, and to develop this text for those music courses which might find the original text too extensive in scope.

This edition, like the original, covers a wider field than the course for which it is designed; it thus allows for supplementary reading and assignments to encourage those students who may wish to pursue their curiosity beyond the material covered in class, and will also guide the further growth of the student after the course is over. Throughout, the main goal has never been lost sight of—to teach the *enjoyment of music*, and in this way to create music lovers.

J. M.

PART ONE

The Materials of Music

❧

"There are only twelve tones. You must treat them carefully."
Paul Hindemith

ᚼ1ᚼ

By Way of Introduction

"What is art? Nature concentrated."
Balzac

WHEREVER men have lived together, art has sprung up among them as a language charged with feeling and significance. The desire to create this language appears to be universal. It shows itself in primitive societies as in our own. It has become a very part of man's need to impose his will upon the universe; to bring order out of chaos; to endow his moments of highest awareness with enduring form and substance.

Art, like love, is easier to experience than define. It would be not easy to find two philosophers who agree on a definition. We may say that art concerns itself with the communication of certain ideas and feelings by means of a sensuous medium—color, sound, bronze, marble, words. This medium is fashioned into a symbolic language marked by beauty of design and coherence of form. It appeals to our mind, arouses our emotions, kindles our imagination, enchants our senses.

A work of art embodies a view of life. It brings us the artist's personal interpretation of human destiny, the essence of his experience both as artist and man. In order to comprehend the work we must enter the secret world out of which it sprang. The greater our understanding, the more complete our possession of the art work; and the better we capture the joy, the illumination that went into its making. In so doing we are carried to heights of awareness, to intensities of experience of which we had hardly thought ourselves capable.

The function of literature, André Malraux has said, is to reveal to man his hidden greatness. The work of art begins by opening to us the landscape of its creator's inner life. It ends by revealing us to ourselves.

THE MEANING OF MUSIC

Music has been called the language of the emotions. This is a not unreasonable metaphor; for music, like language, aims to communicate meaning. But it is a different kind of language. Words are concrete; tone is fluid and intangible. A word taken by itself has a fixed mean-

3

ing; a tone assumes meaning only from its association with other tones. Words convey specific ideas; music suggests elusive states of mind.

Because of this elusiveness music has been subject to a constant attempt to translate its message into words. Writers of a former generation regaled their readers with personal interpretations of musical works. James Huneker saw in Chopin's G-minor Ballade "the slender-hipped girl with the eyes of midnight," while Romain Rolland heard in the first movement of Beethoven's *Appassionata* "a veritable ride to the abyss punctuated with laments." Serious musicians today reject such attempts to chain their art to concrete images. Such images destroy what is the unique glory of music: its freedom from literary— that is, from specific—meaning.

Suppose we say of Schubert's *Moment Musical* that it is graceful, tender, expressive. Will this convey the remotest conception of the music to one who never heard it? The meaning of the piece cannot be translated into words. Precisely this constitutes its nature as music. We are able to define a word through other words. But we are not able to define a melody. It means—itself! Beyond that it will mean something different to each listener.

Even if we reject the possibility of translating the meaning of music into words, there still remains much for us to talk about. It will heighten our perception if we know something about the elements of which music is composed, and the way that composers go about organizing tones into patterns and forms. We may inquire into the forces that have shaped musical activity at various periods, the schools and movements within the art and their relationship to the social-cultural environment. We should have some knowledge of the men whose genius enriched the lives of their fellows, of their style, and of their contribution to the art. This information by no means constitutes the meaning of a musical work, but it will help each one of us to fathom that meaning for himself.

There is only one way to learn to listen to music and that is—to listen, continually and intensively. It will help to focus our listening if we read and talk about music; but this is no more than a preliminary. The true meaning, the ultimate wisdom, is to be found in one place only: the sounds themselves.

THE ENJOYMENT OF MUSIC

People differ greatly in their way of responding to music. During the playing, shall we say, of the Triumphal March from *Aïda*, one listener will summon up a vision of ancient tombs and Pharaohs. Another floats off in a daydream equally far removed from the music and the world. A third is filled with a strange sense of power at the ringing tone of the trumpets. His neighbor for no apparent reason recollects some trivial occurrence in everyday life. This one is pleased with himself for having noticed the reappearance of Theme A. That one has decided the conductor is a shoemaker and wonders how he ever man-

Van Loo, *The Concert.*
"People differ greatly in their way of responding to music."

aged to get an orchestra. The musicologist reflects upon the contribution of Verdi to grand-opera style. The critic polishes a phrase for his next review. The budding composer is oppressed by a suspicion that he was born too late.

Ways of listening to music used to be classified as being on the sensual, the emotional, or the intellectual level. Today it is recognized that such categories are extremely fluid. We listen differently to different kinds of music and we hear the same piece differently on different occasions. In art as in life the physical, emotional, and intellectual elements are too closely interwoven for us to be able to draw rigid boundaries between them. As newcomers to music we fall into the way of listening that comes natural to us. With practice and experience we learn other ways. The goal of our training in the art of listening must be to unite all three levels, so that we will apprehend the floating patterns of sound with all the joy of our senses, the freshness of our emotions, and the power of our understanding.

"To understand," said Raphael, "is to equal." When we completely understand a great work of music we grasp the "moment of truth" that gave it birth. For the nonce we become, if not the equal of the master who created it, at least worthy to sit in his company. We receive his message, we fathom his intention. In effect, we listen perceptively; and that is the one sure road to the enjoyment of music.

≫2≪

Music and Life: the Sources of Musical Imagery

"Art is a human activity having for its purpose the transmission to others of the highest and best feelings to which man has risen."
Tolstoi

THE BEGINNINGS of music are shrouded in pre-history. However, a number of theories have been advanced to explain its origin. One derives music from the inflections of speech, another from mating calls, a third from the cries of battle and signals of the hunt, a fourth from the rhythms of collective labor. Some attribute the rise of music to the imitation of nature, others connect it with the play impulse, with magic and religious rites, or with the need for emotional expression. These explanations have one factor in common: they relate music to the profoundest experiences of the individual and the group. Underlying all is the fact that man possesses in his vocal cords a means of producing song, in his body an instrument for rhythm, and in his mind the capacity to think and perceive musical sounds.

Life in primitive society is saturated with emotion. Speech and body movement alike are intensely expressive. Speech heightened by musical inflection becomes song. Body movement heightened by musical gesture becomes dance. Song is melody, dance is rhythm. Melody and rhythm are the primal sources of music. They are imbued with the imagery of life: love, courtship, and marriage; sowing and reaping; hunting and war—each has its songs and dances, as have the rites of fertility, the exorcism of evil spirits, the burial of the dead.

The art of music has come a long way from its primitive stage; but it has retained its connection with the springs of human feeling, with the accents of joy and sorrow, tension and release. In this sense we may speak of music as a universal language, one that transcends the barriers men put up against each other. Its vocabulary has been shaped by thousands of years of human experience; its rhetoric mirrors man's existence, his place in nature and in society.

SONG

Song is the most natural form of music. Issuing from within the body, it is projected by means of the most personal of all instruments, the human voice. From time immemorial, singing has been the most widespread and spontaneous way of making music.

We have in folk music a treasury of song that reflects all phases of life—work songs, love songs, drinking songs, cradle songs, patriotic songs, dance songs, songs of mourning, marching songs, play songs, narrative songs. Some are centuries old, others are of recent vintage. A folk song originates with an individual, perhaps on the spur of the moment. It is taken up by others, a detail is changed, a stanza added, another version created, and in the course of its wanderings it becomes the collective expression of a group.

One has but to listen to a love song like *Greensleeves* or *Black is the Color of My True Love's Hair* to realize how compellingly a melody may capture the accent of tenderness and longing. Songs such as *Water Boy*, which sprang up among prisoners on the chain gang, or *Lord Randall*, with its theme of betrayal, are surcharged with emotion. Treating of basic human experience, they are understood everywhere. At the same time they are rooted in the speech rhythms, the soil, and the life of a particular place; which is why they possess the raciness and vivid local color that are among the prime attributes of folk song.

The same directness of expression is found on a more sophisticated level in the art song. Here the sentiment is more special, more sharply focused. Text and music are of known authorship, and bear the imprint of a personality. Whereas folk song reflects the pattern of life in rural areas, the art song issues from the culture of cities. Like the folk song, however, its musical content is shaped by human experience and

Della Robbia, *Singing Boys* (*Relief for the Cantoria*).
"Song is the most natural form of music."

has a universal quality. Schubert's *Serenade* has become the archetype of the love song, Brahms' *Lullaby* of the cradle song, Schumann's *Two Grenadiers* of the martial ballad. Such songs carry meaning for the mass of music lovers. They exemplify the power of music to set forth the imagery of life.

Song, however, is not limited to vocal music. There is a large category of instrumental pieces that are in a real sense "songs without words," as Mendelssohn understood when he gave that title to his popular piano miniatures. This melodious type is familiar in the short piano pieces of Schubert, Chopin, and Schumann. More ambitious in scope is the "song" for orchestra, which is best known from the slow movements of various symphonies, where the composer embodies the lyric impulse in an extended movement. In any case, the spirit of song permeates all music, whether vocal or instrumental. It remains the vital link between tone art and man's emotional life.

THE DANCE

Dance springs from man's joy in his body, his love of expressive gesture, his release of tension through rhythmic movement. It heightens the pleasure of being, and at the same time mirrors the life of society. The dance of the countryside is different from the city dance; both, throughout the ages, were set off from the court dance. Folk, popular, and court dances nourished centuries of European art music.

A dance piece may be intended for actual use in the ballroom, like the dance-songs of our commercial popular music. Such was the case with the waltzes of Johann Strauss, who brought to its height the most popular city dance of the nineteenth century. Or a dance rhythm may serve as the basis for an abstract composition. This type of piece evokes images of body movement. In this category is a whole group of dance pieces that retain their popularity with the public, such as the gavottes of Bach, the minuets of Mozart, the country dances of Beethoven, and the waltzes and mazurkas of Chopin. That the twentieth century has retained a fondness for compositions based on dance patterns is evidenced by such works as the Rumanian Dances of Bartók, the *Pavane for a Dead Princess* of Ravel, and the *Circus Polka* of Stravinsky.

Like the song, the dance permeates the abstract forms of orchestral music. The courtly minuet was taken over into the eighteenth-century symphony, retaining its refinement and grace. Also included in the symphony was the more earthy rondo, a dance movement marked by vivacity and charm. Both types figure prominently in the symphonies of Haydn and Mozart, where they take on the formal beauty of the classical style. In these movements the imagery of body movement is sublimated into a pure and serene instrumental music. Certain dance pieces exude a peasant gusto, others idealize the spirit of the dance, but

Primitive drawing of tribal dancers.
"Dance springs from man's joy in his body."

all testify to the persuasive power of rhythm. For it is through rhythm that music mirrors the patterns of man's activity in the physical world.

OTHER SOURCES OF MUSICAL IMAGES

The march, which is related to the dance, descends from the ceremonial processions of tribal life. Its music is associated with trumpets and drums, with the pageantry of great occasions, religious, military, or patriotic. Whether it be the quick march made popular by Sousa, or a grand processional such as the Triumphal March from Verdi's *Aïda* which is played when the conquering hero Radames is welcomed home, this type of music is imbued with the imagery of human experience.

March rhythm may serve too as the basis for an abstract piece that is not intended actually to be marched to. Characteristic is the *Marche Militaire* of Schubert, which tempers the military mood with lyricism; or the Polonaises of Chopin, which recreate the proud processional dance in which the nobles of Poland paid homage to their king. The march creates an atmosphere of pomp and ceremony. Like the dance, it unites appealing melody and decisive rhythm. Like the dance, too, the march captures for music something of the movement and gesture of man's activity in space and time.

The religious impulse has motivated a considerable amount of the world's great music. Most works in this category were composed expressly for use in the church service, others are concert pieces on sacred themes. In either case they hold an expressive content that it is particularly within the domain of music to achieve: the aura of spirituality that surrounds the masses of Palestrina, or the quality of sublimity that we associate with the religious works of Bach and Handel.

The religious spirit animates various kinds of music. In the sphere of popular song there are the Lutheran chorales, those sturdy congregational hymns that nurtured centuries of German music. In America we have produced a rich store of religious folk song in the spirituals, Negro and white. Melodies such as *Go Down, Moses* or *Deep River* are as indestructible as any to be found in the domain of folk art. Both the art song and opera have reflected religious themes; one has but to mention such popular examples of the religious mood as Schubert's *Ave Maria* or the Prelude to Wagner's *Lohengrin,* with its evocation of the Holy Grail. On a more abstract level the religious impulse found expression in many a symphonic movement of the nineteenth century where—especially in the works of the German romantic composers—it was often associated with the worship of nature.

The opera forms another potent link between life and music. Its theme is man, his passions, his conflicts, his actions. Through opera, composers learned to transform into musical images the most varied sentiments and situations. In this way music was encouraged to draw its substance directly from the drama of human existence.

The source of musical imagery, then, is life itself, whether in song or dance, in religious or dramatic music, in the love song, the lullaby, or the warriors' chorus. Nor do composers forget these images when they turn to abstract works such as symphonies and concertos. In these examples of "pure" or absolute music there are still present the impulses of song and dance, of triumph and lamentation, of drama and religious faith—but in sublimated form, lifted from the specific to the abstract, from the particular to the universal. Therefrom springs the dual nature of music. On the one hand it is an art of expressive content rooted in human experience; on the other it is an art of abstraction following purely musical laws and procedures.

This fascinating dualism causes endless argument concerning the nature of music. At one extreme are those who look for a specific meaning, a "story," in every piece of music they hear. At the other are those who deny all connection between music and reality, proclaiming the art to be a self-contained experience whose purity is violated as soon as it is related to anything outside itself. Each of these factions represents half the truth. Music is related to human experience and it has expressive content, otherwise it could not have functioned for thousands of years as a spiritual force in the lives of men. At the same time it presents the stuff of life on a high level of abstraction, purified, lifted from bondage to word meanings, picture meanings, story meanings: an art that obeys purely musical impulses and is truly a song without words. Else it would not be music.

❧ 3 ❦

Melody: Musical Line

> "It is the melody which is the charm of music, and it is that which is most difficult to produce. The invention of a fine melody is a work of genius."
>
> Joseph Haydn

MELODY is that element of music which makes the widest and most direct appeal. It is called the soul of music. It is generally what we remember and whistle and hum. The world has always lavished a special affection upon the creators of melody; nothing is more intimately associated with inspiration, not only in the popular mind but also among musicians, as the quotation from Haydn makes clear.

A melody is a succession of tones perceived by the mind as an entity. When we accept a succession of tones as a melody, we feel that they have not been thrown together in any old way. We derive from them an impression of conscious arrangement: the sense of a beginning, a middle, and an end. A good melody has something inevitable about it. It possesses a distinctive profile, a quality of aliveness.

We hear the words of a sentence not singly but in relation to the thought as a whole. So too we perceive tones, not separately but in relationship to each other within a pattern. Tones move up and down, one being higher or lower than another in musical "space." They also move faster or slower in time, one claiming our attention for a longer or shorter duration than another. From the interaction of the two dimensions—musical space and time—emerges the total unit which is melody. This is the musical line—or curve, if you prefer—which guides our ear through a composition. The melody is the plot, the theme of a musical work, the thread upon which hangs the tale. As Aaron Copland aptly puts it, "The melody is generally what the piece is about."

THE STRUCTURE OF MELODY

Let us examine the pattern of a well-known tune.

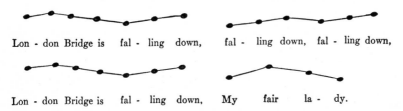

We notice at once that the melody divides itself into two halves. Each half is called a phrase, which in music as in language denotes a unit of meaning. The two phrases together form a sentence, a musical period.

Each phrase is rounded off by a cadence, a term applied to a kind of resting place in music, a formula of conclusion. The first phrase of *London Bridge* ends in an upward inflection, like a question. This is an inconclusive type of cadence indicating that more is to come, like a comma in punctuation. The second phrase answers with a vigorous downward inflection on the word "la-dy": a closing formula known as a full cadence, creating a sense of conclusion.

The composer unifies his structure by repeating the material. Thus, both phrases of *London Bridge* begin in identical fashion. The necessary contrast is supplied by fresh material, which in our example comes on the words "my fair lady." Through repetition and contrast the composer achieves both unity and variety. This combination of traits is basic to musical architecture, for without unity there is chaos, without variety—boredom.

The melody line does not leave off haphazardly, as if it suddenly found something better to do. On the contrary, it gives the impression of having reached its goal. If you will hum the last phrase of several well-known tunes such as *The Star-Spangled Banner*, *America*, and *Old Black Joe*, you will notice they all end on a tone that produces this effect of finality. We encounter here what for centuries has been a cardinal principle in our music: one tone is singled out as the center of the group; it serves as a landmark that gives the other tones their direction, and may be thought of as the point of departure and return.

The up-and-down movement may proceed along the steps of the scale or it may leap to a tone several degrees away. The leap may be narrow or wide, as may be the range of the melody (the distance from its lowest to highest tone). Traits such as these determine the character of the melodic line. Compare the narrow range and stepwise movement of *America* with the bold leaps and far-flung activity of *The Star-Spangled Banner*. Clearly *America* is the quieter, *The Star-Spangled Banner* the more vigorous melody.

The phrase as a whole may follow an upward or downward direction. In the musical scale, as on a staircase, going up is more strenuous than coming down. *The Farmer in the Dell* presents an ascending first phrase which is answered by a descending second phrase—that is, tension followed by relaxation.

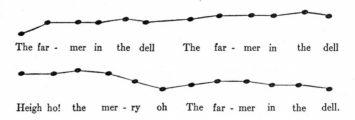

The far - mer in the dell   The far - mer in the dell

Heigh ho! the mer - ry oh   The far - mer in the dell.

The rhythmic pattern of the tones is of crucial importance. Their forward movement in time holds our attention even as does their up-and-down movement in space. Without the rhythm the melody loses its aliveness. Try singing *London Bridge* or *The Farmer in the Dell* in tones of equal duration, and see how much is lost of the quality of the pattern. Of great moment in fixing the character of a melody is its speed or pace. A rapid tune such as *Dixie* or *Oh Susannah!* creates an atmosphere of jaunty activity, whereas a slow and sustained melody like *Silent Night* suggests serenity and rest.

The melodic line may be described as angular or smooth, tense or relaxed, energetic or languid. Above all, the melody must be interesting. We say of a painter that he has a sense of line, meaning that he is able to achieve eventfulness, to sustain movement over the whole of his canvas. The same holds for the unfolding melody line with its rising and falling, its peaks and valleys. A melody has to have what musicians call the "long line." It must build tension as it rises from one level to the next, and must retain its drive up to the final note.

What is apt to make a striking effect on the listener is the climax. Representing the peak of intensity, the climax imparts purpose and direction to the melody line. It creates the impression of crisis met and overcome. Our national anthem contains a fine climax in the last phrase, on the words "O'er the land of the free." There can be no doubt in anybody's mind that this song is about freedom. Clearly, too, freedom must be striven for, to judge from the effort we have to make to get up to the crucial tone.

The principles we have touched upon are to be encountered in the melodies of the masters. Let us take some familiar examples. Brahms' Hungarian Dance No. 5 opens with vigorous upward leaps. The activity of this melodic line contrasts with the gentle stepwise movement and serene flow of Schubert's *Ave Maria*. Similarly the soaring line of the March from *Aïda* contrasts with the restricted activity of the melody in Ravel's *Pavane*. Schumann's *Träumerei* builds to a particularly fine climax in the final phrase, as does Chopin's E-flat Nocturne. The Hallelujah Chorus from Handel's *Messiah* is an excellent example of the way in which rhythm can make a melody memorable. The rhythmic figure on the word "Hallelujah," repeated again and again in the course of the piece, stamps itself unforgettably on the mind.

The question arises: is the composer conscious of these principles or does the melody simply happen that way? One might ask the same about the rhymes and meters of a poem. These, needless to say, do not happen accidentally. Yet if the poet had to think constantly of rules he could not create a living work. The same applies to the composer. Through a combination of talent, training, and practice he learns to think spontaneously—or at least comfortably—within the rules of his art. His melodies uniquely combine the flash of inspiration and the effort that must follow it. Intuition and planning, rapturous vision and technical skill, are here inextricably intertwined.

"Melody," writes Paul Hindemith, "is the element in which the personal characteristics of the composer are most clearly and most obviously revealed." For melody is the essential unit of communication in music: the direct bearer of meaning from composer to listener.

Collection, Museum of Modern Art

Modigliani, *Woman, Head in Hand.*
"We say of a painter that he has a sense of line, meaning that he is able
to sustain movement. The same holds for the unfolding melody line."

≥4≤

Harmony: Musical Space

"The evolution of the harmonic idiom has resulted from the
fact that musicians of all generations have sought new means
of expression. Harmony is a constant stream of evolution, a
constantly changing vocabulary and syntax."

Roger Sessions

WE ARE accustomed to hearing melodies against a background of harmony. To the movement of the melody, harmony adds a third dimension—depth. Harmony is to music what perspective is to painting. It
introduces the impression of musical space. It clarifies direction and
creates meaning. The supporting role of harmony is apparent when a
singer accompanies his melody with chords on the guitar or banjo, or
when the pianist plays the melody with his right hand while the left
strikes the chords. We are jolted if the wrong chord is sounded, for at
that point the necessary unity of melody and harmony is broken.

Harmony pertains to the movement and relationship of chords. A
chord may be defined as a combination of tones that occur simultaneously and are conceived as an entity. Just as the vaulting arch rests
upon columns, so the melody unfolds above supporting chords. Melody
constitutes the horizontal aspect of music; harmony, the vertical.

THE FUNCTION OF HARMONY

The chords are the framework of a composition. They form the
substructure that holds it together. They have meaning only in relation
to other chords; that is, only as each leads into the next. Harmony
therefore implies movement, progression.

The most common chord in our music is a combination of three
tones known as a triad. Such a triad may be built by combining the

17

Tintoretto, *Marriage at Cana*.
"Harmony is to music what perspective is to painting."

first, third, and fifth degrees of the do-re-mi-fa-sol-la-ti-do scale: *do-mi-sol*. Or the second, fourth, and sixth steps: *re-fa-la*. A similar chord may be built on each of the other degrees of the scale.

Although the triad is a vertical block of sound, its three tones often appear horizontally as a melody. The first three tones of the *Blue Danube* waltz form a triad, as do the first three of our national anthem (on the words "O-oh-say"). The foundation tone or *do* may be duplicated an octave above, giving a four-tone version of the triad. This happens at the beginning of *The Star-Spangled Banner*, on the words "say can you see." It is apparent that melody and harmony do not function independently of one another. On the contrary, each constantly influences the other.

The white keys of the piano are named C, D, E, F, G, A, B, C. We may build a triad on C by playing C-E-G (every other tone). A triad with D as root reads D-F-A. The triad on E is E-G-B, and so on. These and other more intricate chords form the materials of our harmonic system. They determine the character of our music, its sounds and its meanings.

ACTIVE AND REST CHORDS

Music is an art of movement. Movement to be purposeful must have a goal. The progressions of chords cannot be left to chance. In the course of centuries musicians have evolved procedures to regulate the movement of chords.

Purposeful movement implies a central point of departure and return. We noticed such a point in the final tone of melodies. This is the *do* which comes both first and last in the do-re-mi-fa-sol-la-ti-do scale. The triad on *do* serves as the chord of rest. But rest has meaning only in relation to activity. The chord of rest is counterposed to other triads which are active. The active chords seek to be completed, or *resolved*, in the rest chord. This striving for resolution is the dynamic force in our music. It shapes the forward movement, imparting direction and goal.

The fifth step of the do-re-mi-fa-sol-la-ti-do scale is the chief representative of the active principle. We therefore obtain two focal points: the active triad on *sol* (the V chord, the *dominant*) which seeks to be resolved to the restful triad on *do* (the I chord, the *tonic*). Dominant moving to tonic constitutes a compact formula of activity completed, of movement come to rest. We learned this formula as children when the two chords were sounded at school assembles as a signal to the group to rise or be seated. This is the traditional final cadence in our music. We hear it asserted over and over again at the end of many compositions dating from the eighteenth and nineteenth centuries. So strong is the tradition that we feel a decided need to hear an active chord resolve to the chord of rest.

Following is the harmonic structure of *London Bridge,* involving a simple progression from tonic to dominant and back.

London Bridge is	falling down,	Falling down,	falling down;
I———————	I————————	V————————	I————————

London Bridge is	falling down,	My fair	la-dy.
I———————	I————————	V————	I————

It will be noticed that the dominant-tonic progression shapes the cadence at the end of each phrase.

The triad built on the fourth scale step *fa* is known as the *subdominant* or IV chord. This too is an active chord, but less so than the dominant. The progression IV–I creates a less decisive cadence than the other. It is familiar to us from the two Amen chords sounded by the organ at the end of hymns.

These three triads, the basic ones of our system, suffice to harmonize many famous melodies.

Way down upon the   Swanee River   Far, far, a-way,
I————————   IV————   I———— V————

There's where my heart is turning ever, There's where the Old Folks stay.
I——————————— IV———— I——————— V———— I——

All the world is   sad and dreary,   Everywhere I   roam,
V————————   I————————   IV————   I—— (V)——

Oh darkies, how my   heart grows weary,   Far from the Old Folks at home.
I————————— IV———————— I———— V———— I——

CONSONANCE AND DISSONANCE

Harmonic movement, we saw, is generated by the tendency of the active chord to be resolved in the chord of rest. This movement receives its maximum impetus from the dissonance. *Dissonance* is restlessness and activity, *consonance* is relaxation and fulfillment. The dissonant chord creates tension. The consonant chord resolves it.

It was during the nineteenth century that the term dissonance took on its inaccurate implication of unpleasantness—inaccurate because, if dissonance is unpleasant, why should every composer have made use of it? The answer is that dissonance introduces the necessary element of expressiveness into music. Without it, a work would be intolerably dull and insipid. What suspense and conflict are to the drama, dissonance is to music. It creates the areas of tension without which the areas of relaxation would have no meaning. Each complements the other; both are a necessary part of the artistic whole.

The history of music teaches us that tone combinations regarded as dissonant in their own time come to be accepted by later generations as consonant. Man's capacity to tolerate novel chords has grown steadily in the last thousand years. The leader in this development has always been the composer, whose imagination grasped the possibilities of new combinations while they were still unacceptable to his fellows. Six hundred years ago Jacob of Liége was protesting against the modernists of his time. "O great abuse, great ignorance, great bestiality whereby an ass parades as a man. . . . For they confound concord with discord, so that it becomes impossible to distinguish the one from the other!" Two and a half centuries later the theorist Artusi excoriated the modernists (especially Monteverdi) for creating "a tumult of sounds, a confusion of absurdities," and for being so enamored of themselves that they substitute their innovations for the traditional rules. How familiar the sentiment, how oft repeated through the ages.

Harmony is a much more sophisticated phenomenon than melody. Historically it appeared much later, about a thousand years ago. Its real development took place only in the West. The music of the Orient to this day is based largely on single-line melody. Indeed, we may consider the great achievement of Western music to be harmony (hearing in depth), even as in painting it is perspective (seeing in depth). Our harmonic system has advanced steadily over the past ten centuries. Today it is adjusting to new needs. These constitute the latest chapter in man's age-old attempt to impose law and order upon the raw material of sound; to perceive tones as the manifestation of a unifying idea, a selective imagination, a reasoning will.

5

Rhythm and Meter: Musical Time

"In the beginning was rhythm."
Hans von Bülow

RHYTHM—the word means "flow" in Greek—denotes the orderly movement of music in time. It is the principle of organization and design that controls the duration of the tones. Rhythm is the element of music most closely allied to body movement, to physical action. Its simpler patterns when repeated over and over have a hypnotic effect upon us. We say admiringly of a dance-band musician that "he's got rhythm," meaning an electrifying quality, an aliveness almost independent of the notes. Rhythm has been called the heartbeat of music, the pulse that betokens life. We have spoken of melody as one of the two basic components of music; the other is rhythm.

THE NATURE OF RHYTHM

Rhythm springs from the need for order inherent in the human mind. Upon the tick-tock of the clock or the clacking of train wheels we automatically impose a pattern. We hear the sounds as a regular pulsation of strong and weak beats, even though in reality they are all alike. In brief, we organize our perception of time by means of rhythm.

The ancients discerned in rhythm the creative principle of the universe, manifested alike in the regular movement of planets, the cycle of seasons and tides, of night and day, desire and appeasement, life and death. Yet these rhythms framed an existence that all too often lacked design and meaning. Rivers overflowed for no good reason, lightning struck, enemies pillaged. Exposed to the caprice of a merciless destiny, man fashioned for himself an ideal universe where the unforeseen was excluded and divine order reigned. This universe was art; and its controlling principle was rhythm. The symmetrical proportions of architecture, the balanced groupings of painting and sculpture, the patterns of the dance, the regular meters of poetry—each in its own sphere represents man's deep-seated need for rhythmical arrangement. But it is in music, the art of ideal movement, that rhythm finds its richest expression.

Byzantine mosaic, *Procession of Female Saints.*
"Rhythm springs from the need for order inherent in the human mind."

METER

Meter pertains to the organization of musical time; specifically, to the arrangement of musical beats in units of time known as measures. The measures contain a fixed number of beats and are marked off by the recurrence of accent.

Meter connotes the fixed time units within which musical events take place. Within these units the rhythm flows freely—now more, now less eventfully. Thus rhythm is the pattern of musical activity, while meter is the pattern of musical time within which that activity unfolds. Meter involves the arrangement of beats into measures, while rhythm pertains to the arrangement of time values within the measure. Every waltz has the same meter: ONE-two-three ONE-two-three. Within that meter, each waltz follows its own rhythm.

The distinction may be noted too in the domain of poetry. In reading a poem metrically we bring out the pattern of accented and unaccented syllables:

> When tó the sés - sions óf sweet sí - lent thóught
> I súm - mon úp re - mém - brance óf things pást.

When we read rhythmically, on the other hand, we bring out the natural flow of the language within the basic meter and, more important, the expressive meaning of the words. It is this distinction between rhythm and meter that the English critic Fox-Strangways has in mind when he observes: "A melody—an Irish reel perhaps—is in strict time, or people could not dance to it correctly; but if it had not also rhythm, they would not dance to it passionately."

METRICAL PATTERNS

The simpler metrical patterns, in music as in poetry, depend on the regular recurrence of accent. Simplest of all is a succession of beats in which a strong alternates with a weak: ONE-two ONE-two—or in marching, LEFT-right LEFT-right. This is known as duple meter and is generally encountered as two-four time ($\frac{2}{4}$). The pattern occurs in many nursery rhymes and marching songs.

Twín - kle	twín - kle	lít - tle	stár - ---,
ONE - two	ONE - two	ONE - two	ONE - two

Hów I--	wón - der	whát you	áre ----.
ONE - two	ONE - two	ONE - two	ONE - two

The best way to perceive rhythm is through physical response. The above tune can be tapped, while singing, with a downward movement of the hand on ONE and an upward movement on *two*.

Duple meter contains two beats to the measure, of which the first is generally accented. Within this meter a tune such as *Yankee Doodle* presents a somewhat more eventful rhythmic pattern than the above example; *Dixie* and *Oh Susannah!* still more so. In these songs there is more than one melody tone to the beat. The meter is the steady ONE-two ONE-two that constitutes the underlying beat, above which flows the rhythmic pattern of the melody.

Yánkee Doodle	wént to town	Ríding on a	pó - ny
ONE - two	ONE - two	ONE - two	ONE - two

The other basic metrical pattern is that of an accented beat followed by two unaccented: three beats to the measure, or triple meter. This is the pattern of three-four time ($\frac{3}{4}$) traditionally associated with the waltz and minuet.

Two celebrated examples of triple meter are *America* and *The Star-Spangled Banner*.

Mý coun - try	'tis of thee,
ONE - two - three	ONE - two - three

Swéet land of	lí - - ber-ty
ONE - two - three	ONE - two - three

Óf thee I	síng ————
ONE - two - three	ONE - two - three

Oh	sáy can you	sée ——— by the
three	ONE - two - three	ONE - two - three

	dáwn's ear - ly	líght ———
	ONE - two - three	ONE - two

Duple and triple are the primary meters; all others are compound. By combining two measures of duple we obtain a measure of four beats, or quadruple meter. The primary accent falls on the first beat of the measure, with a subsidiary accent on the third: óNE-two-Thrée-four. Quadruple meter, generally encountered as four-four time ($\frac{4}{4}$), is found in some of our most widely sung melodies: *Old Folks at Home; Old Black Joe;* the *Battle Hymn of the Republic; Long, Long Ago; Auld Lang Syne,* and a host of others.

Wáy ——— dówn u - pon the	Swá - nee River ———
ONE two Three four	ONE two Three four

Fár, ——— fár a -	wáy ————————
ONE - two - Three - four	ONE - two - Three - four

Two measures of triple time may be combined to make sextuple meter: six-four or six-eight time. This is often marked by a gently flowing effect. Popular examples are *My Bonnie Lies Over the Ocean, Sweet and Low, Silent Night, Believe Me if All Those Endearing Young Charms, Drink to Me Only With Thine Eyes.*

Drínk to me ŏn - - ly	wí - ith thine ěy - es and
ONE - two - three - Four - five - six	ONE - two - three - Four - five - six
í ——— will plě - edge with	míne ———————————
ONE - two - three - Four - five - six	ONE - two - three - Four - five - six

Other compound meters are based on five, seven, nine, eleven, or twelve beats to the measure. However, the four patterns just discussed are the ones most frequent in the music of the nineteenth century.

It will suffice to mention a few familiar examples of each of the various meters. Of two-four time: Brahms' Hungarian Dances Nos. 5 and 6; Schubert's *Marche Militaire;* the Polka of Shostakovitch. Three-four time is well illustrated by the Minuet from Mozart's Symphony in E-flat and the waltzes of Johann Strauss. For examples of quadruple meter listen to the Triumphal March from *Aïda* and the March from the *Love for Three Oranges.* The characteristically flowing effect of six time is set forth in such familiar pieces as the three *Venetian Boat Songs* of Mendelssohn; *Morning* from the *Peer Gynt* Suite of Grieg; and *The Sea and the Ship of Sinbad,* the first movement of Rimsky-Korsakov's *Scheherazade.*

"THE TYRANNY OF THE BAR LINE"

In written music the measures are separated by a vertical bar line. The accent generally falls on the first beat of the measure; in other words, immediately after the bar line. In simple meters such as two-, three-, and four-four time the bar line is consequently a symbol of the regular recurrence of accent.

Such regular meters were of great value in making music understandable to a mass public. They made it possible for people to sing and play in time in large choruses and orchestras. Toward the end of the nineteenth century, however, composers rebelled more and more against "the tyranny of the bar line"—the inevitable recurrence of the accented ONE at the beginning of each measure. What had begun as a support ended by becoming a restraint.

To escape what to them seemed monotony, they disguised the trip-hammer beat of the meter with ever more complex rhythmic patterns within the measure. They also weakened the bar line by causing the rhythm to flow from one measure into the next.

Of the many procedures used for escaping the fixed metrical pattern, the best known is syncopation. This term denotes a deliberate upsetting of the normal accent. Instead of falling on what is supposed to be the strong beat of the measure, the ONE, the accent is shifted to the off-beat. Through this irregularity the accent is made to conflict with the pattern that has been set up in the listener's mind. The pleasure of satisfying his expectations is abandoned for the equally important pleasure of surprise. Syncopation is associated in the popular mind with the Negro dance rhythms out of which modern jazz developed; but it has figured in European art music for centuries and was used by the masters with great subtlety.

To sum up: music is an art of movement in time. Rhythm, the artistic organization of musical movement, permeates every aspect of the musical process. It shapes the melody, the harmony, the form of the music. It binds together the parts within the whole: the notes within the measure, the measures within the phrase, the phrases within the period. Through the power of rhythm the composer achieves a dimension in time comparable to what painter, sculptor, and architect achieve in space.

Time is the crucial dimension in music. And its first law is rhythm.

Palazzo della Cancelleria in Rome, designed by Bramante (1444–1514).

"Through the power of rhythm the composer achieves a dimension in time comparable to what painter, sculptor, and architect achieve in space."

⹂6⹁

Tempo: Musical Pace

"The whole duty of a conductor is comprised in his ability to indicate the right tempo."

Richard Wagner

TEMPO AS AN ELEMENT OF RHYTHM

METER tells us how many beats there are in the measure, but it does not tell us whether these beats occur slowly or rapidly. The tempo, by which we mean the rate of speed, the pace of the music, provides the clue to this vital matter. Consequently the rhythmic organization of music involves three matters: meter, which organizes musical time into measures; rhythm, which organizes time values within the measure; and tempo, which determines the speed of the measures, their duration in actual time.

We respond to musical tempo physically and psychologically. Our pulse, our breathing, our entire being adjusts to the rate of movement and to the feeling engendered thereby on the conscious and subconscious levels. Because of the close connection between tempo and mood, tempo markings have come to indicate not only the pace of the music but its character as well. The tempo terms are generally given in Italian, a survival from the time when the opera of that nation dominated the European scene. Most frequently encountered are the following.

Very slow:	*Largo* (literally, "broad") *Grave* (literally, "heavy")
Slow:	*Lento* *Adagio* (literally, "at ease")
Moderate:	*Andante* (literally, "going")—at a walking pace *Andantino*—somewhat faster than andante, "sauntering" *Moderato*
Fairly fast:	*Allegretto* (literally, "a little lively")—not as fast as allegro
Fast:	*Allegro* (literally, "cheerful," "happy," "lively")
Very fast:	*Vivo*—lively *Vivace*—vivacious *Allegro molto*—very lively *Presto*—quick *Prestissimo*—as quick as possible

Largo has come to imply breadth and dignity; adagio, a tender or elegiac quality; grave, pathos and heaviness. Due to the fact that musical practice changed considerably from the eighteenth century to the nineteenth, some of these terms carry with them a certain ambiguity. To the earlier period andante meant a "going" pace—that is, a fair degree of movement. To the nineteenth century it implied a slowish gait. Both meanings came to be accepted, which caused some confusion. Beethoven was not sure whether andantino was to be understood as being slower or faster than andante.

No less important than the tempo terms are those terms indicating a change of pace. The principal ones are *accelerando* (getting faster) and *ritardando* (holding back, getting slower); *a tempo* (in time), indicates a return to the original tempo.

The flow of a piece, like speech, is an alive thing, now pressing forward, now holding back. No artist playing the same work on two occasions could possibly duplicate the tempo throughout, with its infinite nuances, its subtle accelerations and retardations. The musician adheres to the beat in order to project a clear picture of the meter, rhythm, and tempo; he also departs from the beat in order to achieve the necessary suppleness of movement. In this way he breathes life into what would otherwise be a mechanical thing, transforming the music into a free flow of thought and feeling.

Timbre: Musical Color

THE SAME tone will sound different when produced by a trumpet or a violin. The difference lies in the characteristic color, or timbre, of each instrument. (The word retains its French pronunciation *táhm'br*.) Timbre focuses our musical impressions. It imparts to the tonal image its special and inalienable character. By the way in which the composer chooses his timbres, blending and contrasting them, he creates the particular sound-world that a given piece inhabits.

The composer has at his disposal two basic media—human voices and musical instruments. He may write for any of these alone or in conjunction with others. He has a wide range of choice. He selects the medium that will best express the quality and the meaning of his ideas. Once he has made his choice—a choral piece, let us say, or a string quartet—the medium in turn imposes its character upon the musical conception, shaping it, focusing it, and quite often inspiring fresh ideas. Thus a mutual relationship is set up. The idea determines the choice of medium; the medium determines the fate of the idea.

The composer is constantly aware of the nature of his medium. He takes into account the capacities and limitations of each instrument; he tries to make it do the things for which it is best suited. To write idiomatically for an instrument means to function musically within its limitations—perhaps even to transmute these into fresh sources of beauty. There are, to begin with, the limits of its range—the distance from its lowest to its highest tone, beyond which it cannot go. There is the dynamic limit—the degree of softness or loudness beyond which it cannot play. There are technical peculiarities native to its low, middle, and high register, as a result of which a certain formation of notes will be executed more easily on one instrument than another. An instrument like the tuba, for example, sustains tones well but is unwieldy in rapid scale passages. Another such as the piano is agile in rapid passages but does not sustain tone well. These and a host of similar considerations determine the composer's choice as he clothes his ideas in their instrumental garb.

Certain composers have a more vivid color sense than others. The great masters of orchestration possess it in the highest degree. One thing is clear: tone color is not something that is grafted on to the musical conception; it is part and parcel of the idea, as inseparable from it as are its harmony and rhythm. Timbre is more than an element of sensuous charm that is added to a work; it is one of the shaping forces in music.

≫8≪

Instruments of the Orchestra

"With these artificial voices we sing in a manner such as our natural voices would never permit."
John Redfield: *Music—A Science and an Art*

MUSICAL INSTRUMENTS have always been a source of wonder to those who made, played, and listened to them. The ancients attributed their invention to gods—Apollo, Pan, Mercury—or to legendary figures. Those who mastered their secrets were said to possess supernatural powers. Amphion calmed the raging sea with his lyre. Orpheus charmed the wild beasts and moved even the god of death to pity. Man's first instrument was his body, both for vocal melody and, through slapping and stamping, for rhythm. To enhance the effect, he created the rude rattles, drums, and clappers with which the history of musical instruments began.

An instrument is a mechanism that generates musical vibrations and launches them into the air. It enables us to control the four properties of musical tone: pitch, duration, volume, and color (timbre).

By pitch we mean the location of a tone in the musical scale in relation to high or low. The pitch is determined by the rate of vibration, which in turn depends on the length of the vibrating body. The shorter a string or column of air, the more rapidly it vibrates and the higher the pitch. The longer a string or column of air, the fewer the vibrations per second and the lower the pitch. The width, thickness, density, and tension of the vibrating body also affect the outcome.

Duration depends on the length of time over which vibration is maintained. We hear tones as being not only high or low but also short or long. Volume depends on the degree of force of the vibration, as a result of which the tone strikes us as being loud or soft. The timbre or tone color of an instrument depends on a number of factors. Among these may be mentioned the material of which the instrument is made; its size, shape, and proportions; and the way in which vibration is set up.

Apollo and the Muses.

"The ancients attributed the invention of instruments to gods—Apollo, Pan, Mercury—or to legendary figures."

The oldest and still the most popular of all instruments is the human voice. In no other instrument is the contact between performer and medium so intimate. In none other is expression so personal and direct. The voice is the ideal exponent of lyric melody and has consistently been the model for those who made instruments as well as for those who played them. Instruments can do things that are impossible for the voice to execute, yet it is the highest praise we can bestow upon a performer to say that he makes his instrument sing.

Instruments figure in our music singly; in small groups (chamber music); and as part of that most spectacular of all ensembles, the orchestra. In the orchestra they are divided into four sections: strings, woodwinds, brass, and percussion.

this circumstance comes the term *arpeggio*, which means a broken chord (*arpa* is Italian for "harp"). Arpeggios occur in a variety of forms on many instruments. By breaking up the chord instead of sounding it in block formation, composers are able to extend a harmony over a period of time and to arrange it in diverse rhythmic figures.

The piano, a most popular instrument, is widely used in the home as well as on the concert stage. Whereas the violinist or clarinetist needs someone to accompany him, the pianist is able to play both melody and harmony. This self-sufficiency makes the piano an extremely useful instrument. It is indispensable for accompanying and in small instrumental ensembles, and is of great assistance to musicians in the study of operatic and orchestral scores.

The full name of the instrument is pianoforte, Italian for "soft-loud," which indicates its wide dynamic range and its capacity for nuance. Its strings are struck with little hammers controlled by a keyboard mechanism. The piano is pre-eminent for brilliant scales, arpeggios, and trills, rapid passages and octaves. It has a wide range from lowest to highest tone and commands great rhythmic vitality. Nineteenth-century piano writing leaned toward sensuous beauty and lyricism. Present-day composers have found a new use for the piano as a rhythmic percussion instrument of crisp sonority, both solo and as a member of the orchestra.

The organ, once regarded as "the king of instruments," is a wind instrument into whose pipes the air is fed by mechanical means. The pipes are controlled by two or more keyboards and a set of pedals. Gradations of tone are made possible by means of swell boxes. The organ possesses a multicolored sonority and majestic harmonies that fill a huge space.

The instruments described in this chapter form a vivid and diversified group. To composer, performer, and listener alike they offer a rich palette that embraces manifold possibilities of color and shades of expression.

❧ 9 ❧

The Orchestra

"Orchestration is part of the very soul of the work. A work is thought out in terms of the orchestra, certain tone-colors being inseparable from it in the mind of its creator and native to it from the hour of its birth."

Nicholas Rimsky-Korsakov

FROM the group of approximately twenty that Bach had at his disposal or of the thirty-odd that Mozart knew, the modern orchestra has grown into an ensemble that may call for more than a hundred players. These musicians, many of artist stature, give their full time to rehearsal and performance, achieving a precision of ensemble playing unknown in former times.

The orchestra is constituted with a view to securing the best balance of tone. The performers are divided into the four sections we have described. Approximately two-thirds are string players, one-third are wind players. From three to five men take care of the percussion. The following distribution is typical of our larger orchestras.

Strings, about 65:	18 first violins 16 second violins 12 violas 10 violoncellos 10 double basses
Woodwinds, about 15:	3 flutes, 1 piccolo 3 oboes, 1 English horn 3 clarinets, 1 bass clarinet 3 bassoons, 1 double bassoon
Brass, 11:	4 horns 3 trumpets 3 trombones 1 tuba
Percussion, 5:	2 kettledrum players 3 men for bass and side drum, glockenspiel, celesta, xylophone, triangle, cymbals, tambourine, etc.

It will be noticed that there are about 34 violins which are divided into two groups, first and second. Each functions as a unit and plays a separate part. In the woodwind section one of the players of the principal instrument generally doubles on the related one. The third flutist, for example, also plays the piccolo. Saxophones are added when called for in the score. Certain works call for a larger brass section with additional horns and an extra trumpet. Included in the ensemble are also two harps and, for certain contemporary scores, a piano.

The instruments are arranged so as to secure effective blending and contrast. The softer ones are placed in front, the louder sit farther back. Following is a characteristic seating plan.

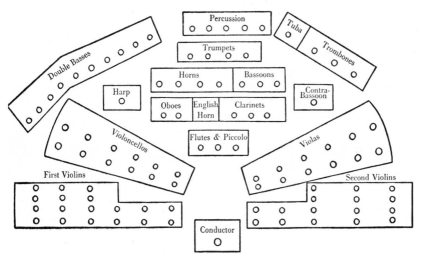

Typical seating plan of a symphony orchestra.

The ensemble is directed by the conductor, who beats time and indicates the entrances of the various instruments, the shadings in the volume of tone, the principal and subordinate lines, and a host of related details that serve to make clear the structure of the work. Poised on the podium, baton raised—some prefer to do without—the conductor may be likened to a commander at the head of his troops. It is his task to bring the ensemble to life, to impose upon it a unifying conception, and to mold the group into a perfectly co-ordinated body.

The conductor has before him the score of the work. This consists of from a few to as many as twenty-five or more lines, each representing an instrumental part. All the staves together comprise a single composite line. What is going on at any moment in the orchestra is indicated at any given point straight down the page. It will be observed from the illustration that the instruments are grouped in families, the woodwinds on top, then the brass, percussion, and strings.

A page from Beethoven's Fifth Symphony, showing the arrangement of instrumental parts in an orchestral score.

THE ART OF ORCHESTRATION

The composer bent over a page of full score may be compared to a weaver intertwining strands of various hues or a painter mixing colors on his palette. He envisions the color scheme in his imagination, blending and contrasting the timbres. He assigns his themes to the instruments that will present them most effectively. He judges accurately the kind of sound he desires, be it powerful, caressing, or delicate; and he uses color to highlight the rhythmic patterns and the architectonic design, to set off the principal ideas from the subordinate, and to weld the innnumerable details into a whole.

The foregoing should dispel the widespread misconception that one man writes the music while another orchestrates it. This is true of popular dance music and in Hollywood, where conditions of mass production make it necessary. But in art music, as the quotation from Rimsky-Korsakov makes clear, the two functions cannot be separated. We could no more imagine Brahms' music with Wagner's orchestration than picture a familiar face with someone else's nose. What the composer says and how he says it are part and parcel of his individual manner of conceiving sound, his musical physiognomy. So personal is this that we can often recognize the composer solely from the way the horns or strings are handled.

Erroneous too is the notion that the composer first writes his orchestral piece for the piano and then arranges it for instruments. An orchestral work is conceived in terms of the orchestra from its inception. Its shape and idiom derive from the nature of the instruments. It cannot come to life in any other medium. If many composers like to have a piano in the room while writing, it is primarily because this gives them contact with the living sound. But the piano is no more able to render a symphonic piece than a black-and-white reproduction can reveal the quality of a Raphael or a Titian.

THE ORCHESTRA IN ACTION

We shall in the course of this book have ample occasion to consider the handling of the orchestra by various composers. At this point, however, the reader may find a helpful introduction to the orchestra in a work such as Prokofiev's perennially popular *Peter and the Wolf*, a "symphonic tale for children young and old." In this work the Russian master set himself the task of acquainting youngsters with the instruments of the orchestra. He therefore associated each character in his tale with a striking tone color. The wolf is represented by the French horns, Peter by the strings, Peter's grandfather by the bassoon, the bird by the flute, the duck by the oboe, the cat by the clarinet in low register, and the shooting of the hunters by the kettledrums and bass drum. For those who have not had much experience in following the various strands of color in the orchestral web, this delightful work will serve as a fine guide to the orchestra in action.

Equally useful for this purpose is Tchaikovsky's *Nutcracker* Suite, which consists of a set of short pieces abounding in distinctive timbres. The concert suite was drawn from a Christmas Eve ballet concerning a little girl who dreams that the nutcracker she received as a gift has turned into a handsome prince. The fairy-tale atmosphere impelled Tchaikovsky to some enchanting music.

The Miniature Overture, marked Allegro, sets the mood. To achieve an effect of lightness and grace Tchaikovsky omitted the bass instruments. No 'cellos or double basses are used; no trombones or tuba; nor are there any trumpets. The percussion section is represented only by the triangle. The dainty effect is enhanced by the use of staccato and the prevalence of the upper register. The sense of climax at the end is achieved through an increase in volume of tone, an acceleration in pace, and a rise in pitch.

There follows the March, in a lively 4/4 time. The characteristic march rhythm is set forth by clarinets, horns, and trumpets. The triplet rhythm is widely associated with military flourishes, but in this setting takes on a fanciful quality. Winds are answered by strings—a widely used orchestral device. Worthy of note is the filigree work in the accompaniment, in this case presented by the violas and 'cellos pizzicato, an effect dear to Tchaikovsky's heart; also the staccato theme in high register, presented by three flutes and clarinet, that so vividly conveys a suggestion of ballet movement.

"I have discovered a new instrument in Paris, something between a piano and a glockenspiel, with a divinely beautiful tone," wrote Tchaikovsky to his publisher in 1891. "I want to introduce this into the ballet." The instrument was the celesta, whose ethereal sound pervades the Dance of the Sugar-Plum Fairy. The piece opens with four bars of pizzicato introduction, whereupon the celesta tone is effectively contrasted with that of the bass clarinet. There is a passage for celesta alone, after which the opening theme is repeated. In the theater this music is inevitably associated with a ballerina swathed in diaphanous veils.

The Trepak or Russian Dance, marked Molto vivace (very lively), is in 2/4 time. The short measure and heavy accents create the suggestion of vigorous physical movement proper to a peasant dance. The full orchestral sonority is enlivened, especially in the final measures, by the presence of the tambourine. Tchaikovsky, at the end, achieves a climax through an increase in the volume of sound (crescendo), an acceleration of pace (accelerando), and a rise to the upper pitches of the orchestral gamut.

The little girl and her prince are entertained by various sweetmeats in the castle of the Sugar-Plum Fairy. Coffee dances the Arab Dance, a subdued number marked Allegretto that forms an effective contrast with the Trepak that preceded. Muted violas and 'cellos set up a rhythmic *ostinato*—that is, a rhythmic figure repeated over and over with an almost hypnotic insistence. Against this dark curtain of sound, after introductory chords on the woodwinds, the muted violins unfold an oriental-sounding melody. The steady throb of a small drum adds the properly exotic touch. Striking is the long-drawn-out wail of the oboe, in upper register, over the quiet movement of the melody and harmony in the strings below. The music dies away at the end, *pppp*.

Tea, not to be outdone, presents the Chinese Dance, Allegro moderato. Bassoons, playing staccato, establish a rhythmic *ostinato* against which flute and piccolo trace a somewhat shrill melody. Whether this music bears any resemblance to that heard in Peking is beside the point. It is sufficiently close to what Western ears have come popularly to regard as Chinese—which means that it is pleasantly exotic and orchestrally colorful.

The Dance of the Toy Flutes, marked Moderato assai (very moderate) and in 2/4 time, has always been a favorite with devotees of Tchaikovsky. Against a pizzicato accompaniment of violas, 'cellos, and double basses, three flutes outline a suave and beguiling melody. A short solo on the English horn arrests the ear, after which the opening theme returns. The middle section of the piece is devoted to a telling idea on the trumpets, with a crescendo as the melodic line ascends and a decrease in volume as it moves downward. After this the gracious melody of the flutes is heard again.

The Waltz of the Flowers that closes the suite displays to the full Tchaikovsky's gifts as a composer of ballet music. Flowing melody and brilliancy of color are here associated with that sense of movement and gesture which are of the essence in the dance theater. The introduction alternates chords on woodwinds and horns with arpeggios on the harp. After an extended solo passage for the latter instrument, the waltz proper begins with a phrase on the horns answered by the clarinets. A contrasting melody emerges on the strings, punctuated by a measure on the woodwinds—always an effective orchestral procedure. The horn melody returns, now set off by ornamentation on the flutes. Notable, in the middle section, is the full-throated melody of the violas and 'cellos. The opening section is repeated and works up to the climactic finale through a steady increase in pace and volume, together with a rise to the brilliant upper register. With its suggestion of swirling ballerinas, this music conjures up everything we have come to associate with the romantic ballet.

It is clear that in a piece such as this, as in many that we will examine in later chapters, color is at the heart of the conception. The orchestral timbre is used to highlight the melodies, harmonies, and rhythms; to balance these, one against the other; and to weld them into lucid and convincing forms. Beyond this purely structural use of color, the composer—being one who is fascinated by sound—indulges his sheer love of sonority, his sense of the orchestra as a thing of wonder and beauty.

With its amplitude of tonal resources, its dynamic range and infinite variety of color, the modern orchestra offers a memorable experience both to the musician and music lover. There is good reason for the widespread conviction that it is one of the wonders of our musical culture.

The New York Philharmonic Symphony Orchestra.

≥10≤
Dynamics: Musical Volume

DYNAMICS denotes the degree of loudness or softness at which the music is played. In this area, as in that of tempo, certain responses seem to be rooted in the nature of our emotions. Mystery and fear call for a whisper, even as jubilation and vigorous activity go with full resonance. A lullaby or love song moves in another dynamic range than a triumphal march. Modern instruments place a wide gamut of dynamic effects at the composer's disposal.

The principal dynamic indications are:

Very soft: *pianissimo (pp)*
Soft: *piano (p)*
Moderately soft: *mezzo piano (mp)*
Moderately loud: *mezzo forte (mf)*
Loud: *forte (f)*
Very loud: *fortissimo (ff)*

As the modern orchestra increased in size and precision, composers extended the range of dynamic shadings in both directions, so that we find *ppp* and *fff*. In late nineteenth-century scores, four and even five *p*'s or *f*'s were used.

Of special importance are the changes in dynamics. The commonest are:

Growing louder: *crescendo* (⟨)
Growing softer: *decrescendo* or *diminuendo* (⟩)
Sudden stress: *sforzando (sf)*, (literally, "forced")—accent on a single note or chord

Tempo and dynamic markings are so many clues to the expressive content of a piece of music. These so-called "expression marks" steadily increased in number during the late eighteenth century and during the nineteenth, as composers tried ever more precisely to indicate their intentions. In this regard it is instructive to compare a page of Bach with one of Tchaikovsky. (See pp. 56–57.)

A number of terms embrace both tempo and dynamics. This is true especially of those used in the nineteenth century to fix the mood and character of a piece. *Andante maestoso* (fairly slow and majestic) implies a stately pace and full sonority. *Morendo* (dying away) indicates that the music is to become slower and softer. *Scherzando* (playful)

A page from the score of Bach's Brandenburg Concerto No. 2 (note the lack of expression marks).

A page from the score of Tchaikovsky's *Pathétique* Symphony showing the profusion of expression marks in nineteenth-century scores.

requires a light tone and brisk movement. *Con brio* (with vigor) suggests an energetic pace and vibrant sonority.

TEMPO AND DYNAMICS AS ELEMENTS OF MUSICAL EXPRESSION

Crescendo and diminuendo are among the important expressive effects available to the composer. Through the gradual swelling and diminishing of the tone volume, the illusion of distance enters music. It is as if the source of sound were approaching us and then receding. As orchestral style developed, composers quickly learned to take advantage of this procedure. Rossini, for example, was so addicted to employing a long-drawn-out swell of tone for the sake of dramatic effect that he was caricatured in Paris as "Monsieur Crescendo." The impact of such a crescendo can be little short of electrifying, as is apparent from the closing section of his Overture to *The Barber of Seville*. A similar effect is to be observed in Ravel's *Bolero*, in which two ideas are repeated over and over with steadily growing force. The piece builds up to a climax whose cumulative power used to hold audiences enthralled.

In such cases the crescendo becomes the shaping force of the music, the element that determines the conception as a whole. This is true, too, of Wagner's Prelude to *Lohengrin*, which is intended to depict the descent from heaven of the Holy Grail. The image of a band of angels approaching from the distance and then receding is translated into what has become a basic pattern in music, the crescendo-and-decrescendo (◁▷).
A stunning example of this dynamic scheme is to be found also in Debussy's nocturne for orchestra, *Fêtes* (Festivals).

Crescendo in conjunction with accelerando (louder and faster) creates excitement as surely as decrescendo together with ritardando (softer and slower) slackens it. The effect of an intensification of volume and pace is exemplified in Honegger's *Pacific 231*, in which the composer tries to suggest the sense of power conjured up by a locomotive tearing through the night. Here crescendo and accelerando are translated into the imagery of motion, as is the case in the finale of Tchaikovsky's Waltz of the Flowers, which is designed to build up to a rousing curtain for the *Nutcracker* ballet of which it is the last number. In the Tchaikovsky piece as in the Honegger, the music climbs steadily from the dark lower register to the bright and nervous high, so that the three elements—acceleration of pace, increase in volume, and rise in pitch—reinforce one another to create the climax.

Devices of this kind are infallible in their effect upon audiences, which would seem to indicate that they are not the arbitrary procedures of a single imagination but are rooted in certain basic responses inherent in our nature.

⊱11⊰

Form: Musical Structure and Design

"The principal function of form is to advance our understanding. It is the organization of a piece which helps the listener to keep the idea in mind, to follow its development, its growth, its elaboration, its fate."

Arnold Schoenberg

THE IDEA must have a visible embodiment, a dwelling not only beautiful in itself but suitable to the content. Out of this need comes form in art: the principle of organic unity that shapes the structure to the idea. Form and content, the *how* and the *what*, are as indissoluble as body and mind. Form is of decisive importance in architecture, painting, and sculpture; in poetry, drama, and the novel. But in music, where the material is so intangible, where an impression is no sooner received than it is succeeded by another, form is of the essence. How much so may be seen from the fact that the word "composing" derives from the Latin *componere*, "to put together." For the musicians of old the problem of composing was not so much to create elements as to weld them together.

Form is that quality in a work of art which presents to the mind of the beholder an impression of conscious choice and judicious arrangement. It represents law and order in art. It shows itself in the selection of certain details and the rejection of others. Form is manifest too in the relationship of the parts to the whole. It helps us to grasp the work of art as a unity, and can be as potent a source of beauty as the content itself.

Whether in the domestic arts—the setting of a table, the weaving of a basket—or in the loftier ones, a balance is required between unity and variety, between symmetry and asymmetry, activity and repose. Nor are these qualities confined to art. Nature has embodied them in the forms of plant and animal life and in what man likes to think of as her supreme handiwork—his own form.

FORM IN MUSIC

Our lives are composed of sameness and differentness: certain details are repeated again and again, others are new. Music mirrors this dualism. Its basic law of structure is repetition and contrast—unity and variety. Repetition fixes the material in our minds and ministers to our need for the familiar. Contrast sustains our interest and feeds our love of change. From the interaction of the familiar and the new, the repeated elements and the contrasting ones, result the lineaments of musical form.

The principle of form is embodied in a variety of musical forms. These utilize procedures worked out by generations of composers. No matter how diverse, they are based in one way or another on repetition and contrast. The forms, however, are not fixed molds into which the composer pours his molten material. What gives a piece of music its aliveness is the fact that it adapts a general plan to its own requirements. All faces have two eyes, a nose, and a mouth. In each face, though, these features are to be found in a wholly individual combination. The forms that students in composition follow are ready-made formulas set up for their guidance. The forms of the masters are living organisms in which external organization is delicately adjusted to inner content. No two symphonies of Haydn or Mozart, no two sonatas of Stravinsky or Hindemith are exactly alike. Each is a fresh and unique solution of the problem of fashioning musical material into a logical and coherent form.

STATEMENT-DEPARTURE-RETURN (A-B-A)

A basic type of musical form is that known as A-B-A. Here the composer presents a musical idea, next presents a contrasting idea, and then repeats the first. The repetition safeguards the unity, while variety is supplied by the middle section.

It often happens that as soon as the idea is set forth it is repeated, so as to engrave it on the mind. In such cases the A-B-A pattern becomes A-A-B-A, as in the following song.

A   Way down upon the Swanee River, far, far, away,
A   There's where my heart is turning ever, there's where the Old Folks stay.
B   All the world is sad and dreary, everywhere I roam,
A   Oh darkies, how my heart grows weary, far from the Old Folks at home.

This formation is to be found in many familiar melodies such as *Long, Long Ago; Believe Me if All Those Endearing Young Charms; Maryland, My Maryland; Ach du lieber Augustin;* and *Old Man River.* It is the standard formula for the tunes of Tin Pan Alley. Our need for repetition simplifies the composer's task: of the four phrases of the song, he has to compose only two.

The phrases do not have to follow the A-A-B-A pattern. Any number of variants are possible. For that matter the phrases do not have to be four in number, although this formation prevails in the music of the eighteenth and nineteenth centuries. But no matter what their structure, most melodies will be found to repeat certain material and to intersperse this with fresh material. The principle of statement-departure-return is found in Gregorian chants of fifteen hundred years ago as well as in the popular songs of today. It figures in our music from the simple folk song to the elaborate movements of symphonies and sonatas.

THREE-PART OR TERNARY FORM

The four phrases in the A-A-B-A formation make up a unit that corresponds roughly to a paragraph in prose. Such a unit may be built up through repetition and expansion into a larger formation. For instance, a contrasting section may be fashioned from new material, after which the composer repeats the first section, either as before or with some variation. There results what is known as a ternary form consisting of three symmetrical sections. In the following diagram, capital letters indicate the independent sections, and small letters the distribution of phrases within the section.

A	B	A
a-a-b-a	c-c-d-c	Exact repetition
or	*or*	
a-b-b-a,	c-d-d-c,	*or*
a-b-a-b,	c-d-c-d,	
etc.	*etc.*	variation

Three-part form became the standard pattern for innumerable short pieces of a simple song or dance type—nocturnes, waltzes, marches, impromptus, romances, and the like. The pattern is clear in many familiar compositions such as Schubert's *Marche Militaire*, Chopin's F-sharp major Nocturne, and Beethoven's Country Dance in E-flat. A-B-A is the pattern, too, of the minuet movement of the classical symphony. The reader will have no difficulty recognizing in these pieces the underlying pattern of statement-departure-return.

So as not to interrupt the musical flow, a transition passage may be inserted to lead from one section to the next. All the same, each section is an independent unit, and the middle one must present a contrast to the first and last. This may show itself in a number of ways. An agitated first section may be opposed to a lyric middle part. A dynamic rhythmic idea in the one section may be counterposed to a songlike idea in the other. The first part may lie in the dark lower register, the second in the middle or upper range. There may be contrasts in tempo and dynamics, in timbre and in the type of accompaniment. All of these serve to emphasize the contrast between the A and B sections.

Brown Brothers

New York City Hall (an example of A-B-A or three-part form in architecture).
"The middle section must present a contrast to the first and last sections."

With its attractive symmetry and its balancing of the outer sections against the contrasting middle one, the three-part or ternary form constitutes a simple, clear-cut formation that is a favorite in painting and architecture no less than in music.

TWO-PART OR BINARY FORM

This type of structure is based on the question-and-answer or A-B formation observed in such tunes as *London Bridge*, *The Farmer in the Dell*, and *America*. By repeating each phrase we get the A-A-B-B form encountered in such pieces as Brahms' *Lullaby* and the Italian folk song *Santa Lucia*.

Binary form is much in evidence in the short dance pieces that made up the suite of the seventeenth and eighteenth centuries, a period of lively experimentation in the realm of musical structure. The harpsichord pieces of François Couperin exhibit this form, as do certain pieces in the suites of Bach. Binary structure is readily apparent to the ear because each part ends in a complete cadence. However, the second section invariably repeats certain features of the first, so that many of these ostensibly two-part forms bear some resemblance to three-part structure. For this reason, certain musical theorists do not recognize two-part form as a separate category.

We will examine in subsequent chapters the great forms of Western music. No matter how imposing their dimensions, they all show the principle of repetition and contrast, of unity in variety, that we have traced here. In all its manifestations our music displays the striving for organic form that binds together the individual tones within the phrase, the phrases within the musical sentence, the sentences within the section, the sections within the movement, and the movements within the work as a whole; even as, in a novel, the individual words are bound together in phrases, sentences, paragraphs, sections, chapters, and parts.

It has been said that architecture is frozen music. By the same token, music is a floating architecture. Form is the architectural principle in music: it distributes the areas of activity and repose, tension and relaxation, light and shade, and integrates the multitudinous details, large and small, into the spacious and coherent structures that are the glory of Western music.

≥12≤

Musical Notation

> "Musical notation is so familiar to us that few are aware of the difficulty of the problems which had to be solved, and the innumerable experiments undertaken for the invention and perfection of a satisfactory method of recording musical sounds."
> Sylvia Townsend Warner

MUSICAL NOTATION presents a kind of graph of the tones in regard to their pitch and duration. The notes are written on the staff, a series of five horizontal lines with four spaces between, each representing another degree of pitch. The tones are C, D, E, F, G, A, B, C. From one C to the next is a distance of an octave. The series is duplicated in each octave.

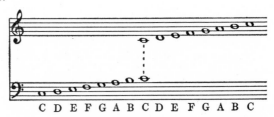

C D E F G A B C D E F G A B C

Accidentals are used to alter the pitch. The sharp (♯) raises the pitch by a half tone (or semitone); the flat (♭) lowers the pitch by a half tone. The natural (♮) cancels these, restoring the original pitch. Also in use are the double sharp (✖) and double flat (♭♭) which respectively raise and lower the pitch by two half tones.

The piano keyboard exemplifies this arrangement of whole and half tones. From one key to the next is a distance of half a tone, as from C to its upper neighbor C-sharp or from B to its lower neighbor B-flat. It will be noticed that C-sharp is identical with D-flat, D-sharp with E-flat, F-sharp with G-flat, and so on.

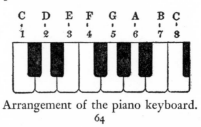

Arrangement of the piano keyboard.

64

The distance between two white keys is a whole tone (two semitones). The same holds for two black keys. Notice, however, two significant exceptions: there is no black key between E and F or between B and C, which are a semitone apart. By playing the eight white keys from one C to the next we sound the do-re-mi-fa-sol-la-ti-do scale, which we will examine more closely in a later chapter.

The clef is a letter sign placed on the staff in order to indicate the pitch of the notes. It is written on a certain line from which are reckoned the others. The G or treble clef establishes the second line of the staff as G above middle C. The F or bass clef establishes the fourth line as F below middle C. The treble clef is used in music for instruments of high range such as the violin or flute; in piano music, for the upper (generally the right-hand) part. The bass clef is used for instruments of low range such as the 'cello or trombone; in piano music, for the lower (generally the left-hand) part. There is also a C clef for instruments of middle range, which establishes middle C either on the third line of the staff (alto or viola clef) or on the fourth line (tenor clef, used by bass instruments in the upper part of their range).

Treble Clef   Bass Clef   Alto Clef   Tenor Clef

TIME VALUES

The duration of the notes is indicated by a system of relative values. When the whole note receives four beats, a half note receives two, and a quarter note one beat. The quarter note may be divided into two eighth notes (or three, which become a triplet); an eighth note divides into two sixteenths. Smaller subdivisions such as thirty-second and sixty-fourth notes are also used.

whole   half   quarter   eighth   sixteenth   thirty-second   sixty-fourth

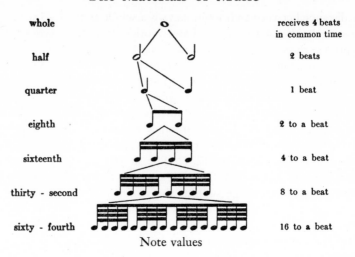

Note values

A tie connects two successive notes of the same pitch, prolonging the first by the value of the second. A dot after a note prolongs its time value by half.

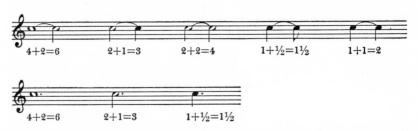

Dotted rhythms break up the musical flow, creating those terse pointed patterns that composers have used extensively. A familiar example of dotted rhythm occurs in the opening strophe of *The Battle Hymn of the Republic*, on the words "Mine eyes have seen the glory of the coming of the Lord"; the dotted rhythm continues through the next two lines. (For other examples see the musical illustrations on pp. 67–68.)

Time never stops in music, even when there is no sound. Silence is indicated by rests, which correspond in time value to the notes.

Rests

The time signature indicates the metrical pattern—that is, the basic scheme of accents and the note values. The upper numeral shows the number of beats in the measure; the lower shows the unit of value, the note value receiving one beat. The time signature 3/4 means there are three beats to a measure, with a quarter note receiving one beat. In 6/8 time there are six beats to the measure, an eighth note receiving one beat. Following are the most frequently encountered time signatures.

Duple meter	$\frac{2}{2}$	$\frac{2}{4}$	$\frac{2}{8}$
Triple meter	$\frac{3}{4}$	$\frac{3}{8}$	$\frac{3}{16}$
Quadruple meter	$\frac{4}{4}$	$\frac{4}{8}$	
Sextuple meter	$\frac{6}{4}$	$\frac{6}{8}$	

Also in use are $\frac{9}{8}$ (3 groups of 3) and $\frac{12}{8}$ (4 groups of 3). Contemporary music shows a wide use of nonsymmetrical patterns such as $\frac{5}{4}$ or $\frac{5}{8}$ (2 plus 3) and $\frac{7}{4}$ or $\frac{7}{8}$ (4 plus 3).

Four-four ($\frac{4}{4}$) is known as common time and is often indicated by the sign C. A vertical line drawn through this sign (¢) indicates *alla breve* or quick duple time, with the half note receiving one beat instead of the quarter; in other words, $\frac{2}{2}$ time instead of $\frac{4}{4}$.

The following examples show how the system works. It will be noticed that the measures are marked off by vertical bar lines. This makes the metrical pattern more readily apparent to the eye.

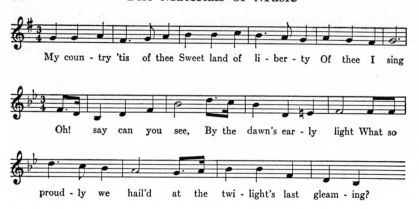

My coun - try 'tis of thee Sweet land of li - ber - ty Of thee I sing

Oh! say can you see, By the dawn's ear - ly light What so

proud - ly we hail'd at the twi - light's last gleam - ing?

NOTATION AND THE PERFORMER

The printed lines of a play do not indicate the many nuances of expression—the continual shifting of pace, the changes in emotional tension, the accenting of one word rather than another, the pauses, inflections, movements, and gestures—that create a living character. It is here that actor and director make their personal contribution, as a result of which one performer's interpretation of a role differs markedly from another's. The notation of music is even more limited in this regard than language. The composer is able to set down the pitches and their values in time; he indicates whether a passage should go fast or slow, soft or loud; and he may add other details that serve as clues to the character of the piece. But the life of the music, its mood and feeling, cannot be written down in symbols. This is where the sympathetic imagination of the performer comes into play, his intuition, his sense of timing, above all his understanding of style. The performer makes the notes come alive, he unlocks the composer's intention, his temperament serves as a kind of colored glass through which is refracted the creator's.

There is no single recipe for the proper performance of a work. Two great artists will differ in their interpretation of the same piece, yet each will be convincing on his own grounds. Precisely this flexibility makes for the excitement of the concert, and for the enormous interest that the public today takes in the interpretation of this artist or that. The performer's freedom of choice, naturally, is valid only within certain limits. If he goes beyond those, if he is too personal in his interpretation, he becomes capricious and arbitrary; he is no longer faithful

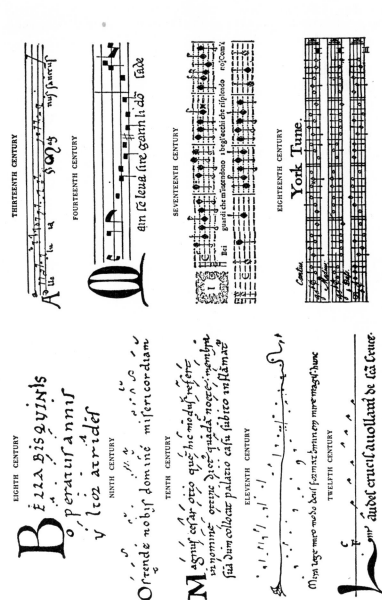

The evolution of notation in Western Music.

to the spirit of the composer. The great artist is one who strikes an exceedingly difficult balance. He asserts his own personality sufficiently to re-create and effectively project the music, while on the other hand he enters imaginatively into the spirit of the creator and reverently transmits the latter's intention.

It is the performer's high duty to transform the symbols on the page of music into glowing sound. To this task he brings the insights that talent, training, and years of experience have given him. When he discharges it well he makes a real contribution to our musical experience; he becomes the vital link between the composer and ourselves.

PART TWO

Nineteenth-Century Romanticism

"Music is the most romantic of all the arts—one might almost say, the only genuinely romantic one—for its sole subject is the infinite. Music discloses to man an unknown realm, a world in which he leaves behind him all definite feelings to surrender himself to an inexpressible longing."

E. T. A. Hoffmann (1776–1822)

❧13❧

The Romantic Spirit

"Romanticism is beauty without bounds—the beautiful infinite."
Jean Paul Richter (1763–1825)

HISTORIANS of art observe that the life of style moves between two opposite poles. In one period art leans toward order, poise, serenity. In another it exalts strangeness and wonder and ecstasy. During one era the artist views life objectively; he expresses emotion through universal symbols. During another he becomes fiercely individualistic; he seeks a manner of expression that is personal and subjective. One generation of artists adheres to traditional forms, striving above all for beauty of design and proportion; another rebels against tradition and loosens the inherited designs, enthroning in their place picturesque detail and striking color, mood, and atmosphere. One art style embraces the rational, another yearns for the irrational and the infinite. We call the one art classic, the other romantic.

Nietzsche in his writings on art dramatized the contrast between the two through the symbol of Apollo, god of light and measure, as opposed to Dionysus, god of intoxication and passion. Neither the Apollonian nor the Dionysian is confined to one epoch or country. Classic and romantic have alternated and even existed side by side from the beginning of time, for they correspond to two basic impulses in man's nature: on the one hand, his love of traditional standards, his need to have emotion purged and controlled; on the other, his desire for intoxication and ecstasy, his longing for the unknown and the unattainable.

It is important to avoid the common misconception that classical art is form without feeling while romantic art is feeling without form. There can be no art without feeling, nor can there be art without form. Thus classical art contains profound emotion and drama, just as romantic art often exhibits a most subtle sense of form. The difference between them is one of emphasis; it has to do with the way in which form and content are fused. Classicism purifies emotion by subjecting it to the discipline of an all-embracing design. In romantic art the emotion often struggles against this discipline, it floods and threatens to burst asunder the form. From this is derived the inner tension of romantic art, the sense of strain that is alien to the classical spirit.

73

Specifically, the classic and romantic labels are attached to two important periods in European art. The one held the stage in the late eighteenth century, the other came to the fore in the decades following the French Revolution. Romanticism dominated the art output of the nineteenth century; gave its name to a movement and an era; and created a multitude of colorful, intensely lyrical works that are still very much with us.

THE ROMANTIC MOVEMENT

The French Revolution was the outcome of momentous social forces. It signalized the transfer of power from the feudal-agricultural aristocracy to the industrial middle class. The new society, based on free enterprise, emphasized the individual as never before. Freedom—political, economic, religious, personal—was its watchword. On the artistic front this urge for individualism found expression in the romantic movement.

The breakdown of the aristocratic way of life, with its formal code of behavior, opened the door to the unashamed expression of feeling. One of the prime traits of romantic art was its emphasis on emotion. The slogans of liberty, fraternity, and equality inspired hopes and visions to which few artists failed to respond. Love of nature, interest in simple folk and in children, sympathy with the oppressed, faith in man and his destiny—all these, so intimately associated with the time, point to the democratic character of the romantic movement.

For centuries the artist had functioned under the patronage of princely courts or the Church. Under the patronage system he had been a commoner creating for aristocrats who were interested in his product rather than in him. Now he addressed an audience of his equals. His joys and sorrows became a legitimate subject for his art, his personality grew to be his most important asset. "I am different from all the men I have seen," proclaimed Jean-Jacques Rousseau. "If I am not better, at least I am different." In an age of individualistic empire builders the artist too emerged as an individual. The change is apparent in poetry where, it has been well said, the pronoun "I" now made its appearance. Gone were the elegant couplets of eighteenth-century poetry. The new age responded with sighs and tears to the passionate lyricism of Byron and Shelley, Keats, Heine, and de Musset.

The new freedom of the artist proved a not unmixed blessing. He confronted a philistine world from which he felt himself more and more cut off. A new type emerged—the artist as bohemian, the rejected

Delacroix, *Dante and Virgil in Hell.*

"One of the prime traits of romantic art was its emphasis on emotion."

dreamer who starved in an attic and through peculiarites of dress and behavior "shocked the bourgeois." This was the sensitive individual who was both too good for the moneyed world about him and not good enough. Increasingly the romantic artist found himself arrayed against the established order. He prized his freedom but paid dearly for it in loneliness, in knowing himself apart from his fellows. Withdrawal from the world brought a preoccupation with inner problems. Eternal longing, regret for the lost happiness of childhood, an indefinable discontent that gnawed at the soul—these were the ingredients of the romantic mood.

This malaise was reflected in the art of the time. Thus, Balzac's *Human Comedy* depicted the warping of human relationships in the new society. Hugo dedicated *Les Misérables* "to the unhappy ones of the earth." The nineteenth-century novel found its great theme in the conflict between the individual and society. Jean Valjean and Heathcliffe, Madame Bovary and Anna Karenina, Oliver Twist, Tess of the d'Urbervilles, and the Karamazovs—a varied company rises from those impassioned pages to point up the frustrations and guilts of the nineteenth-century world.

Hardly less persuasive was the art of those who sought escape. Some glamorized the past, as did Walter Scott and Alexandre Dumas. Longing for far-off lands inspired the exotic scenes that glow on the canvases of Turner and Delacroix. Whereas the eighteenth century had found

Turner, *Grand Canal, Venice.*

"Longing for far-off lands inspired the exotic scenes that glow on the canvases of Turner and Delacroix."

its inspiration in ancient Greece, the romantics discovered the so-called Dark Ages. King Arthur and Siegfried, fairy tale and medieval saga usurped the place formerly held by the gods and heroes of antiquity. The romantics also discovered nature, but nature as a backdrop for the inner conflicts of man. Theirs was a world of "strangeness and wonder": the eerie landscape of a Coleridge or a Poe. The fantastic and the macabre, traits of the medieval imagination, had returned to European art.

Poetry and painting, drama and the novel fulfilled as best they might the demands laid upon them by the romantic temperament. But it was in music that the romantics found their fulfillment. Music by its very indefiniteness spoke directly to the heart. It alone could appease the longing for the happiness that was nowhere to be found. "Every passion," wrote Hoffmann, author of the fantastic *Tales*, "is clothed by music with the purple luster of romanticism." Music became *the* romantic art, to the condition of which—in Walter Pater's celebrated phrase—all the other arts aspired. The magic potion drunk by the lovers in the first act of *Tristan* was an apt symbol. Their public no less than they yearned for oblivion, the highest bliss; and this only music—romantic music—could give them.

Romanticism has a youthful exuberance. Its ardor, its idealism, and its discontents are the attributes of youth. An atmosphere of adolescence surrounds the lives and works of its leading figures. Significantly, some of the greatest among them died at what is ordinarily the threshold of maturity: Keats at twenty-six, Shelley at thirty, Schubert at thirty-one; Chopin, Mendelssohn, Byron, and Poe before they reached forty. They burned with the "hard gemlike flame" and were consumed.

There is an immense excitement about the romantic era—the consciousness of reaching for things that had never been attempted before. Romantic art manifests a hunger for life and a fervor of emotion that are nothing short of formidable. It is an intensely expressive art that still holds millions in thrall.

≥14≤

Romanticism in Music

"Music is the melody whose text is the world."
Schopenhauer

EMOTION in art differs in one important respect from the emotions of life: it is presented within a form. In the course of shaping his ideas into a form the artist endows them with beauty. He also lifts them from the personal level, where they would be of interest only to himself and his friends, to the enduring realm of art.

It is through the form, then, that private feelings are transformed into public art. The classical era evoked elaborate forms to effect this transformation: the sonata, the symphony, the concerto. But the romantics chafed under the restraints of form. Desiring to keep emotion at maximum intensity, they loosened the classical design and flooded it with lyricism. Or they developed free supple forms that strove for direct contact with the listener.

The early nineteenth century therefore saw a departure from the grand form of the preceding age—the classical sonata and symphony. The romantic composers could no more follow the forms of Haydn, Mozart, and Beethoven than they could transport themselves back to the time of those masters. What they had to say—what the age demanded of them to say—constituted a new content that had to find its own form. Romantic melody had a wide and immediate appeal, as is evidenced by the enduring popularity of the tunes of Schubert, Chopin, Verdi, and their fellows. It is the romantic concept of melody that is most familiar to our present-day public. Of even greater moment was the romantic contribution to harmony. Nineteenth-century musicians, in their attempt to expand the expressive powers of music, experimented widely in this domain. Especially they investigated the capacity of dissonant harmony to generate emotional tension. Chopin, Liszt, and Wagner were among the innovators who exerted a decisive effect on the further evolution of our harmonic system. Their piquant chord progressions teased the ear, imparting to the musical fabric a bewitching variety of colors. They revealed a new harmonic language that stands as one of the foremost achievements of the romantic era. The interest in folklore and the rising tide of nationalism impelled the romantic musicians to utilize the folk songs and dances of their native lands. As a result, a number of national idioms—Hungarian, Polish, Russian, Bohemian, Scandinavian—came to the fore and opened up new areas to European music, greatly enriching its melody and harmony.

In the domain of tone color romanticism made what is perhaps its most signal contribution. For the classical period color had been a means of clarifying architecture. The romantics regarded color as a value in itself. They strove for sensuous beauty, for tonal enchantment. Now the horn, the romantic instrument par excellence, came into its own; as did those expressive combinations of woodwinds and strings that were so dear to the romantic imagination.

Romanticism found an enchanting path of escape from the heritage of the classical sonata and symphony. This was by way of the short lyric forms—the piano piece and song—which came to occupy a central place during the first phase of the romantic movement. But the desire for intimate lyricism was only part of the picture. The romantic interest in tone color went hand in hand with a steady growth in the size and importance of the orchestra. The center of musical life in the nineteenth century was no longer church or palace, but concert hall. The new patrons of music, the middle-class public, were ready to support large bodies of musicians for whom playing was a full-time occupation. Interest came to center in the orchestra and, among musicians, in the art and science of orchestration.

The desire for direct communication led composers to use a large number of expressive terms intended to serve as clues to the mood of the music, with the result that a highly characteristic vocabulary sprang up. We encounter again and again *espressivo* (expressively), *dolce* (sweetly), *cantabile* (songful); *agitato, misterioso, lamentoso, trionfale; dolente* (weeping), *mesto* (sad), *maestoso* (majestic); *pastorale* and *gioioso* (joyous); *con amore* (with love, tenderly), *con passione, con fuoco* (with fire). These suggest not only the character of the music but the frame of mind behind it.

THE UNION OF THE ARTS

The romantic wished to encompass all experience at its maximum intensity. He was enchanted in turn by poetry, music, painting. How much more intoxicating, he reasoned, would be the effect of combining all three. Music in the nineteenth century drew steadily closer to literature and painting—a typically romantic phenomenon. The romantics were unable to accept music as an abstract, purely esthetic experience. For them it was linked to dreams and passions; to philosophy and religious faith; to profound meditations on life, death, and destiny; to love of nature, pride in one's country, desire for freedom, and to the fierce political struggles of the age. The result was that music took on an intensely human content. It began to evoke moods and visions in a way that it never had before.

Romantic music, then, was marked on the one hand by intimate lyricism, on the other by the grand orchestral gesture. It developed harmony and color, exploited folklore and national sentiment, painted exotic scenes. It brought music close to literary and pictorial values, it exalted passion and intoxication. The romantic attitude enabled music to achieve a unique position in the nineteenth century: as a moral force, a vision of man's greatness, and as a direct link between the outer world and his interior life.

Song and Piano Piece

⊰15⊱

The Short Lyric Forms as an Expression
of Romanticism

"Out of my great sorrows I make my little songs."
Heinrich Heine

THROUGH the short lyric forms the romantic movement satisfied its need for intimate personal expression. Coming into prominence in the early decades of the century, the song and piano piece emerged as one of the purest manifestations of the new lyricism.

THE SONG

The repertory of song—folk, popular, and art—is more extensive than that of all other types of music. For song combines two musical elements of universal appeal—melody and the human voice. A song is a short lyric composition for solo voice based on a poetic text. The vocal melody is presented as a rule with an instrumental accompaniment. The melodic line follows the natural inflections of the language. For this reason vocal music reflects the speech patterns of a nation and is rooted in the native soil. It is this that makes Debussy's vocal line seem so French, Brahms' so German, Stephen Foster's so American.

The accompaniment furnishes harmonic background and support to the vocal melody. It creates the proper atmosphere and the frame; and in addition may offer a commentary on the words through independent passages such as a prelude, interludes, and postlude. In the art song of the past hundred years the accompaniment has taken on increasing prominence and sophistication.

81

TYPES OF SONG STRUCTURE

We distinguish between two main types of song structure. In strophic form the same melody is repeated with every stanza, or strophe, of the poem. This formation, which occurs very frequently in folk and popular song, permits of no great closeness between words and music. Instead it sets up a general atmosphere or feeling-tone that accommodates itself equally well to all the stanzas. The first may tell of the lover's expectancy, the second of his joy at seeing his beloved, the third of her father's harshness in separating them, and the fourth of her sad death, all these being sung to the same tune. The prevalence of strophic song throughout the ages points to one conclusion: the folk learned early that a lovely tune is a joy in itself, and that it heightens emotion no matter what the content of a particular stanza.

The other type is what the Germans call *durchkomponiert*, literally "through-composed" (that is, composed throughout). Here the music follows the story line, changing with each stanza according to the text. This affords the possibility of subtle characterization that captures every shade of meaning in the words.

The strophic form is used for lyric moods, simple emotions, and songs in folk or popular style. The "through-composed" song is suited for narrative, for dramatic ballads, and for the introspective poetry that the romantic composers and their successors set with such refinement.

THE ROMANTIC SONG

Despite the prominence of song throughout the ages, the art song as we know it today was a product of the romantic era. It was created by the union of romantic poetry and music in the early nineteenth century. This union was consummated with such artistry by Franz Schubert and his successors, notably Robert Schumann and Johannes Brahms, that the new genre came to be known all over Europe by the German word for song—*Lied*.

The lied depended for its flowering on the upsurge of lyric poetry that marked the rise of German romanticism. Goethe (1749–1832) and Heine (1799–1856) are the two leading figures among a group of poets who, like Wordsworth and Byron, Shelley and Keats in our literature, cultivated a subjective mode of expression through the short lyric poem. The lied brought to flower the romantic desire for the union of music and poetry. Projected through the most expressive of instruments—the human voice—the lied ranged from tender sentiment to dramatic balladry. Its favorite themes were love and longing, the beauty of nature, the transience of human happiness. Within a short time the lied achieved immense popularity and made a durable contribution to world art.

THE PIANO PIECE

The short lyric piece was the instrumental equivalent of the song. The favored medium was the piano, whose literature in this domain far surpasses in interest and variety that for any other instrument. This species of intimate composition, which illumines a particular mood rather than a general idea, is known as a characteristic piece (or character piece). Among the titles most frequently used are bagatelle (literally, "a trifle"), impromptu (on the spur of the moment), intermezzo (interlude), nocturne (night song), novelette (short story), moment musical, song without words, album leaf, prelude, romance, caprice; and, of larger dimensions, the rhapsody and ballade. In the dance category are the waltz, mazurka, polka, écossaise, polonaise, march, and country dance (or contredanse).

Many of these pieces follow a simple A-B-A structure that presents two contrasting moods. The first may be rhythmic and the second lyric, or the other way around. The return of the first section gives these pieces a rounded form, imparting balance and symmetry to the design. The general titles gradually gave way to specific ones of a fanciful and descriptive nature. Typical are *In the Night, Soaring, Whims, Forest Murmurs, Fireflies.*

Before the romantic period, composers lavished their attention upon the large musical forms. Sonata, symphony, concerto, string quartet, and the like achieved their effects through the logical development of musical ideas. In such works intellectual factors played an important role. The character piece, on the other hand, emphasized new values in musical expression: freshness, simplicity, spontaneity, and the presentation of musical material in such a way as to underline the element of pure feeling.

The short lyric forms occupied a central position in the musical output of the romantic era. They did so because the nineteenth-century composer recognized that size is no criterion in art, and that an exquisitely wrought miniature may contain as much beauty as an hour-long symphony. In the song and lyric piano piece romanticism, especially in its early phase, found one of its most characteristic means of expression.

❧16❦
Franz Schubert (1797-1828)

"When I wished to sing of love it turned to sorrow. And when
I wished to sing of sorrow it was transformed for me into love."

IN THE popular mind Franz Schubert's life has become symbolic of the
romantic artist's fate. He wrote music of inexpressible poignancy. He
knew poverty. He died young. And after his death he was enshrined
among the immortals.

Franz Schubert.

HIS LIFE

He was born in a suburb of Vienna, the son of a schoolmaster. The
boy learned the violin from his father, piano from an elder brother;
his beautiful soprano voice gained him admittance to the imperial

chapel and school where the court singers were trained. His creative gift asserted itself in boyhood, and his teachers were duly astonished at the musicality of the shy dreamy lad. One of them remarked that Franz seemed to learn "straight from Heaven."

His schooldays over, young Schubert tried to follow in his father's footsteps, but he was not cut out for the routine of the classroom. He found escape in the solitude of his attic, immersing himself in the lyric poets who were the first voices of German romanticism. "Everything he touched turned to song." With a spontaneity comparable to Mozart's, the melodies took shape that gave to the new romantic lyricism its ideal expression. *Gretchen at the Spinning Wheel,* to Goethe's verses, was written in a single afternoon—when he was seventeen. A year later came his setting of the same poet's *Erlking.* One of his greatest songs, it was the work of a few hours.

Schubert's talent for friendship attracted to him a little band of followers. Their appreciation of his genius solaced him for the neglect and incomprehension of the world. Poets, painters, musicians, these young enthusiasts were the advance guard of the romantic movement. With their encouragement Schubert, not yet twenty, broke with the drudgery of his father's school. In the eleven years that were left him he occupied no official position (although he occasionally made half-hearted attempts to obtain one). He lived with one or another of his friends in that mixture of poverty and camaraderie, hope and despair, that operetta writers of a later age have found it all too easy to glamorize. And steadily, with an almost self-devouring intensity, the music came pouring from the bespectacled young man. "How do you compose?" he was asked. "I finish one piece," was the answer, "and begin the next."

Schubert was singularly unable to stand up to the world. Songs that in time sold in the hundreds of thousands he surrendered literally for the price of a meal. It was borne in upon him that the creative gift is not enough for an artist. "The state should support me," he remarked sadly, "so that I may be untroubled and free to compose." As the years passed, the buoyancy of youth gave way to a sense of loneliness, the tragic loneliness of the romantic artist. "No one feels another's grief," he wrote, "no one understands another's joy. People imagine that they can reach one another. In reality they only pass each other by." Yet he comprehended—and in this he was the romantic—that his very suffering must open to his art new layers of awareness. "My music is the product of my talent and my misery. And that which I have written in my greatest distress is what the world seems to like best."

He still yielded to flurries of optimism when success appeared to lie within his grasp. Again and again he directed his efforts to opera. But he was not destined for success in the theater. His repeated defeats had a devastating effect upon his impressionable nature. He describes himself as "the most unfortunate, most miserable being on earth . . . whose brightest hopes have come to nought, to whom love and friendship are but torture, and whose enthusiasm for the beautiful is fast vanishing." There came to him an intimation that the struggle had been decided against him. "It seems to me at times that I no longer belong to this world."

This was the emotional climate of the magnificent song cycle *Die Winterreise* (The Winter Journey), in which he struck a note of somber lyricism new to music. Depressed by illness and poverty, he abandoned himself to the mournful images of Wilhelm Müller's poems. The long dark journey—was it not the symbol of his own life? Now he nerved himself to his last effort. To the earlier masterpieces was added, in that final year, an amazing list that includes the Symphony in C major, the Mass in E-flat, the String Quintet in C, the three posthumous piano sonatas, and thirteen of his finest songs, among them the *Serenade*.

With the great C-major Symphony behind him he made arrangements to study counterpoint. "I see now how much I still have to learn." Ill with typhus, he managed to correct the proofs of the last part of *Die Winterreise*. The sense of defeat accompanied him through the final delirium; he fancied that he was being buried alive. "Do I not deserve a place above the ground?" His last wish was to be buried near the master he worshiped above all others—Beethoven.

He was thirty-one years old when he died. His possessions consisted of his clothing, his bedding, and "a pile of old music valued at ten florins": his unpublished manuscripts. In the memorable words of Sir George Grove, "There never has been one like him, and there never will be another."

HIS MUSIC

Schubert stood at the confluence of the classical and romantic eras. His symphonic style bespeaks the heir of the classical tradition; but in his songs and piano pieces he was wholly the romantic, an artist whose magical lyricism impelled Liszt to call him "the most poetic musician that ever was." Like every composer of the nineteenth century, he was

weighed down by the greatness of his predecessors. "Who can do anything more after Beethoven?" he complained. Yet within the orbit of
that towering figure he developed a symphonic idiom of his own. His
symphonies, for all their romantic ardor, are classical in their dramatic
momentum and continuity. They rank as the finest since Beethoven.

Chamber music was Schubert's birthright as a Viennese. To the
tradition of intimate social music he brought his own inwardness of
spirit. The string quartets, the Quintet in C, the two trios, and the
Trout Quintet bear the true Schubertian stamp. They end the line of
Viennese classicism.

In the Impromptus and *Moments Musicaux* (Musical Moments) the
piano sings the new lyricism. Caprice, spontaneity, and the charm of
the unexpected take their place as elements of romantic art. Of comparable freshness is the popular tone of the dance pieces, Waltzes,
Ländlers, and Écossaises. As for his piano sonatas, they have never
established themselves because of their length. Single movements are of
surpassing loveliness, but on the whole they lack conciseness and unity.

Finally there are the songs, more than six hundred of them. Many
were written down at white heat, sometimes five, six, seven in a single
morning. In popular manuals Schubert is named "Father of the Song."
The title is misleading on two counts: it ignores his position among the
masters of instrumental music, and it ignores the history of the art
song throughout Europe. But it does indicate how closely his genius is
linked in the popular mind with the lyric song as we know it today.
Certain of his melodies achieve the universality of folk song, others
display the highest sophistication. In either case they issue directly
from the heart of the poem. Their eloquence, their freshness of feeling,
has never been surpassed. Of special moment are the accompaniments:
a measure or two, and the rustling brook is conjured up, the dilapidated
hurdy-gurdy, or the post-horn announcing the eagerly awaited letter.
The themes treated by Schubert are as diverse as life itself. Upon the
poets whose verses he set he conferred a dubious immortality: never
again would their poems seem complete without his music.

DER ERLKÖNIG (THE ERLKING)

The "strangeness and wonder" of romanticism are set forth in Goethe's celebrated ballad, which is based on the legend that whoever is
touched by the King of the Elves must die. The poem has four characters: the narrator, the father, the child, and the seductive Elf.

Wer reitet so spät durch Nacht und Wind?
Es ist der Vater mit seinem Kind;
er hat den Knaben wohl in dem Arm,
er fasst ihn sicher, er hält ihn warm.

Who rides so late through night and wind?
It is the father with his child.
He holds the boy within his arm,
He clasps him tight, he keeps him warm.

"Mein Sohn, was birgst du so bang dein Gesicht?"
"Siehst, Vater, du den Erlkönig nicht?
den Erlenkönig mit Kron' und Schweif?"
"Mein Sohn, es ist ein Nebelstreif."

"My son, why hide your face in fear?"
"See, father, the Erlking's near.
The Erlking with crown and wand."
"Dear son, 'tis but a misty cloud."

"Du liebes Kind, komm, geh' mit mir!
gar schöne Spiele spiel' ich mit dir;
manch' bunte Blumen sind an dem Strand,
meine Mutter hat manch' gülden Gewand."

"Ah, sweet child, come with me!
Such pleasant games I'll play with thee!
Such pleasant flowers bloom in the field,
My mother has many a robe of gold."

"Mein Vater, mein Vater, und hörest du nicht
was Erlenkönig mir leise verspricht?"
"Sei ruhig, bleibe ruhig, mein Kind;
in dürren Blättern säuselt der Wind.

"Oh father, father, do you not hear
What the Erlking whispers in my ear?"
"Be still, my child, be calm;
'Tis but the withered leaves in the wind."

"Willst, feiner Knabe, du mit mir geh'n?
meine Töchter sollen dich warten schön;
meine Töchter führen den nächtlichen Reih'n
und wiegen und tanzen und singen dich ein."

"My lovely boy, wilt go with me?
My daughters fair shall wait on thee,
My daughters nightly revels keep,
They'll sing and dance and rock thee to sleep."

"Mein Vater, mein Vater, und siehst du nicht dort
Erlkönigs Töchter am düstern Ort?"

"Oh father, father, see you not
The Erlking's daughters in yon dark spot?"

"Mein Sohn, mein Sohn, ich seh' es genau.
es scheinen die alten Weiden so grau."

"My son, my son, the thing you see
Is only the old gray willow tree."

"Ich liebe dich, mich reizt deine schöne Gestalt;
und bist du nicht willig, so brauch' ich Gewalt."
"Mein Vater, mein Vater, jetzt fasst er mich an!
Erlkönig hat mir ein Leids gethan!"

"I love thee, thy form enflames my sense;
And art thou not willing, I'll take thee hence!"
"Oh father, father, he grasps my arm,
The Erlking has done me harm!"

Dem Vater grauset's, er reitet geschwind
er hält in Armen das ächzende Kind,
erreicht den Hof mit Müh' und Noth:
in seinen Armen das Kind war todt!

The father shudders, he speeds ahead,
He clasps to his bosom the sobbing child,
He reaches home with pain and dread:
In his arms the child lay dead!

The eerie atmosphere of the poem is established by the piano part. Galloping triplets are heard against a rumbling figure in the bass. This motive, so romantic in tone, pervades the canvas and imparts to it an astonishing unity.

The characters are vividly differentiated through changes in the melody, harmony, rhythm, and type of accompaniment. The child's terror is suggested by clashing dissonance, pitched higher each time. The father, allaying his son's fears, is represented by a more rounded vocal line. As for the Erlking, his cajoling is given in suavely melodious phrases.

The song is through-composed; the music follows the unfolding of the narrative with a steady building up of tension to the climax. Abruptly the obsessive triplet rhythm breaks off, giving away to declamation. "In his arms the child"—a pause—"lay dead."

The thing seems strangely simple, inevitable. The doing of it by a marvelous boy of eighteen was an event in the history of romanticism.

MOMENT MUSICAL IN F MINOR

In title, form, and substance the most famous of the "Musical Moments" epitomizes the short lyric piece. It is intimate and unassuming; one would almost say artless, were it not for the omnipresence of art. It appears to have been tossed off on the spur of the moment, yet it is anything but a sketch. It bears the finest qualities of the miniature: chiseled line, fastidious speech, and epigrammatic thought.

The piece consists of brief symmetrical sections, each of them repeated. So small a frame does not allow for great contrasts. The mood

of the opening prevails more or less throughout. In this compact little work are manifest the qualities that set Schubert apart, in the eyes of his devotees, from all others: his charm of melody, his tenderness, his gentle sorrow, and that ineffably romantic longing which can only be described as Schubertian.

⪧17⪦

Robert Schumann (1810-1856)

"Music is to me the perfect expression of the soul."

THE TURBULENCE of German romanticism, its fantasy and subjective emotion, found their voice in Robert Schumann. His music is German to the core, yet he is no local figure. A true lyric poet, he rose above the national to make his contribution to world culture.

HIS LIFE

Robert Schumann was born in Zwickau, a town in Saxony, son of a bookseller whose love of literature was reflected in the boy. At his mother's insistence he undertook the study of law, first at the University of Leipzig, then at Heidelberg. The youth daydreamed at the piano, steeped himself in Goethe and Byron, and attended only an occasional lecture. His aversion to the law kept pace with his passion for music; it was his ambition to become a pianist. At last he won his mother's consent and returned to Leipzig to study with Friedrich Wieck, one of the foremost pedagogues of the day. "I am so fresh in soul and spirit," he exulted, "that life gushes and bubbles around me in a thousand springs."

The young man practiced intensively to make up for his late start. In his eagerness to perfect his technique he devised a contrivance that held the fourth finger immobile while the others exercised. The gadget was so effective that he permanently injured the tendons of his right hand. The end of his hopes as a pianist turned his interest to composing. In a burst of creative energy he produced, while still in his twenties, his most important works for the piano.

The spontaneity of his production astonished him. "Everything comes to me of itself," he wrote, "and indeed, it sometimes seems as if I could play on eternally and never come to an end." He refers again and again to the almost automatic quality of his inspiration. "Often I feel such a compulsion to compose that even if I were on a lonely island in the middle of the sea I could not stop. . . . It makes me altogether happy, this art."

He was engaged concurrently in an important literary venture. With a group of like-minded enthusiasts he founded a journal named *The New Magazine for Music*. The leading spirit in the enterprise, he regarded it as his mission "to help prepare and hasten the coming of a new poetic era." Schumann threw himself into his editorial activities as impetuously as he had into composing. Under his direction the periodical became one of the most important music journals in Europe.

Schumann's critical essays revealed the composer as a gifted literary man. Cast in the form of prose poems, imaginary dialogues, or letters, they were as personal as his music. He fought the taste of the bourgeois —the Philistines, as he liked to call them. He agitated for the great works of the past and for the new romanticism. In sketches that were half fact, half fiction he portrayed his friends and associates. Felix Meritis was Mendelssohn, whom at that time he admired above all living musicians. Master Raro was the judicious critic modeled after his teacher Friedrich Wieck. Chiarina was the latter's young daughter Clara, already known as one of the gifted pianists of the time. Schumann himself assumed two pen names to express the two sides of his personality: Florestan was gay and impetuous, Eusebius dreamy and introspective. The two carried on great arguments that mirrored the conflict between exuberance and restraint, between rebellious content and controlling form: the basic conflict in the soul of the romantic artist.

The hectic quality of this decade was intensified by his courtship of Clara Wieck. When he first came to study with her father she was an eleven-year-old prodigy who forthwith lost her heart to the young man. She was about sixteen when Robert realized that he loved her. Wieck's opposition to the marriage bordered on the psychopathic. Clara was the supreme achievement of his life and he refused to surrender her to another. For several years she was cruelly torn between the father she revered and the man she loved. At length, since she was not yet of age, the couple was forced to appeal to the courts against Wieck. The marriage took place in 1840, when Clara was twenty-one and Robert thirty. His happiness overflowed into a medium more personal even than the piano. This was his "year of song," when he produced over a hundred of the lieder that represent his lyric gift at its purest.

The two artists settled in Leipzig, pursuing their careers side by side. Clara became the first interpreter of Robert's piano works and in the ensuing decade contributed substantially to the spreading of his fame. Yet neither her love nor that of their children could ward off his increasing withdrawal from the world. Moodiness and nervous exhaustion culminated, in 1844, in a severe breakdown. The doctors counseled a change of scene. The couple removed to Dresden where Schumann seemingly made a full recovery. But the periods of depression returned ever more frequently. "In these years I have been very industrious. One must work as long as day lasts. . . ."

In 1850 Schumann was appointed music director at Düsseldorf. But he was ill-suited for public life; he could neither organize music festivals nor deal with masses of men, and was forced to relinquish the post. During a tour of Holland, where Clara and he were warmly received, he began to complain of "unnatural noises" in his head. His last letter to the violinist Joachim, two weeks before the final breakdown, is a farewell to his art. "The music is silent now . . . I will close. Already it grows dark."

He fell prey to auditory hallucinations, during which he was kept awake by a single maddening tone. Once he rose in the middle of the night to write down a theme that he imagined had been brought him by the spirits of Schubert and Mendelssohn. It was his last melody. A week later, in a fit of melancholia, he threw himself into the Rhine. He was rescued by fishermen and placed in a private asylum near Bonn. Despite occasional flashes of lucidity, the darkness did not lift. He died two years later at the age of forty-six.

HIS MUSIC

Schumann's art exemplifies the conflict between classical form and romantic content that his generation was heir to. He fought to save for romanticism the heritage of Beethoven, and bravely tackled the great classical forms—symphony, sonata, concerto, and chamber music. But he was essentially a lyricist and made his major contribution in the romantic realm of the lied and the piano piece.

As a piano composer Schumann was one of the most original figures of the century. Whimsy and ardent expressiveness pervade his miniatures, which brim over with impassioned melody, novel harmonies, and vigorous rhythms. The titles of the collections strike the romantic note;

among them we find *Fantasy Pieces*, *Papillons* (Butterflies), *Romances*, *Scenes from Childhood*. No less characteristic are the names affixed to individual numbers: *In the Night*, *Why?*, *The Poet Speaks*. Schumann emphasized that he added the titles *after* the music was written. All the same he illustrates the tendency of his time to "literarize" musical emotion, to associate it with specific images. He was less successful with the abstract forms. Although his three sonatas contain lovely things, they fall short of the organic unity that was the classical ideal. He did, however, succeed in producing three large works that stand in the top class of the repertoire: the Fantasy in C, the Symphonic Etudes and the Piano Concerto in A minor.

As a lieder writer he ranks second only to Schubert. His songs are finely wrought and rich in poetic suggestion. His favorite theme is love, particularly from the woman's point of view. His favored poet was Heine, for whom he had an affinity like that of Schubert for Goethe. The piano accompaniments are integrated with the vocal line in the highest degree. Schumann followed Schubert in cultivating the song cycle. Among his supreme achievements are the cycles *Frauenliebe und -Leben* (Woman's Love and Life, verses by Chamisso) and *Dichterliebe* (Poet's Love, by Heine).

Thoroughly romantic in feeling are the four symphonies. Schumann has been taken to task for his inability to develop thematic material and to orchestrate. The difficulty lies deeper, in the lyrical rather than symphonic nature of his thinking. Yet even when his instrumental writing is awkward, it fits peculiarly his forceful ideas. The best of his symphonies, the First and Fourth, communicate a lyric freshness that has kept them alive long after many more adroitly fashioned works have fallen by the way. What could be closer to the essence of German romanticism than the "nature sound" of the horns and trumpets at the opening of the *Spring* Symphony? "Could you infuse into the orchestra," he wrote the conductor, "a kind of longing for spring? At the first entrance of the trumpets I should like them to sound as from on high, like a call to awakening."

Through his writings on music he stands in the forefront of nineteenth-century critics. His propagandizing on behalf of Bach, Beethoven, and Schubert helped enormously to raise the level of public taste. And he singled out the creative forces of his own time with sure intuition. His first article, a review of a set of variations by an unknown young composer named Frédéric Chopin, began with the famous words: "Hats off, gentlemen—a genius!" More than twenty years later, in his last essay, he prophesied the future eminence of another unknown—Johannes Brahms. His writings prove, if proof were needed, that there is no better critic of music than the composer who is articulate. Many a paragraph applies amazingly to our own time.

DIE BEIDEN GRENADIERE (THE TWO GRENADIERS)

Heinrich Heine's ballad about two homecoming Napoleonic soldiers furnished the text for Schumann's most celebrated song. Here is exemplified the vigorous, Florestan side of Schumann's genius.

Nach Frankreich zogen zwei Grenadier',	To France came from Russia two grenadiers
die waren in Russland gefangen,	Who had been captives in battle,
und als sie kamen in's deutsche Quartier	And as they reached the German frontiers
sie liessen die Köpfe hangen.	Their heads were bowed with grief.
Da hörten sie beide die traurige Mähr,	For there they heard the sorrowful news
dass Frankreich verloren gegangen,	That France had been defeated,
besiegt und geschlagen das tapfere Heer,	Defeated and scattered her valiant army,
und der Kaiser, der Kaiser gefangen!	And the Emperor, the Emperor taken.
Da weinten zusammen die Grenadier'	Then wept the two grenadiers
wohl ob der kläglichen Kunde;	Such sorrowful tidings to learn;
Der Eine sprach: "Wie weh wird mir	The first one said: "Woe is me,
wie brennt meine alte Wunde."	Now fiercely my old wounds burn."
Der And're sprach: "Das Lied ist aus,	The other said: "My song is done,
auch ich möcht" mit dir sterben,	Would that I were dead,
doch hab' ich Weib und Kind zu Haus,	Yet I've a wife and child at home
die ohne mich verderben."	Who are helpless without me."
"Was schert mich Weib, was schert mich Kind	"What matters wife or child?
ich trage weit bess're Verlangen,	By nobler desires I am shaken,
lass sie betteln geh'n wenn sie hungrig sind,	Let them go beg if they hungry be,
mein Kaiser, mein Kaiser gefangen!	My Emperor, my Emperor is taken.
Gewähr mir, Bruder, eine Bitt':	Grant me, brother, one request:
Wenn ich jetzt sterben werde,	If I now should die,
So nimm meine Leiche nach Frankreich mit	Take my body to France with you,
begrab' mich in Frankreich's Erde.	In my native soil let me lie.
Das Ehrenkreuz am rothen Band	My cross of honor with band of red
sollst du auf's Herz mir legen;	Lay upon my heart;
die Flinte gieb mir in die Hand,	My musket place in my hand,
und gürt mir um den Degen.	And my sword beside me.
So will ich liegen und horchen still,	So will I lie within the grave,
wie eine Schildwach', im Grabe,	A sentry still, and faithful,
bis einst ich höre Kanonengebrüll	Till I hear the roar of the cannon
und wiehernder Rosse Getrabe.	And the galloping hoofbeats.

Dann reitet mein Kaiser wohl über mein Grab,	Then over my grave will my Emperor ride
viel Schwerter klirren und blitzen;	While swords flash and descend.
dann steig' ich gewaffnet hervor aus dem Grab,	Then armed to the teeth will I rise from the grave
den Kaiser, den Kaiser zu schützen!"	The Emperor, the Emperor to defend.

The song is an example of the dramatic ballad that is through-composed. A martial figure in the piano part, in 4/4 time, immediately sets the mood.

This prelude, marked by the dotted rhythms beloved by Schumann, recurs. The little motive of sixteenth notes at its end is heard again and again throughout the song. There is a slackening of intensity as the soldiers learn the sorrowful news. Their mounting agitation is reflected in an acceleration of pace. The request of the second grenadier (stanzas 3 and 4) steadily builds up tension. The climax is very grand: as the soldier pictures himself in the grave, the vocal line rises to the strains of the *Marseillaise*. It is one of those exciting effects that never fail. In the final stanza Schumann repeats the line about the flashing swords—the only repetition of text in the whole song—to allow for the necessary musical expansion. A postlude of sustained chords in the piano part adds a thoughtful commentary. The heroics of this ballad belong to a former era; but it would be difficult to surpass its sweeping line, its virile tone, and its effectiveness in the concert hall.

"Music still devours me. I must often tear myself from it by violence." This remark indicates the passionate creativity of the decade and a half in which Schumann was at his peak. His peak was the spring tide of German romanticism, during which he nobly discharged what he conceived to be the artist's mission: "To send light into the depths of the human heart!"

Program Music

18

The Nature of Program Music

"More an expression of feeling than tone painting."
Beethoven (on the *Pastoral* Symphony)

FROM the mating of orchestral music with literature came the genre known as program music, which carries associations lying outside the realm of tone. The nature of these associations is indicated by a literary title or an explanatory note—the "program"—which is appended to the score. Program music is distinguished from absolute or pure music, which deals with musical patterns devoid of literary connotations.

Program music has existed for thousands of years. Every age has produced its quota of compositions intended to depict storms, battles, bird calls, the ringing of bells, the murmur of waterfalls, and the outlines of a story. However, it was only in the nineteenth century that this type of music came to play a major part in the output of an era.

There is one essential point to be remembered in connection with program music. The composer is *not* trying to tell a story or paint a scene. If this were his goal he would become a writer or painter. He is a musician—which means two things: first, that thoughts and feelings, poetic associations and images, take shape in his mind as musical ideas; and second, that once these ideas come into being they exist for him as musical material, to be molded into musical forms according to the laws of his art. To regard the music as telling a story, to listen to it as a kind of musical scenario or accompaniment to an imaginary animated cartoon, is to miss its nature as music A musical work expresses a frame of mind and a state of form. It is not a painting in tones.

What the program does is to give us a clue to the frame of mind out of which the work issued. It stands as a link between the composer's experience as a musician and his experience as a human being. The program serves an orchestral work in much the same way as the poem does a song or the plot does an opera. It becomes the point of departure for the musical conception.

The distinction between absolute and program music is not as rigid as many suppose. A work entitled Symphony No. 1 or Third String Quartet falls into the former category. Yet the composer in the course of writing it may very well have had in mind specific images and associations that he has not seen fit to divulge. Conversely, a piece called *Romeo and Juliet* Overture comes under the heading of program music. Yet if we were not told the title we would listen to it as a piece of pure music. This is what we are apt to do in any case once we get to know the work. What concerns us ultimately is the destiny not of the lovers but of the themes.

It is well for us to take note of the program, as this indicates the emotional and intellectual framework of the composition. But it is even better, with each rehearing of the work, to let the program recede into the background—where it belongs—and to concentrate on the music.

VARIETIES OF PROGRAM MUSIC

THE CONCERT OVERTURE

One impulse toward program music derived from the theater. Many overtures to operas and spoken plays achieved an independent popularity in the concert hall. This pointed the way to a new type of overture much in favor with the romantic era: a one-movement concert piece for orchestra based on a striking literary idea. Such a work might be descriptive, like Mendelssohn's seascape *Hebrides* (*Fingal's Cave*); or it might be of a sharply defined character, such as Brahms' *Tragic Overture*. It could embody a patriotic idea, as did Tchaikovsky's *Overture 1812;* or a dramatic one, like the same composer's *Romeo and Juliet.*

The concert overture, despite its literary program, presented and developed its ideas in accordance with the procedures of absolute music. Its design, in fact, was the same as that of the first movement of the symphony. It offered romantic composers an attractive compromise form between program and absolute music. On the one hand, they could avail themselves of the abstract musical procedures of the classical era. On the other, they were able to invest their music with poetic or pictorial images of a romantic cast.

INCIDENTAL MUSIC

An engaging species of program music is that written for plays, generally consisting of an overture and a series of numbers to be performed between the acts and during the important scenes. Nineteenth-century composers produced a number of works in this genre that were notable for tone painting, characterization, and theater atmosphere. The most successful numbers were generally arranged into concert suites, certain of which became vastly popular. Mendelssohn's music for *A Midsummer Night's Dream* is one of the most felicitous works in this category. Hardly less appealing are the two suites from Bizet's music for Alphonse Daudet's play *L'Arlésienne* (The Woman of Arles) and the two from Grieg's music for Henrik Ibsen's poetic drama *Peer Gynt*.

THE PROGRAM SYMPHONY

The impulse toward program music was so strong that it invaded even the hallowed absolute form of the classical era—the symphony. This represented an attempt to reconcile classical form and romantic content; to retain the grand form of Beethoven and at the same time to associate it with a literary theme. Thus came into being the program symphony, a type best known through the works of Berlioz.

The last quarter of the century witnessed the triumph of what has been called the poematic symphony: a large work without a literary program but highly emotional in tone, retaining the imagery of nature worship and religious faith, of despair and affirmation, conflict and ultimate triumph, that appealed to the romantic mentality. As cultivated by César Franck, Tchaikovsky, Mahler, and Sibelius, this poetic but storyless type of symphony achieved immense popularity.

THE SYMPHONIC POEM

More and more the need was felt for a free form of orchestral music that would serve the romantic era as well as the symphony had served the classical. Toward the middle of the century the long awaited step was taken with the creation of the symphonic poem, the nineteenth century's one original contribution to the large forms. This was the achievement of Liszt, who first employed the term in 1848.

A symphonic poem is a piece of program music for orchestra in one movement, which in the course of contrasting sections develops a poetic idea, suggests a scene, or creates a mood. The name is used interchangeably with *tone poem*; except that the latter is not restricted to orchestral music. The symphonic poem as cultivated by Liszt and his disciples was an immensely flexible form that permitted its course to be shaped by the literary idea. The programs were drawn from poets and painters dear to the romantic temperament: Shakespeare, Dante, Petrarch; Goethe and Schiller; Michelangelo and Raphael; Byron and Victor Hugo. A strong influence was the "return to nature" that had been advocated by Rousseau. Before long the new form, assimilating the force of nationalism, turned to patriotic themes and native landscapes.

The varieties of program music just described—overture, incidental music, program symphony, and symphonic poem—comprise one of the striking manifestations of nineteenth-century romanticism. This type of music emphasized color, mood, and atmosphere; it led composers to express specific feelings; and it proclaimed the direct relationship of music to life.

≥19≤

Felix Mendelssohn (1809-1847)

"People often complain that music is too ambiguous; that what they should think when they hear it is so unclear, whereas everyone understands words. With me it is exactly the opposite, and not only with regard to an entire speech but also with individual words. These too seem to me so ambiguous, so vague, so easily misunderstood in comparison to genuine music which fills the soul with a thousand things better than words."

FELIX MENDELSSOHN stands out in the roster of musicians for the fortunate circumstances that attended his career: he was born to wealth; he found personal happiness; and he was the idol of a vast public.

HIS LIFE

Felix Mendelssohn was the grandson of Moses Mendelssohn, the Jewish philosopher who expounded Plato to the eighteenth century. His father was an art-loving banker; his mother read Homer in the original. They joined the Protestant faith when Felix was still a child. The Mendelssohn home was a meeting place for the wit and intellect of Berlin. The garden house, seating several hundred guests, was the scene of memorable musicales where an orchestra under the boy's direction performed his numerous compositions. Here, when he was seventeen, his Overture to *A Midsummer Night's Dream* was presented to an enraptured audience.

The youth's education was thorough and well rounded. He visited the venerable Goethe at Weimar and attended Hegel's lectures at the University of Berlin. He worshiped Bach, Mozart, and Beethoven. In 1829 the twenty-year-old enthusiast organized a performance of the *St. Matthew Passion,* which had lain neglected since the death of Bach. The event proved to be a turning point in the nineteenth-century revival of that master.

Mendelssohn's misfortune was that he excelled in a number of roles— as pianist, conductor, organizer of musical events, and educator. For the last fifteen years of his life his composing was carried on amid the distractions of a public career that taxed his energies and caused his early death even as poverty and neglect might have done. At twenty-six he was conductor of the Gewandhaus Orchestra at Leipzig, which he transformed into the finest in Europe. He was summoned to Berlin by Frederick William IV to carry out that monarch's plans for an Academy of Music. Later he founded the Conservatory of Leipzig, which set new standards for the training of musicians. He made ten visits to England, where his appearances elicited a frenzy of enthusiasm. All this in addition to directing one or another of the provincial festivals that formed the backbone of musical life in Germany. Mendelssohn composed with a speed and facility that invite comparison with Mozart or Schubert, but he seldom allowed himself the inner repose that might have imparted to much of his music the profundity it lacks.

His last major composition, the oratorio *Elijah,* was produced in 1846 at the Birmingham Festival. The following year he won fresh triumphs in England, appearing as pianist and conductor of his works. He returned to Germany in a state of nervous exhaustion. The happiness he found in the company of his wife and children was shattered by a severe blow—the death of his sister Fanny, to whom he was deeply attached. Six months later, at the age of thirty-eight, he succumbed to a stroke. Huge throngs followed his bier. Condolences came from all over Europe. A world figure had died.

HIS MUSIC

Mendelssohn was dedicated to a mission: to preserve the purity of the classical forms in an age that was turning from them. His fastidious craftsmanship links him to the great tradition. Serene and elegant expression was the characteristic trait of a mind as orderly as it was conservative. Mendelssohn represents the classicist trend within the romantic movement. But it should not be supposed that he was untouched by romanticism. In his early works he is the ardent poet of nature, a landscape painter of gossamer brush. Tenderness and manly fervor breathe from his music, and a gentle melancholy that is very much of the age. As he matured, however, traditionalism permeated his outlook.

Of his symphonies the best known are the *Scotch* and *Italian*— mementos of his youthful travels—and the *Reformation* Symphony. The Concerto for Violin and Orchestra retains its position as one of the most popular ever written. In chamber music Mendelssohn was a leading figure of the century. As a composer for the piano he was too conventional to attain the highest rank. Yet the short lyric pieces known as *Songs without Words* enjoy undiminished popularity with young pianists. The titles appended by Mendelssohn's friends indicate the contents of the famous collection; among them are the *Spinning Song, Hunting Song, Venetian Boat Songs, Consolation*, and the perennial *Spring Song*.

Mendelssohn was a prolific writer for the voice; his songs are suavely melodious. His choral music used to be widely sung, especially the psalms, hymns, anthems, and motets that hit off the religious taste of his time. The oratorio *Elijah* represents the peak of his achievement in this category.

In England Mendelssohn was revered as no composer had been since Handel and Haydn. The first edition of Grove's Dictionary, the musical bible of the British, which appeared in 1880, devoted its longest article to him—sixty-eight pages. Bach received eight.

A MIDSUMMER NIGHT'S DREAM: OVERTURE AND INCIDENTAL MUSIC

The overture to Shakespeare's fairy play is in Mendelssohn's happiest vein. Four prolonged chords on the woodwinds open the portals to the realm of Oberon and Titania. The fairy music is introduced by the violins in high register, allegro di molto (very lively) and very softly. The dots over the notes indicate that they are to be played short and detached (staccato).

Allegro di molto

The fairy music is expanded. A transition leads into the second idea. This is a lyric theme presented by the strings in the songful middle register, suggestive of the young lovers in the play.

The third idea is the boisterous dance of the clowns who appear in the last act of the play. Energetic rhythm and wide leaps set the character of this theme, which is presented by the violins against a background of wind tone.

Now that the themes have been expounded, there follows the development section, an extended fantasy on the first theme. The composer gives free rein to his imagination in exploring a mood close to his heart. When the development of the idea has run its course the four mystic chords are heard again, the thematic material is restated substantially as we heard it before, and the work ends on a note of gentle retrospection. As the youthful composer explained, "After everything has been satisfactorily settled and the principal players have joyfully left the stage, the elves follow them, bless the house and disappear with the dawn. So ends the play, and my overture too."

The Scherzo serves to launch Act II. To Puck's query, "How now, spirit? Whither wander you?" the Elf makes his famous reply: "Over hill, over dale, through bush, through brier. . . ."

The scherzo (pronounced sker′tso and derived from the Italian word meaning "jest," "joke") had been elevated by Beethoven into a symphonic movement of great driving force. Mendelssohn transformed it into an independent piece compounded of elfin grace and humor. The Scherzo from *A Midsummer Night's Dream* music is in 3/8 time and marked Allegro vivace. The first idea is a staccato rhythmic pattern played by the woodwinds softly in the upper register. This is set off against a theme in lower register which is introduced pianissimo by the strings. The two ideas alternate throughout the work. Characteristic is the pianissimo ending in which an agile run on the flute trails off into the distance.

The Nocturne is played while the lovers, lost in the enchanted wood, sleep. Here Mendelssohn is the poet of nature. The beauty of the forest is evoked by the horns in a melody tender and serene.

Finally confusion is righted and all ends happily with the wedding of the Duke. A fanfare on the trumpets introduces the march without which no bride today considers herself properly married. The movement is an Allegro vivace in 4/4 time, for the most part forte. Two sections of quieter character supply the necessary contrast to the recurrent festive theme.

As the romantic tide swept over Europe, Mendelssohn was one of the first idols to be engulfed. The later nineteenth century was as extreme in its censure of him as the earlier had been in its adulation. His reserve was disparaged as superficiality, his elegance as incapacity to feel. But posterity is more changeable than we realize. Our generation, turning away from the full-blown romanticism of its grandparents, has restored Mendelssohn to favor. His particular virtues—sovereign command of form, refinement of feeling, fastidious workmanship and economy of means—recommend him to an era that is not partial to the fervor of the late romantics. The time is ripe for him again.

⚘20⚘
Franz Liszt (1811-1886)

"Sorrowful and great is the artist's destiny."

THE CAREER of Franz Liszt is one of the legends of the romantic era. As piano virtuoso he captured the imagination of Europe. As composer and conductor, teacher, and organizer of musical events, he occupied a central position in the artistic life of the century. Yet this fabulously successful artist did not escape the romantic melancholy. "To die and die young—" he once exclaimed, "—what happiness!"

HIS LIFE

Liszt was born in Hungary, son of a steward in the employ of a wealthy family. A stipend from a group of Hungarian noblemen enabled him to pursue his musical studies in Paris. There he came under the spell of French romanticism, with whose leaders—Victor Hugo, Delacroix, George Sand, Berlioz—he formed close friendships.

The appearance in Paris of the sensational violinist Paganini made Liszt aware of the possibilities of virtuoso playing. The new mass public required spectacular soloists. Liszt met the need. He was one of the greatest of pianists—and showmen. An actor to his fingertips, he possessed the personal magnetism of which legends are made. Instead of sitting with his back to the audience or facing it, as had been the custom hitherto, he introduced the more effective arrangement that prevails today. It showed off his chiseled profile, that reminded people of Dante's. He crouched over the keys, he thundered, he caressed. Countesses swooned. Ladies less exalted fought for his snuffbox and tore his handkerchief to shreds. Liszt encouraged these antics as a necessary part of the legend. But behind the façade was a true musician. For his friends and disciples he played the last sonatas of Beethoven; they never forgot the experience.

Inseparable from the legend of the pianist was that of the lover. Liszt never married. His path for the better part of fifty years led through a thicket of sighs, tears, and threats of suicide. Among those briefly smitten were George Sand—they toured Switzerland for a summer— and Marie Duplessis, the original of Dumas's Lady of the Camellias.

More important in his intellectual development was his relationship with Countess Marie d'Agoult, who wrote novels under the name of Daniel Stern. They eloped to an idyll in Switzerland that lasted for a number of years. Of their three children, Cosima subsequently became the wife of Wagner. Liszt and the Countess parted in bitterness. She satirized him in her novels.

An afternoon at Liszt's. Grouped around the pianist are Kriehuber, Berlioz, Czerny, and Ernst.

He withdrew from the concert stage at the height of his fame in order to devote himself to composing. His twelve years as court conductor to the Grand Duke of Weimar (1849–61) saw the production of his chief orchestral works. As director of the ducal opera house he was in a position to mold public taste. He used his influence unremittingly on behalf of the "Music of the Future," as he and Wagner named the type of program music, both dramatic and symphonic, which they along with Berlioz advocated. At Weimar, Liszt directed the first performances of Wagner's *Lohengrin*, Berlioz' *Benvenuto Cellini*, and many other contemporary works. History records few instances of an artist so generous, so free from envy in his dealings with his fellow artists.

The Weimar period saw his association with the woman who most decisively influenced his life. Princess Caroline Wittgenstein, wife of a powerful noble at the court of the Tsar, fell in love with Liszt during his last concert tour of Russia. Shortly thereafter she came to Weimar to unite her life with his. For years their home, the Altenberg, was a center of artistic activity. A woman of domineering will and intellect, the Princess assisted Liszt in his later literary efforts. These include a book on Gypsy music and a *Life of Chopin*. Both are eloquent and inaccurate.

In his last years Liszt sought peace in the bosom of the Church. He took minor orders and was known as Abbé Liszt. This was the period of his major religious works. He divided his time between Rome, Weimar, and Budapest, the friend of princes and cardinals. The gloom of old age was dispelled by fresh triumphs. At seventy-five he was received with enthusiasm in England, which had always been reluctant to recognize him as a composer. He journeyed to Bayreuth to visit the widowed Cosima and died during the festival of Wagner's works, with his last breath naming the masterpiece of the "Music of the Future"— Wagner's *Tristan*.

HIS MUSIC

Liszt believed in "the renewal of music through its inner connection with poetry." But it was not his aim to make music usurp the function of the other arts. The poetic idea served as point of departure for his fancy. His goal was pure lyric expression through what he called "the mysterious language of tone."

To give his lyricism free scope he created the symphonic poem. The form was held together by the continuous transformation of a few basic themes. By varying the melodic outline, the harmony and rhythm of a theme, by shifting it from soft to loud, from slow to fast, from low to high register, from strings to woodwinds or brass, he found it possible to transform its character so that it might suggest romantic love in one section, a pastoral scene in another, tension and conflict in a third, and triumph in the last.

His twelve symphonic poems exercised incalculable influence on the nineteenth century. His masterpiece for orchestra is the *Symphony after Goethe's Faust*, comprising three portraits: Faust, Gretchen, Mephistopheles. A companion work is the *Symphony after Dante's Divine Comedy*. In these program symphonies he honored his companions in arms. The *Faust* is dedicated to Berlioz, the *Dante* to Wagner.

Liszt is one of the creators of modern piano technique. His exploitation of the resources of the instrument—octaves, trills, runs, arpeggios—is of the highest ingenuity. The piano in his hands became an orchestra, capable of colors and sonorities that were without precedent in his time. Through hundreds of arrangements and transcriptions, many of hair-raising difficulty (yet eminently playable), he extended the piano repertoire to include a wealth of symphonic, operatic, organ, and vocal music. These have dropped from view, but they performed yeoman service—in an age without radio or recordings—in bringing to a worldwide public the knowledge of Beethoven's symphonies, Schubert's songs, Bach's organ works, and Wagner's operas.

The best of his piano pieces, like his songs, are in the vein of true romantic lyricism. The fifteen Hungarian Rhapsodies did much to advance the cause of musical nationalism. In a class apart is his chief work for the piano, the Sonata in B minor, a single movement of great dramatic tension. Here is the Liszt of impassioned rhetoric and grandiose gesture, the contemporary in every sense of Victor Hugo.

LES PRÉLUDES (THE PRELUDES)

Liszt appended to the score a program note of his own devising that had some connection in his mind with one of the *Méditations Poétiques* of the mystical poet Alphonse Lamartine. "What is our life but a series of preludes to that unknown song whose first solemn note is tolled by Death? The enchanted dawn of every life is love. But where is the destiny on whose first delicious joys some storm does not break? . . . And what soul thus cruelly bruised, when the tempest rolls away, seeks not to rest its memories in the pleasant calm of pastoral life. Yet man does not long permit himself to taste the kindly quiet that first attracted him to Nature's lap. For when the trumpet sounds he hastens to danger's post, that in the struggle he may once more regain full knowledge of himself and his strength." Such a program related the music to one of the favorite themes of the age—the image of man pitted against Fate—unfolding a series of moods, dramatic, lyric, pastoral, triumphal, that appealed immensely to the romantic mentality.

The work is fashioned from a basic motif of three notes announced at the outset by the strings. The ascending interval of a fourth (at x) imparts to the motif a questioning upward inflection.

There follows a passage for full orchestra, Andante maestoso (at a going pace, majestic), the "prelude to that unknown song." Notice that the characteristic upward leap is present both in the melody and accompaniment.

Two themes in Liszt's suavest manner evoke the image of love that he calls "the enchanted dawn of every life." The first, espressivo cantando (expressively, in singing style), is assigned to violins and 'cellos. The germ motif is embedded in the melody (under bracket).

The second amorous theme is played by muted strings and a quartet of horns, espressivo ma tranquillo (expressive but tranquil). This melody contrasts with the preceding. On closer examination, however, it too turns out to be an ingenious expansion of the basic motif.

The tempo quickens, tension mounts. The basic material is presented Allegro tempestoso. The atmosphere of struggle is associated with chromatic scales. (The chromatic scale takes in all twelve tones of the octave. On the piano it includes the seven white and five black keys—that is, all the sharps and flats. Chromatic scales became a favorite device of the romantic composers for whipping up orchestral excitement.) Naturally the tempestuous passage features trumpets and horns.

An area of relaxation ensues with the Allegretto pastorale, a peaceful nature scene. The motif is now expanded into a bucolic theme on the oboe. The return to the fray is marked by an Allegro marziale animato (lively, marchlike). Through changes in pace, register, dynamics, and color, the two love themes are transformed into rousing battle calls. Finally the mood of exaltation returns, to round off the action with the typically romantic "apotheosis." The basic motif has triumphed along with Man.

A pioneer in respect to harmony, form, and orchestral color, Liszt had an abiding effect on the musical practice of the latter nineteenth century. He was the first to give a full piano recital. (Before his time piano solos were interspersed with orchestral or vocal numbers.) He introduced the grand style in piano playing and established new standards of virtuosity. He injected the picturesque personality—embodiment of romantic individualism—into the concert hall, where it has remained ever since. A great teacher, he raised a generation of giants of the keyboard. He was a master of orchestral technique. He gave impetus to musical nationalism, and his easily accessible music helped create the modern mass public. He influenced composers from Wagner and César Franck to Ravel and George Gershwin.

His defect was one of character rather than genius. It lay in his too great eagerness to please, to dazzle, to be adored. This was the fatal flaw in an otherwise great man. His shortcomings have, for many people, obscured the qualities of a genuinely musical personality. The "Music of the Future" has become that of the past. Yet he remains— man and musician—the voice of an era. "In art," he said, "one must work on a grand scale." This he did.

❧21❧

Nationalism and the Romantic Movement

"There is no patriotic art and no patriotic science. Both belong,
like everything nobly good, to the whole world."

Goethe

THE RISE OF MUSICAL NATIONALISM

NATIONAL sentiment was an all-important factor in the political development of nineteenth-century Europe. Its influence extended to the
sphere of art, where it became a determining force within the romantic
movement. National tensions on the Continent—the pride of the conquering nations and the struggle for freedom of the subjugated ones—
gave rise to emotions that found an ideal expression in music. Romanticism exalted the popular tone and exploited picturesque local color,
encouraging musicians to make use of the songs and dances of their
people. The emphasis upon program music fit in with this trend. Composers focused their symphonic poems and operas on a national hero,
or an event or place of patriotic significance. Romantic interest in the
Middle Ages opened up to the musician a fanciful world of national
legend and saga. In addition, the nationally conscious composer made
a contribution to his country's art by uniting his music with the lyrics
of a national poet.

Examples of musical nationalism abound in the output of the romantic
era. The folk idiom is prominent in the Mazurkas of Chopin, the Hungarian Rhapsodies of Liszt, the Slavonic Dances of Dvořák, and the
Norwegian Dances of Grieg. The life of the peasantry furnishes the
theme for Weber's *Freischütz*, Glinka's *A Life for the Tsar*, Smetana's
Bartered Bride, as well as the fairy-tale operas and ballets of Tchaikovsky and Rimsky-Korsakov. Native scenes and place names figure
in any number of musical landscapes from Smetana's *The Moldau* to
Musorgsky's *Night on Bald Mountain* and Johann Strauss's *Tales from
the Vienna Woods*. The beauty of the Rhine, of German forest and
mountain, pervades Wagner's *Ring of the Nibelung*. The gods and
heroes of the ancient sagas live again in this vast epic that centers about
the life and death of Siegfried. Tchaikovsky's *Overture 1812* commem-
orates a national victory. The symphonic poems of Smetana, Dvořák,
and Sibelius glorify the exploits of national heroes. German art was

enriched in the early romantic period by settings of native poetry such as the songs of Schubert and Schumann; as was French art in the post-romantic period through the songs of Debussy and Ravel based on Baudelaire, Mallarmé, and Verlaine. Russia's national poet Alexander Pushkin (1799–1837) was the source of a number of operas by Tchaikovsky, Musorgsky, and Rimsky-Korsakov. Bizet wrote music for Alphonse Daudet's *L'Arlésienne*, Grieg for Henrik Ibsen's *Peer Gynt*.

Nationalism encouraged the nations that had no established tradition of art music to develop their own manner of musical speech. It brought these newcomers to their rightful place in the concert of nations, alongside the older musical cultures such as Italy, Germany, and France. The nationalist impulse was naturally most prominent among the musically "young" nations, but the older ones felt it too. For national consciousness pervaded every manifestation of the European spirit in the nineteenth century. The romantic movement is unthinkable without it.

EXOTICISM

Once nationalism showed the way, local color became a decorative element in musical art to be exploited for its own sake. This gave rise to one of the most arresting offshoots of the romantic movement: the evoking of a distant locale for the sake of picturesque effect. Exoticism glamorized the far-off and the unknown, "the land that never was." It was nourished by the romantic interest in atmosphere, in instrumental color and orchestration.

In the nineteenth century exoticism manifested itself, in the first place, as a longing of the northern nations for the warmth and color of the South; in the second, as a longing of the West for the fairy-tale splendors of the Orient. The former impulse found expression in the works of German, French, and Russian composers who turned for inspiration to Italy and Spain. The long list stretches from Glinka's two Spanish Overtures and Mendelssohn's *Italian* Symphony to Tchaikovsky's *Caprice Italien*, Rimsky-Korsakov's *Capriccio on Spanish Themes*, Chabrier's *España*, Lalo's *Symphonie Espagnole*, and Richard Strauss's *Aus Italien*. The masterpiece in this category is of course Bizet's *Carmen*.

The glamor of the East was brought to international prominence by the Russian national school. In an empire that stretched to the borders of Persia, exoticism was really a form of nationalism. The fairy-tale background of Asia pervades Russian music. Rimsky-Korsakov's orchestrally resplendent *Scheherazade* and his opera *Sadko*, Alexander Borodin's opera *Prince Igor* and symphonic poem *In the Steppes of Central Asia*, and Ippolitov-Ivanov's *Caucasian Sketches* are among the many orientally inspired works that for a time found favor throughout the world. A number of French composers also utilized exotic themes, as did Verdi in *Aïda* and Puccini in his operas *Madame Butterfly* and *Turandot*.

Nationalism added to the language of European music a variety of idioms of immense charm and vividness. By associating music with the love of homeland, nationalism aligned the art with the great social and political movements of the age, and enabled composers to give expression to the cherished aspirations of millions of people.

⤳22⤶
Bedřich Smetana (1824-1884)

"I am no enemy of the old forms in the old music. But I do not hold that we now have to follow them. I have come to the conclusion that the forms of the past are finished. Absolute music is quite impossible for me."

BEDŘICH SMETANA was the founder of the Czech national school. As in the case of several nationalist composers, Smetana's career unfolded against a background of political agitation. Bohemia stirred restlessly under Hapsburg rule, caught up in a surge of nationalist fervor that culminated in the uprisings of 1848. Young Smetana aligned himself with the patriotic cause. He composed a march for the Students' Legion and a *Solemn Overture* that was an affirmation of his political faith. After the revolution was crushed, Smetana accepted a post as conductor in Sweden, where he remained for five years.

During his stay abroad, Smetana turned to the writing of symphonic poems. On his return to Bohemia in 1861 he resumed his career as a national artist and worked for the establishment of a theater in Prague where the performances would be given in the native tongue. Prague had always been in the orbit of Vienna's musical culture, so that Smetana's effort on behalf of native art was an important gesture against the supremacy in Central Europe of Germanic music. Although influenced by the German tradition, he succeeded in fashioning a specifically Czech idiom. The hope of national liberation that inspired his art was inseparable from his vision of a better life for his people. Folklore and local color were never used by him as picturesque ends in themselves; they constituted the very soul of what he had to say.

Of his eight operas on patriotic themes, several still hold the boards in the theaters of his native land. One—*The Bartered Bride*—attained world-wide fame. Hardly less important in the establishing of Smetana's reputation was the cycle of six symphonic poems entitled *My Country* which occupied him from 1874 to 1879. These works are steeped in the beauty of Bohemia's countryside, in the pomp and pageantry of her legends. Best known of the series is the second, *The Moldau*, Smetana's finest achievement in the field of orchestral music.

THE MOLDAU (VLTAVA)

In this tone poem the famous river becomes a poetic symbol that suffuses the musical imagery with patriotic associations. The program appended to the score explains the composer's intention. "Two springs pour forth in the shade of the Bohemian forest, one warm and gushing, the other cold and peaceful." These join in a brook that becomes the river Moldau. "Coursing through Bohemia's valleys, it grows into a mighty stream. Through thick woods it flows as the gay sounds of the hunt and the notes of the hunter's horn are heard ever closer. It flows through grass-grown pastures and lowlands where a wedding feast is being celebrated with song and dance. At night, wood and water nymphs revel in its sparkling waves. Reflected on its surface are fortresses and castles—witnesses of bygone days of knightly splendor and the vanished glory of martial times." The stream races ahead through the Rapids of St. John, "finally flowing on in majestic peace toward Prague and welcomed by historic Vyšehrad"—the legendary site of the castle of the ancient Bohemian kings. "Then it vanishes far beyond the poet's gaze."

The work opens at a moderate allegro with a rippling figure heard as a dialogue between two flutes against a pizzicato accompaniment on violins and harp. From this emerges a broadly flowing melody played by oboes and violins—the theme of the river:

After a suitable expansion of this idea, horn calls evoke a hunting scene. The section labeled *Peasant Wedding* is in the spirit of rustic dance. The mood changes to one of mystery. The score is marked *Moonlight—Nymphs' Revels*. Woodwinds, horn, and strings, creating a typical romantic sonority, conjure up a poetic landscape. The principal theme returns. The pace quickens as the music graphically depicts the seething rapids near Prague. As the composer envisions the river passing the ancient site of the royal castle, the brass proclaims a triumphal chorale, a promise to his countrymen that their former glory will be restored. (A chorale is a hymn or a hymnlike tune.) There is a diminuendo to the end as the river "vanishes far beyond the poet's gaze."

The Czechs regard this symphonic landscape as a national tone poem that mirrors the very soul of their land. The rest of the world sees in it one of the more attractive examples of late romantic tone painting.

≫23≪

The Awakening of Russia

"I grew up in a quiet spot and was saturated from earliest childhood with the wonderful beauty of Russian popular song. I am therefore passionately devoted to every expression of the Russian spirit. In short, I am a Russian through and through!"

Tchaikovsky

THE ENTRANCE of Russia into the family of musically productive nations was a striking phenomenon in the art life of the nineteenth century, and one that had far-reaching effects. The Russians arrived on the scene too late to be dominated by the Germanic tradition. Instead, they were in the forefront of those who in the latter part of the century successfully challenged the world supremacy of the German symphony.

Modern Russia began with the attempt of Peter the Great (1672–1725) forcibly to westernize his empire. Throughout the eighteenth century the Russian aristocracy imported French ideas, German tutors, and Italian operas. It was Mikhail Glinka (1804–57) who launched the national school with his folk opera *A Life for the Tsar*. The aristocratic audience that gathered for its opening night in 1836 pronounced it to be "music for coachmen." But the work accorded with the political plans of Emperor Nicholas I, whose approval launched it on its triumphal career.

The emancipation of the serfs in 1861 spelled the end of feudal Russia. Some felt that the nation's future lay in a rapprochement with the West, others clung nostalgically to the old traditions. The two attitudes were reflected in the group of gifted young musicians who appeared during the 1860s to create the Russian national school. The cosmopolites advocated Western techniques and forms. The Slavophiles demanded independence from the West, drawing inspiration from native folk song and religious music.

The Western camp was led by the pianist-composer Anton Rubinstein (1829–94), a disciple of the Mendelssohn-Schumann school. His operas, symphonies, and oratorios are no longer performed. To Americans he is known chiefly by his *Melody in F*. He founded the Conservatory of St. Petersburg, patterned after the Leipzig model. His brother, the pianist Nicholas Rubinstein, established the equally important Conservatory of Moscow. Out of the system of education inaugurated by these two came Russia's first native-trained professional composer, Peter Ilyich Tchaikovsky.

"THE MIGHTY FIVE"

Russian nationalism fired the imaginations of a group of youthful enthusiasts who came to be known as "The Mighty Five." (It has become apparent since that the adjective applied to only one of their number.) Leader of this dedicated band was Mily Balakirev (1837–1910). A self-taught musician, he persuaded himself and his four disciples—César Cui, Alexander Borodin, Nicholas Rimsky-Korsakov, and Modest Musorgsky—that they had no need of exercises in German counterpoint to give expression to the pan-Slavic dream.

Of the five, Balakirev and Cui may be dismissed at once; they hardly rose above the level of the salon composer. Alexander Borodin (1834–87) was a gifted scientist who lectured at the Academy of Medicine and wrote important treatises in his field. He managed, amid the distractions of a crowded life, to create several works that are still heard: the Second Symphony and the String Quartet No. 2; the national opera *Prince Igor*, notable for its fine choral writing and the exotic *Polovetsian Dances;* and the symphonic sketch *In the Steppes of Central Asia.* Although Rimsky-Korsakov was the most successful of the group during his lifetime, it remained for the fifth among them to fathom the depths of his nation's soul. Modest Musorgsky was looked upon with condescension by his four comrades because of what they considered the technical ineptness of his writing. They never suspected that he was incomparably the greatest among them.

Russia's musical awakening, like her achievement in literature, was an expression on the artistic front of her coming of age as a European power. The Russian national school was destined to exert a strong influence on Debussy, Ravel, and their contemporaries. In this way it made a fruitful contribution to our present-day musical culture.

⚜24⚜

Nicholas Rimsky-Korsakov (1844-1908)

"Our epoch, the post-Wagnerian age, is the age of brilliance and imaginative quality in orchestral tone color."

RIMSKY-KORSAKOV is one of the chief representatives of nineteenth-century exoticism. His was an imagination haunted by fairy-tale landscapes, by luminous seas and skies. His music has a picture-book quality and the gorgeousness of color that goes with it. He was one of the great orchestrators of the nineteenth century.

His career as a naval officer was cut out for him by family tradition. The squadron to which he was assigned visited the United States in 1863. "Niagara Falls made the most marvelous impression on us," he records in his *Autobiography*. "We rowed in a boat as near as possible up to the falls." Since England during the Civil War espoused the southern cause, her traditonal enemy Russia sided with the North. "We followed the course of events with deep interest, though we kept exclusively within Northern territory. The expected war with England had not materialized, and we did not have to privateer and threaten English merchantmen in the Atlantic."

The flotilla proceeded to South America. During the three years of the cruise he wrote his First Symphony. This was performed upon his return to Russia, and brought him his first success as a composer. At twenty-seven he was appointed professor of composition and orchestration at the Conservatory of St. Petersburg. Two years later he resigned from the navy.

In his capacity as conductor and teacher Rimsky exercised a formidable influence on the course of Russian music. His fifteen operas continue to delight his countrymen. Almost all are based on subjects drawn from Russian history or fairy tale. The librettos of several are derived from the leading writers of his country—Pushkin, Gogol, Ostrovsky. A few excerpts have caught the fancy of the American public: the Song of India from *Sadko,* Hymn to the Sun from *Le Coq d'Or* (The Golden Cockerel), and the Flight of the Bumblebee from *Tsar Saltan.*

SCHEHERAZADE

Rimsky-Korsakov is best known to the West through his orchestral evocation of *A Thousand and One Nights.* The prefatory note tells of the Sultan Schahriar who, "convinced of the faithlessness of women, had resolved to put to death each of his wives after the wedding night. But the Sultana Scheherazade saved her life by diverting him with tales which she told him on a thousand and one nights. Conquered by his curiosity the Sultan postponed from one day to the next the execution of his wife and in the end renounced completely his bloody vow."

The introduction, marked Largo e maestoso (very broad and majestic), presents two contrasting themes that conjure up the main characters. The brusque theme of the Sultan is announced fortissimo in low register by most of the orchestra.

The motive of the Narrator is given by a violin solo in high register above arpeggios on the harp. It is an oriental-sounding melody that reappears throughout the four movements in various guises, serving as a unifying thread.

The movement proper, *The Sea and the Ship of Sinbad,* is an ample seascape in 6/4 time, marked Allegro non troppo. This is frankly descriptive music, sensuous and atmospheric. The main theme is a vigorous idea derived from the Sultan theme. For contrast there is the relaxed sequence of chords presented by the woodwinds, which commentators generally associate with the calm of the sea, as well as the crescendo passages in which Rimsky whips up an exciting orchestral tempest. The movement is too long for the meager thematic material, which instead of being developed is simply repeated over and over again in the fairy-tale manner beloved by the Russian school. It is the orchestration that supplies the variety, now shot with flame as the brass give out their pronouncements, now silvered with the sheen of woodwinds and strings.

The Tale of the Prince Kalender is an *Arabian Nights* narrative. It opens with a repetition of the Narrator theme. An artless tune in folk style, played by the bassoon andantino and capriccioso, gives an attractive picture of the happy-go-lucky prince who went disguised as a beggar. The melody contains several grace notes (at x). (This term refers to a very short note having no time value of its own, which is interpolated before a longer note as an ornament.)

Tension increases in the middle part of the movement. Tremolos on the strings and ominous pronouncements by trumpets and trombones suggest that our hero has run into trouble. But he extricates himself and proceeds on his untroubled way, satisfying both the listener and the demands of A-B-A form.

The first movement is descriptive in character; the second, narrative. The third is lyric. *The Young Prince and Princess* is a love scene in three-part form. The meter is 6/8, the tempo Andantino quasi allegretto. The Prince's song is played by violins and repeated against decorative runs on the flutes and clarinets.

The dance of the Princess is given by clarinet solo against a strongly rhythmic accompaniment, at the completion of which the music returns to the languorous melody of the opening.

The finale, *Festival at Bagdad*, is a tumultuous dance scene, marked Allegro molto. The headlong dance in duple meter is interspersed with

a procession of themes from the earlier movements—Scheherazade, the Sultan, the Kalender Prince, the Young Princess. This not only offers the listener the charm of reminiscence, but ties the work together, a procedure much in favor, we shall find, with nineteenth-century composers.

The movement mounts to a climax through a steady rise in pitch, volume, and pacing. At the height of the excitement there is a return to the broadly flowing 6/4 time of the first movement. "The Ship is dashed to pieces against a rock surmounted by a Bronze Warrior." A graphic musical hurricane is whipped up by means of chromatic scales. Tumult builds inexorably to the point where stentorian trumpets pronounce the motive of doom. A great calm descends upon the orchestra. The Coda strikes a note of reconciliation between the two primal themes, suggesting the Sultan's resolve to let Scheherazade keep her clever head.

Scheherazade occupies its own niche in the romantic heritage. Its position is analogous to certain literary classics such as *The Mill on the Floss* or *Oliver Twist*. We may not feel impelled to return to them in our maturity, yet we should be immeasurably the poorer for not having known them in our youth.

❧25❦
Peter Ilyich Tchaikovsky (1840-1893)

"Truly there would be reason to go mad were it not for music."

FEW COMPOSERS typify the end-of-century mood as does Peter Ilyich Tchaikovsky. He belonged to a generation that saw its truths crumble and found none to replace them. He expressed as did none other the pessimism that attended the final phase of the romantic movement.

HIS LIFE

Tchaikovsky was born at Votinsk in a distant province of Russia, son of a government official. His family intended him for a career in the government. He graduated at nineteen from the aristocratic School of Jurisprudence at St. Petersburg and obtained a minor post in the Ministry of Justice. Not till he was twenty-three did he reach the decision to resign his post and enter the newly founded Conservatory of St. Petersburg. "To be a good musician and earn my daily bread"—his was a modest goal.

He completed the course in three years and was immediately recommended by Anton Rubinstein, director of the school, for a teaching post at the new Conservatory of Moscow. Despite the long hours and large classes, the young professor of harmony applied himself assiduously to composition. His twelve years at Moscow saw the production of some of his most successful works.

Extremely sensitive by nature, Tchaikovsky was subject to attacks of depression aggravated by his irregular personal life. "Regretting the past and hoping for the future without ever being satisfied with the present—this is how my life is spent." Could there be a better characterization of the late romantic artist? In the hope of achieving some degree of stability Tchaikovsky entered into an ill-starred marriage with a student of the Conservatory, Antonina Miliukov, who was hopelessly in love with him. His sympathy for Antonina soon turned into uncontrollable aversion, and in a fit of despair he wandered into the icy waters of the Moscow River. Some days later he fled, on the verge of a serious breakdown, to his brothers in St. Petersburg.

In this desperate hour, as in one of the fairy tales he liked to turn

Peter Ilyich Tchaikovsky.

into ballets, there appeared the kind benefactress who enabled him to go abroad until he had recovered his health, freed him from the drudgery of teaching, and launched him on the most productive period of his career. Nadezhda von Meck, widow of an industrialist, was an imperious and emotional woman. She lived the life of a recluse in her mansion in Moscow, from which she ran her railroads, her estates, and the lives of her eleven children. Her passion was music, especially Tchaikovsky's. Bound by the rigid conventions of her time and her class, she had to be certain that her enthusiasm was for the artist, not the man; hence she stipulated that she was never to meet the recipient of her bounty.

Thus began the famous friendship by letter which soon assumed a tone of passionate attachment. For the next thirteen years Mme. von Meck made Tchaikovsky's career the focal point of her life, providing for his needs with exquisite devotion and tact. She resisted all temptation to remove the relationship from its ideal plane. Save for an accidental glimpse of one another at the opera or during a drive, they never met.

The correspondence gives us an insight into Tchaikovsky's method of work. "You ask me how I manage the instrumentation. I never compose in the abstract. I invent the musical idea and its instrumentation simultaneously." Mme. von Meck inquires if the Fourth Symphony (which he dedicated to her) has a definite meaning. Tchaikovsky replies, "How can one express the indefinable sensations that one experiences while writing an instrumental composition that has no definite subject? It is a purely lyrical process. It is a musical confession of the soul, which unburdens itself through sounds just as a lyric poet expresses himself through poetry. The difference lies in the fact that music has far richer resources of expression and is a more subtle medium. . . . As Heine said, 'Where words leave off music begins.'"

Tchaikovsky was the first Russian whose music caught on in the West, and in 1891 he accepted an invitation to come to America to participate in the ceremonies that marked the opening of Carnegie Hall. From New York he wrote, "These Americans strike me as very remarkable. In this country the honesty, sincerity, generosity, cordiality, and readiness to help you without a second thought are extremely pleasant. . . . I am convinced that I am ten times more famous in America than in Europe."

The letters of his final years breathe disenchantment and—that bugbear of middle-aged artists—the suspicion that he had nothing more to say. "Is it possible that I have completely written myself out? I have neither ideas nor inclinations!" But ahead of him lay his two finest symphonies.

Immediately after finishing his Sixth Symphony, the *Pathétique*, he went to St. Petersburg to conduct it. The work met with a lukewarm reception, due in part to the fact that Tchaikovsky, painfully shy in public, conducted his music without any semblance of conviction. Some days later, although he had been warned of the prevalence of cholera in the capital, he carelessly drank a glass of unboiled water and contracted the disease. He died within the week, at the age of fifty-three. The suddenness of his death and the tragic tone of his last work led to rumors that he had committed suicide, and almost immediately there accrued to the *Symphonie Pathétique* the sensational popularity it has enjoyed ever since.

HIS MUSIC

"He was the most Russian of us all!" said Stravinsky. In the eyes of his countrymen Tchaikovsky is a national artist. He himself laid great weight on the Russian element in his music. "Why is it that the simple Russian landscape, a walk in summer through Russian fields and forest or on the steppes at evening can affect me so that I have lain on the ground numb, overcome by a wave of love for nature." At the same time, in the putting together of his music Tchaikovsky was a cosmopolite. He came under the spell of Italian opera, French ballet, German symphony and song. These he assimilated to the strain of folk melody that was his heritage as a Russian, setting upon the mixture the stamp of a sharply defined personality.

Tchaikovsky cultivated all branches of music. Of prime importance are the last symphonies, the Fourth, Fifth, and Sixth. In the domain of program music two symphonic poems continue to be played: the overture-fantasy *Romeo and Juliet* and the symphonic fantasy *Francesca da Rimini*. Hardly less popular is the colorful *Caprice Italien*. Of his eight operas, two hold the stage in his native land: *Eugene Onegin* and *Pique Dame* (Queen of Spades). Unlike the operas, Tchaikovsky's ballets maintain themselves on the international scene. *Swan Lake, Sleeping Beauty*, and the *Nutcracker* are widely appreciated both in the ballet theater and the concert hall.

The Piano Concerto in B-flat minor and the Violin Concerto are staple display pieces of the virtuosi. The four suites for orchestra have dropped from sight. Tchaikovsky wrote a fair amount of chamber music. The First String Quartet is remembered because of the perennial Andante cantabile. Tchaikovsky's piano pieces are of the salon variety.

Several—*Romance, Barcarolle, Song without Words, Troika*—are firmly entrenched in the repertory of dinner music. Of his more than one hundred songs a single one—*None But the Lonely Heart*, in his familiar vein of romantic melancholy—has obscured many that are more representative of him at his best.

We shall in a later section consider Tchaikovsky as a symphonist. In this chapter we are concerned with his most successful effort in the domain of program music.

OVERTURE-FANTASY *ROMEO AND JULIET*

Tchaikovsky was twenty-nine when he wrote this, the first work that fully revealed his gifts. The term "overture-fantasy" is intended to suggest his free handling of the traditional form. The form is similar to the one that we encountered in Mendelssohn's Overture to *A Midsummer Night's Dream:* a large three-section structure that allows for the presentation, development, and restatement of musical ideas (exposition-development-recapitulation). In this case the form is enlarged by means of a spacious introduction. It was in no sense the composer's intent to give a musical depiction of the Shakespearean drama. Rather, he selected three salient images that lent themselves to musical treatment—the gentle Friar Laurence, the feud between the two noble families of Verona, and the lovers.

Ecclesiastical harmonies evoke the good friar. They are in the style of a chorale which is presented in four-part harmony by two clarinets and two bassoons, Andante quasi moderato (fairly slow, almost moderate). The chords, archaic in effect and moving in parallel motion, create a medieval atmosphere.

The Allegro proper begins with the Feud theme.

The brusque rhythm with its strong syncopation suggests violent action, as do the full orchestral tone and explosive accompaniment. Characteristic of Tchaikovsky are the sweeping runs, ascending and descending, on the violins.

The love theme is a melody long of line and tenderly lyrical sung by English horn and muted violas. The youthful composer created here a broadly spun song whose ardor is not unworthy of Shakespeare's lovers.

The mood is rounded off by a subsidiary idea of great expressiveness, played by the muted strings. With this the exposition section—that is, the presentation of the musical material—comes to an end.

The agitated development section is based mainly on the Feud theme, interspersed with references to the Friar Laurence music in a transformed version. The Recapitulation brings back the Feud theme substantially as before. The love music is now expanded and rises, wave upon wave of sumptuous orchestral sound, to one of those torrential climaxes that only an uninhibited romantic could achieve. The epilogue is fashioned out of the love theme. Muffled drums beat a dirge for the dead lovers, and the chorale of the opening is heard again, balancing the architecture.

This is young man's music, fervid, communicative, and fashioned along broad simple lines. It captures a characteristic moment in the thought and feeling of the late romantic era. Beyond that it remains one of the more beguiling—and solidly wrought—examples of nineteenth-century program music.

Symphony and Concerto

⚹26⚹

The Nature of Absolute Music

"A great symphony is a man-made Mississippi down which we irresistibly flow from the instant of our leave-taking to a long foreseen destination."

Aaron Copland

WE HAVE in the past few chapters established two types of meaning that coexist in a musical work. On the one hand, music has an expressive content that may be associated in the composer's mind with certain emotions, scenes, or even an action. On the other, a composition exists as a piece of musical material which is fashioned into a balanced structure according to principles having to do solely with the nature of sound.

We now come to a class of music in which the two meanings are present in a somewhat different relationship. In the large forms of absolute music—symphony and concerto, sonata and chamber music—the expressive content is no longer chained to a program. The emotional content of the music is projected in abstract forms. The musical ideas are rooted, of course, in the composer's way of feeling and his need to communicate that feeling. But they are organized in such a way that, without any aid at all from external images, they will give the listener a satisfying sense of order and continuity.

The most important type of large-scale absolute music is known as sonata (from the Italian *suonare*, "to sound," indicating a piece to be sounded on instruments, as distinct from *cantata*, a piece to be sung). A sonata is an instrumental work consisting of a cycle of contrasting movements, generally three or four in number, in the sequence fast-slow-fast or fast-slow-moderately fast-fast. (There are many exceptions to this, as to all rules in art.) The movements contrast in character and mood. Taken together they form an architectural entity. The name sonata is used when the music is intended for one or two instruments. If more than two are involved, the work is called a trio, quartet, quintet, sextet, septet, octet, or nonet as the case may be. A sonata for solo instrument and orchestra is called a concerto; for full orchestra, a symphony. The sonata cycle, obviously, accounts for a large part of the instrumental music we hear.

THE SYMPHONY

The symphony is one of the most impressive forms of instrumental music, mobilizing as it does all the resources of the orchestra. The most highly organized and characteristic member of the three or four movements that make up the symphonic cycle is the opening allegro. This is in what is known as first-movement or sonata-allegro form; often it is referred to simply as sonata form. The movement is based on the contrast between two theme groups, one strongly rhythmic in character, the other lyrical. It consists of three sections—*exposition, development*, and *recapitulation* (or restatement).

The symphony may open with a slow introduction which sets the stage for the ensuing action; or the music may plunge directly into the allegro. The exposition sets forth the two contrasting thematic groups. Between them is a bridge or transitional passage that leads from one theme group to the next. The section is rounded off by a closing passage, a codetta (from Italian *coda*, "a tail"). Thus, the contents of the exposition section may be summarized as: slow introduction (optional), first theme group, bridge, second theme group, and codetta. In the nineteenth century, when the first-movement form was much expanded, there might also be a third theme group.

In the middle section of the movement, the development, the composer proceeds to reveal the potentialities of his themes. He breaks them into their component motives, recombines them into fresh patterns; he views them in a new light and explores their potentialities for dynamic growth. The character of the development section is indicated by the names sometimes given to it—"free fantasia" or "working-out section." Conflict and action are the essence of drama. In the development section the conflict erupts, the action reaches maximum intensity. We hear a fragment of a theme thrown out by one group of instruments, imitated by another, contracted, expanded, turned upside down, combined with other motives or with fresh material. Now it appears in the upper register, now deep in the bass. Suddenly a hitherto inconspicuous motive joins the fray and flowers into a fanciful design. The manifold transformations of the themes appear to grow inevitably out of the material. They turn out to have been implicit therein from the start, waiting for the master hand to release them. In the development section the composer marshals all his resources of imagination and ingenuity. He functions as the supreme architect, or as the general hurling his forces into battle. Each measure seems to grow out of the preceding by an inescapable law of cause and effect. Each adds to the drive and the momentum.

In the third section of the movement, the restatement or recapitulation, we hear again the themes of the exposition more or less in their original guise, but with the wealth of new meaning that these have taken on in the course of their wanderings. We experience the charm of returning to familiar ground, of recognizing old friends who have grown immeasurably since first we knew them. The movement ends with the *coda*, which rounds off the action and brings it to its preordained conclusion. The coda crowns the movement and reaffirms its basic idea for the last time.

First-movement or sonata-allegro form, while it is indissolubly associated with the cycle of three or four movements that make up the sonata, concerto, and symphony, may also be encountered as an independent piece, as in the overture. We encountered first-movement form in the *Midsummer Night's Dream* Overture and the *Romeo and Juliet* Overture.

The second movement of the nineteenth-century symphony is generally a slow movement of tenderly lyric nature. It may, however, vary in mood from the whimsical, even playful, to the tragic and passionate. Third (sometimes second) in the cycle, in the symphonies of the romantic period, is the strongly rhythmic and impetuous scherzo, with overtones of humor, surprise, whimsy, or folk dance. The form is an A-B-A, the middle section being of a quieter nature. A suggestion of the outdoors is often introduced into this movement through the use of horn and woodwind tone. The reader will recall that *scherzo* derives from the Italian word for "jest"; but the mood may range from the elfin lightness of the Mendelssohnian scherzo to a mood of Cyclopean energy or intensity. The fourth and last member of the cycle is a large movement to balance the first. It brings the symphony to a close, at any rate during the latter nineteenth century, on a note of triumph—the glorification or "apotheosis" dear to the romantic temperament. In most of the romantic symphonies to be discussed in the next chapters the final movement is cast in the exposition-development-recapitulation structure of first-movement or sonata form.

We have here given the barest outline of symphonic form, not attempting a complete picture until after we shall have heard several representative symphonies. What is important at this point is to understand that the symphony is an ideal tone-drama whose action concerns the unfolding, expansion, and development of musical ideas. The essence of its style is dramatic contrast and development within a tight frame of thematic continuity. It arouses emotion in the listener, but emotion not directed to any specific image. For the symphony is a highly charged communication in the language of absolute music, whose glory is its freedom from definiteness. From our knowledge of the romantic era, from the letters and statements of composers concerning their symphonic works, we may glean some idea of the emotional climate that a given symphony inhabits. Certain characteristic symbolisms recur, as the movement "from doubt to faith" of César Franck's Symphony, or the progression from conflict to triumphal affirmation that appealed to the nineteenth-century mind. However, what the doubt, faith, conflict, or triumph is about is left unspecified. We may be specific about the formal content of a symphony—the disposition of the themes, their growth and development. The emotional content is left for each listener to determine for himself.

The word "theme" is apt to figure prominently in any discussion of musical form. By a theme we mean a distinctive musical idea that serves as a building block, a germinating element in a large musical work. The theme may be a fully rounded melody or it may be a compact melodic-harmonic-rhythmic kernel that is capable of further growth and flowering. The theme may be broken down into its constituent fragments which are known as motives. For example, the melody of *London Bridge* might serve as a theme in a large work. The first four notes (on the words "London Bridge is") could constitute one motive, the next three notes (on the words "falling down"), another. In the unfolding of a work this theme and its motives might undergo continual development, in the course of which their capacity for growth would be explored, their latent energies brought to light. We shall have more to say on theme and motive when we discuss the classical form in detail.

THE CONCERTO

In the concerto, attention is focused upon the solo performer. This circumstance helps determine the form. The concerto has to be a "grateful" vehicle that will enable the artist to display his gifts, technical and musical. The concerto has three movements instead of four.

(The Piano Concerto in B-flat of Brahms is an unusual exception.) A massive allegro in first-movement form is followed by a songful slow movement and a brilliant finale.

In several of the concertos that we will discuss, the final movement is in the form of a *rondo*. This is a lively movement suffused with the spirit of the dance. Its distinguishing feature is the recurrence of a central idea—the rondo theme—in alternation with one or more subsidiary themes. Its symmetrical sections create a balanced architecture that is esthetically satisfying and easy to grasp. In its simplest form, A-B-A-B-A, the rondo is an extension of the A-B-A principle. If there are two subordinate themes, the sections may follow an A-B-A-C-A or similar pattern. Vivacity, brilliance, and charm are native to the rondo.

The dramatic tension between soloist and orchestra may be compared to that between protagonist and chorus in Greek tragedy. This opposition of forces constitutes the essential nature of the concerto. The massive harmonies of the piano may be pitted against the orchestral mass. The sweetness of violin or 'cello tone may be counterposed to the orchestral harmony. As in the symphony, contrasting themes are "exposed," developed, and restated. In this case, however, the tension is twofold: not only between the contrasting ideas but also between the opposing forces—solo as against the group.

Each of the basic themes may be announced by the *tutti* (literally, "all"; i.e., the orchestra as a whole) and then taken up by the solo part. Or the latter may introduce the ideas and the orchestra expatiate upon them. The classical masters of the concerto—Mozart and Beethoven— favored a clear-cut opposition in which a passage for orchestra alternated with one for solo, both joining forces at the climactic points. The romantics preferred a more intimate relationship between the two. Often a phrase in the orchestra is echoed immediately by the solo part or the other way around, in the manner of a tender dialogue.

A characteristic feature of the concerto is the *cadenza*, a flowery solo passage in the manner of an improvisation that is interpolated in the movement. The term originally signified the display of trills and roulades indulged in by opera singers near the close, or cadence, of a scene in order to display their virtuosity and arouse the house to enthusiasm. The cadenza came out of a time when improvisation was an important element in art music, as it still is today in jazz. Taken over into the solo concerto, it made a dramatic effect: the orchestra fell silent and the soloist launched into a free play of fantasy on the themes of the movement.

Before the nineteenth century, the performer as like as not was also the composer; consequently the improvisation was apt to be of the highest caliber. With the rise of a class of professional players who interpreted the music of others but did not invent their own, the art of improvising declined. Thus, the cadenza came to be written out beforehand, either by the composer or the artist; or else, now that it was no longer a functional part of the occasion, it was omitted altogether.

SYMPHONY AND CONCERTO IN THE ROMANTIC ERA

The sonata form was the crowning achievement of eighteenth-century classicism. Brought to artistic maturity by Haydn, Mozart, and Beethoven, it embodied the thought and feeling of the classical age. The romantic composers were at a disadvantage: they tried to adapt the grand form to a content for which it had not been intended. The struggle between classical form and romantic content was the central issue of nineteenth-century music. As more than one composer complained, it was not easy to write a symphony after Beethoven.

The classical symphony was based on the clash of ideas; romanticism preferred the battle of emotions. Classical form called for tight structure, careful planning, thematic logic, abstract thought; romanticism loved diffuseness and caprice, mood and atmosphere, and literary associations. The classical symphony was a dramatic form; romanticism was avid for lyricism. In the first flush of the romantic movement the symphony lost its supremacy. Composers turned on the one hand to program music, on the other to short lyric forms such as the romantic song and piano piece. To Liszt, Berlioz, Wagner, and other adherents of the "Music of the Future" it seemed that the symphony as the classical era had known it was a thing of the past.

Once the initial fervor of romanticism had subsided, however, the symphony began to regain its central position: its appeal to the purely musical instincts of composers was too great to be long ignored. Imperceptibly it accommodated itself to the needs of a new age. Its structure was loosened by lyricism and by the grand rhetoric of the nineteenth-century style. It absorbed the romantic love of spectacular effect and grandiose gesture. It could not recapture the ideal balance of form and content, the Olympian serenity of Haydn and Mozart, or the tightness of construction of Beethoven. But it became an intensely human document packed with action, with turbulent climax and spine-tingling proclamation, with purple patches and with upwellings of song.

Romantic symphony and concerto cannot be judged, strictly speaking, by the standards of the classical era. They aspired to something else. Only in this way could they truthfully reflect their own time. Only in this way were brought into being the exuberant works that continue to delight multitudes of music lovers.

✿27✿

A Romantic Concerto

MENDELSSOHN: CONCERTO FOR VIOLIN AND ORCHESTRA

THE VIOLIN CONCERTO in E minor, Op. 64, dates from the latter part of Mendelssohn's career. The work reveals Mendelssohn's gifts: clarity of form and grace of utterance, a subtle orchestral palette, and a vein of sentiment that is tender but reserved. The first movement, Allegro molto appassionato (very fast and impassioned), is a spacious sonata-allegro form. The customary orchestral introduction is omitted, and the violin at once announces the main idea of the movement, a resilient and active melody in the upper register.

The expansion of this idea gives the violinist opportunity for brilliant passage work. The theme is then proclaimed by full orchestra (tutti).

A transitional idea appears. This leads to the contrasting lyric theme, narrow of range and characterized by stepwise movement along the scale and by narrow leaps. It is introduced by flutes and clarinets, tranquillo and pianissimo over a sustained tone on the open G string of the solo instrument.

The development section is marked by genuine symphonic momentum, culminating in the cadenza which, instead of coming at the end of the movement as is customary, serves as a link between the second and third sections (the Development and Recapitulation). Under a curtain of widely spaced arpeggios on the violin the opening theme emerges in the orchestra. From here to the Coda the movement gains steadily in power and is exemplary for its elegant handling of the large form.

The Andante follows without a break, an A-B-A form in 6/8 time. Mendelssohn could not command the pathos of the Beethovenian slow movement. Within his own limits he was well able, however, to create an atmosphere of calm meditative sentiment. The middle section in somber elegiac vein marks the romantic in him; after which the serene opening melody returns.

Brave flourishes on bassoons, horns, and trumpets, *ff*, lead into the Allegro molto vivace (very fast and lively), a rondo in 4/4 in the light breezy manner that is Mendelssohn's most characteristic vein. The movement demands agile fingers and high spirits, a crisp staccato and brilliance of tone. Excitement builds steadily to the pyrotechnics of the Coda.

Felicitous in melody, form, and texture, the Concerto displays the Mendelssohnian blend of tender sentiment and classic moderation. It deservedly remains a favorite with performers and listeners alike.

❧28❧
Johannes Brahms (1833-1897)

"It is not hard to compose, but it is wonderfully hard to let the superfluous notes fall under the table."

AGAINST the colorful program art of Berlioz, Liszt, and Wagner there arose an austere, high-minded musician dedicated to the purity of the classical forms. His veneration for the past and his mastery of the architecture of absolute music brought him closer to the spirit of Beethoven than were any of his contemporaries.

HIS LIFE

Brahms was born in Hamburg, son of a double-bass player whose love of music was greater than his attainments. As a youngster of ten Johannes helped increase the family income by playing the piano in the dance halls of the slum district where he grew up. By the time he was twenty he had acquired sufficient reputation as a pianist to accompany the Hungarian violinist Reményi on a concert tour.

His first compositions made an impression on Joseph Joachim, leading violinist of the day, who made possible a visit to Robert Schumann at Düsseldorf. Schumann recognized in the shy young composer a future leader of the camp dedicated to absolute music. He published in his journal the famous essay entitled "New Paths" in which he named the twenty-year-old "young eagle" as the one who "was called forth to give us the highest ideal expression of our time." Brahms awoke to find himself famous.

Robert and Clara took the fair-haired youth into their home. Their friendship opened up new horizons for him. Five months later came the tragedy of Schumann's mental collapse. Brahms hastened to Clara's side, and with a tenderness and strength he had not suspected in himself, tided her over the ordeal of Robert's illness.

The older man lingered for two years while the younger was shaken by the great love of his life. Clara Schumann was then at the peak of her fame. Fourteen years his senior and the mother of seven children, she appeared to young Brahms as the ideal of womanly and artistic perfection. What had begun as filial devotion ripened into romantic passion. She for her part found a necessary source of strength in the loyalty of the "young eagle." She watched his genius unfold as once she had watched Robert's. For Johannes this was the period of storm and stress, as his letters to her reveal. "I regret every word I write you which does not speak of love. You have taught me and every day teach me more and more to marvel at the nature of love, affection, and self-denial. I can do nothing but think of you." At the same time he was rent by feelings of guilt, for he loved and revered Schumann, his friend and benefactor, above all others. He thought of suicide and spoke of himself, as one may at twenty-two, as "a man for whom nothing is left."

The conflict was resolved the following year by Schumann's death; but another conflict took its place. Now that Clara was no longer the unattainable ideal, Brahms was faced with the choice between love and freedom. Time and again in the course of his life he was torn between the two, with the decision going always to freedom. His ardor subsided into a lifelong friendship. Two decades later he could still write her, "I love you more than myself and more than anybody and anything on earth." Toward the end of his life, when the forty-year-old relationship was almost broken because of a misunderstanding, he wrote to Clara, "Today you must allow me to repeat to you that you and your husband represent the most beautiful experience of my life, that you stand for its greatest wealth and noblest meaning."

His appointment as musician to the Prince of Detmold inaugurated his professional career. After four years at this post he returned to Hamburg to devote himself to composition. But he failed to obtain an official appointment in his native city—the directors of the Philharmonic never forgot that Johannes came from the waterfront—and settled in Vienna, which remained the center of his activities for thirty-five years. In the stronghold of the classical masters he found a favorable soil for his art, his northern seriousness refined by the grace and congeniality of the South. The time was ripe for him. His fame filled the world and he became the acknowledged heir of the Viennese masters.

This exacting artist had a curiously dual nature. He could be morose and withdrawn, yet he loved lusty humor. A bohemian at heart, he craved bourgeois respectability. Behind a rough exterior he hid the tenderness that found expression in his music and his love of children. He fought the softness in himself and came to be feared for his caustic wit. To a musician fishing for compliments he remarked, "Yes, you have talent. But very little!" The elderly ladies whom he was rehearsing in *The Creation* were admonished: "Why do you drag it so? Surely you

Johannes Brahms.

took this much faster under Haydn." When a renowned quartet played his work the viola player inquired if he was satisfied with the tempo. Brahms snapped, "Yes—especially yours!" Thus the crotchety bachelor went his way through the middle-class circles of Vienna, the center of an adoring coterie. Although he complained of loneliness and on occasion fell in love, he was unable to accept the responsibility of a sustained relationship. His motto was *Free—but happy!* "It would be as difficult for me to marry," he explained, "as to write an opera. But after the first experience I should probably undertake a second!"

Just as in early manhood his mother's death had inspired *A German Requiem,* so the final illness of Clara Schumann gave rise to the *Four Serious Songs.* Her death profoundly affected the composer, already ill with cancer. He died ten months later, at the age of sixty-four, and was buried not far from Beethoven and Schubert.

HIS MUSIC

Hans von Bülow called Brahms' First Symphony the "Tenth." He thereby indicated its kinship with Beethoven's nine. From the same source came the remark about "the three B's—Bach, Beethoven, Brahms." Although both descriptions are meaningless from a historical point of view, they sum up what Brahms meant to his generation.

He was a traditionalist. His gaze was directed back to the classical era whose splendor it was no longer possible to resurrect. This sense of being a latecomer imparts to his music its gently retrospective flavor, its autumnal resignation. Endowed with the historic sense, Brahms looked upon himself as a preserver of the great tradition. His aim was to show that new and important things could still be said in the forms inherited from the classical masters. In this he differed from avowed innovators such as Berlioz, Liszt, and Wagner.

A romantic who was drawn to introspection and lyricism, he buttressed himself with the austere architecture of the large forms. He was one of the very few of his generation who came to grips with the main issues of classical structure and handled the large forms with something of the mastery of the past. His melodies have a rugged strength. The harmonies are subtly archaic in quality, colored by his interest in old music. Certain progressions are recognizable at once as being his and no other's. His rhythm is vigorous, dynamic; he is fond of syncopations and cross rhythms. His loyalty is to idea rather than color; not for him the brilliant orchestration of Liszt or Wagner. Woodwinds and brass are much used in their low register, blending with the strings in a silver-gray sonority that has a warmth all its own. The interweaving of the separate lines in his music gives it its intricate texture. He was a master at varying and combining themes.

Brahms' four symphonies are among the most important in the literature after Schubert. They are unsurpassed in the late romantic period for breadth of conception and design. Best known of the other orchestral works are the *Variations on a Theme by Haydn* and the concert overtures—the *Academic* and the *Tragic*. The two concertos for piano and orchestra and the one for violin are justly regarded as the finest since Beethoven.

In greater degree than any of his contemporaries Brahms captured the tone of intimate communion which is the essence of chamber-music style. The duo sonatas, trios, quartets, quintets, and sextets for string and wind instruments, with and without piano, comprise a body of works marked by lyricism and a quality of introspection peculiarly his own. He is an important figure too in piano music. The three sonatas are works of his youth. The *Variations and Fugue on a Theme by Handel* represents his top achievement in this field. A favorite with concert performers is the set of *Variations on a Theme by Paganini*, a composition that requires supreme virtuoso playing. The romantic in Brahms also found expression in short lyric pieces; the Rhapsodies, Ballades, Capriccios, and lyrical meditations known as Intermezzi are among the treasures of the literature. On the popular level are the Hungarian Dances and the set of sixteen Waltzes.

As a song writer Brahms stands in direct line of succession after Schubert and Schumann. His output includes about two hundred solo songs and an almost equal number for two, three, and four voices. The favorite themes are love, nature, death. His finest choral work is the *German Requiem*, written to texts from the Bible selected by himself. A song of acceptance of death, this work more than any other spread his fame during his lifetime.

The national element is strong in Brahms. His lyricism was fed by German folk song. He spoke of himself as *echt Deutsch* (thoroughly German). When it was pointed out to him that art has no fatherland, "That is true," he retorted, "for those who listen but not for those who write." His love of the national inspired his arrangements of German folk and children's songs as well as the popular tone of many of his art songs. In his Waltzes he paid tribute to the popular dance of his beloved Vienna, but he knew he was too much the north German to capture the real Viennese flavor. When he gave his autograph to Johann Strauss's daughter—composers customarily inscribed a few bars of their music—he wrote the opening measures of the *Blue Danube* waltz and noted beneath it, "Not, alas, by Johannes Brahms."

THE THIRD SYMPHONY

The Symphony No. 3 in F major, Op. 90, was completed in 1883 when Brahms was fifty years old. It is a picturesque work that serves well as an introduction to the composer's style. The first movement, Allegro con brio (lively, with vigor), is in sonata-allegro form. The opening three notes constitute a kind of motto that pervades the first movement and returns in the last.

The motto becomes an accompaniment to the first idea. This is a downward striding, vigorous theme of commanding gesture. Played passionato by the violins, it outlines the tones of the tonic chord.

The contrasting idea, pastoral in character, is presented by the clarinet grazioso and mezza voce (in half voice). The same pattern of notes recurs on different beats within the measure, a favorite device of Brahms that makes the melody appear to be "chasing its tail."

Brahms requires the exposition section to be repeated. This practice of classical times was falling into discard in the romantic period, when considerations of form were made subordinate to dramatic effectiveness. Brahms' revival of the practice underlines his classicist bent.

The two themes are subjected to a brief and intense development, the motto theme serving as a unifying element. The Recapitulation is followed by an ample coda. Characteristic throughout is the prominence of horn tone, the warm but subdued resonance, the wide spacing of the harmonies, and the quality of reticent emotion that is Brahms' own.

The slow movement is an Andante in 4/4 time. Brahms marks it espressivo and semplice (with simplicity). The theme is announced by clarinets supported by bassoons and horns. A contrasting idea appears that is destined to take on significance in the final movement of the symphony. The first theme returns with variation in rhythm and harmony, register, accompaniment, and orchestration. The movement ends on a serene note.

For the impetuous scherzo of Beethoven's symphony Brahms substituted a lyrical third movement in moderate tempo. This Allegretto in triple meter is an impassioned, darkly colored orchestral song. The lyric theme on the 'cellos is contrasted with a lighter idea in the middle section, after which the first is repeated with changes in orchestration.

The finale is a dramatic sonata-allegro marked by concise themes and abrupt changes of mood. The first idea is a searching melody, narrow in range and with a well-defined curve. It is played in unison by bassoons and strings. The low register and the instrumentation combine to give it its somber coloration.

For contrast there is a festive theme molded to the nature of the wind instruments. Brahms is thoroughly German in his fondness for wind sound. The movement proceeds with classical logic and impulsion. There is an extensive development; the first idea returns in longer note values. A tender allusion by the violins to the opening theme of the symphony casts a nostalgic glow over the closing measures of the work.

❧ 29 ❧
Antonin Dvořák (1841-1904)

> "In the Negro melodies of America I discover all that is needed
> for a great and noble school of music. These beautiful and varied
> themes are the product of the soil. They are American. They
> are the folk songs of America, and your composers must turn
> to them."

ANTONIN DVOŘÁK is one of several late romantic composers who based
their personal style on the songs and dances of their native lands. He
stands alongside Bedřich Smetana as a founder of the Czech national
school.

HIS LIFE

Dvořák was born in a village near Prague where his father kept an
inn and butcher shop. Poverty for a time threatened to rule out a
musical career. However, the boy managed to get to Prague when he
was sixteen. There he mastered his craft and wound up as viola player
in the orchestra of the Czech National Theater. Success as a composer
came slowly, but in time he was able to resign his orchestra post and
devote himself to composing, teaching, and conducting. By the time
he was forty Dvořák had left behind the material cares that plagued
the first years of his career. As professor of composition at the Conservatory of Prague he was able to influence the younger generation
of Czech musicians.

The spontaneity and melodious character of his music assured its
popularity. When the last decade of the century arrived, Dvořák was
known throughout Europe. In 1892 he was invited to become director
of the National Conservatory of Music in New York City. He received
fifteen thousand dollars a year at the Conservatory—a fabulous sum
in those days—as compared with the six hundred dollars that made up
his annual salary as a professor in Prague. His stay in the United States
was fruitful. He produced what has remained his most successful symphony, *From the New World*; a number of chamber works, including
the *American* Quartet; and the Concerto for 'Cello and Orchestra.
Dvořák spent a summer at the Czech colony in Spillville, Iowa, in an
atmosphere congenial to his simple tastes. Although every effort was
made to induce him to continue at the Conservatory, his homesickness

overrode all other considerations. After three years he returned to his beloved Bohemia. His joy at the prospect of going home found expression in a series of little Humoresques for piano, of which the seventh became one of the world's most overplayed pieces.

He spent his remaining years in Prague in the happy circle of his wife and children, students and friends. He died in his sixty-third year, revered as a national artist throughout his native land.

HIS MUSIC

Dvořák was a natural musician, a type that has always been abundant in Bohemia. Songfulness was native to a temperament in which intuition predominated over the intellectual process. Having sprung from the village, he never lost touch with the soil that was the source of his strength. At the same time, he achieved a solid craftsmanship in his art that enabled him to shape his musical impulses into large forms notable for their clarity and rightness.

Dvořák's large output covered all branches of his art: operas, a national oratorio, symphonies, concertos, chamber music, overtures, rhapsodies, symphonic poems, songs, piano pieces, Slavonic dances. A good part of this work never established itself outside his native land. Though much of it has fallen into discard, enough remains to endear him to many.

Coming to the United States as one of the leading nationalists of Europe, Dvořák tried to influence his American pupils toward a national art. American musicians at that time went to study either at Leipzig, where they steeped themselves in the tradition of Mendelssohn, or at Weimar, where they absorbed the teachings of Liszt. Dvořák held up to them the necessity of creating a native music free from European influence. In the melodies of the Negroes, as in the cowboy tunes of the West, he discerned the raw material for such an art. One of his pupils was Henry T. Burleigh, the Negro baritone and arranger of spirituals. The melodies he heard from Burleigh stirred the folk poet in Dvořák, and strengthened him in his conviction that American composers would find themselves only when they had thrown off the European past and come to grips with the indigenous material of the New World.

The time was not ripe for his advice to be heeded. But his instinct did not mislead him concerning the future of American music. One has but to regard the rich harvest of contemporary American works based on folklore to realize how correct, in the main, was his view.

THE *NEW WORLD* SYMPHONY

The subtitle *From the New World* defines the scope and intent of the Symphony in E minor, Op. 95. Dvořák was too much the Czech to presume to write an American work. His aim was to record the impressions of a visitor, his response to the exuberance and vastness of a young and growing land. He wished also, as a folk composer, to pay homage to the spirit of Negro folk music even while he longingly evoked the landscape of his own Bohemia. The work is consequently a mixture of Czech and American elements.

The symphony opens with an introduction marked Adagio which leads into a vigorous Allegro molto. This is a clearly wrought first-movement form based on three ideas. The first is an energetic theme which opens with an upthrusting arpeggio figure, wide of span and syncopated in rhythm.

The second idea is a plaintive tune of Bohemian folk character which is introduced by flutes and oboes. It has the narrow range and repetition of tones associated with melodies born of the soil.

Third is a songful theme announced by flute solo and taken over, in the answering phrase, by the violins. Its outlines suggest Dvořák's favorite Negro spiritual, *Swing Low, Sweet Chariot.*

The Development is brief, clear-cut, imbued with forward drive. Its vivid contrasts of soft and loud, high and low, and its broad crescendos and lively colors please ear and mind without taxing either. The Recapitulation restates the thematic material. There is a grandiose coda based on descending chromatic scales, culminating in a fortissimo statement of the basic arpeggio figure.

The slow movement is the famous Largo, in 4/4 time. Out of the remote chords of the introduction, marked *ppp*, issues the nostalgic melody assigned to the English horn. As the folk song *Going Home* this has become famous in many lands, even as far away as China. Dvořák here caught the accents of the weary ones of the earth. The son of peasants set down what he felt. What he felt rings true.

The movement is an A-B-A form. Just before the return of the Largo melody, the orchestra works up a climax from which emerges, as an effective reminiscence, the arpeggio figure of the first movement. This bringing back of a theme from an earlier movement is known as *cyclical structure*, and serves to knit the work as a whole together.

The Scherzo, marked Molto vivace (very lively), is a dance movement in 3/4 time, unmistakably Czech in atmosphere. The middle section reinforces the character of Czech folk song and dance. Then the first section is heard again. In this movement, as in the Largo, Dvořák uses cyclical form to unify his symphonic framework: there are a number of references to the first movement.

The finale, Allegro con fuoco (fast, with fire), is an ample sonata form in 4/4 time. The stormy introduction leads into a vigorous melody, in the character of a march, played by trumpets and horns.

This is counterposed to a flowing lyric idea, a reverie sung by the clarinet. The third idea is in the nature of a popular song. Its symmetrical phrases end in three descending notes that appear to be derived from the familiar round, *Three Blind Mice*. This little figure takes on prominence as it is bandied about by the various instrumental groups. In the development and recapitulation sections we meet a grand procession of themes from the earlier movements. At the last there is the rousing sort of finale that we have come to expect in works of this period.

The *New World* Symphony has always been a favorite in the United States. Its continuity of thought, clarity of outline, and vivacity of detail command the respect of musicians; while its appealing melodies and accessible ideas are such as make the popular classic.

❧30❧
Edvard Grieg (1843-1907)

"The fundamental trait of Norwegian folk song is a deep melancholy that may suddenly change to a wild unrestrained gayety. Our traditional tunes, handed down from an age when the Norwegian peasantry was isolated from the world in its solitary mountain valleys, bear the stamp of an imagination as daring as it is bizarre."

EDVARD GRIEG occupies a position in his homeland similar to that of Dvořák in his. To the international music public he came to represent "the Voice of Norway." The nationalist movement of which his music was an expression had a political background. Agitation for independence from Sweden came to a head during the last quarter of the nineteenth century. This cause, to which Grieg was devoted with all his heart, was crowned with success not long before his final illness. "What has happened in our country this year," he wrote, "seems like a fairy tale. The hopes and longings of my youth have been fulfilled. I am deeply grateful that I was privileged to live to see this."

Scandinavia's art music, up to the time of Grieg, remained within the orbit of German musical culture. Her composers studied in Leipzig or Weimar and came home to continue the traditions of Mendelssohn and Schumann or Wagner and Liszt. Grieg's first attempts at composition, after several years at the Leipzig Conservatory, followed the formula that has been well described as "Mendelssohnacid Schumannoxide." It was only when he returned to Norway, after several years at the Leipzig Conservatory, that he became aware of the need for a national art. In so doing he found his personal tone. "The more he sang about his land the more truly he spoke about himself."

His development in this direction was spurred by his friendship with Richard Nordraak, a gifted young composer one year older than himself, who made him see that only by asserting his national heritage would he contribute something original to art. The two young men spent some time in Denmark and founded a musical society in Copenhagen whose purpose it was to present the works of Norwegian composers. Nordraak's death at the age of twenty-four profoundly affected his friend. Grieg's anguish found vent in the *Funeral March for Richard Nordraak*, the first work in which his gifts are apparent.

Copenhagen was the home of his cousin Nina Hagerup. To her he wrote his most famous song *I Love Thee (Ich liebe dich)*, to the verses of Hans Christian Andersen. Grieg and Nina were in their early twenties when they embarked on their ideally happy marriage. For forty years she was his constant companion. A woman of great charm and intelligence, she was an accomplished singer and became one of the finest interpreter's of her husband's songs.

Grieg benefited from the enlightened policy of the Scandinavian countries toward their creative artists. At thirty-one he was granted what many an artist has dreamed of: a life annuity from the government that made it possible for him to devote all his energies to composing. The first fruit of this leisure was the incidental music for Henrik Ibsen's poetic drama *Peer Gynt*. Four numbers from this work, arranged as a concert suite, did more than any of his other compositions to spread Grieg's name throughout the world.

The folk songs of Scandinavia are based on scales sufficiently different from the traditional ones to sound exotic. Grieg was most successful in assimilating their novel charm to his personal style. He added a new dialect to the musical speech of the late romantic period; he introduced a spontaneous tone and revealed the northern landscape.

The final decades of his life were spent at his villa Troldhaugen (Hill of the Trolls), overlooking the fiords outside his native town of Bergen. In these years he was much in demand all over Europe as an interpreter of his works, and appeared in the various capitals as conductor and pianist. He received many tempting offers to visit the United States, but declined because of his uncertain health. His death at the age of sixty-four was mourned throughout the world. For his compatriots it had the nature of a personal loss.

THE PIANO CONCERTO

Grieg was one of a rather large group of artists who start off with a lucky hit that they never quite duplicate. He was twenty-five when he wrote the Piano Concerto in A minor. It remained his masterpiece.

The first movement, Allegro molto moderato (moderately lively), is in sonata form. It opens with a dramatic roll on the kettledrums and precipitously descending octaves in the solo part. The opening melody, with its tinge of melancholy, evokes the northern scene. We find here one of Grieg's mannerisms: a fragment of melody is repeated at once on a higher degree of the scale. This is the method of the miniaturist.

An animated bridge passage leads to the contrasting idea, tranquillo e cantabile (tranquil and songful), which shows the same construction by fragments as the first theme. Set forth by the 'cellos and taken over by the piano, this lyric melody is in Grieg's characteristic vein.

The development section is brief and intense. The harmonies are familiar to us now, but they sounded altogether novel to Grieg's contemporaries. The Recapitulation is climaxed by an impressive cadenza that presents the main theme embellished by ornate runs, massed chords, and octaves.

The Adagio, an A-B-A form in 3/4 time, captures the lyric charm of a Grieg song. The finale, Poco animato (somewhat animated), counterposes a dance and a song mood in the formation A-B-A-B. A vigorously rhythmic theme of folk-dance character, in duple meter, is presented with bravura effect on the piano. This is followed by an idyllic melody marked Poco più tranquillo (somewhat calmer), first heard on the flute. At the finale this melody is transformed into a sumptuous Andante maestoso. This characteristically romantic "apotheosis" brings the work to a triumphal close.

It was given to Edvard Grieg to reveal to the world the Norwegian landscape and the musical imagery of its people. He fulfilled his mission with taste and imagination. Overshadowed by the more robust figures of his time, his attractive figure continues to exercise its own wistful charm.

❧ 31 ❧

A Late Romantic Symphony
TCHAIKOVSKY'S *PATHÉTIQUE*

"I have put my whole soul into this work."

TCHAIKOVSKY's symphonies and concertos achieved a prominence in the international repertoire rivaled by few works of the late romantic period. His Sixth Symphony, the *Pathétique*, is representative of his style and esthetic. Early in the last year of his life he wrote his nephew, to whom it was dedicated, that he was occupied with a new work. "This time with a program—but a program of the kind that will remain an enigma to all. Let them guess it who can. The work will be entitled *A Program Symphony*. The program is penetrated with subjective sentiment. During my journey, while composing it in my mind, I frequently shed tears."

The adagio introduction is somber in color and sets the tone of brooding intensity. A solo bassoon in low register moves sluggishly along the chromatic scale, foreshadowing the material of the Allegro proper.

The Allegro non troppo (not too fast) is a first-movement form based upon two vividly contrasted ideas. First is a tense rhythmic theme penetrated, as Tchaikovsky put it, with subjective sentiment.

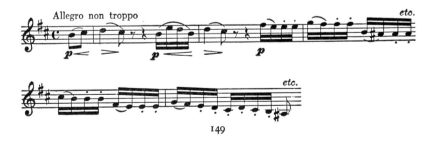

149

The area of relaxation comes with the famous lyric theme sung by muted violins and 'cellos, andante. Tchaikovsky marks the passage teneramente, molto cantabile, con espansione (tenderly, very songfully, expansively).

An explosive chord, fortissimo, opens the development. Based on the first theme, this section is a veritable catalogue of Tchaikovsky's favorite orchestral devices. Violins sweep furiously up and down the scale. Brusque accented chords spread across the orchestral gamut. The richly colored tone mass is whipped up to excitement, thrusting its way step by step to the higher register.

The Recapitulation presents the two fundamental ideas with changes in instrumental color. A new passage is introduced in which the massed brass is pitted against woodwinds and strings in spectacular fashion. The Coda sounds the tragic tone. A descending scale reiterated in the bass, pizzicato, invariably suggests to commentators the footfalls of fate.

Next is the Allegro con grazia (lively, with grace), a dance mood vivid and quite ballet-like in quality. This is an A-B-A form in what was, in the 1890s, a most unusual meter—5/4 time. The alternation within the measure of groups of two and three beats imparts to the movement a wayward charm.

The third movement, Allegro molto vivace (very fast and lively), is in 4/4 time. Within a tightly knit frame, a scherzo alternates with a march in an A-B-A-B formation. The March is based on an incisive rhythm ending with a syncopated "snap." From modest beginnings this characteristic pattern infiltrates the orchestral tissue and works up to an electrifying climax.

Last is the Adagio lamentoso (very slow, lamenting) in 4/4 time. The dolorous theme, introduced by the violins, unfolds a bleak landscape of the soul.

The atmosphere of sorrow is dispelled for a space by the consoling middle section, marked Andante. The orchestral sound is lashed to a furious climax. The lament returns. At the end we hear a combination of bassoon and string tone similar to that with which the symphony opened. The music descends to the dark regions whence it issued.

Thus the arc of the nineteenth-century symphony is completed: from the optimism, the spirit of affirmation of a dawning revolutionary epoch that found its gesture in the triumphal finale of Beethoven's symphonies, to the twilight anguish of Tchaikovsky's last statement. The Beethovenian pathos celebrated man the master of his fate. The Tchaikovskian pathos was compounded of futile regret, impotent fury, torturing doubt. The artist is bound by mysterious threads to his age. In distilling the poison from his soul Tchaikovsky voiced the illness of an era.

Yet the Beethovenian vision of art as healing, of art as victory over life, sustained this end-of-century figure. Through art he conquered the forces of disunity within himself, he lifted himself above despair and won his place in history. He left his mark on the musical practice of the late romantic period. He established a kind of utterance that is unmistakably Tchaikovskian, in much the same way that we recognize another kind as Dickensian. He captured in his music the mood of a time and a place, endowed it with artistic form, and, by an act of will and imagination, made it comprehensible to men everywhere.

Opera

≥32≤
The Nature of Opera

"It is better to invent reality than to copy it."
Giuseppe Verdi

FOR WELL over three hundred years the opera has been one of the most alluring forms of musical entertainment. A special glamor attaches to everything connected with it—its arias, singers, and roles, not to mention its opening nights. Carmen, Mimi, Aïda, Tristan—what character in fact or fiction can claim, generation after generation, so constant a public?

An opera is a drama which is sung. It combines the resources of vocal and instrumental music, soloists, ensembles, and chorus, orchestra and ballet, with poetry and drama, acting and pantomime, scenery and costumes. To weld the diverse elements into a unity is a problem that has exercised some of the best minds in the history of music.

OPERA AND REALITY

At first glance opera would seem to make impossible demands on the credulity of the spectator. It presents us with human beings caught up in dramatic situations who sing to each other instead of speaking. The reasonable question is—and it was asked most pointedly throughout the history of opera by literary men—how can an art form based on so unnatural a procedure be convincing? How can it bring about that "suspension of disbelief" which is the essence of the theater experience? The question ignores what must always remain the fundamental aspiration of art: not to copy nature but to heighten our awareness of it.

True enough, people in real life do not sing to each other. Neither do they converse in blank verse, as Shakespeare's characters do; nor live in rooms of which one wall is conveniently missing so that the audience may look in.

All the arts employ conventions that are accepted both by the artist and his audience. Lyric poetry gives the impression of being a spontaneous utterance; yet much of it is arranged in the most artful patterns of meter and rhyme. We respond to the illusion of depth in a painting even though we know that the canvas is flat. The conventions of opera are more in evidence than those of poetry, painting, or drama, but they are not different in kind. Once we have accepted the fact that the carpet can fly, how simple to believe that it is also capable of carrying the prince's luggage.

Opera functions in the domain of the poetic drama. It uses the human voice to impinge upon the spectator the basic emotions—love, hate, jealousy, joy, grief—with an elemental force possible only to itself. The logic of reality gives way on the operatic stage to the transcendent logic of art, and to the power of music over the life of the heart.

THE COMPONENTS OF OPERA

In the classic type of opera the explanations necessary to plot and action are presented in a kind of musical declamation known as *recitative*. This vocal style imitates and emphasizes the natural inflections of speech; its rhythm is curved to the rhythm of the language. Recitative gives way at the lyric moments to the *aria*, which releases the emotional tension accumulated in the course of the action. The aria is pure melody. It is what audiences wait for, what they cheer, and what they remember.

Grand opera is sung throughout. In opera of the more popular variety the recitative is generally replaced by spoken dialogue. This is the type known among us as operetta or musical comedy, which has its counterpart in the French *opéra-comique* and German *Singspiel*. Interestingly enough, in Italy—the home of opera—even the comic variety, the *opera buffa*, is sung throughout.

The emotional conflicts in opera are linked to universal types and projected through the contrasting voices. Soprano, mezzo-soprano, and contralto are counterposed to tenor, baritone, and bass. The dramatic soprano is preferred for dynamic range and striking characterization, the lyric for gentler types. The coloratura has the highest range and greatest agility in the execution of trills and rapid passages. Corresponding to these are the dramatic tenor and the lyric tenor. German opera has popularized the *Heldentenor* (heroic tenor) who, whether as Siegfried or Tristan, is required to display endurance, brilliance, and expressive power. The palette is completed by the rich resonance of the bass, a figure often associated with age and royal dignity.

An opera may contain ensemble numbers—trios, quartets, quintets, sextets, septets. In these the characters pour out their respective emotions, creating a rich interplay of independent melody lines. The chorus is used in conjunction with the solo voices or it may function independently in the mass scenes. It may comment and reflect upon the action, in the manner of the chorus in Greek tragedy, or it may be integrated into the action. The orchestra provides the accompaniment. It sets the mood and creates the atmosphere for the different scenes. It also functions independently, in the overture, preludes to the acts, interludes, and postludes.

The ballet proves an eye-filling diversion in the scenes of pageantry that are an essential feature of grand opera. In the folk operas of the nineteenth century the ballet was used to present peasant and national dances. The libretto or book of the opera must be devised so as to give the composer his opportunity for the set numbers—the arias, duets, ensembles, choruses, marches, ballets, and finales that are the traditional features of this art form. The librettist must not only create characters and plot with some semblance of dramatic insight, but he has also to present these in terms of the lyric theater, fashioning situations that justify the use of music and could not be fully realized without it.

An important component of opera is the grand style. The pomp and splendor of its great scenes are survivals from a time when opera was the chief diversion of princely courts. The operatic is an exuberant style. Everything is presented larger than life-size. The spoken drama may concern itself with the clash of ideas; the opera concentrates on sentiments and passions.

Opera appeals primarily to those composers and music lovers who are given to the magic of the theater. It exerts its fascination upon those who love to hear singing. Thousands who do not feel at home with the abstract instrumental forms warm to opera, find there a graphic kind of music linked to action and dialogue, whose meaning it is impossible to mistake. Countless others are attracted for the very good reason that opera contains some of the grandest music ever written.

THE LANGUAGE PROBLEM

The composer of opera translates the imagery of life into music in the most direct and immediate way. The drama transforms itself in his mind, line by line, into sound. One has but to read the letters of composers to their librettists to realize how the masters extended themselves to capture in their music every nuance of the dialogue.

It is no less true that the vocal line takes its shape from the contours of the language. The composer releases the music inherent in its vowels and consonants; he reveals the melody of the language. That is one reason why opera is so intimately connected with national culture. What could be more German than Wagner, more Italian than Verdi?

A difficult problem arises when opera is exported to foreign lands. If it is given in the original tongue, the spectators lose the connection between text and music. If on the other hand the libretto is translated into the language of the audience, the authentic relationship between speech melody and vocal melody is destroyed.

Most European nations have preferred to sacrifice authenticity to the pleasure of understanding the proceedings on stage. Paris listens to Wagner in French, Berlin hears Verdi in German. Vienna, Prague, Moscow, Budapest translate opera into their respective tongues, thereby making it possible for the audience to participate in the dramatic experience. England and the United States, on the other hand, retain the original language. In these countries audiences do not understand what the characters are saying, nor do they seem to care.

There are opera lovers who tell you that they prefer *not* to know what the characters are singing about. For such listeners, the meticulous effort of the great masters to render accurately the sentiments and the passions is transformed into a series of pear-shaped tones that might just as well be sung in Sanskrit or to a string of la-la-la's. Opera cannot become a living part of a nation's culture until it has shed its foreign origin and adapted itself to the native scene and the native tongue. Opera began as an international form imported from Italy. Then one nation after another adapted it to its own genius—first France, subsequently Germany, Russia, Bohemia, Hungary. Today in our own country we witness successful attempts to present the great operas of the past in English, in lively and literate translations. We are seeing the beginnings of a native school of opera written by American composers for American singers and audiences. And we already have, of course, a tradition of popular opera in the musical shows of Broadway and Hollywood which, like the popular operas of former times in France, Germany, and England, contain spoken dialogue, spirited action, and pointed allusions to the topics of the day.

The future of opera in America lies not with the one or two celebrated opera houses that serve as repositories of the European tradition, but with the small lyric theaters and opera workshops scattered throughout the country. It rests also with the television studios that are beginning to bring opera into the American home in a form more closely related to our theater tradition than has been the case hitherto. Out of these and our popular musical theater will emerge a specifically American operatic culture. Signs are not lacking that it is on its way.

⪨ 33 ⪩

Opera in the Romantic Period

"It is at the Théâtre-Français, from the lips of the great actors, that declamation accompanied by theatrical illusion gives us ineffaceable impressions. It is there that the musician learns to interrogate the passions, to sound the depths of the human heart."
André Grétry (1742–1813)

THROUGHOUT its history the opera house was a center of novel ideas and experimentation whose influence permeated every branch of music. It was in the opera house that composers of the romantic period strove for the union of the arts so ardently desired by their time. Impelled by a hunger to encompass all facets of human experience, the romantic opera—like the world of which it was the bejeweled mirror—offered to eye and ear a feast of color, movement, and sound.

FRANCE

The grand opera that ruled the lyric stage in the post-Napoleonic era was very grand indeed. It was a conglomerate work based on heroic plots and "strong" situations drawn from history, abounding in purple rhetoric, brilliant solos and ensembles, spectacular ballets and décor.

Parisian grand opera was an exportable commodity whose triumphs extended to Berlin, London, and New York. Acknowledged master of the style was Giacomo Meyerbeer (1791–1864), a resourceful man of the theater whose dramatic power, striking declamation, and original orchestration exerted a more widespread influence than is generally realized. Meyerbeer had the advantage of working with one of the most accomplished librettists in history. Eugène Scribe understood the possibilities of the stage as thoroughly as he did the taste of the public. Meyerbeer's life work is summed up in three heroic operas: *Les Huguenots* (1836), based on the massacre of St. Bartholomew's Eve; *Le Prophète;* and *L'Africaine*, which is laid in an exotic setting and centers about the explorer Vasco da Gama. To the same category of operas belongs *La Juive* (The Jewess) by Jacques Halévy (1799–1862).

The Paris Opéra was reserved for works sung throughout. Those containing spoken dialogue were presented at a more intimate house, the Opéra-Comique. This type of opera outgrew its humble beginnings in the popular theater and took over certain traits of grand opera. It was out of the *opéra-comique* tradition that there came a work which captured the imagination of the world—*Carmen*.

Several composers of French opera achieved more than passing fame in the latter part of the century. Charles Gounod (1818–93) is remembered today chiefly for *Faust* (1859), one of the most successful operas of the century. Camille Saint-Saëns (1835–1921) scored a hit with his spectacular biblical opera *Samson and Delilah*. To this group belongs also Jules Massenet (1842–1912). His masterpiece is of course *Manon*, after the touching novel of Abbé Prévost.

On the comic side, none is more intimately associated with the spirit of Paris than Jacques Offenbach (1819–80), a highly gifted musician of German-Jewish parentage. His saucy operettas presented to French society of the era of Napoleon III the mirror in which it could laugh at its foibles. The Paris of Offenbach was perhaps no more real than the Vienna of Johann Strauss. Each created a legendary city that became a symbol of delight to millions.

ITALY

The most important figure in Italian opera during the first part of the century was Gioacchino Rossini (1792–1868), whose infectious melodies made him the idol of the musical world. *The Barber of Seville* (1816), his finest work, displays a vitality and electrical excitement that stamp him one of the great musicians of the theater.

Of the many composers active in Italian opera at this time only two others are known to the American public. Gaetano Donizetti (1797–

1848) is remembered chiefly for his tragic opera *Lucia di Lammermoor*, based on Walter Scott's novel *The Bride of Lammermoor*. Vincenzo Bellini (1801–35) is best known for *Norma, La Sonnambula* (The Sleepwalker), and the historical *I Puritani* (The Puritans). His untimely death prevented him from leading Italian opera toward the romantic lyricism that was native to his temperament.

Rossini, Donizetti, and Bellini left a rich legacy to their successors. They set the stage for developments that were to carry the national art form of Italy to new heights.

GERMANY

Of the men active in German opera during the early romantic period, only one captured the imagination of the world—Carl Maria von Weber (1786–1826).

His *Songs of War and Fatherland* inflamed a nation that was discovering its identity in the face of the Napoleonic invasion. These melodies were set to the lyrics of Theodor Körner, the poet of Young Germany who fell in battle at the age of twenty-two. Popular in the best sense, they caught the spirit of a vast stirring and aroused indescribable enthusiasm among the students and soldiers. Weber thus became the first national artist of the new age.

His most celebrated opera, *Der Freischütz* (The Marksman, 1821) is rooted in folklore. Popular superstition and peasant humor, the supernatural and the idyllic, are fused in a work pervaded by the beauty and mystery of the German forest, and by the touching simplicity of German folksong. *Euryanthe* and *Oberon* were less successful, but indicated the path that German romantic opera was to follow in the mid-nineteenth century.

Oberon was written for London, where Weber died—shortly after the première of the work—at the age of forty. Eighteen years later Richard Wagner, newly installed as royal conductor in Dresden, initiated the movement to bring back to Germany the remains of his idol. The composer was interred in Dresden in the presence of a vast throng. Wagner delivered the oration, and summed up what Weber meant to his countrymen: "Never was there a more German composer than you. In whatever fathomless realms of fancy your genius bore you, it remained bound by a thousand tender links to the heart of your German people, with whom it wept or smiled like a believing child listening to the legends and tales of its country."

≥ 34 ≤
Richard Wagner (1813-1883)

"The error in the art genre of opera consists in the fact that a means of expression—music—has been made the object, while the object of expression—the drama—has been made the means."

RICHARD WAGNER looms as probably the single most important phenomenon in the artistic life of the latter nineteenth century. Historians, not without justice, divide the period into "Before" and "After" Wagner. The course of post-romantic music is unthinkable without the impact of this complex and fascinating figure.

HIS LIFE

He was born in Leipzig, son of a minor police official who died when Richard was still an infant. A year later the widow married Ludwig Geyer, a talented actor, playwright, and painter who encouraged the artistic inclinations of his little stepson. The future composer was almost entirely self-taught. He had in all about six months of instruction in music theory. At twenty he abandoned his academic studies at the University of Leipzig and obtained a post as chorus master in a small opera house. In the next six years he gained practical experience conducting in provincial theaters. He fell in love with the actress Minna Planer whom he married when he was twenty-three. He absorbed the current repertory that centered about Meyerbeer, Bellini, and Donizetti. Under these influences he produced his first operas, *Die Feen* (The Fairies) and *Das Liebesverbot* (Love Prohibited, after Shakespeare's *Measure for Measure*). As with all his later works, he wrote the librettos himself. He was in this way able to achieve a unity of the musical-dramatic conception beyond anything that had been known before.

While conducting at the theater in Riga he began *Rienzi, Last of the Tribunes*, a grand opera based on Bulwer-Lytton's historical novel. This dealt with the heroic figure who in the fourteenth century led the Roman populace against the tyrannical nobles and perished in the struggle. With the first two acts of *Rienzi* under his arm he set out with Minna to conquer the world. His destination was Paris. But the world, then as now, was not easily conquered; Wagner failed to gain a foothold at the Opéra.

Richard Wagner.

The two and a half years spent in Paris were fruitful nevertheless. He completed *Rienzi* and produced *A Faust Overture*, the first music that bears the imprint of his genius. To keep alive he did hack work, such as arranging popular arias for the cornet, and turned out a number of articles, essays, and semifictional sketches. He also wrote the poem and music of *The Flying Dutchman*.

Just as the harassed young musician was beginning to lose heart, a lucky turn rescued him from his plight: *Rienzi* was accepted by the Dresden Opera. Suddenly his native land was wreathed in the same rosy mist as had formerly enveloped Paris. He started for Dresden, gazed on the Rhine for the first time, and "with great tears in his eyes swore eternal fidelity to the German fatherland." *Rienzi*, which satisfied the taste of the public for historical grand opera of the Meyerbeer stripe, was extremely successful. As a result, its composer in his thirtieth year found himself appointed conductor to the King of Saxony.

With *The Flying Dutchman* Wagner had taken an important step from the drama of historical intrigue to the idealized folk legend. He continued on this path with the two dramas of the Dresden period—*Tannhäuser* and *Lohengrin*—which bring to its peak the German romantic opera as established by Weber, his revered model. The operas use subjects derived from folklore, display a profound feeling for nature, employ the supernatural as an element of the drama, and glorify the German land and people. But the Dresden public was not prepared for these poetic works. They had come to see another *Rienzi* and were disappointed.

A dedicated artist who made no concessions to popular taste, Wagner dreamed of achieving for opera something of the grandeur that had characterized the ancient Greek tragedy. To this task he addressed himself with the fanaticism of the born reformer. He was increasingly alienated from a frivolous court that regarded opera as an amusement; from the bureaucrats in control of the royal theaters, who thwarted his plans; and from Minna, his wife, who was delighted with their social position in Dresden and had no patience with what she considered his utopian schemes. He was persuaded that the theater was corrupt because the society around it was corrupt. His beliefs as an artist led him into the camp of those who, as the fateful year 1848 approached, dreamed of a revolution in Europe that would end the power of the reactionary rulers. He came under the influence of August Röckel, a musician turned revolutionary, and of the Russian anarchist Bakunin who was then in Dresden. With reckless disregard of the consequences, Wagner appeared as speaker at a club of radical working-men. He published two articles in Röckel's journal: "Man and Existing Society" and "The Revolution." "The present order," he wrote, "is inimical to the destiny and the rights of man. The old world is crumbling to ruin. A new world will be born from it!"

The revolution broke out in Dresden in May 1849. King and court fled. Troops dispatched by the King of Prussia crushed the insurrection. Röckel and Bakunin were captured. Wagner escaped to his friend Liszt at Weimar, where he learned that a warrant had been issued for his arrest. With the aid of Liszt he was spirited across the border.

In the eyes of the world—and of Minna—he was a ruined man, but

Wagner did not in the least share this opinion. "It is impossible to describe my delight when I felt free at last—free from the world of torturing and ever unsatisfied desires, free from the distressing surroundings that had called forth such desires." He settled in Zurich and entered on the most productive period of his career. He had first to clarify his ideas to himself, and to prepare the public for the novel conceptions toward which he was finding his way. For four years he wrote no music, producing instead his most important literary works, *Art and Revolution, The Art Work of the Future,* and the two-volume *Opera and Drama* which sets forth his theories of the music drama, as he named his type of opera. He next proceeded to put theory into practice in the cycle of music dramas called *The Ring of the Nibelung.* He began with the poem on Siegfried's death which came to be known as *Götterdämmerung* (Dusk of the Gods). Realizing that the circumstances prior to this action required explaining, he added the drama on the hero's youth, *Siegfried.* The need for still further explanation led to a poetic drama concerning the hero's parents, *Die Walküre* (The Valkyrie). Finally, the trilogy was prefaced with *Das Rheingold* (The Rhinegold), a drama revolving about the curse of gold out of which the action stems.

Although he wrote the four poems in reverse order he composed them in sequence. When he reached the second act of *Siegfried,* he grew tired, as he said, "of heaping one silent score upon the other," and laid aside the gigantic task. There followed his two finest works— *Tristan und Isolde* and *Die Meistersinger von Nürnberg* (The Mastersingers of Nuremberg). The years following the completion of *Tristan* (1859) were the darkest of his life. The mighty scores accumulated in his drawer without hope of performance: Europe contained neither theater nor singers capable of presenting them. Wagner succumbed to Schopenhauer's philosophy of pessimism and renunciation—he who could never renounce anything. He was estranged from Minna, who failed utterly to understand his artistic aims. His involvement with a series of women who did understand him—but whose husbands objected—obtruded the *Tristan* situation into his own life and catapulted him into lonely despair. As he passed his fiftieth year, his indomitable will was broken at last. He contemplated in turn suicide, emigration to America, escape to the East.

At this juncture intervened a miraculous twist of events. An eighteen-year-old boy who was a passionate admirer of his music ascended the throne of Bavaria as Ludwig II. One of the young monarch's first acts was to summon the composer to Munich. The King commissioned

him to complete *The Ring*, and Wagner took up the second act of
Siegfried where he had left off a number of years before. A theater
was planned especially for the presentation of his music dramas, which
ultimately resulted in the festival playhouse at Bayreuth. And to crown
his happiness he found, to share his empire, a woman his equal in will
and courage—Cosima, the daughter of his old friend Liszt. For the
last time the *Tristan* pattern thrust itself upon him. Cosima was the
wife of his fervent disciple, the conductor Hans von Bülow. She left
her husband and children in order to join her life with Wagner's. They
were married some years later, after Minna's death. Their son was
named Siegfried and their home, like a dwelling out of the sagas of
The Ring, Wahnfried.

The Wagnerian gospel spread across Europe, a new art-religion.
Wagner societies throughout the world gathered funds to raise the
temple at Bayreuth. The radical of 1848 found himself, after the
Franco-Prussian War, the national artist of Bismarck's German Empire. The *Ring* cycle was completed, twenty-six years after Wagner
had begun it, and the four dramas were presented to worshipful audiences at the first Bayreuth festival in 1876.

One task remained. To make good the financial deficit of the festival
the master undertook his last work *Parsifal*, a "consecrational festival
drama" based on the legend of the Holy Grail. He finished it as he
approached seventy. He died shortly after, in every sense a conqueror,
and was buried at Bayreuth.

HIS MUSIC

Wagner gave shape to the desire of the romantic era for the closest
possible connection between music and dramatic expression; and beyond that, for the closest connection between music and life. "Every
bar of dramatic music," he maintained, "is justified only by the fact that
it explains something in the action or in the character of the actor."
Nature worship, national feeling, and the painting of specific moods
and emotions find in his art their ultimate embodiment.

He insisted that music in the theater is not an end in itself, only a
means of achieving dramatic effect. His theories notwithstanding, the
music dwarfs all the other elements in his stage works; for he was a
musician first and a dramatist afterward. He did away with the old
"number" opera with its arias, duets, ensembles, choruses, and ballets.
His aim was a continuous tissue of melody that would never allow the
emotions to cool. This meant abandoning the old distinction between

recitative and aria. He evolved instead an "endless melody" that was molded to the natural inflection of the German language, more melodious than traditional recitative, more flexible and free than traditional aria. By moving away from the formal tune based on four-measure phrases, he brought his listeners to a broader conception of what melody is. Whenever possible he avoided definite cadences and sections, achieving a continuous flow and the highest degree of musical-dramatic unity.

The focal point of Wagnerian music drama, however, is not the melody but the orchestra. Here is the nub of his operatic reform. He had inherited the orchestral language and the symphonic art of Beethoven, and it became his mission to introduce these into the lyric theater. In so doing he developed a type of symphonic opera as native to the German genius as vocal opera is to the Italian. The orchestra is the unifying principle of his music drama. It is both participant and ideal spectator; it remembers, prophesies, reveals, comments. The orchestra is fate and primal force, flooding the action, the characters, and the audience in a torrent of sound that incarnates the sensuous ideal of the romantic era: a sumptuous sound shot with color and light, which for sheer imaginativeness is unsurpassed in nineteenth-century art.

The orchestral tissue is fashioned out of concise themes, the *Leitmotifs,* or "leading motives"—Wagner called them basic themes—that recur throughout the work, undergoing variation and development even as the themes and motives of a symphony. The leitmotifs carry specific meanings. They have an uncanny power of suggesting in a few strokes a personage, an emotion, or an idea; an object—the Gold, the Ring, the Sword; or a landscape—the Rhine, Valhalla, the lonely shore of Tristan's home. Through a process of continual transformation the leitmotifs trace the course of the drama, the changes in the characters, their experiences and memories, their thoughts and hidden desires. As the leitmotifs accumulate layer upon layer of meaning, they themselves become characters in the drama, symbols of the relentless process of growth and decay that rules the destinies of gods and heroes.

The orchestra, in Wagnerian usage, is the sea of harmony over which rises and falls the wave of melody. Here harmony usurps the prime position previously held by melody and rhythm. Wagner tied together the harmonic discoveries of his age into a system. *Tristan* represents the farthermost limit of chromatic harmony. Its poignant dissonances voice the longing and the unfulfillment of an era. Never before had the unstable tone combinations been used so eloquently to portray states of soul.

A cardinal tenet of Wagner's philosophy was his desire to merge the different arts into one super-experience. He believed his music drama to be the "universal art work" in which were combined on an equal basis music, poetry, drama, acting, dance, painting (the scenery), architecture, and sculpture (the plastic poses of the actors). He prophesied that once the music drama had established itself the different arts would never again exist separately. Such a notion could occur only to one who had no real appreciation of either painting, sculpture, or poetry. He never suspected that each art is most fully itself precisely when it does the things that are impossible for the others. All the same, he was able at Bayreuth to lavish attention upon every phase of the "art work of the future," as he mistakenly called his music drama. There resulted a unity of conception and effect until then unknown in the European theater.

EXCERPTS FROM *TRISTAN UND ISOLDE*

For unity of mood, sustained inspiration, and intensity of feeling *Tristan und Isolde* is the most perfectly realized of Wagner's lyric tragedies. He overcame here the diffuseness and awkward plot construction that mar the dramas of *The Ring*. In *Tristan*, he wrote, "Life and death, the whole significance of existence of the external world, turn on nothing but the inner movements of the soul." Certainly no more eloquent tribute has ever been offered to consuming passion.

Isolde, proud princess of Ireland, has been promised in marriage to the elderly King Mark of Cornwall. Tristan, the King's nephew and first knight of his court, is sent to bring her to her new home. They had met before when Tristan fought against her country. What had begun as hate, wounded pride, and desire for revenge turns to overpowering love.

The Prelude to the drama depicts the passion that enmeshes them. This extraordinary tone poem evolves from a leitmotif that recurs throughout the opera. Used always to suggest the yearning, tenderness, and rapture of the lovers, the famous progression is the epitome of Wagnerian (that is, of romantic) harmony.

"There can be no greater pleasure," Wagner wrote in regard to *Tristan*, "than an artist's perfect abandon whilst composing." Abandon is possible only when one has achieved complete control over the means of expression. It is the quality that brings this prelude as close as any piece ever came to those twin goals of musical romanticism, intoxication and ecstasy.

Langsam und schmachtend (Slowly and languidly)

The Love Duet is from Act II which takes place outside King Mark's castle. The King leaves, ostensibly on a hunt. Tristan and Isolde meet in the garden. The scene between them is one of the high points of Wagnerian drama. The lovers hymn the night: "O rest upon us, night of love, Grant us forgetfulness of life. Take us within thine embrace, Free us forever from the world." Day represents the loathed reality that stands between them, the pretense and hopelessness of their worldly existence. Night is the symbol of their inner life—the real life. In this scene is consummated the great romantic theme of the individual estranged from society. Love is the dream and the search; the longing for oblivion. Since happiness is not to be attained in life, love leads beyond its confines, becoming the ultimate escape. Thus the impulse that generates life is transformed, by a magnificently romantic gesture, into the self-destroying passion whose fulfillment is death. The use of horn and woodwinds that envelop man and woman in the nature sound of German romanticism; the interpolation of Brangäne, Isolde's confidante, as she stands watch on the tower; the intangible suggestion of the beauty of the night; the sustained exaltation—it is Wagner at his most compelling.

At the high point of the Duet, King and retinue burst in upon the lovers. Tristan has been betrayed by his false friend Melot. He takes leave of Isolde and in the ensuing scuffle suffers himself to be mortally wounded. The doom they knew was inescapable is now upon them.

Act III is laid before Tristan's castle in Brittany, where he has been brought by his faithful servant Kurvenal. In his delirium he fancies himself back in the garden with Isolde. She arrives in time to see him die. The opera culminates in her hymn to love and death, the *Liebestod*. She envisions herself united with Tristan, the obstacles that kept them apart in life surmounted at last. Transfigured, she sinks lifeless on Tristan's body.

The Love Death follows a basic design in music. Beginning softly and from a low pitch it builds up in a steadily mounting line to the torrential climax, whence it subsides. The aria—and aria it is, although the perfect Wagnerite would never call it that—is fashioned from a motive first heard during the love scene in Act II. There it was cruelly interrupted by the arrival of the King. Now, ascending wave upon wave, it achieves its resolution. "In the billowing air, in the resounding blare, in the world's encompassing breath—To drown, to sink, unknowing—Highest bliss!"

Wagner satisfied the need of an era for sensuous beauty and intoxication, for the heroic, the mystical, the grandiloquent. He glorified the

medieval past, he sang the womanly woman and the manly man, he upheld intuition against reason, he mused upon mighty issues, and he
commanded a wider public than composer ever had before. Rarely have
the time, the place, and the personality come together so fortunately
to create an international career. He found a means, wrote Nietzsche,
of stimulating tired nerves "and in this way he made music ill." But
this was the illness of a century, for which he furnished the magic
potion.

Greatness in music as in other spheres proceeds from the supreme
height of spiritual tension. Wagner justly stands among the giants of
his art. Yet his music issues from a lower level of spirituality than
theirs. He knew hate and ruthlessness, lust for power and devouring
passion. The creative energy of that imperious soul hid profoundly
destructive forces. His music, rooted in the irrational, is truly demonic;
by the same token it is not always healing. It enchants and overpowers
the senses, but it does not always reach the secret places of the heart.

His impact upon his own time and the half century that followed was
nothing short of overwhelming. Indeed, we are the first generation that
is able to view him objectively. He takes his place in history as the most
commanding figure of the romantic era; a master whose unique achievements have become part and parcel of our musical heritage.

ঌ35ঌ

Giuseppe Verdi (1813-1901)

"Success is impossible for me if I cannot write as my heart dictates!"

IN THE case of Giuseppe Verdi, the most widely loved of operatic composers, it happened too—as with Wagner—that the time, the place,
and the personality were happily met. He inherited a rich tradition, his
capacity for growth was matched by masterful energy and will, and
he was granted a long span of life in which his gifts attained their full
flower.

HIS LIFE

Born in a hamlet in northern Italy where his father kept a shop, the
shy taciturn lad grew up amid the poverty of village life. His talent at-

tracted the attention of a prosperous merchant in the neighboring town of Busseto, a music lover who made it possible for the youth to pursue his studies. After two years in Milan he returned to Busseto to fill a post as organist. When he fell in love with his benefactor's daughter, the merchant in wholly untraditional fashion accepted the penniless young

Giuseppe Verdi.

musician as his son-in-law. Verdi was twenty-three, Margherita sixteen.

Three years later he returned to the conquest of Milan with his wife, two infant children, and the manuscript of an opera. *Oberto, Count of San Bonifacio* was produced at La Scala with only moderate success; but the work brought him a commission to write three others. Shortly after, Verdi faced the first crisis of his career. His two children were carried off by fever, a catastrophe followed several weeks later by the death of his wife. "My family had been destroyed, and in the midst of these trials I had to fulfill my engagement and write a comic opera!" The opera failed miserably. "In a sudden moment of despondency I despaired of finding any comfort in my art and resolved to give up composing."

The months passed; the distraught young composer adhered to his decision. One night he happened to meet the impresario of La Scala who forced him to take home the libretto of *Nabucco* (Nebuchadnezzar, King of Babylon). "I came into my room and throwing the manuscript angrily on the writing table, I stood for a moment motionless before it. The book opened as I threw it down. My eyes fell on the page and I read the line *Va pensiero sull' ali dorate*" ["Go, my thought, on golden wings"—first line of the chorus of captive Jews who by the waters of Babylon mourn their ravished land]. "Resolved as I was never to write again, I stifled my emotion, shut the book, went to bed, and put out the candle. I tried to sleep, but *Nabucco* was running a mad course through my brain." In this fashion the musician was restored to his art. *Nabucco*, presented at La Scala the following season, was a triumph for the twenty-nine-year-old composer; it inaugurated a spectacular career.

Italy at this time was in the process of birth as a nation. The patriotic party aimed at liberation from the Hapsburg yoke and the establishment of a united kingdom under the House of Savoy. Verdi from the beginning identified himself with the national cause. "I am first of all an Italian!" In this charged atmosphere his works took on special meaning for his countrymen. No matter in what time or place the opera was laid, they interpreted it as an allegory of their plight. The chorus of exiled Jews from *Nabucco* became a patriotic song. As the revolutionary year 1848 approached, Verdi's works—despite the precautions of the Austrian censor—continued to nourish the zeal of the nationalists. In *Attila* the line of the Roman envoy to the leader of the Huns, "Take thou the universe—but leave me Italy!" provoked frenzied demonstrations. When, in *The Battle of Legnano*, a chorus of medieval Italian knights vowed to drive the German invaders beyond the Alps, audiences were aroused to indescribable enthusiasm.

But the impact of Verdi's operas went deeper than the implications of the plot. The music itself had a dynamic force, a virility that was new in the Italian theater. This was truly, as one writer called it, "agitator's music." It happened too that the letters of Verdi's name coincided with the initials of the nationalist slogan—Vittorio Emmanuele Re d'Italia (Victor Emmanuel King of Italy). The cries of *Viva Verdi* that rang through Italian theaters not only hailed the composer but voiced the national dream. Rarely has a musician more ideally filled the role of a people's artist.

Although he was now a world-renowned figure, Verdi retained the simplicity that was at the core both of the artist and man. He returned to his roots, acquiring an estate at Busseto where he settled with his second wife, the singer Giuseppina Strepponi. She was a sensitive and intelligent woman who had created the leading roles in his early operas and who was his devoted companion for half a century. He acquired in later life an interest in agriculture and developed a model farm that gave employment to two hundred workers and their families, in whose welfare he displayed a patriarchal interest. During the period of economic distress that caused a mass emigration of Italians to America, Verdi declared with pride that from his district they did not emigrate. After Italy had won independence he was urged to stand for election to the first parliament because of the prestige his name would bring the new state. The task conformed neither to his talents nor inclinations, but he accepted and sat in the chamber of deputies for some years.

The outer activities of this upright man framed an inner life of extraordinary richness. It was this that enabled him to move with unflagging creative tension from one masterpiece to the next. He was fifty-seven when he wrote *Aïda*. At seventy-three he completed *Otello*, his greatest lyric tragedy. On the threshold of eighty he astonished the world with *Falstaff*. Such sustained productivity invites comparison with the old masters, with a Monteverdi, Michelangelo, or Titian.

His death at eighty-eight was mourned throughout the world. He bequeathed the bulk of his fortune to a home for aged musicians founded by him in Milan. Italy accorded him the rites reserved for a national hero. From the thousands who followed his bier there sprang up a melody—*Va pensiero sull' ali dorate* . . . It was the chorus from *Nabucco* that he had given his countrymen as a song of solace sixty years before.

HIS MUSIC

Verdi's music is the epitome of dramatic energy and passion. Endowed with an imagination that saw all emotion in terms of action and conflict—that is, in terms of the theater—he was able to imbue a dramatic situation with shattering expressiveness. True Italian that he was, he based his art on melody, which to him was the most immediate expression of human feeling. Using rhythm, harmony, and orchestration with a sure hand, he never permitted these to overshadow the soaring line—now soulful, now explosive—of those tense indestructible tunes that have survived several generations of organ grinders. He sought dramatic truth with all the strength of his uncompromising nature. The element of variety in Verdi's scores derives from the fact that each character speaks his own language, and speaks it with the utmost directness. "Art without spontaneity, naturalness, and simplicity," he maintained, "is no art."

Of his first fifteen operas the most important is *Macbeth*, in which for the first time he derived his story material from Shakespeare, whom he called "the great searcher of the human heart." There followed in close succession the three operas that established his international fame: *Rigoletto* in 1851, based on Victor Hugo's drama *Le Roi s'Amuse* (The King is Amused); *Il Trovatore* (The Troubadour) in 1853, derived from a fanciful Spanish play; and *La Traviata* (The Lost One) also produced in 1853, which he adapted from the younger Dumas's play *La Dame aux Camélias* (Camille). In these works of sustained pathos the musical dramatist stands before us in full stature.

The operas of the middle period are on a more ambitious scale, showing Verdi's attempt to assimilate elements of the French grand opera. The three most important are *Don Carlos, Un Ballo in Maschera* (The Masked Ball), and *La Forza del Destino* (The Force of Destiny). In these the master fights his way to a higher conception of dramatic unity. "After *La Traviata*," he declared, "I could have taken things easy and written an opera every year on the tried and true model. But I had other artistic aims."

These aims came to fruition in *Aïda*, the work that ushers in his final period; it was commissioned by the Khedive of Egypt to mark the opening of the Suez Canal in 1870. Delayed by the outbreak of the Franco-Prussian War, the production was mounted with great splendor in Cairo the following year. In 1874 came the Requiem Mass in memory of Alessandro Manzoni, the novelist and patriot whom Verdi revered as a national artist. Although the composer was, as his devout wife put it, a man of little faith, he employed the dramatic ritual of the Church with the naturalness that was his birthright as an Italian.

Verdi found his ideal librettist in Arrigo Boito (1842–1918), himself a composer whose opera *Mefistofele* was popular in Italy for years. For their first collaboration they turned to Shakespeare. The result was *Otello*, the apex of three hundred years of Italian lyric tragedy. After its opening night the seventy-four-year-old composer declared, "I feel as if I had fired my last cartridge. Music needs youthfulness of the senses, impetuous blood, fullness of life." He disproved his words by completing six years later, again with Boito, *Falstaff*. Fitting crown to the labors of a lifetime, this luminous comic opera ranks with Mozart's *Figaro*, Rossini's *Barber of Seville*, and Wagner's *Meistersinger*. Shakespeare's bedraggled knight, whom Verdi called "the eternally true type of jovial scoundrel" cavorts before us in all his glory—but given a new realization through music. When the action is resolved in the magical scene in Windsor Forest, the concluding fugue tells us that "man is born a clown and all the world's a jest." Thus on a note of infinite compassion the aged enchanter bade farewell to his art.

AÏDA

In *Aïda* Verdi achieved an ideal fusion of the diverse elements that comprise grand opera. The dramatic story revolves about emotions that lend themselves to musical treatment. The action exploits all the resources of the opera house in terms of picturesque scenery, spectacular display, ballets, and striking mass scenes. Characters and situations are conceived in the grand manner, and the exotic setting admirably frames the inner experiences of the protagonists.

The action is laid in Egypt in the time of the Pharaohs during a war with the Ethiopians. Aïda, princess of Ethiopia, has been captured and is slave to Amneris, the Egyptian princess. The latter is in love with the conquering general Radames but rightly suspects that he loves Aïda rather than herself. Aïda's father Amonasro, the Ethiopian king, is brought into captivity, his identity unknown to his enemies. He still hopes to break the Egyptian power. Radames, torn between his passion for the enemy princess and devotion to his country, is induced to flee with Aïda and her father. The plan is foiled by the jealous Amneris. Aïda and Amonasro make their escape, Radames surrenders to the High Priest. He is sentenced to die by being entombed in a subterranean vault. Amonasro having been killed while leading the revolt, Aïda returns in time to make her way into the crypt. The lovers die together.

The Prelude is evolved from the lyrical phrase associated with Aïda throughout the opera. Act I is in two scenes, the first of which is laid in the palace of the Pharaohs at Memphis. The famous *romanza*, *Celeste Aïda* (Heavenly Aïda), in which Radames reveals his love, displays the composer's preference for melodies that move along the scale with occasional effective leaps along the chord.

The basic conflict is established in a dramatic trio in which Amneris voices her jealousy, Radames fears she suspects the truth, and Aïda is torn between love and her devotion to the Ethiopian cause. The en-

trance of the King and court introduces the note of pomp that alternates throughout the play with the expression of personal emotion.
Radames is appointed leader of the Egyptian forces against the Ethiopians. Aïda, alone, is tormented by the knowledge that the man she
loves is to war against her father. She appeals to the gods in a grand
scena.

The second scene takes place in the temple of Ptah. Priests invoke
the god. The music assumes an oriental coloring as priestesses perform
a sacred dance. Radames receives the consecrated arms and is blessed
by the High Priest.

Act II opens in the royal palace. Moorish slaves perform a lively
dance to distract the Princess. Aïda enters. A tense scene ensues between the women, at the climax of which Amneris in a jealous rage
threatens to destroy her rival.

There follows the great scene outside the walls of Thebes where the
returning hero is welcomed by King, court, and populace. Trumpets
sound the theme of the Triumphal March.

Ablaze with color and movement, the tableau culminates in a stirring
sextet. Amneris and the High Priest demand death for the prisoners.
Amonasro, in chains, implores the King to be merciful. Pharaoh in a
magnanimous mood releases the prisoners—all except Amonasro—and
bestows the hand of his daughter upon the victorious general. Radames
and Aïda hide their consternation. This mass scene, with its interplay of
personal drama and regal splendor, has come to represent everything
we associate with grand opera.

Act III is packed with action of the kind that Verdi needed for the
full deploying of his powers. The scene—"Night: stars and a bright
moon"—is on the bank of the Nile. Amneris, accompanied by the High
Priest, arrives to pray in the temple of Isis on the eve of her marriage.
Events move swiftly and with ever mounting intensity. Aïda's aria *O
patria miâ* (O my native land) in which she bemoans her fate leads to

Photo by Sedge Le Blang

Triumphal Scene from *Aïda*.

"This mass scene, with its interplay of personal drama and regal splendor, has come to represent everything we associate with grand opera."

a furious encounter with her father. Amonasro orders her to find out from her lover the plan of the forthcoming campaign. He curses her when she refuses, and his rage breaks her will. Amonasro conceals himself at the approach of Radames. In the rapturous duet of the lovers Aïda persuades him that they can never find happiness within reach of the vengeful Amneris. He consents to fly with her, and divulges the plan of attack against Ethiopia. Amonasro appears and reveals himself as the enemy king, and Radames realizes that he has betrayed his country. At this point Amneris, who has come out of the temple, grasps the situation and accuses Radames of treason. Amonasro, drawing his knife, rushes upon her, but Radames interposes and saves her life. He implores Aïda and her father to save themselves. Soldiers appear before the temple and give pursuit. Radames, lost, surrenders to the implacable High Priest.

Act IV opens in a hall in the palace. Amneris orders Radames to be brought before her. She tells him she can save him if he will renounce

Aïda. He spurns her offer and is led back to his cell. Overcome with remorse, the Princess curses the jealousy that has brought ruin to her beloved and endless misery to herself. The priests are heard pronouncing the death sentence.

In the final scene we see the subterranean vault and the temple above it. As the fatal stone is lowered Radames voices his hope that Aïda will never learn his fate. Then he discovers her in the crypt. Against the chorus of the priests in the temple above, the eerie chant of the priestesses, and the lamenting of Amneris, the lovers sing their final duet, a farewell to earth, a vision of eternal bliss to come.

Fare-well, oh earth, fare-well thou vale___ of sor-row

The creator of this majestic drama incarnated the soul of his nation. Boito recognized this when he saluted in Verdi "the genius of our race. He revealed to the world the ardor, the dash, the affection, the force of the Italian spirit."

⋙36⋘

Other Composers of the Romantic Period

I. HECTOR BERLIOZ (1803–1869)

> "The prevailing characteristics of my music are passionate expression, intense ardor, rhythmic animation, and unexpected turns. To render my works properly requires a combination of extreme precision and irresistible verve, a regulated vehemence, a dreamy tenderness, and an almost morbid melancholy."

HECTOR BERLIOZ is the towering figure of the romantic movement in France. He was one of the boldest innovators of the nineteenth century, particularly in his handling of the orchestra. Berlioz from the first had an affinity for the literary program; he stood alongside Liszt and Wagner as an advocate of the "Music of the Future." His vivid imagination found outlet in a magnificent attempt to dramatize the symphony. Significantly, he called his symphonies "instrumental dramas." For the abstract development of themes he substituted a luminous orchestral fabric shot through with literary meanings. A recurrent theme serves to unite the several movements. This is the *idée fixe* which, even as the Wagnerian leitmotif, returns in various guises according to the progress of the literary program.

In his choice of program Berlioz was the product of his age. The emotions are violent, the settings theatrical. Idyllic landscapes alternate with scenes of the supernatural and the macabre. He sometimes fell into a realism that shocked the purists. But he was too much the musician to try to imitate nature or tell a story in tone. He knew quite well, as he said, that "music is a substitute neither for speech nor for the art of painting."

Berlioz' best-known work, the *Symphonie Fantastique*, dates from 1830. He was then twenty-seven, and at the height of his infatuation with the English actress Harriet Smithson. (He subsequently married the lady, whereupon his ardor cooled.) The program concocted by the composer reveals the sultry atmosphere whence this work issued. "A young musician of morbid sensibility and ardent imagination in a paroxysm of lovesick despair has poisoned himself with opium. The drug, too weak to kill, plunges him into a heavy sleep accompanied by strange visions. The beloved one herself becomes for him a melody, a recurrent theme that haunts him everywhere." Thus, the *idée fixe* in all its transformations, becomes the musical thread uniting the five movements. First is *Reveries, Passions*, which pictures the growth of his infatuation. There follows *A Ball*, amidst whose tumult and excitement the enamored one "glimpses the loved one again." The third movement, *In the Fields*, is a tender landscape in which nature herself becomes the backdrop for his emotions. Then "he dreams that he has killed his beloved, that he has been condemned to die and is being led to the scaffold." The *March to the Gallows* is a processional "now somber and wild, now brilliant and solemn," whose fanciful sonorities were to haunt the imagination of composers for generations to come. The final movement is the *Dream of a Witches' Sabbath*, a satanic fantasy in which the theme of the Beloved returns in a vulgar caricature. It is hardly to be believed that this "novel in tones" was conceived by a young musician only three years after the death of Beethoven.

For all his flamboyance, Berlioz never loses his refinement of thought and texture. It is the Latin in him. There is a bigness of line and gesture about his music, an overflow of vitality and invention. He remains one of the major prophets of the romantic era.

II. FRÉDÉRIC FRANÇOIS CHOPIN (1810–1849)

"My life . . . an episode without a beginning and with a sad end."

In the annals of his century Chopin is known as the "Poet of the Piano." The title is a valid one. His art, issuing from the heart of romanticism, constitutes the golden age of that instrument.

Chopin was one of the most original artists of the romantic era. He decisively influenced the course of nineteenth-century music. His idiom is so entirely his own that there is no mistaking it for that of any other composer. He was the only master of first rank whose creative life centered almost exclusively about the piano. From the first his imagination was wedded to the keyboard, to create a universe within that narrow frame. "Everything must be made to sing," he told his pupils. Delicate ornaments—trills, grace notes, runs of gossamer lightness—magically prolong the single tones. The widely-spaced chords in the bass, sustained by pedal, set up masses of tone that wreathe the melody in enchantment. And all this lies so well to the hand that the music seems almost to play itself.

In harmony he was one of the daring innovators of the century. His melodies are models of romantic lyricism; his rhythms are the idealization of body movement. So personal a message could hardly be set in the great classic forms. Chopin is a master of the miniature; his lyric forms draw their sustenance from the spirit of song and dance. His Nocturnes—night songs, as the name implies—are tender avowals tinged with varying shades of melancholy. The twenty-four Preludes are visionary fragments; some are only a page in length, several consist of two or three lines. Of these Schumann said, "In each piece we find in his own hand, 'Frédéric Chopin wrote it!' He is the boldest, the proudest poet of his time." The twenty-four Etudes crown the literature of the study piece. The problems of piano technique are here transformed into poetry. The four Impromptus are fanciful, capricious, yet they have a curious rightness about them. The Waltzes capture the brilliance and coquetry of the salon. They are veritable dances of the spirit. The Mazurkas, derived from a Polish peasant dance, with their elusive rhythms evoke the idealized landscape of his youth.

Among the larger forms are the four Ballades. These are tone poems of spacious structure, sagas related by a bard. The Polonaises revive the stately processional dance in which Poland's nobles were wont to hail their kings. Epic in tone, they resound with the clangor of battle and brave deeds. In reminding his countrymen of their ancient glory the national poet strengthens their will to freedom. The *Berceuse* (Cradle Song), the *Barcarolle* (Boat Song), the *Fantasy*, and the dramatic Scherzos reveal the composer at the summit of his art. The two sonatas, one in B minor and the other in B-flat minor, are thoroughly romantic in spirit; they dissolve the outlines of sonata form in rhapsodic lyricism. The two concertos, one in E minor and one in F minor, are works of his youth. Chopin's was not an orchestral imagination, nor was he at home in the classical form. Yet these contain some wonderfully felicitous moments, like the romantic sonority of horn and piano tone in the E-minor Concerto.

Chopin's style stands before us fully formed when he was twenty. It was not the result of an extended intellectual development, as was the case with masters like Beethoven or Wagner. In this he was the true lyricist, along with his contemporaries Schumann and Mendelssohn. All three died young, and all three reached their peak through the spontaneous lyricism of youth. In them the first period of romanticism—its idealist phase—found pure and noble expression.

His countrymen have enshrined Chopin as the national composer of Poland. Withal he is a spokesman of European culture. It is not without significance that despite his homesickness he spent the whole of his adult life in Paris. Thus Poland was idealized in his imagination as the symbol of that unappeasable longing which every romantic artist carries in his heart: the longing for the lost land of happiness that may never be found again. Heine, himself an expatriate, divined this when he wrote that Chopin is "neither a Pole, a Frenchmen, nor a German. He reveals a higher origin. He comes from the land of Mozart, Raphael, Goethe. His true country is the land of poetry."

III. CÉSAR FRANCK (1822–1890)

"What Wagner did for human love, I have done for divine."

César Franck was the most important figure in French instrumental music of the late nineteenth century. Confronted with a public for whom music was chiefly synonymous with opera, he fought for the cause of instrumental music and helped prepare the way for the emergence of a French school of symphonists.

Franck was a religious mystic for whom music was an act of faith. The progression of the sonata form from tension to repose became in his mind a spiritual advance from darkness to light, from inner struggle and doubt to the serenity of belief. His music dealt in symbolic meanings and states of soul. In this he was of the romantic age. At the same time he was attuned to the classical heritage. He strove to inject into French music the constructional logic of the German tradition. (Appropriately enough, he was born in the country that lies between the two cultures—in Belgium, at Liége.) He found his true expression in the large forms of absolute music. The works by which he is best known today include one each of the important instrumental types: a symphony, a string quartet, a quintet for piano and strings, a sonata for violin and piano, a concerto for piano and orchestra—the *Symphonic Variations*—and a large-scale work for piano, the *Prelude, Chorale and Fugue*.

Franck sought to knit together the movements of the sonata structure through adherence to cyclical form. This, as we saw in our discussion of the *New World* Symphony, involves the use of the same material in the various movements. Often the cyclical idea takes the shape of a motto theme that comes back at climactic moments, serving both as reminiscence and unifying thread. Franck carried the principle still further by deriving all the material from a few basic themes, which appear in manifold transformations and disguises in each movement.

Franck's most widely played work is the Symphony in D minor, an ample and communicative work abounding in opulent harmonies and heaven-storming proclamation. The germinal motive, with its upward inflection, is like the questioning three-note motive that opens Liszt's *Les Préludes*. It flowers into a tempestuous Allegro non troppo (not too lively), in which dramatic and lyrical elements are counterposed within a spacious frame. The second movement, the Allegretto, combines within one structure both a slow movement and a scherzo. The famous opening melody, first outlined by harp and strings, is sung by the English horn. The impetuous finale, marked Allegro non troppo, completes the progression from conflict and doubt to the triumphal affirmation of faith. Themes from the earlier movements are much in evidence here, exemplifying the cyclical structure so closely associated with this composer. The work ends in a blaze of glory—the romantic "apotheosis." With its breadth of gesture, hymnic exaltation and opulent orchestral garb, the Symphony of César Franck is an eloquent memorial to the late romantic style. It is the work of a musician whose dedication to lofty ideals assures him a niche in the history of his art.

IV. GEORGES BIZET (1838–1875)

> "The composer gives the best of himself to the making of a work. He believes, doubts, enthuses, despairs, rejoices, and suffers in turn."

Bizet's tragically short career moved in a straight line towards its culminating point. His three earlier operas—*The Pearl Fishers*, *The Fair Maid of Perth*, and *Djamileh*—were only moderately successful. Along with his incidental music to Alphonse Daudet's drama *L'Arlésienne* (The Woman of Arles), they prepared the way for the greatest French lyric drama of the nineteenth century.

Carmen was not the fiasco that popular legend makes it out to have been. It did fail, incomprehensibly, to conquer its first audience. The Opéra-Comique, where it was first presented, was a "family theater" where the bourgeois of Paris brought their wives and marriageable daughters. Passion on the stage was acceptable as long as it concerned kings and duchesses long dead. The passionate Gypsy and her band of smugglers and brigands were too close for comfort.

The rumor that the piece was not quite respectable helped to give it a run of thirty-seven performances in the next three months, an average of three a week. In addition, the manager offered the composer and his librettists a contract for their next work. The failure of *Carmen* was really in Bizet's mind. He had put every ounce of his genius into the score. Its reception was a bitter disappointment. His delicate constitution, worn out by months of rehearsals and by the emotional tension that had attended the production, was ill prepared to take the blow. Exactly three months after the première he succumbed to a heart attack, at the age of thirty-seven. His death came just as he had found his mature style.

Immediately the work was dropped by the Opéra-Comique. Yet within three years it had made its way to Vienna and Brussels, London and New York. Eight years after its uncertain reception, *Carmen* returned to Paris and triumphed. Along with Verdi's *Aïda* and Puccini's *La Bohème* it remains one of the best-loved operas of the world. (The spoken dialogue was turned into musical recitative after Bizet's death by his friend Ernest Guiraud, so that the work might be presented at the Paris Opéra. It is in this grand-opera version that *Carmen* is usually heard.)

The power of this lyric drama stems from the impact with which it projects love, hate, desire. The story line follows one of the most compelling themes literature has to offer—the disintegration of a personality. The action is swift and unfaltering as the characters are carried step by step to their doom. The libretto is a tightly knit affair revolving around a few key words—love, fate, death, nevermore—all of them eminently singable, at any rate in French. Carmen dominates the action, by turn tender, cruel, seductive, imperious, sensual, arch. She remains one of the great characters of operatic fiction. Invested with Bizet's music, the heartless Gypsy takes on a certain nobility. She is fearless in the face of death. Even then she must be free. As for Don José, the simple soldier who is brought to ruin through his obsessive love; the swaggering bull-fighter Escamillo; and Micaela, José's childhood sweetheart—they are realized on the highest plane of operatic art. They come to life through the music; they are unthinkable without it.

It was a German philosopher who, awakening from the intoxication of Wagnerian music drama, discovered in *Carmen* the ideal lyric tragedy. This music, wrote Friedrich Nietzsche, "possesses the refinement not of an individual but of a race. I envy Bizet for having had the courage of this sensitiveness, this southern, tawny, sunburnt sensitiveness. I know of no case in which the tragic irony that constitutes the kernel of love is expressed with such severity or in so terrible a formula as in the last cry of Don José: 'Yes, it is I who killed her—Ah, my adored Carmen!'"

V. MODEST MUSORGSKY (1839–1881)

"The artist believes in the future because he lives in it."

Modest Musorgsky appeared at a time when the initial force of romanticism had spent itself. He regarded it as his mission to seek fresh modes of expression that would stand closer to the realities of human existence. "*Life* wherever it shows itself, *truth* no matter how bitter—this is what I want!"

He prepared for a military career and became an officer in a fashionable regiment of Guards. As his true vocation asserted itself, he found his military duties increasingly irksome, and at the age of twenty-two resigned his commission. He established himself in St. Petersburg, where a post at the Ministry of Transport gave him a modest subsistence. He soon became one of the mainstays of the "Mighty Five." Almost immediately there asserted itself in his music a personality that would accept neither tradition nor guidance. He was one of those artists who must follow their own path.

At twenty-nine Musorgsky was ready for the great task of his life. In *Boris Godunov* he found a worthy theme out of his country's past. He fashioned the libretto himself, after Pushkin's drama and the old chronicles. The opera was presented in 1874. It was damned by the critics, but made a deep impression on the public. Nor were its political implications lost on the young intelligentsia, at that time seething with unrest under the tsarist regime. The choruses depicting the revolt against Tsar Boris were soon heard on the streets of St. Petersburg. The opera, it was rumored, aroused the displeasure of the imperial family. In the following season it was presented with drastic cuts and soon was practically dropped from the repertory.

The withdrawal of *Boris* ushered in the bitter period of Musorgsky's life. In the six years that remained to him he moved ever farther from his comrades of the "Mighty Five." He had outgrown his admiration for Balakirev. César Cui, who was now an influential critic, had betrayed him by attacking *Boris*. Rimsky-Korsakov and Borodin, he felt, had capitulated to the academic spirit that he regarded as the enemy of true art. He remained alone, a rebel to the end.

But the lonely struggle demanded sterner stuff than he was made of. Moods of belief in himself alternated with periods of depression. Poverty, lack of recognition, and the drudgery of his clerical post played their part. His need for escape revived a craving for stimulants that he had kept more or less under control since early manhood. Increasingly his life lost its direction and followed the erratic course of the alcoholic. Now the arc was complete, from the debonair young officer of the Guards to the slovenly, tragic figure of Repin's famous portrait. Having resigned his post, he tried to support himself by accompanying singers. He was soon destitute. While attending a musical evening he collapsed and was placed in a hospital, suffering from delirium tremens. His former comrades rallied to his side. But he died— as he had lived—alone, on his forty-second birthday, crying out, "All is ended. Ah, how wretched I am!"

In *Boris Godunov* Musorgsky gave his country its great national drama. It has been well said that the real hero of the opera is the Russian people. In the magnificent choral tableaux we encounter, instead of the conventional operatic chorus, vivid types drawn from the peasantry. Musorgsky's genius for dramatic characterization reveals itself in the delineation of the main personages. The drama centers about Boris who, having contrived the murder of the boy Dmitri, the rightful heir to the throne, has himself proclaimed Tsar. As the years pass, the usurper is tormented by remorse. The scene in which the guilt-ridden Tsar sees the ghost of the murdered Dmitri and struggles in vain with his hallucination is on the level of Shakespearean tragedy. "O conscience, thou art cruel . . ." This is but one of the high points in a role which, in the hands of a great singing actor, creates an unforgettable impression.

The creator of this profound drama of conscience was forgotten by his countrymen for several decades after his death. It was in the Paris of the nineties that his work first came to be understood. Musicians of the new generation, among them Debussy and Ravel, discovered in him the first exponent of the modern temper, and found in his daring harmonies an inspiration for their own. The twentieth century has made amends for the incomprehension of the nineteenth. He who died so abjectly is recognized today as one of the most prophetic figures of the late romantic era. As far as certain contemporary musicians are concerned, he is Russia's greatest composer.

PART THREE

More Materials of Music

❧❧

"In any narrative—epic, dramatic or musical—every word or tone should be like a soldier marching towards the one, common, final goal: *conquest of the material.* The way the artist makes every phrase of his story such a soldier, serving to unfold it, to support its structure and development, to build plot and counter-plot, to distribute light and shade, to point incessantly and lead up gradually to the climax—in short, the way every fragment is impregnated with its mission towards the whole, makes up this delicate and so essential objective which we call FORM."

Ernst Toch

❧ 37 ❧

Key, Scale, Mode: the Organization of
Musical Space

"All music is nothing more than a succession of impulses that
converge towards a definite point of repose."
                                                    Igor Stravinsky

AT THE beginning of this book we discussed various elements of music.
Now that we have had occasion to hear how these are interwoven in a
number of works, we are ready to consider the materials of music on a
more advanced level, particularly as they relate to the organization of
the large classical forms.

TONALITY

A system of music must have set procedures for organizing tones
into intelligible relationships. One of the first steps in this direction is to
select certain tones and arrange them in a family or group. In such a
group one tone assumes greater importance than the rest. This is the
do, the tonic or keynote around which the others revolve and to which
they ultimately gravitate.

By a key we mean a group of related tones with a common center or
tonic. The tones of the key serve as basic material for a given composition. When we listen to a composition in the key of A we hear a
piece based in large part upon the family of tones that revolve around
and gravitate to the common center A.

This "loyalty to the tonic" is inculcated in us by most of the music
we hear. It is the unifying force in the do-re-mi-fa-sol-la-ti-do scale that
was taught us in our childhood. The reader can test for himself how
strong is the pull to the tonic by singing the first seven tones of this
pattern, stopping on *ti*. He will experience an almost physical compulsion to resolve the *ti* up to *do*.

The sense of relatedness to a central tone is known as tonality. It has
been building up in mankind for thousands of years. Tonality, in the
larger sense, indicates the whole system of relationships among tones
as summed up in keys, scales, and the harmonies based on those, such
relationships converging upon the "definite point of repose"—the
keynote.

THE OCTAVE

By an octave we mean the distance from one *do* to the next; that is, from any tone in the scale to the next that carries the same name, as from C to C, D to D, E to E, and so on. The method of dividing the octave determines the scales and the character of a musical system. It is precisely in this particular that one system differs from another. In Western music the octave is divided into twelve parts. The fact is apparent from the look of the piano keyboard, where we find twelve keys—seven white and five black—between any tone and its octave. These twelve tones are a half tone apart. From C to C-sharp is a half tone; from C-sharp to D the same. From C to D is a whole tone. Half tone and whole tone are the units of distance in our musical system.

Oriental music is based on other units. Hindu scales, for example, use quarter tones. The Javanese divide the octave into five nearly equal parts, each equivalent to a whole tone plus a quarter. Arabic music contains a scale which divides the octave into seventeen parts. We are not able to play oriental music on the piano, which is tuned in half and whole tones. Nor could we readily sing it, as our vocal cords have been trained to produce only the whole and half tone intervals of our system.

The twelve semitones into which Western music divides the octave constitute what is known as the chromatic scale. They are duplicated in higher and lower octaves. No matter how vast and intricate a musical work, it is made up of the twelve basic tones and their higher and lower duplications.

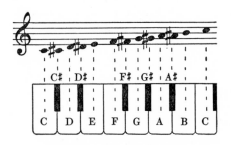

THE MAJOR SCALE

A scale is an arrangement of a series of tones. Specifically, a scale presents the tones of the key in consecutive order, ascending or descending. The word is derived from the Latin *scala*, "ladder." A scale, essentially, is a musical alphabet revealing at a glance the principle whereby tones are selected and related to one another in a given system. The scale is derived from actual musical practice. That is to say, the songs and dances come first. From this living music the theorist codifies his scales.

The music of the classic-romantic period was based on two contrasting scales, the major and the minor. These consist of seven tones —eight, if you prefer, as the *do* is duplicated at the end of the series. The major scale is the familiar do-re-mi-fa-sol-la-ti-do pattern. Its seven tones are picked out of the possible twelve in order to form a centralized family or key out of which musical compositions may be fashioned. The relationship of the major scale to the chromatic scale is made clear by the piano keyboard. The chromatic scale includes the seven white and five black keys, whereas the major scale can be sounded by the seven white keys from C to C. It becomes clear that the music of the eighteenth and nineteenth centuries, which was based upon the major scale, represents a "seven out of twelve" way of hearing music.

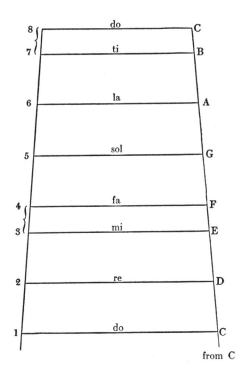

from C

The seven tones of the major scale are not equally distant from one another. Where the white keys have a black between, they are a whole tone (two half tones) apart. This is the rule, with two important exceptions: there is no black key between the third and fourth steps E-F and between the seventh and eighth steps B-C, which are a semitone apart. Consequently, when we sing the do-re-mi-fa-sol-la-ti-do sequence we are measuring off a pattern of eight tones that are a whole tone apart except steps 3–4 (*mi-fa*) and 7–8 (*ti-do*). The reader will find it instructive to sing this scale trying to distinguish between the half- and whole-tone distances.

This scale implies certain relationships based upon tension and resolution. We have already indicated one of the most important of these —the thrust of the seventh step to the eighth (*ti* seeking to be resolved to *do*). There are others: if we sing *do-re* we are left with a sense of incompleteness which is resolved when *re* moves down to *do; fa* gravitates to *mi; la* descends to *sol*. These tendencies, needless to say, reside not in the tones but in our minds. They are the meanings attached by our musical culture to the raw material of nature.

Most important of all, the major scale defines the two poles of classical harmony: the *do* or tonic, the point of ultimate rest; and the *sol* or dominant, representative of the active harmony. Upon the trackless sea of sound this relationship imposes direction and goal. Tonic going to dominant and returning to tonic becomes a basic progression of classical harmony. It will also serve, we shall find, as a basic principle of classical form.

THE KEY AS AN AREA IN MUSICAL SPACE

The major scale, we said, is a "ladder" of whole and half tones. A ladder may be placed on high ground or low, but the distance between its steps remains the same. So too the major scale may be measured off from one starting point or another without affecting the sequence of whole and half steps within the pattern.

Any one of the twelve tones of our octave may serve as starting point for the scale. Whichever it is, that tone at once assumes the function of the tonic or key center. The other tones are chosen according to the pattern of the ladder. They immediately assume the functions of activity and rest implicit in the major scale. Most important, they all take on the impulse of gravitating more or less directly to the tonic.

With each different tonic we get another group of seven out of the possible twelve. In other words, every major scale has a different number of sharps or flats. The scale of C major is the only group that has no sharps or flats. If we build the major scale from G we must include an F-sharp in order to conform to the pattern of whole and half steps. (Try building the pattern whole step, whole step, half step, whole step, whole step, whole step, half step, from G. You will find that there is no F in this group.) If we build the major scale pattern from D, we get a group of seven that includes two sharps. If F is our starting point the scale includes B-flat. (The twelve major scales are listed in Appendix IV.) When we play *America* on the piano with C as keynote— that is, in the key of C major—we use only the white keys. Should we play it with G as a keynote—that is, in the key of G major—we should in the course of it have to sound F-sharp, not F. Were we to play F we would be off key.

It becomes clear that the meaning of a tone, its direction, and drive are determined not by its intrinsic nature but by its position in the scale. The tone C may be the tonic or point of rest in one scale. In another it may be the seventh step seeking to be resolved by ascending to the eighth. In still another it may be the second step thrusting down to the first. In any case its impulse of activity or rest depends not on its character as the tone C, but on its function as the *do*, the *ti*, or the *re*— the 1, 7, or 2—of that particular key and scale. The classical system is based on the eminently social doctrine that the significance of a tone depends not upon itself but upon its relationship to other tones.

The key serves as a means of identification. The title "Symphony in A major" refers to a work based in large measure upon the tones of the A major scale and the harmonies fashioned from those, with the keynote A serving as the central tone to which the others gravitate. The key signature at the head of a piece announces the number of sharps or flats, so that the performer may see at a glance which group of seven furnishes the basic tones for that particular composition.

G major D major A major E major F major B♭ major E♭ major A♭ major

He forthwith adjusts his thinking—and his fingers—to that particular key. This adjustment presented some difficulty when musicians were not yet familiar with the system. The custom persists to this day of repeating the key signature on each line of music as a reminder, although the time signature is given only once at the beginning of a section.

To sum up: When we sing the sequence do-re-mi-fa-sol-la-ti-do we are marking off a series of whole and half steps that constitute the basic units of measurement in our musical system. We are setting forth these whole and half steps according to the pattern of the major scale. We are selecting seven tones out of twelve to constitute a key with a common center or keynote. We are setting up among these seven tones certain relationships of activity and rest, of tension and resolution; especially the tonic and dominant as the two poles of activity within the group. Finally, we are marking off an area in musical space that has the characteristics of geographical space—distance, direction, a fixed point of departure and return.

THE MINOR MODE

Whether the major scale begins on C, D, E, or any other tone, it follows the same model in the arrangement of the whole and half steps. This model is known as a mode. Thus, all the major scales exemplify the major mode of arranging whole and half steps.

There is also a minor mode, which complements and serves as a foil to the major. This differs primarily from the major in that its third degree is flatted; that is, the scale of C minor has E-flat instead of E. In the pure or natural minor scale the sixth and seventh steps are also flatted: C-D-E♭-F-G-A♭-B♭-C. (For two other versions of the minor scale—harmonic and melodic—see Appendix IV.) The minor is pronouncedly different from the major in mood and coloring. *Minor*, the Latin word for "smaller," refers to the fact that the distinguishing interval C-E♭ is smaller than the corresponding interval C-E in the major ("larger") scale.

Like the major, the pattern of the minor mode may be duplicated from each of the twelve tones of the octave. In each case there will be another group of seven out of twelve—that is, another number of sharps or flats. It becomes clear that every tone in the octave may serve as starting point or keynote for a major and a minor scale. This gives us twelve keys according to the major mode and twelve keys according to the minor mode. If the mode is not specified, the major is implied; as when we speak of the Melody in F, Minuet in G, or Symphony in A. The minor is always specified, as in the case of Schubert's Symphony in B minor or Mendelssohn's Violin Concerto in E minor.

Is the minor "sadder" than the major? Such connotations exist only in reference to the music of a particular time and place. The nineteenth century seems to have regarded the minor as more somber than the major. The funeral music of Beethoven, Mendelssohn, Chopin, Wagner, and Grieg is conspicuously in the minor, while the triumphal finales of a number of symphonies and overtures of the same period are as conspicuously in the major.

The minor mode has a certain exotic ring to Western ears and is associated in the popular view with oriental and east European music. This aspect of the minor is prominent in such works as the *Turkish* Rondo of Mozart; in a number of pieces in Hungarian style by Schubert, Liszt, and Brahms; in the main theme of Rimsky-Korsakov's *Scheherazade*, César Cui's *Orientale*, and similar exotica. The folk songs of certain regions appear to incline to the major while others lean toward the minor. There are, however, so many exceptions that such a generalization must be viewed with caution.

The contrast between minor and major became an element of musical structure during the classic-romantic period. For example, in A-B-A form, the outer sections might be in one mode and the contrasting middle section in the other. Or a symphony might start out in the minor and shift to the major in an access of triumph, as in Beethoven's Fifth, Franck's D-minor, and Tchaikovsky's Fifth.

In the classical system of harmony, then, each of the twelve tones may be the keynote of a scale according to the major mode and of a scale according to the minor mode. Each of these twenty-four scales contains a different group of seven tones out of the possible twelve—that is, another selection of sharps or flats. The twelve major and twelve minor keys make up the classical system of harmony.

There had to come into existence an art form that would mobilize the resources of this system, that would bring into focus its capacities for dramatic conflict and architectural expanse. It was the great achievement of the eighteenth century to evolve and perfect this form.

The Major-Minor System

> "Tonality should be understood as the principal means which the composers of the seventeenth, eighteenth and nineteenth centuries evolved of organizing musical sounds and giving them coherent shape."
>
> Roger Sessions

TRANSPOSITION

JUST AS we are able to build a scale from any one of the twelve tones, we are able to sing or play the same melody beginning on C, C-sharp, D, and so on. In each case the tune will be in another key. The pitch and the keynote will be different, as will the number of sharps or flats. But the melody line will remain unchanged because the pattern of whole and half steps is retained in the new key as in the old. This is why the same song can be published in various keys for soprano, alto, tenor, or bass.

When we shift a piece of music from one key to another we *transpose* it. In singing this is done by ear. A group of children, for example, will begin a song from a certain note. If the melody moves too high or too low for comfort, their teacher will stop them and have them begin again from another tone. On an instrument, transposing is a more complicated matter. The player must adjust his fingers to another arrangement of sharps and flats. If he is a pianist or organist he must shift not only the melody but the harmonies as well. The ability to transpose a piece at sight is a skill that musicians regard with respect. It is a necessity for professional accompanists who are constantly required to transpose songs to higher or lower keys to suit the range of singers.

MODULATION

If a piece of music can be played in one key as in another, why not put all music in the key of C and be done with it? Because the contrast between keys and the movement from one key to another is an essential element of musical structure. We have seen that the tones of the key form a closed circle of "seven out of twelve" that imparts coherence and focus to the music. But the circle may be opened up, in which case we are shifted—either gently or abruptly—to another area centering about another keynote. Such a change gives us a heightened sense of activity. It is an expressive gesture of prime importance.

The act of passing from one key to another is known as *modulation*. There is no way to describe in words something that can be experienced only in the domain of sound. Suffice it to say that the composer has at his disposal a number of ways of modulating; therewith he "lifts" the listener from one tonal area to another.

The twelve major and twelve minor keys of classical harmony may be compared to so many rooms in a house, with the modulations equivalent to corridors leading from one to the next. The "rooms" were arranged in ascending order of sharps and flats: C major with none, G major with one sharp, D major with two, A major with three, and so on. The composer firmly established the home key, then embarked on a leisurely journey to the next related key. The "rooms" and corridors were spacious, imparting to the forms of the classical era an amplitude of structure that was the musical counterpart of the rolling sentences of the eighteenth-century novel and the balanced façades of eighteenth-century architecture.

Nineteenth-century romanticism, on the other hand, demanded a whipping up of emotions, an intensifying of all musical processes. The corridors between the "rooms" steadily shrank; modulations were ever more frequent and more daring. There came into being a hyperemotional music that wandered restlessly from key to key in accord with the need for excitement of the mid- and late romantic era. By the same token, the balanced structure of the classical system, with its key areas neatly marked off one from the other, began to disintegrate.

CHROMATICISM

When seven tones out of twelve are selected to form a key, the other five become extraneous in relation to that particular tonic. They enter the composition as transients, mainly to embellish the melody or harmony. Their status is summed up in the term *accidentals*, meaning the sharped or flatted notes that appear in the course of a piece without belonging to the prevailing key.

If the piece is to sound firmly rooted in the key, the seven tones that are directly related to the tonic must prevail. Should the composer introduce into his melody and harmony too many of the five foreign tones—the accidentals—the relationship to the key center will be weakened and the key feeling become ambiguous. The distinction between the tones that do not belong within the key area and those that do is made explicit in the contrasting terms *chromatic* and *diatonic*. "Chromatic" refers to the twelve-tone scale that includes all the semitones of the octave. Chromatic melody or harmony moves by half steps, taking in the tones that are extraneous to the key. The word comes from *chroma*, which in Greek means "color." "Diatonic," on the other hand, refers to musical progression based upon the seven tones of the scale, and to harmonies that are firmly rooted in the key.

Diatonic harmony went hand in hand with the discreet modulations and clear-cut key feeling of eighteenth-century classicism. We may say that the music of Haydn, Mozart, and Beethoven tends to be diatonic. (There are of course many passages in their music, especially in their late works, that belie this generalization.) Chromatic harmony, on the other hand, characterized the ceaseless modulation and surcharged emotional atmosphere of nineteenth-century music. From Schubert to Wagner and on to Richard Strauss and Mahler, the romantic and post-romantic composers indefatigably explored the possibilities of chromaticism. In an earlier section of this book we described the musical traits of nineteenth-century romanticism. We may now isolate its most important characteristic: the predominance of chromatic harmony.

THE KEY AS A FORM-BUILDING ELEMENT

By marking off an area in musical space with a fixed center, the key provides the framework within which musical growth and development take place. The three main harmonies of the key—tonic (I), dominant (V), and subdominant (IV)—become the focal points over which melodies and chord progressions unfold. In brief, the key is the neighborhood inhabited by a tune and its harmonies. Thus the key becomes a prime factor for musical unity.

At the same time the contrast between keys may further the cause of variety. The classical composer pitted one key against another, thereby achieving a dramatic opposition between them. He began by establishing his home key. Presently he modulated to a related key (for example, from C major with no sharps or flats to G major, one sharp; or from G major to D major, two sharps). In so doing he established a tension, as the new key was unstable compared to the tonic. This tension required resolution, which was provided by the return to the home key.

The progression from home key to contrasting key and back outlined the basic musical pattern of statement-departure-return. Through such a progression the movement came to do precisely what its name implied: it moved! The home key was the anchorage, the safe harbor; the foreign key represented adventure. The home key was the symbol of unity; the foreign key ensured variety and contrast.

The tension between two keys and their ultimate reconciliation became the motive power of the music of the classical era. This conflict-and-resolution found its frame in the grand form of the latter eighteenth century—the ideal tone-drama known as the sonata.

⪼ 39 ⪻

The Development of Themes: Musical Logic

"I alter some things, eliminate and try again until I am satisfied. Then begins the mental working out of this material in its breadth, its narrowness, its height and depth."

Ludwig van Beethoven

THINKING, whether in words or tones, demands continuity and sequence. Every thought must flow out of the one before and lead logically into the next. In this way is created a sense of steady progression toward a goal.

When a melodic idea, we noted, is used as a building block in the construction of a larger work it is known as a theme or subject. The theme is the first in a chain of musical situations. All of these must grow out of the basic idea as naturally as does the plant from the seed. Hence the term *germ theme* which indicates the capacity of the initial idea to flower, to expand, and to develop in such a way as to create an effect of organic unity. The net result of this expansion and development is to make the audience feel, as they would in the case of a convincing drama or novel, that each situation is a necessary link in the chain: given this particular premise, what happens at any point is inevitable; or must seem so.

The most tightly knit kind of expansion in our music is known as *thematic development*. To develop a theme means to unfold its latent energies, to search out its capacities for growth and bring them to fruition. Thematic development represents the constructional element in music. It is one of the most important techniques in musical composition, demanding of the composer imagination, master craftsmanship, and intellectual power.

In expanding and manipulating his ideas the composer treats the tone material in the manner of the sculptor or goldsmith: he molds, hews, and joins, deriving inspiration from the stuff in his hands, allowing it to dictate forms and shapes peculiar to itself. He is engaged in a kind of thinking possible only in music. In the process of development, certain procedures have proved to be particularly effective. The simplest is repetition, which may occur either at the same pitch or at another. For example, in *America*, the melodic idea on the words "Land where my fathers died" is duplicated immediately, but a tone lower, on the words "Land of the pilgrims' pride." Such a repetition on a higher or lower pitch is known as a *sequence*. The repetition may be either exact or with variations in the melody, harmony, rhythm, timbre, dynamics, and register. It may be attended by expansion or contraction of the note values as well as by bold and frequent changes of key.

A basic technique in thematic development is the breaking up of the theme into its constituent fragments, the *motives*. A motive is the smallest fragment of a theme that forms a melodic-rhythmic unit. The motives are the germ cells of musical growth. Through fragmentation of themes, through repeating and varying the motives and combining them in ever fresh patterns, the composer imparts to the musical organism the quality of dynamic evolution. As we watch this process of flowering and growth we experience the joy of recognizing the basic idea throughout its ever-changing manifestations.

The intricacies of thematic development are out of place in short lyric pieces of song or dance character. In such compositions a simple contrast between sections and a modest expansion within each section supplies the necessary continuity. By the same token, thematic development is of the essence in the large forms. To those forms it furnishes an epic-dramatic quality, along with the clarity, coherence, and logic that are the indispensable attributes of this most advanced type of musical thinking.

❧ 40 ❧

The Cycle of Movements in
Sonata and Symphony

"To write a symphony means, to me, to construct a world."
Gustav Mahler

IN AN earlier part of this book we viewed sonata form as a flexible
framework for the statement, development and recapitulation of musical ideas. We may now examine it under its other aspect—as an ingenious structural device allowing for the departure from and return to
the home key.

FIRST-MOVEMENT FORM AND THE PRINCIPLE OF
TONALITY

The basic assumption underlying first-movement form is that a musical movement takes on direction and goal if it establishes itself in the
home key, modulates to a related key, and returns to the home key.
The tension will be heightened if, before the return home, there is
modulation farther afield through a series of keys. We may therefore
regard sonata form as a drama between two contrasting key areas. The
"plot," the action, and the tension derive from this contrast. Sonata
form, in brief, is the musical device that most effectively embodies the
principles and exploits the resources of the major-minor system.

In a drama or novel, the various human traits—courage, cowardice,
love, avarice—are presented not abstractly, but as embodied in specific
characters. So too, the home key and the related key are made manifest
to the ear by two contrasting themes or thematic groups. In this way
the opposition between the two key areas is sharpened—dramatized,
as it were—and presented to the listener as a conflict between two
ideas. In other words, the basic conflict is not so much between Theme
1 and Theme 2 as between the two tonalities—home key and contrasting key—which they represent.

The first theme group, then, establishes the home key; the second,
the contrasting key. In the classical sonata the two keys were closely
related. The bridge between the two serves to carry us from the home

key to the other; in a word, it modulates. Each of the two ideas flowers into a section or a group of themes. Then comes the closing passage or codetta that rounds off the exposition and establishes a cadence in the related key. The adventurous quality of the exposition derives in no small measure from the fact that it "lifts" us from one key area to another. The cadence in the foreign key promises that much is to happen before we get back.

We have said that in the development section the conflict between the two theme groups erupts, the action reaches maximum intensity. This is done not only through the dynamic "working out" of the themes and their motives, but also through a corresponding intensification of the key relationships. Temperature is kept at fever pitch through continual modulation, that "wandering farther afield" which creates an impression of breathless activity and builds up tension against the inevitable return home. Indeed, the impression of breathless activity and tension achieved in the development section is due mainly to the fact that the music modulates freely, carrying the listener from one key area to the next without allowing him to settle down anywhere.

When the developmental surge has run its course, tension simmers down to a transition passage back to the home key. The beginning of the third section, the recapitulation, is in a sense the psychological climax of sonata form—just as the peak of many a journey is the return home. The first theme appears as we first heard it, in the home key, proclaiming the victory of unity over diversity, of continuity over change. The warring elements are reconciled, with the home key emerging triumphant over the foreign key.

The recapitulation, we saw, follows the general path of the exposition, restating the first and second themes more or less in their original form. With one important difference. When the composer comes to the second theme group, which originally was in the contrasting key, he shifts it into (or as close as possible to) the home key; so that, although the material of the second theme group unfolds pretty much as before, we now hear it transposed into the home key. There follows the ultimate pronouncement, the coda, which rounds off the movement and asserts the victory of the home key with a vigorous final cadence.

The procedure just described is summed up in the following outline.

SONATA FORM

Exposition	Development	Recapitulation (or Restatement)
(Slow introduction) First theme or theme group in home key	Frequent modulation (away from home key) Fragmentation and ma-	First theme or thematic group in home key Bridge

Exposition	Development	Recapitulation (or Restatement)
Bridge—modulates	nipulation of themes	Second theme or thematic group transposed to home key (or close to it)
Second theme or thematic group in contrasting key	Building up of tension against return to home key	
Codetta. Cadence in contrasting key	Retransition to home key	Coda. Cadence in home key

An outline such as this is an oversimplification. It implies a ready-made mold into which the material is poured, whereas living form springs out of the material itself. The main features of the above outline are present in one shape or another in innumerable sonata-allegro movements. Yet no two are exactly alike in their disposition of the material. Each constitutes a unique solution of the problem in terms of character, mood, and relation of forces, just as every novel, play, or sonnet—and every living organism besides—is a particular and unique example of general structural principles. First-movement form proved capable of being adapted to the most diverse temperaments and ideas. The true artists—and it is their work alone that has endured—allowed the content to shape the form; so that what looks on paper like a fixed plan becomes, when transformed into living sound, a supple framework of infinite variety.

Even as the dramatist creates opposing personalities as the chief characters of his work, so the composer achieves a vivid contrast between the musical ideas that form the basis of the movement. The opposition between two themes may be underlined in a number of ways. Through a contrast in dynamics—loud against soft; in register—low against high; timbre—strings against winds, one instrumental combination against another; rhythm and tempo—an animated pattern against one that is sustained; tone quality—legato against staccato, type of melody, harmony, and accompaniment. One contrast is required, being the basis of the form: the contrast of key. And the opposition may be further intensified by putting one theme in the major and the other in minor. From the interaction of all these emerged the conception of a first theme vigorously rhythmic and energetic, imparting to the movement its forward impulsion, as against a quietly lyrical second theme.

The novel is distinguished from the short story by its development of characters over a spacious canvas. Similarly, sonata-allegro is distinguished from the simple lyric forms by its development of themes over a large canvas. In a well-devised novel the characters are motivated by the inner forces of their personality. They seem at every juncture to have a choice; yet in the profoundest sense their decisions are inevitable. So in first-movement form the action springs inevitably from the germinal themes. The music follows one course rather than another not because the composer arbitrarily wills it so but because, given these premises, it must be so.

The reader should be cautioned, in conclusion, against a widespread misconception. The conventional description of sonata form, by its emphasis upon the two or three themes that serve as building blocks for an instrumental movement, seems to imply that everything between these themes is in the nature of transitional material. But from everything we have said it is clear that the sonata movement is an organic unity in which the growth, the development, the destiny of the idea is no less important than the idea itself (just as, in assessing a human action, we consider its consequences no less than the deed proper). From the symphonic point of view the theme includes not only the germinal idea *but also its expansion and development*. The musical examples in the past chapters and in those to come represent what is generally regarded as "Theme 1" or "Theme 2" of a sonata movement. They are actually only the kernels, the beginnings of themes. The theme, in the profoundly musical sense, must be considered to include not only the few notes on the page but also the "etc."—that is, the passage or section into which the initial idea flowers. It is only when we take this larger view of the theme that we come to understand the symphonic movement for what it is: a continuous expansion and growth of musical ideas from first note to last, from which not a measure may be omitted without disturbing the equilibrium and the organic oneness of the whole.

Sonata and symphony are generally regarded as musical forms. It might perhaps be closer to the truth to speak of sonata style—that is, to consider sonata and symphony as a manner of thinking; specifically, a manner of thinking for instruments that combines in the highest degree logical continuity, dynamic development, and emotional intensity. Sonata form has been a living force in our music for two hundred years, and in that time has survived vast changes in musical taste and thought. It has done so because it affords the composer the fullest opportunity to work out purely musical ideas in a purely musical way.

THE OTHER MOVEMENTS

Sonata form proved to be so challenging to the musicians of the classical era that on occasion they used it also for the slow movement of the cycle. This movement also might be a simple song form in A-B-A structure, with the middle section presenting a contrast not only in thematic material but also in regard to the key. Or it might be cast in the shape of a theme and variations.

THEME AND VARIATIONS

The theme is stated at the outset, so that the audience will know the basic idea which serves as point of departure. The theme is apt to be simple in character, so as to allow room for elaboration. There follows a series of variations in which certain features of the original idea are retained while others are altered. Each variation sets forth the idea with some new modification—one might say in a new disguise—through which the listener glimpses something of the original theme.

To the process of variation the composer brings all the techniques of musical embellishment. He may vary the melody or harmony; the rhythm, meter, and tempo; the dynamics and tone color. The texture may be enriched by interweaving the melody with new themes. Or the original theme may itself become an accompaniment for a new melody. By combining these methods in an infinite variety of ways, the character of the theme may be changed, so that it is presented now as a funeral march, now as a serenade, folk dance, caprice, or boat song. This type of character variation was much in favor in the romantic era.

The theme with variations, like the development section in first-movement form, challenges the composer's inventiveness and crafts-manship. One understands why variation form has attracted composers for the last three hundred years. The theme and variations appeared not only as the slow movement of the sonata cycle; it might also serve as the fourth or final movement, and occasionally even as the first. Also, it was much cultivated as an independent piece, with the variations sometimes based on an idea borrowed from another composer, as in the case of Brahms' *Variations on a Theme by Handel*. In any case, the theme with variations presents a challenging manifestation of unity in diversity, and a manipulation of purely musical material in a purely musical way.

MINUET AND TRIO

The *minuet* was the favored dance of the courts of Europe; its stately 3/4 time embodied the ideal of grace of an aristocratic age. In the eighteenth century the minuet was taken over into the sonata cycle, where it served as the third movement. Since dance music lends itself to symmetrical construction, we often find in the minuet a clear-cut structure based on phrases of four and eight measures. In tempo the minuet ranges from stateliness to a lively pace and whimsical character.

The custom prevailed in the seventeenth century of presenting two dances as a group, the first being repeated at the end of the second (A-B-A). The one in the middle was frequently arranged for three instruments; hence the name *trio*, which persisted even after the customary setting for three was abandoned. The trio as a rule is lighter in texture and quieter of gait. Frequently woodwind tone predominates, creating an out-of-doors atmosphere that lends a special charm to this section. At the end of the trio we find *Da Capo* or *D. C.* (from the beginning), signifying that the first section is to be played over again. Minuet and trio, then, is a symmetrical three-part structure in which each part in turn is a small a-b or a-b-a form.

In the nineteenth-century symphony the minuet was displaced by the scherzo. The scherzo is usually the third movement, sometimes the second, and like the minuet is in 3/4 time. Like the minuet, too, it is a three-part form (scherzo-trio-scherzo), the first section being repeated after the middle part. But it differs from the minuet in its headlong pace and vigorous rhythm. The scherzo—the name, it will be recalled, derives from the Italian for "jest"—is marked by abrupt changes of mood ranging from the humorous or the whimsical to the mysterious and even demonic. In the hands of Beethoven the scherzo became a movement of immense driving force.

THE RONDO

The *rondo* is a lively movement suffused with the spirit of the dance, whose main characteristic is the recurrence of a central idea—the rondo theme—in alternation with one or more subsidiary themes; as in the pattern A-B-A-C-A.

The true rondo as developed by the classical masters was more ambitious in scope. In effect, the gay rondo took on some of the architectural breadth of first-movement form. Characteristic was the formation A-B-A-C-A-B-A. The first A-B-A was in the nature of an exposition and the corresponding A-B-A at the end was a recapitulation. Between them was the C section, which served as a kind of development. What with contrast of key and elaborate transitional passages, the classical rondo assimilated the spaciousness of sonata form and came to be known as a rondo-sonata.

The essence of the rondo is its vivacity and good humor. Because the theme is to be heard over and over again it must be catchy and relaxing. The rondo figured in eighteenth- and nineteenth-century music both as an independent piece and as a member of the sonata cycle. In the sonata it served as the final movement, rounding off the work with a happy ending.

THE SONATA AS A WHOLE

The four-movement cycle of the classical masters, as exemplified in their sonatas, symphonies, string quartets, and other types of chamber music, consisted of two large outer movements balanced by two inner movements of song and dance character. The following outline will be helpful to the reader, provided he remembers that it is no more than a general scheme and does not necessarily apply to all works of this kind. In Beethoven's Ninth Symphony, for example, the scherzo is the second movement while the adagio comes third.

| | | | TEMPO | |
MOVE-MENT	FORM	CHARACTER	*Mozart: Symphony No. 40*	*Beethoven: Symphony No. 5*
First	Sonata form	Epic-dramatic	Allegro molto	Allegro con brio
Second	A-B-A Sonata form Theme and variations	Slow lyrical movement. May range, however, from the whimsical to the tragic	Andante	Andante con moto
Third	A-B-A	Dance movement: Minuet (18th century) Scherzo (19th century) Both in ¾ time	Allegretto	Allegro
Fourth	Rondo Sonata form Rondo-sonata Theme and variations	Lively finale (18th century) Triumphal ending: the romantic "apotheosis" (19th century)	Allegro molto	Allegro

The classical masters of the sonata thought of the four movements of the cycle as self-contained entities connected by identity of key. First, third, and fourth movements were generally in the home key, with the second movement in a contrasting key. The nineteenth century sought a more obvious connection between movements. This need was met by cyclical structure, in which a theme from the earlier movements appeared in the later ones as a kind of unifying thread.

The sonata cycle satisfied the need of composers for an extended work of an abstract character. It derived its being from the nature of the instruments. It mobilized the contrasts of key and mode inherent in the major-minor system. Upon the insubstantial stuff of sound it implanted the heroic dimensions of architecture—length, width, and depth; spaciousness and symmetry. And it achieved all this according to principles deriving exclusively from the nature of sound. The sonata cycle has an epic-dramatic quality, leaving the listener with the sense of a vast action consummated, an eventful journey brought to its predestined conclusion. With its fusion of sensuous, emotional, and intellectual elements, its intermingling of lyric contemplation and action, the sonata cycle may justly claim to be one of the most ingenious art forms ever devised by man.

PART FOUR

Eighteenth-Century Classicism

❧

"When a nation brings its innermost nature to consummate expression in arts and letters we speak of its classic period. Classicism stands for experience, for spiritual and human maturity
which has deep roots in the cultural soil of the nation, for the
mastery of the means of expression in technique and form, and
for a definite conception of the world and of life; the final com-
pression of the artistic values of a people."
Paul Henry Lang: Music in Western Civilization

⇗41⇖

The Classical Spirit

'Tis more to guide, than spur the Muse's steed;
Restrain his fury, than provoke his speed;
The winged courser, like a gen'rous horse,
Shows most true mettle when you check his course.
Alexander Pope (1688–1744)

THE DICTIONARY defines classicism in two ways: as pertaining to the highest order of excellence in literature and art; or pertaining to the culture of the ancient Greeks and Romans. Implicit in the classical attitude is the notion that supreme excellence has been reached in the past and may be attained again through adherence to tradition and rule. In this regard classicism is opposed to the romantic revolt against established norms.

Being part of a tradition implies a relationship to something outside oneself. The classical artist participates in the common practice of his time. Unlike the romantic, he neither glories in nor emphasizes his apartness from other men. Rather he accepts the fact that he is different and moves on to other things. His prime aim is to achieve the highest with the materials and procedures inherited from the past. The romantic is preoccupied chiefly with self-expression; the classicist with the manipulation of the material—that is to say, with communication.

The classical artist regards neither his individuality nor his personal experience as the primary material of his art. The work exists for him as an entity in its own right rather than as an emanation of his ego. His attention is directed rather to beauty of form, purity of line, and exquisite craftsmanship. He strives for an objective view of reality. Freed from the domination of the self, he seeks symbols that will have universal validity. This wholeness of view encourages the qualities of order, stability, and poise, clarity, restraint, and harmonious proportion that we associate with the classical style.

In classical art the emotion is purified, transfigured under the aegis of beauty into an ideal serenity. Classicism upholds the ethical nature of art, its moral discipline, its power to purge the soul. Romanticism exploits the wonder and ecstasy of art, its demonic energy, its intimations of the unknown and the irrational. Both spring from the nature of man. Both minister to his nature.

The Theseum.

"The qualities of order, stability, and harmonious proportion that we associate with the classical style."

EIGHTEENTH-CENTURY CLASSICISM

Conditions in the nineteenth century were extraordinarily congenial to the romantic temper. By the same token the latter part of the eighteenth century formed a favorable climate for the triumph of classicism. The culture of that era was under the patronage of an aristocracy for whom the arts were a necessary adornment of life. In such a society, where the ruling caste enjoys its power through hereditary right, tradition is apt to be prized and the past revered. The emphasis is on elegance of manner and beauty of expression.

The artist under patronage creates for a public high above him in social rank; his patrons are interested in his product rather than in him. To be too personal in such circumstances would be an impertinence. He is thus led from the egocentric temper of the romantic to classical objectivity and reserve. The art of the eighteenth century bears the imprint of the spacious palaces and formal gardens, with their balanced proportions and finely wrought detail, that formed the setting for enlightened despotism. In this milieu the artist was a master craftsman, an artisan working on direct commission. He was not concerned, as was his nineteenth-century counterpart, with posterity. The artist of the classical era produced works for immediate use, sustained by daily contact with his public. This was a public of connoisseurs for whom familiarity with art was part of their birthright. He could be as fastidious, as subtle as he pleased. No trouble he might take was too great, no detail too nice for so knowing an audience.

In point of social status the artist in livery was little better than a servant. This was not quite as depressing as it sounds, for in that society

Classicism, old and new. Ancient Roman sculpture, *Ariadne Sleeping.*
Madame Récamier by David.
"An art of noble simplicity . . ."

everybody was a servant of the prince save other princes. The patronage system gave the artist security. It also marked off the limits within
which he might function. The court artist might rise to lofty pathos,
but this had to be of a formalized kind. He was not encouraged to seek
new worlds; and he most definitely had to avoid ideas and emotions that
might disturb his princely patrons.

The eighteenth century—the age of the Enlightenment—witnessed
the appearance in France of the Great Encyclopedia, the result of a
majestic attempt to systematize all knowledge and subject it to the
scrutiny of reason. The spirit of rationalism pervaded the culture of
the era. Unlike the romantic, who discerned a fundamental antagonism
between intellect and emotion, the eighteenth-century man strove to
reconcile them, to strike an ideal balance between mind and heart.

Classical art sang of enduring values. The glittering world for which
it sang appeared to be no less enduring. But beneath the polished surface, tremors were shaking the foundations of European society. The
disinherited of the earth were stirring. The new middle class, its
strength based on industry and commerce, was moving forward to
challenge and to overthrow the landed nobility. In England, indus-
trially the most advanced country of Europe, the rising bourgeois
culture had already created its characteristic art form in the novel. In
France, even as the magnificent festivities unfolded in the gardens of
Versailles, philosophers were formulating the doctrines that before
long would destroy the *ancien régime*. Far off in the new world a
revolutionary belief was emerging in the inalienable rights of man.
Eighteenth-century classicism mirrored the unique movement in history when the old world was dying and the new was in process of being
born. From the meeting of two historic forces emerged an art of "noble
simplicity and quiet greatness," whose achievement in music constitutes
one of the pinnacles of Western culture.

≫42≪

Classicism in Music (c. 1770-1820)

"Ought not the musician, quite as much as the poet and painter, to study nature? In nature he can study man, its noblest creature."
Johann Friedrich Reichardt (1774)

IN OUR discussion of nineteenth-century music we cautioned the reader against the widespread misconception that classical art is all form and no emotion while romanticism is all emotion and no form. Any attempt to differentiate between the classical and romantic spirit in music must emphasize throughout that there can be no art without emotion, for the work of art begins as an intimation of beauty, a rapturous vision glimpsed by the artist and held fast. So, too, there can be no art without form, for the creative act by its very nature implies discipline, the conscious selection of certain details and exclusion of others. No artist ever says to himself, "I will restrain my emotions." No artist ever says to himself, "I will cast away all forms." Every artist makes use of *all* the expressive resources and *all* the technical resources available in his time, striving always to find the form that will best fit what he has to say. Where the distinction between classic and romantic holds is in the nature of the relationship between the form and the emotion, between the rapture and the discipline. This distinction has been drawn, in retrospect, by later generations. It is a valid distinction as long as it is not pushed too far.

Musical classicism is in many respects the direct opposite of romanticism. Whereas the latter sought to bring music into close relation with literature and painting, classicism upheld the independence of music as a self-contained art. Romanticism leaned toward program music, classicism toward absolute. Romanticism glorified folklore and exploited peasant song and dance. The music of classicism came out of the culture of cities and the sophistication of courts (although the popular tone, significantly, makes its appearance in the vivacious finales of Haydn). Romantic music is a democratic art; classical music is aristocratic. Romantic music was intensely national; classical music created a universal style disseminated through two international art forms— Italian opera and Viennese symphony. Romantic music evoked atmosphere and mood, whereas classical music concentrated upon the development of abstract ideas. The masters of the classical era favored a clean sensible music, limpid and discreet; not for them the rhetoric and gesture that marked the nineteenth-century style.

Romantic music was given to excess; classical music favored moderation. Romantic music sounded the nature tone in its land- and seascapes; classical music on the whole ignored the scenic element, fastening instead upon the landscape of the spirit. For the romantics music was an enchantment, a religion, a way of life. The classical era enjoyed music as an embellishment of gracious living. Hence romantic pessimism is alien to this urbane and essentially optimistic art.

For the romantic composer color and harmony, melody and rhythm often existed as ends in themselves. For the classicist these functioned in the closest possible relationship, serving a single goal: unity of form: form as the principle of artistic law and order, born of the mating of reason and emotion. Out of this union came the chiseled structures of Haydn, Mozart, and Beethoven which for a century and a half have remained models of musical clarity and coherence. Never before or since have all the elements of music operated in so harmonious a conjunction.

The climate of rationalism that pervaded the Enlightenment brought forth the great rational form of eighteenth-century music: the sonata cycle. This offered a perfect frame for the classical impulse toward logical organization of the parts within the whole. The form sprang out of the material, the material demanded the form. It is this unparalleled unity of form and content that constitutes the truly classical element in eighteenth-century music.

We have made reference before to Nietzsche's distinction between the Dionysian and the Apollonian. The classical temper finds a fit symbol in the god of light whose sculptured beauty so eloquently proclaims the cult of harmonious proportion.

MAIN CURRENTS IN CLASSICAL MUSIC

The opera house was a focal point of musical activity and experimentation in the classical era. Classical opera was based on principles directly opposite to those that prevailed in the romantic music drama. The music was the point of departure and imposed its forms on the drama. Each scene was a closed musical unit. The separate numbers were conceived as parts of the whole and held together in a carefully planned framework. There was the greatest possible distinction between the rapid patter of recitative and the lyric curve of aria. The voice reigned supreme, yet the orchestra displayed all the vivacity of the classical instrumental style.

A significant development was the importance of comic opera (*opera buffa*). Far from being an escapist form of entertainment, comic opera was directly related to the life of the time. Its emphasis was on the affairs of "little people," on swift action, spontaneous emotion, and sharpness of characterization. This popular lyric theater showed an abundance of racy melody, brilliant orchestration, and lively rhythms. Characteristic were the ensemble numbers at the end of the act, of a verve and drive that influenced all branches of music. Classical *opera buffa* steadily expanded its scope until it culminated in the works of the greatest musical dramatist of the eighteenth century—Mozart.

As a center of music making the Church retained its importance alongside opera house and aristocratic salon. The masters of the classical Viennese school—Haydn, Mozart, Beethoven, Schubert—produced a great deal of church music, masses, vespers, litanies, and the like. The notion has been advanced that the masses of the classical era are not true church music because of their operatic and symphonic elements. Such reasoning sets up a distinction between church and secular style —between religion and life—that simply did not exist for the musicians of the classical period. They did as composers had done for centuries before them: they used the living idiom of their day (an idiom based on opera and symphony) to express their faith in God and man.

INSTRUMENTAL MUSIC

The piano sonata became the most ambitious form of solo music. The piano was newly established as the main keyboard instrument, having supplanted the two favorites of the early eighteenth century, the harpsichord and clavichord. Through the piano sonata, composers worked out new conceptions of keyboard style and sonata structure, creating a rich literature for both amateur and virtuoso.

The heart of the classical orchestra was the string choir. Woodwinds, used with great imaginativeness, ably seconded the strings. The brass sustained the harmonies and contributed body to the tone mass, while the kettledrums supplied rhythmic life and vitality. The eighteenth-century orchestra numbered from thirty to forty players. Foreign to classical art were the swollen sonorities of the late nineteenth century. The orchestra of Haydn and Mozart lent itself to delicate nuances in which each timbre stood out radiantly. The masters used their medium with surpassing economy, attaining a variety of color, a transparency and lightness of texture, that are among the most enchanting manifestations of the classical temper.

The classical orchestra brought to absolute music a number of effects long familiar in the opera house. The gradual crescendo and decrescendo established themselves as staples of the new symphonic style. Hardly less conspicuous were the abrupt alternations of soft and loud, sudden accents, dramatic pauses; the use of tremolo, pizzicato, and similar devices of operatic music. Within the orchestral domain, the sonata cycle took on ample proportions. Of paramount importance was the sonata for solo instrument and orchestra—the concerto, which combined a virtuoso part for the featured player with the full resources of the instrumental ensemble. The piano concerto was the chief type, although other solo instruments were not neglected. But the central place in instrumental music was reserved, naturally, for the "sonata for orchestra"—the symphony. This grew rapidly in dimension and significance until, with the final works of Mozart and Haydn, it became the most important type of absolute music.

The symphony was descended from the operatic overture. Within its spacious confines the masters of the classical era worked out all those problems of musical organization that we discussed in the chapters on sonata form. In so doing they achieved the true symphonic style, projected in a musical language of such expressiveness and élan that musicians everywhere still regard it as an unsurpassable ideal.

Chamber music enjoyed a great flowering in the classical era, as did a type of composition that stood midway between chamber music and symphony, known as *divertimento*. The title fixes the character of this category of music as sociable diversion or entertainment. Contemporary accounts tell of groups of street musicians who performed these works—for strings, winds, or both—outside the homes of the wealthy or in a quiet square before an appreciative audience of their townsmen. Salzburg and Vienna were pre-eminent in the richness and variety of their street music. The unique distinction of this popular music lies in the fact that its literature was enriched by the great masters. For once "popular" and "classical" were united, giving rise to one of the most attractive species of eighteenth-century music.

FURTHER ASPECTS OF MUSICAL CLASSICISM

Audiences of the classical era differed from those of our time in one important respect. Their attention was directed mainly to the hearing of new works by living composers; whereas our public shies away from

contemporary music but flocks to hear the standard repertoire rein-
terpreted by one virtuoso or another. The star of the classical scene
was the creator of music. The spotlight in our scene belongs, as far as
the big public is concerned, to the performer. The composer was
directly involved in the playing of his music. Mozart and Beethoven
were outstanding pianists in their time; Haydn appeared in England as
conductor of his symphonies. Eighteenth-century eagerness for new
music may be compared to the present-day appetite for new films. The
classical era, in brief, was an ideal climate for the living composer;
whereas ours is pre-eminently devoted to the dead one.

The classical era created an all-European culture that transcended
national boundaries. In this it reflected the international character of
the two most powerful institutions in social life: the aristocracy and
the Church. Indeed, the eighteenth century was the last stronghold of
internationalism in art (until the twentieth began). German, French,
and Italian influences intermingled in the art of Haydn and Mozart.
These masters were not German in the way that Wagner was, or
Schumann, or Brahms. Romantic nationalism, we saw, opened up new
dialects to composers. By the same token something was lost of the
breadth of view that made artists like Beethoven or Goethe in the
highest sense citizens of the world.

This inter-European language was shared by all the contemporaries,
greater and lesser, of Haydn and Mozart, in Austria and Germany,
Italy and France. We have but to hear a few bars of their music to
recognize that they spoke the same idiom as the two Viennese masters.
They did not speak it as profoundly or as eloquently, which is why
many of them have survived only in the history books; but they spoke
it with utter assurance, for it was the one musical language of the age.
Eighteenth-century classicism struck the ideal balance between passion
and intellect, between external form and inner content. So delicate an
equilibrium springs only from the perfect fusion of matter and spirit.
It is as rare in art as in life.

❧43❧
Joseph Haydn (1732-1809)

"I have only just learned in my old age how to use the wind instruments, and now that I do understand them I must leave the world."

THE LONG career of Joseph Haydn spanned the critical decades of the classic era. He absorbed all that the eighteenth century had achieved and succeeded in bringing its diverse elements into a remarkable unity of style. The legacy he left was a contribution to music in scope and significance second to none.

HIS LIFE

He was born in a village in Lower Austria, son of a wheelwright. Folk song and dance were his natural heritage. Displaying uncommon musical aptitude as a child, he was taught the rudiments by a distant relative, a schoolmaster. The beauty of his voice secured him a place as chorister in St. Stephen's Cathedral in Vienna, where he remained till he was sixteen. With the breaking of his voice his days at the choir school came to an end. He established himself in an attic in Vienna, managed to obtain a dilapidated clavier, and set himself to master his craft. Those were the lean years. He eked out a living through teaching and accompanying, and often joined the roving bands of musicians who performed in the streets. In this way the popular Viennese idiom entered his style along with the folk idiom he had absorbed in childhood.

Haydn before long attracted the notice of the music-loving aristocracy of Vienna, and was invited to the country house of a nobleman who maintained a modest musical establishment. His next patron kept a small orchestra, so that he was able to experiment with more ample resources. In 1761, when he was twenty-nine, he entered the service of the Esterházys, a family of enormously wealthy Hungarian princes famous for their patronage of the arts. He remained in this post for almost thirty years—that is, for the greater part of his creative career.

The palace of Esterház was one of the most splendid in Europe, and music played a central part in the constant round of festivities there.

The musical establishment under Haydn's direction included an orchestra, an opera company, a marionette theater, and the chapel. His creativity was stimulated by a constant demand for new works and by

Joseph Haydn.

the intelligent appreciation of his patron. The agreement between prince and composer sheds light on the social status of the eighteenth-century artist. Haydn is required to abstain "from undue familiarity and from vulgarity in eating, drinking, and conversation . . . It is especially to be observed that when the orchestra shall be summoned to perform before company the said Joseph Haydn shall take care that he and all the members of his orchestra do follow the instructions given and appear in white stockings, white linen, powdered, and with a pig-tail or tie-wig."

Haydn's life is the classic example of the patronage system operating at its best. Though he chafed occasionally at the restrictions imposed on his freedom at Esterház, he inhabited a world that questioned neither the supremacy of princes nor the spectacle of a great artist in livery. His final estimate of his position in the Esterházy household was that the advantages outweighed the disadvantages. "My Prince was always satisfied with my works. I not only had the encouragement of constant approval but as conductor of an orchestra I could make ex-periments, observe what produced an effect and what weakened it, and was thus in a position to improve, alter, make additions or omissions, and be as bold as I pleased. I was cut off from the world, there was no one to confuse or torment me, and I was forced to become *original*."

Haydn had married when still a young man, but did not get on with his wife; he found consolation elsewhere. By the time he reached middle age his music had brought him fame throughout Europe. He was asked to appear at various capitals but accepted none of these invitations as long as his patron was alive. After the Prince's death he made two visits to England, where he conducted his works with phe-nomenal success. He returned to his native Austria laden with honors and financially well off.

When he was seventy-six a memorable performance of *The Creation* was organized in his honor by the leading musicians of Vienna and members of the aristocracy. At the words "And there was light"—who that has heard the work can forget the grandeur of the C-major chord on the word "light"?—the old man was deeply stirred. Pointing up-ward he exclaimed, "It came from there!" As he was carried out in his armchair his admirers thronged about him. Beethoven, who had briefly been his pupil, kissed his hands and forehead. At the door he turned around and lifted his hands as if in blessing. It was his farewell to the public.

He died a year later, revered by his countrymen and acknowledged throughout Europe as the premier musician of his time.

HIS MUSIC

Haydn set himself to master a new instrumental language and to adapt it to the new things that music had to say: specifically, to achieve the dynamic development of themes and motives that was the kernel of the new symphonic style, and to mold those high-strung themes of his into convincing forms. These goals he encompassed with such success that for the next hundred years he was represented in popular manuals as the father of the symphony, of the string quartet, of the modern orchestra, and of instrumental music in general. Such allegations of paternity, it goes without saying, are vastly exaggerated. The sonata was the product of an age, not an individual. Haydn's pre-eminence stems from the fact that he solved its problems with greater force and brilliance of imagination than did most of his contemporaries.

The string quartet occupied a central position in Haydn's art. The eighty-odd examples he left are an indispensable part of the repertory. Like the quartets, the symphonies—over a hundred in number—extend across the whole of Haydn's career. In them he solved what he considered to be the basic problem of large-scale musical architecture: the unity of the idea. His fame as a symphonist rests mainly on the twelve works that he wrote, in two sets of six, for his appearances in England. Known as the *Salomon* Symphonies, after the impresario who arranged the concerts, they abound in effects that the public associates with later composers—syncopation, sudden crescendos and accents, dramatic contrasts of soft and loud, daring modulation, and an imaginative color scheme in which each choir and instrument plays its allotted part. Of Haydn's symphonies it may be said, as it has been of his quartets, that they are the spiritual birthplace of Beethoven.

Haydn was a prolific composer of church music. His fourteen masses form the chief item in this category. The prevailing cheerfulness of these works reflects a trusting faith undisturbed by inner travail or doubt. "At the thought of God," he said, "my heart leaps for joy and I cannot help my music doing the same." *The Creation*, written in his mid-sixties after his return from England, is a hymn to nature and its Creator. In this oratorio, based on Milton's *Paradise Lost*, the earth and its beauties are described with that capacity for wonder which only children and artists know. The oratorio attained a popularity second only to that of Handel's *Messiah*. Haydn followed it with another on a text drawn from English literature—*The Seasons*, based on James Thomson's celebrated nature poem. Completed when the composer was on the threshold of seventy, it was his last major work.

Haydn enriched the literature of the divertimento, the concerto, and the song. His piano sonatas, of late years unjustly neglected, are returning to favor. His numerous operas and marionette plays were designed specifically for the entertainment needs of the Esterházy court. "My operas are calculated exclusively for our own company and would not produce their effect elsewhere." But several, revived in recent years, have given delight. Haydn had the humility and striving for perfection of the true artist, but he knew the value of his works. "There are some bad ones among the good," he said. "Some of my children are well-bred, some ill-bred, and here and there is a changeling among them." How touching is the remark of the aged master quoted at the head of this chapter. Finally, in summing up his life's work: "I think I have done my duty and been of use in my generation by my works. Let others do the same."

THE *SURPRISE* SYMPHONY

The best known of Haydn's symphonies, No. 94 in G major (*Surprise*), is one of the set of six written for the first visit to London in 1791. The orchestra that presented these compositions to the world consisted of about thirty-five players: a full string section; two each of flutes, oboes, bassoons, and horns; and drums.

The first movement opens with a brief introduction marked Adagio cantabile. The movement proper is a forceful Allegro assai (very lively) in sonata form, imbued with the symphonic drive and forthrightness of the classical style.

The first theme establishes the home key, G major.

It expands into a vigorous section, after which a bridge passage leads to the contrasting key, D major. This is set forth by the second theme.

As often happens in Haydn, the two basic ideas do not present a marked contrast to one another. The movement is built rather on the opposition between home and foreign key. One theme flowers into the next in a continuous self-evolving fabric that is the essence of Haydn's symphonic thinking. A graceful closing theme rounds off the exposition.

The Development opens with a reference to the main theme, its principal interval enlarged. Motives are expanded and developed, each measure seeming to give rise to the next. Throughout the section there is that sense of exploring possibilities, of releasing hidden energies, that makes the classical development. The Recapitulation presents the material in shortened form. The second theme is transposed from foreign to home key. A shapely coda affirms the triumph of the home key. Haydn's codas served as models for Beethoven.

The second movement is the Andante, a theme and variations in C major. The theme is of a folk-song simplicity. It is announced by the violins, staccato.

The eight-bar phrase is repeated and ends in an abrupt fortissimo crash —the "surprise" that gives the symphony its name. "There," Haydn told a friend, "all the ladies will scream." But despite the famous anecdote, in an artist of Haydn's stature one must seek a deeper motivation for the effect. The contrast between soft and loud was one of the dynamic elements of the new orchestral language and was bound to fascinate an innovative artist like Haydn, quite apart from the ladies.

Haydn's variations are notable for their ease, taste, humor, and workmanship. The theme returns in a number of versions. It is, to begin with, combined with a countermelody; then shifted into the minor mode (lowered third step) with further changes in dynamics and color, and varied rhythmically. It undergoes a continuous process of growth at the end of which we hear the melody wreathed in new harmonies. This andante is one of the famous examples of the desire to make much out of little, to achieve unity in variety, that appealed so strongly to the classical temper.

Third is the Minuet in G major, a rollicking Allegro molto that leaves far behind it the manner of the courtly dance. Peasant humor and the high spirits of folk dance permeate this movement. It is earthy, vital, symphonic.

The A section opens with one of Haydn's delicious irregularities in structure: an eight-bar phrase is answered by a phrase of ten. The B or middle part, the Trio, is quieter in movement, combining bassoon and string tone. The Minuet is repeated da capo.

The finale, Allegro di molto (very lively) in G major, is brisk, vigorous, and thoroughly orchestral. The popular dance tone of the rondo is here amalgamated with the expansive frame of sonata form. The principal theme establishes the home key of G.

An energetic bridge passage leads to a roguish little tune in the contrasting key, D major. The first theme is subjected to forceful development. In the Restatement, the second theme is transposed from dominant to tonic key. A jovial coda leads to the energetic cadence in G major.

Haydn's is the music of a man rooted in the world, an optimistic music that even in its darker moments accepts life and finds it good. The nineteenth century with its love of the grandiose was not overly responsive to this clean, sensible music. Thus was created the stereotype of an amiable "Papa Haydn" in court dress and powdered wig who purveyed harmless pleasantries to the lords of the old regime. It has remained for the twentieth century to rescue this great musician from such incomprehension and to restore to its rightful place his deeply felt, finely wrought art—an art of moderation and humor, polished and lucid, profoundly human and unfadingly fresh.

Wolfgang Amadeus Mozart (1756-1791)

> "People make a mistake who think that my art has come easily to me. Nobody has devoted so much time and thought to composition as I. There is not a famous master whose music I have not studied over and over."

SOMETHING of the miraculous hovers about the music of Mozart. One sees how it is put together, whither it is bound, and how it gets there; but its beauty of sound and perfection of style, its poignancy and grace defy analysis and beggar description. For one moment in the history of music all opposites were reconciled, all tensions resolved. That luminous moment was Mozart.

HIS LIFE

He was born in Salzburg, son of Leopold Mozart, an esteemed composer-violinist attached to the court of the Archbishop. The child's career presents the most extraordinary example of precociousness in the history of art. He began to compose before he was five, and performed at the court of the Empress Maria Theresa at the age of six. The following year his ambitious father organized a grand tour that included Paris, London, and Munich. By the time he was thirteen the boy had written sonatas, concertos, symphonies, religious works, an *opera buffa* and the operetta *Bastien and Bastienne*.

He reached manhood having attained a mastery of all forms of his art. The speed and sureness of his creative power, unrivaled by any other composer, is best described by himself: "Though it be long, the work is complete and finished in my mind. I take out of the bag of my memory what has previously been collected into it. For this reason the committing to paper is done quickly enough. For everything is already finished, and it rarely differs on paper from what it was in my imagination. At this work I can therefore allow myself to be disturbed. Whatever may be going on about me, I write and even talk." In similar vein he writes to his father: "You know that I am, so to speak, immersed in music, that I am busy with it all day—speculating, studying, considering."

His relations with his patron, Hieronymus von Colloredo, Prince-

Archbishop of Salzburg, grew steadily worse. The high-spirited young artist rebelled against the restrictions imposed by the patronage system. "The two valets sit at the head of the table," he writes his father. "I at least have the honor of sitting above the cooks." At length he could endure his position no longer. He quarreled with the Archbishop, was dismissed, and at twenty-five established himself in Vienna to pursue the career of a free artist, the while he sought an official appointment. Ten years remained to him. These were spent in a tragic struggle to achieve financial security and to find again the lost serenity of his childhood. Worldly success depended on the protection of the court. But the Emperor Joseph II—who referred to him as "a decided talent"— either passed him by in favor of lesser men or, when he finally took Mozart into his service, assigned him to tasks unworthy of his genius such as composing dances for the court balls. Of his remuneration for this work Mozart remarked with bitterness, "Too much for what I do, too little for what I could do."

In 1782 he married Constanze Weber, against his father's wishes. The step signalized Mozart's liberation from the close ties that had bound him to the well-meaning but domineering parent who strove so futilely to ensure the happiness of the son. Constanze brought her husband neither the strength of character nor the wherewithal that might have shielded him from a struggle with the world for which he was singularly unequipped. She was an undistinguished woman to whom Mozart, despite occasional lapses, was strongly attached. It was not till many years after his death that she appears to have realized, from the adulation of the world, the stature of her husband.

With the opera *The Marriage of Figaro*, written in 1786 on a libretto by Lorenzo da Ponte, Mozart reached the peak of his career as far as success was concerned. The work made a sensation in Vienna and in Prague, and his letters from the latter city testify to his pleasure at its reception. Noteworthy is his cheerful acceptance of the fact that the main arias of the opera had been transformed into popular dance tunes, a practice that people today regard as an irreverence. "At six o'clock I drove with Count Canal to the so-called Bretfield ball, where the cream of Prague's beauties gather. I neither danced nor flirted with any of them, the former because I was too tired, the latter owing to my natural timidity. I looked on however with the greatest pleasure while all these people flew about in sheer delight to the music of my *Figaro* arranged for quadrilles and waltzes. Here they talk about nothing but *Figaro*. Nothing is played, sung, or whistled but *Figaro*. No opera is drawing like *Figaro*. Nothing, nothing but *Figaro!*"

Wolfgang Amadeus Mozart.

He was commissioned to do another work for the following year. With da Ponte again as librettist he produced *Don Giovanni*. The opera baffled the Viennese. His vogue had passed. The composer whom we regard as the epitome of clarity and grace was, in the view of the frivolous public of his time, difficult to understand. His music, it was said, had to be heard several times in order to be grasped. What better proof of its inaccessibility? In truth, Mozart was entering regions beyond the aristocratic entertainment level of the day. He was straining toward an intensity of utterance that was new in the world. Of *Don Giovanni* Joseph II declared, "The opera is heavenly, perhaps even more beautiful than *Figaro*. But no food for the teeth of my Viennese." Upon which Mozart commented, "Then give them time to chew it." One publisher advised him to write in a more popular style. "In that case I can make no more by my pen," he answered. "I had better starve and die at once."

The last years of his life were spent in growing want. The frequent appeals to his friends for aid mirror his despair and helplessness. He describes himself as "always hovering between hope and anxiety." He speaks of the black thoughts that he must "repel by a tremendous effort." He asks for a loan so that he may work "with a mind *more free* from care and *with a lighter heart* and thus *earn more*. . . . If only I had at least 600 gulden I should be able to compose with a fairly easy mind. Ah! I must have peace of mind." The love of life that had sustained him through earlier disappointments began to desert him. Again and again he embarked on a journey that seemed to promise a solution to all his difficulties, only to return empty-handed. A note of defeat crept into the gay tender letters he wrote his wife. "I cannot describe what I have been feeling. A kind of emptiness that hurts me dreadfully—a kind of longing that is never satisfied, that never ceases, that persists—no, rather increases daily."

In the last year of his life, after a falling off in his production, he nerved himself to the final effort. For the popular Viennese theater he wrote *The Magic Flute*, on a libretto by the actor-impresario-poetaster Emanuel Schikaneder. Based on the symbols of Freemasonry, this gigantic fantasy issued out of the native *Singspiel* tradition. Then a flurry of hope sent him off to Prague for the coronation of the new Emperor, Leopold II, as King of Bohemia. The festival opera he composed for this event, *The Clemency of Tito*, failed to impress a court exhausted by the protracted ceremonies of the coronation. Mozart returned to Vienna broken in body and spirit. With a kind of fevered desperation he turned to his last task, the *Requiem*. It had been commissioned by a music-loving count who fancied himself a composer and intended to pass off the work as his own. Mozart in his over-wrought state became obsessed with the notion that this Mass for the Dead was intended for himself and that he would not live to finish it. A tragic race with time began as he whipped his faculties to this master-work steeped in visions of death.

The gentle resignation that many find in his music comes through in the letter he supposedly wrote da Ponte in England, in response to the latter's suggestion that he join him there.

I wish I could follow your advice, but how can I do so? My mind is con-fused, I reason with difficulty and cannot free myself from the image of this stranger. I see him perpetually entreating me, pressing me and impatiently demanding the work. I go on writing because composition tires me less than resting. Otherwise I have nothing more to fear. I know from what I suffer that the hour has come. I am at the point of death. I have come to the end without having had the enjoyment of my talent. Life was so beautiful, my career began under such fortunate auspices. But no one can change his destiny. No one can measure his days. One must resign oneself, it will be as providence wills. I must close. Here is my death-song. I must not leave it incomplete.

His last days were cheered by the growing popularity of *The Magic Flute*. The gravely ill composer, watch in hand, would follow the performance in his mind. "Now the first act is over . . . Now comes the aria of the Queen of Night. . . ." His premonition concerning the *Requiem* came true. He failed rapidly while in the midst of the work. His favorite pupil, Süssmayer, completed the mass from the master's sketches, with some additions of his own.

Mozart died shortly before his thirty-sixth birthday. In view of his debts he was given "the poorest class of funeral." His friends followed to the city gates; but as a violent storm was raging they turned back, leaving the hearse to proceed alone. "Thus, without a note of music, forsaken by all he held dear, the remains of this prince of harmony were committed to the earth—not even in a grave of his own but in the common paupers' grave."

HIS MUSIC

Mozart's art sprang from the European culture of his time. He assimilated the suave, sensuous vocal melody of the Italians, the ad-vanced orchestral-symphonic conception of the Germans, the elegance and lucidity of the French. His music acknowledged no national bound-aries. Like Haydn and Beethoven he addressed the world.

Many picture Mozart as one in whom the dainty elegance of court art reached its apogee. To others he represents the spirit of artless youth untouched by life. Both views are equally far from the truth. Neither the simplicity of his forms nor the crystalline clarity of his texture can dispel the intensity of feeling that pervades the works of his maturity. Because of the mastery with which everything is carried out, the most complex operations of the musical mind are made to appear effortless. This deceptive simplicity is truly the art that conceals art.

It has been said that Mozart taught the instruments to sing. Into his exquisitely wrought instrumental forms he poured the lyricism of the great vocal art of the past. There resulted a pure and spiritualized idiom. The peasant touch is missing from Mozart's music, which draws its inspiration neither from folk song nor nature. It is an indoor art, sophisticated, rooted in the culture of two musical cities—Salzburg and Vienna. Haydn, who adjusted both his life and music to the needs of the aristocracy, was the natural man and the democratic artist; while Mozart, whose life was one long gesture of rebellion against the old regime, in his art was essentially aristocratic. His music is the acme of refinement, the product of a ripe civilization lifted to universality through the profoundly human insights of its creator.

The Salzburg years saw the composition of a quantity of social music, divertimentos and serenades of great variety. In chamber music he favored the string quartet. His works in this form range in expression from the buoyantly songful to the austerely tragic. The last ten quartets rank with the finest specimens in the literature, among them being the set of six dedicated to Haydn, his "most celebrated and very dear friend." Worthy companions to these are the string quintets, in which he invariably used two violas. The somber Quintet in G minor represents the peak of his achievement in this medium.

One of the outstanding pianists of his time, Mozart wrote copiously for his favorite instrument. Among the solo works the Fantasia and Sonata in C minor occupy the first rank. He was less experimental than Haydn in regard to formal structure, yet he led the way in developing one important form: the concerto for piano and orchestra. He wrote more than twenty works in this medium. Intended primarily as display pieces for his own public performances, they abound in the brilliant flourishes characteristic of eighteenth-century entertainment music. With these works the piano concerto achieved a leading position in the art of the classical era.

The more than forty symphonies that extend across his career tend toward ever greater richness of orchestration, freedom of part writing, and depth of emotion. The most important are the six written in the final decade of his life—the *Haffner* in D, the *Linz* in C, the *Prague* in D, and the three composed in 1788. The last three, significantly, were never performed during Mozart's lifetime. They were composed for no specific occasion but from inner necessity—a momentous departure in an age when artists wrote only on commission. They came into being because the composer had something in him that had to be said, no matter who heard.

But the central current in Mozart's art that nourished all the others was opera. Here were embodied his joy in life, his melancholy, all the impulses of his many-faceted personality. None has ever surpassed his power to delineate character in music and to make his puppets come alive. No one solved more masterfully the age-old problems of opera— the balance of voice and orchestra, of recitative and aria, solos and ensembles, dramatic action and musical expressiveness. In Lorenzo da Ponte, an Italian-Jewish adventurer and poet who was one of the pic- turesque figures of the age (he ultimately emigrated to America, operated a distillery, taught Italian at Columbia College, and wrote a fascinating book of memoirs), Mozart found a librettist whose dramatic vitality was akin to his own. The collaboration produced three works: *The Marriage of Figaro*, which da Ponte adapted from the comedy of Beaumarchais satirizing the old regime; *Don Giovanni*, "the opera of all operas"; and *Così fan tutte*, which has been translated in a variety of ways from "So do all women" to "Girls will be girls!" These crown the history of classical *opera buffa*, just as *The Abduction from the Seraglio* and *The Magic Flute* bring to its apex the German *Singspiel* (song-play). The grandly human conception of Mozart's lyric theater unfolds under the mask of comedy—but comedy elevated, as in *Don Giovanni*, to encompass all human experience. Mozart's music brings to life the eighteenth-century world with its class distinctions, its amorous intrigue, its molding of the individual to a set pattern. Abounding in irony and satire, these masterworks reach beyond the gallant world of satin and lace whence they issued. They achieve what da Ponte set forth as his and Mozart's intention: "To paint faithfully and in full color the divers passions."

SYMPHONY NO. 40

It was in the summer of 1788, during the darkest period of his life, that Mozart in the space of a little over six weeks composed his last three symphonies: No. 39 in E-flat (K. 543); No. 40 in G minor (K. 550); and No. 41 in C, the *Jupiter* (K. 551). (The K. followed by a numeral included in the listing of Mozart's works refers to the catalogue of Ludwig Köchel, who enumerated them all in the order of their composition.)

The G-minor Symphony represents that aspect of Mozart's art which pointed to a new expressive goal in music. Along with several important works that preceded it, the symphony strikes a tenderly impassioned note. The fact that Mozart throughout his maturity moved steadily closer to this goal played its part in losing him the favor of an aristocracy to whom his music spoke in new and disquieting accents.

The first movement, in sonata form, plunges immediately into the tumultuous Allegro molto. The intense opening theme is played by the violins, establishing the home key of G minor. It flowers out of a three-note germ motive that is genuinely symphonic in its capacity for growth and development. Note the symmetrical phrase-structure of the melody.

A vigorous bridge passage leads into the contrasting key, the related major—B-flat. The second theme, shared by woodwinds and strings, provides an area of relaxation in the headlong drive of the movement. This serene melody is in direct contrast with the restlessness of the first subject.

The Codetta, in which we hear echoings of the germ motive, establishes the cadence in the foreign key. The Exposition is repeated.

The Development is brief and packed with action. It searches out the possibilities of the opening theme, concentrating on the three-note motive. There is modulation far afield. The principal melody appears in altered guise, revealing unsuspected aspects of its nature. Now it is heard in the bass, given out by bassoon and lower strings against a countermelody high above. Now it appears in the upper register. Suddenly we hear it in inversion. Never slackening in its course, the Development is crowned by the transition to the Recapitulation, one of those miraculous passages that only one figure in all of music could have written. With the reappearance of the initial theme we are back in the home key of G minor.

The Restatement follows the course of the first section. The bridge is expanded and circles about the home key. The second theme is shifted into G minor, taking on a strangely tender tone. The Coda energetically affirms the triumph of the home key.

The second movement is the Andante in E-flat, which is pitched on a less subjective level. It is almost as if the composer, having revealed more than he had intended, were retreating behind the formal elegance of the eighteenth-century style. The use of sonata-allegro form for a slow movement is a classical trait, one that keeps lyricism subservient to the demands of structure. Classical too is the independence of the instrumental lines as violas, second violins, then first violins enter in turn with the main subject.

Horn tone provides a background for the strings. There is Viennese grace in the characteristic dip of the melody in the answering phrase.

The theme unfolds amid an abundance of ornament in thirty-second notes. The Development has the dynamic quality that goes with the growth of themes. The transition to the Restatement is accomplished through a dialogue for woodwinds—bassoon, clarinets, flutes. *Andante*

here, as in the case of the Haydn symphonies, is to be understood in the eighteenth-century sense, meaning a "going" pace. The movement too often is dragged, which makes it seem overlong. With its ceremonious gestures and embellishments it looks back to the courtly refinement of an era that was drawing to a close.

The third movement in G minor recaptures the emotional tension of the first. In this minuet Mozart reaches out beyond the aristocratic dance that gave the movement its name. The opening section is marked by a type of nonsymmetrical phrase structure which appears in Mozart, as in Haydn, more frequently than is generally realized. Two phrases of three bars each are followed by a phrase of five measures and one of three.

The Trio, in G major, is in a relaxed mood, although there is no trace here of Haydn's down-to-earth jollity. Color becomes an element of form as oboe, flute, and bassoon in turn take the phrase. Horn tone is pitted against string. The Minuet is repeated da capo, giving a balanced three-part form in which each part consists of little sections that contrast with one another and are repeated.

The finale, Allegro molto, is a compact sonata form, abrupt and imperious. A tragic restlessness lurks beneath its polished surface. The first subject in G minor is of the upward bounding type dear to the classical era and known as a *rocket theme*. Note the symmetrical phrase-structure of the melody.

The contrasting theme in the related key of B-flat major provides the necessary foil in point of serenity and grace.

The Development is tense and resilient. The rocket motive is bandied about by various instruments that crowd upon one another in hurried imitation as they spin out a complex orchestral fabric. The Recapitulation presents the material again with certain changes, most important of which is the shifting of the second theme into the home key of G minor. From that moment of enchantment until the final cadence we witness the exciting spectacle of a great artist functioning at the summit of his powers.

SERENADE EINE KLEINE NACHTMUSIK (A LITTLE NIGHT MUSIC)

The elegance and delicacy of touch commonly associated with Mozart are embodied in this serenade for strings. The piece was composed, or at any rate written down, in a single day in August 1787. Intended for a festive occasion, it stems from the tradition of Viennese social music exemplified in the divertimento. The score calls for first and second violin, viola, 'cello, and bass, the last two doubling the same part. In performance there were probably several players to each part, so that this work (K. 525) stands between chamber and orchestral music. It is in four movements, compact, intimate, and beautifully proportioned.

The opening Allegro is a sonatina in G in 4/4. As was customary in music of this type, the first movement has a marchlike character—as if the musicians were arriving for their cheerful task. Second is the Romanze, an eighteenth-century andante that maintains the balance between lyricism and a pleasant reserve. The Minuet, marked Allegretto, is in G major and in regular four-bar structure. The rondo finale, Allegro, is in 2/2 in the home key of G, and is based on the alternation of a principal and subordinate theme. We have said that there is a rondo style as well as a rondo form. This is the perfect example, bright, jovial, and—a trait inseparable from this master—stamped with an aristocratic refinement.

In the music of Mozart subjective emotion is elevated to the plane of the universal. The restlessness and the longing are exorcised by the ideal loveliness of Apollonian art. It is the duality of this music, its trembling between laughter and tears, its noble serenity amid grief and pain, that constitutes its special magic. The classic and the romantic, the impassioned and the elegant fuse in a style of miraculous unity and control. Mozart is one of the supreme artists of all time; the voice of pure beauty in music, and probably the most sheerly musical composer that ever lived.

≥45≥
Ludwig van Beethoven (1770-1827)

"Freedom above all!"

BEETHOVEN belonged to the generation that received the full impact of the French Revolution. He was nourished by its vision of the freedom and dignity of the individual. The time, the place, and the personality combined to produce an artist sensitive in the highest degree to the impulses of the new century. He created the music of a heroic age and in accents never to be forgotten proclaimed its faith in the power of man to shape his destiny.

HIS LIFE

He was born in Bonn, in the Rhineland, where his father and grandfather were singers at the court of the Elector. The family situation was unhappy, the father being addicted to drink, and Ludwig at an early age was forced to take over the support of his mother and two younger brothers. At eleven and a half he was assistant organist in the court chapel. A year later he became harpsichordist in the Elector's orchestra. A visit to Vienna in his seventeenth year enabled him to play for Mozart. The youth improvised so brilliantly on a theme given him by the master that the latter remarked to his friends, "Keep an eye on him—he will make a noise in the world some day."

Arrangements were made some years later for him to study with Haydn in Vienna at the Elector's expense. He left his native town when he was twenty-two, never to return. One of his admirers, Count

Ludwig van Beethoven.

Waldstein, inscribed in his album at parting, "Work well and receive the spirit of Mozart from the hands of Haydn." Despite this sound advice the relationship between pupil and teacher left much to be desired. The aging Haydn was ruffled by the young man's volcanic temperament and independence of spirit. Beethoven worked with other masters, the most academic of whom declared that "he has learned nothing and will never do anything in decent style."

Meanwhile his powers as a pianist took the music-loving aristocracy by storm. He was made welcome in the great houses of Vienna by the powerful patrons whose names appear in the dedications of his works—

Prince Lichnowsky, Prince Lobkowitz, Count Razumovsky, and the rest. Archduke Rudolph, brother of the Emperor, became his pupil and devoted friend. These connoisseurs, no less than the public, were transported by his highly personal style of improvisation, by the wealth of his ideas, the novelty of their treatment, and the surging emotion behind them.

To this "princely rabble," as he called them, the young genius came —in an era of revolution—as a passionate rebel, forcing them to receive him as an equal and friend. "It is good to move among the aristocracy," he observed, "but it is first necessary to make them respect you." The day had passed of the artist in livery waiting in the antechamber for his instructions. Beethoven, sensitive and irascible, stood up for his rights. When a nobleman at the home of Count von Browne persisted in talking during his performance, he left off and in a loud voice remarked, "For such pigs I do not play!" Prince Lichnowsky, during the Napoleonic invasion, insisted that he play for some French officers. Beethoven stormed out of the palace in a rage, demolished a bust of Lichnowsky that was in his possession, and wrote to his exalted friend: "Prince! what you are, you are through the accident of birth. What I am, I am through my own efforts. There have been many princes and there will be thousands more. But there is only one Beethoven!" Such was the force of his personality that he was able to make the aristocrats about him accept this interesting proposition. Beneath the rough exterior they recognized an elemental power akin to a force of nature.

The growth of a middle-class public, of concert life, and of music publishing freed Beethoven from dependence on patrons. He was the first professional composer in the modern sense; the first, that is, to live off the sale of his works. At the age of thirty-one he was able to write, "I have six or seven publishers for each of my works and could have more if I chose. No more bargaining. I name my terms and they pay." A youthful exuberance pervades the first decade of his career, an almost arrogant consciousness of his strength. "Power is the morality of men who stand out from the mass, and it is also mine!" Thus spoke the individual, in the new era of individualism.

Then, as the young eagle was spreading his wings, fate struck in a vulnerable spot: he began to lose his hearing. His helplessness in the face of this affliction dealt a shattering blow to his pride. "Ah, how could I possibly admit an infirmity in the one sense that should have been more perfect in me than in others. A sense I once possessed in highest perfection. Oh I cannot do it!" As his deafness closed in on him— the first symptoms appeared when he was in his late twenties—it became the symbol of his terrible sense of apartness from other men; of all the defiance and insecurity and hunger for love that had rent him for as long as he could remember. "Forgive me when you see me draw back when I would gladly mingle with you. My misfortune is doubly painful because it must lead to my being misunderstood. For me there can be no recreation in the society of my fellows. I must live like an exile." His malady brought to a focus what was to become one of the main themes of the nineteenth century—the loneliness of man. Upon the mistaken advice of his doctors he retired in 1802 to the oppressive solitude of a summer resort outside Vienna called Heiligenstadt. A titanic struggle shook him, between the destructive forces in his soul and his desire to live and create. It was one of those searing experiences that either break a man or leave him stronger. "But little more and I would have put an end to my life. Only art it was that withheld me. Ah, it seemed impossible to leave the world until I had produced all that I felt called upon to produce, and so I endured this wretched existence."

It was slowly borne in on him that art must henceforth give him the happiness life withheld. Only through creation could he attain the victory of which fate had threatened to rob him. The will to struggle asserted itself; he fought his way back to health. "I am resolved to rise superior to every obstacle. With whom need I be afraid of measuring my strength? If possible I will bid defiance to my fate, although there will be moments in life when I will be the unhappiest of God's creatures . . . I will take Fate by the throat. It shall not overcome me. Oh how beautiful it is to be alive—would that I could live a thousand times!"

Having conquered the chaos within himself he came to believe that man could conquer chaos. This became the epic theme of his music: the progression from despair to conflict, from conflict to serenity, from serenity to triumph and joy. The revelation that had come to him through suffering was a welcome message to the world that was struggling to be born. The concept of man the master of his fate hit off the temper of the new middle-class society in its most dynamic phase. In giving expression to his personal faith Beethoven said what his generation most wanted to hear. He became the major prophet of the nineteenth century, the architect of its heroic vision of life. "I am the Bacchus who presses out the glorious wine for mankind. Whoever truly understands my music is freed thereby from the miseries that others carry about in them." He had stumbled on an idea that was to play a decisive part in nineteenth-century thought: the concept of art as refuge, as compensation for the shortcomings of reality; art as sublimation, atonement, faith—the idealized experience, the ultimate victory over life.

The remainder of his career was spent in an unremitting effort to subjugate the elements of his art to the expressive ideal he had set himself. Fellow musicians and critics might carp at the daring of his thoughts, but his victory was assured. A growing public, especially among the younger generation, responded to the powerful thrust of his music. His life was outwardly uneventful. There were the interminable quarrels with associates and friends—he grew increasingly suspicious and irritable, especially after he became totally deaf. There were the complicated dealings with his publishers, in which he displayed an impressive shrewdness; his turbulent love affairs (he never married); his high-handed interference in the affairs of his brothers; his tortured relationship with his nephew Carl, an ordinary young man upon whom he fastened a tyrannical affection. All these framed an inner life of extraordinary intensity, an unceasing spiritual development that reached down to ever profounder levels of insight and opened up new domains to tonal art.

Biographers and painters have made familiar the squat sturdy figure —he was five foot four, the same as that other conqueror of the age, Napoleon—walking hatless through the environs of Vienna, the bulging brow furrowed in thought, stopping now and again to jot down an idea in his sketchbook; an idea which, because he was forever deprived of its sonorous beauty, he envisioned all the more vividly in his mind. A ride in an open carriage in inclement weather brought on an attack of dropsy that proved fatal. He died in his fifty-seventh year, famous and revered.

HIS MUSIC

Beethoven is the supreme architect in music. His genius found expression in the structural type of thinking embodied in sonata and symphony. His was an instrumental conception. In this respect he differs from the masters who infused into the instruments the spirit of vocal melody. (It is no accident that his name is missing from the list of composers whose symphonic themes are converted year after year into popular songs.) The sketchbooks in which he worked out his ideas show how gradually they reached their final shape and how painstakingly he molded the material into its one inevitable form. It is significant that when he describes the creative process in himself he stresses the development of the idea. "I carry my thoughts within me long, often very long before I write them down. In doing this my memory stands me in such good stead that even years afterward I am sure not to forget a theme I have once grasped . . . As I know what I want, the fundamental idea never deserts me. It mounts, it grows in stature. I hear, I see the picture in its whole extent standing all of a piece before my spirit, and there remains for me only the task of writing it down."

Significant too is his comment regarding the source of his material. "You will ask where I get my ideas. I am not able to answer that question positively. They come directly, indirectly; I can grasp them with my hands. Out amid the freedom of nature, in the woods, on walks, in the silence of the night, early in the morning, called forth by such moods as in the minds of poets translate themselves into words, but in mine into tones that ring, roar, storm until at last they stand as notes before me."

Inheriting the grand form from Haydn and Mozart, he adapted it to his personal needs. His ideas required a spacious frame. He expanded the dimensions of the first movement, especially of the slow introduction, the coda, and the development section. He transformed the latter into the dynamic center of sonata form. His short incisive themes offer limitless opportunity for expansion and development. They unfold with volcanic energy and momentum. The slow movement became in his hands a hymnic adagio, the embodiment of Beethovenian pathos. He transformed minuet into scherzo, making it a movement of rhythmic energy ranging from "cosmic laughter" to mystery and wonder. He enlarged the rondo finale of the eighteenth century into a movement comparable in size and scope to the first, ending the symphony—as the new age required—on a note of triumph.

The piano occupied a central position in Beethoven's art. His thirty-two sonatas are an indispensable part of its literature, whether for the amateur pianist or concert artist. They are well called the pianist's New Testament, the Old being the *Well-Tempered Clavier* of Bach. Dynamic contrasts, explosive accents, opposition of low and high register, syncopation, and powerful crescendos are essential features of his idiom. Characteristic is his fondness for the theme and variations. Here he becomes the master builder, marshaling his inexhaustible wealth of ideas to fashion out of the simplest material a towering edifice.

In the symphony Beethoven found the ideal medium wherein to address mankind. His nine symphonies are spiritual dramas of universal appeal. Their sweep and tumultuous affirmation of life mark them a pinnacle of the rising democratic art. They are conceived on a scale too grand for the aristocratic salon; they demand the amplitude of the concert hall. The composer's personal tone is manifest in the first two symphonies. With the Third, the *Eroica*, he achieved the expanded architecture of his mature style. The work was originally dedicated to Napoleon, First Consul of the Republic, in whom he saw incarnated the spirit of revolution and the freedom of man. When the news came that Napoleon had proclaimed himself Emperor he was disenchanted. "He too is just like any other! Now he will trample on the rights of man and serve nothing but his own ambition." The embittered composer tore up the dedicatory page of the just-completed work and renamed it "Heroic Symphony to celebrate the memory of a great man." A conqueror himself—did he not once declare, "I too am a king!"—he understood the Corsican. "It is a great pity I do not comprehend the art of war as well as I do the art of music. I would conquer him!"

The Fifth Symphony has fixed itself in the popular mind as the archetype of all that a symphony is. The Seventh was regarded by Wagner as "the apotheosis of the dance." The Ninth, the *Choral* Symphony, strikes the searching tone of Beethoven's last period. The finale, in which soloists and chorus join with the orchestra, contains the famous line, "Be embraced, ye millions!" The choral movement is a setting of Schiller's Ode to Joy, a ringing prophecy of the time when "all men shall be brothers." In these works there sounds the rhetoric of the new century. Complementing them are the Fourth and Eighth, two buoyant and serene symphonies; and the Sixth, the hymn to nature known as the *Pastorale*.

The concerto offered Beethoven a congenial public form in which he combined virtuosity with symphonic architecture. Most popular of his works in this medium are the Fourth Piano Concerto in G, and the Fifth (the *Emperor*) in E-flat; and the noble Concerto for Violin in D. He wrote much chamber music, the string quartet being closest to his heart. His supreme achievements in this area are the last five quartets which, together with the Grand Fugue, Op. 133, occupied the final years of his life. In these, as in the last five piano sonatas, Beethoven found his way to a skeletal language from which all nonessentials had been rigidly pared—a language far transcending his time. The master's gaze is focused within, encompassing depths that music never before had plumbed.

Although his most important victories were won in the instrumental field, Beethoven enriched the main types of vocal music. Of his songs the best known is the cycle of six *An die Ferne Geliebte* (To the Distant Beloved). His sole opera *Fidelio* (originally called *Leonora*) centers about wifely devotion, human freedom, and the defeat of those who would destroy it. There is much memorable music in it. All the same, Beethoven's imagination was hampered by the trappings of the stage. He is at his most dramatic in abstract forms. Although the pious Haydn considered him an atheist, he hymned "Nature's God" through the traditional form of religious music. The *Missa Solemnis* (Solemn Mass) in D ranks in importance with the Ninth Symphony and the final quartets, although its length makes it impracticable for use in the church. Beethoven's altar is the world, his faith embraces all creeds. Above the Kyrie of the mass he wrote a sentence that applies to the whole of his music: "From the heart . . . may it find its way to the heart."

His creative activity, extending over a span of thirty-five years, bears witness to a ceaseless striving after perfection. "I feel as if I had written scarcely more than a few notes," he remarked at the end of his career. And a year before his death: "I hope still to bring a few great works into the world." Despite his faith in his destiny he knew the humility of the truly great. "The real artist has no pride. Unfortunately he sees that his art has no limits, he feels obscurely how far he is from the goal. And while he is perhaps being admired by others he mourns the fact that he has not yet reached the point to which his better genius like a distant sun ever beckons him."

THE FIFTH SYMPHONY

The most popular of all symphonies, Beethoven's Fifth in C minor, Op. 67, is also the most concentrated expression of the frame of mind and spirit that we have come to call Beethovenian. It embodies in supreme degree the basic principle of symphonic thinking—the flowering of an extended composition from a kernel or germ theme by a process of organic growth. The popular story that Beethoven, when asked for the meaning of the opening theme, replied, "Thus Fate knocks at the door," is probably not authentic. Such literalness seems unlikely in one who was so completely the tone poet. If the work continues to be associated with Fate it is rather because of the inevitable, the relentless logic of its unfolding.

The first movement, marked Allegro con brio (lively, with vigor) springs out of the rhythmic idea of "three shorts and a long" that dominates the symphony. Announced in unison by strings and clarinet

(Beethoven holds his full forces in reserve), the motive establishes the home key of C minor. It is the most compact and commanding gesture in the whole symphonic literature.

Out of this motive flowers the first theme, which is nothing more than a repetition, at different levels of the scale and with altered intervals, of the germinating rhythm.

The power of the movement springs from the almost terrifying single-mindedness with which the underlying idea is pursued. It is rhythm, torrential yet superbly controlled, that is the generating force behind this "storm and stress." Beethoven here achieved a vehemence that was new in music. We reach an area of relaxation in the lyric second theme, in the related key of E-flat major. Yet even here the headlong course of the movement does not slacken. As the violins, then clarinets sound the gentle melody in the treble, the 'cellos and double basses persist with the "three shorts and a long" in the bass.

Basic rhythm

The Development is a tightly knit fabric woven out of the basic rhythm. Characteristic of Beethoven's style are the powerful contrasts between soft and loud. The retransition to the home key culminates in a fortissimo proclamation of the underlying rhythm by full orchestra. Before the Restatement gets under way, a note of pathos is introduced by the oboe solo, which momentarily slackens the tension. The second theme is transposed into C major. There is an extended coda in which the basic rhythm reveals a new fund of explosive energy, and the movement ends with an affirmation of the home key.

Beethovenian serenity and strength imbue the second movement, Andante con moto (at a going pace, with movement). The key is A-flat; the form, a theme and variations. There are two melodic ideas. First is a broadly spun theme sung by violas and 'cellos. It is followed

by one of those hymnic upward thrusting subjects so characteristic of the master, which echoes the "three shorts and a long" of the opening movement.

In this Andante the constructive impulse prevails over the lyrical. It is not a romantic slow movement; rather is it classical in its reserve, its symphonic drive, its architectural cohesion.

Beethoven varies the opening melody by embellishing it first in sixteenth, then in thirty-second notes. The second theme is varied in color, dynamics, register, and type of accompaniment, gathering strength until it is affirmed triumphantly by the full orchestra. The Coda opens with a motive on the bassoon against syncopated chords in the strings. A dynamic crescendo rounds off the movement.

Third in the cycle of movements is the Allegro in 3/4 which returns to the somber C minor that is the home key of the work. This is a genuinely symphonic scherzo marked by rhythmic élan. From the depths of the bass rises a characteristic subject, a rocket theme played by 'cellos and double basses.

The first eight notes are identical with those of the last movement of Mozart's G-minor Symphony. Beethoven was aware of the resemblance, for he copied out the Mozart theme in his sketchbook opposite his own. Our "tune detectives" who specialize in such discoveries fail to point out that the important thing in such cases is not the theme but its destiny—what the composer does with it. Because of differences in rhythm, mood, and treatment, Beethoven's movement—despite the re-semblance of theme—is as far removed as could be from Mozart's.

The "three shorts and a long" reappear fortissimo in the horns. The Trio is based on a gruffly humorous motive of running eighth notes stated in the bass by 'cellos and double basses and imitated in turn, in ever higher register, by violas, second violins, and first violins.

The motive of the double basses was described by Berlioz in a cele-brated phrase as the "gambols of a frolicsome elephant." Beethoven's cosmic laughter resounds through these measures: a laughter that shakes—and builds—a world.

The Scherzo returns in a modified version, followed by a transition that leads directly into the fourth movement. This highly dramatic passage, punctuated by the mysterious tapping of the kettledrum, is spun out of the scherzo theme and the basic rhythm. There is a steady accumulation of tension until the orchestra, in a blaze of light, surges into the triumphal Allegro in C major.

Beethoven's changes of mode are instructive. The first movement is in a somber minor. The second, with its classical serenity, is in major. The third, save for the jovial Trio, returns to minor. Now the dark C minor is dispelled for good by the opening fanfare of the finale. At this point three instruments make their appearance in symphonic music that were previously used only in opera—piccolo, double bassoon, and trombone, lending brilliance and body to the orchestral sound.

The fourth movement is a monumental sonata form in which Beethoven overcomes what would seem to be an insuperable difficulty: to fashion an ending that will sustain the tension of what has gone before. Actually the ideas are less striking than those of the earlier movements. What carries the work to its victorious end is the rhythmic energy, the bigness of conception, and the orchestral sonority. The main idea is based on a chord-and-scale pattern. This theme and a transitional sub-

ject are in C major, as opposed to a vigorous theme group in G. The Restatement is followed by an extensive coda fashioned from materials already heard. The pace accelerates up to the concluding Presto, with a final appearance of the basic rhythm in the lower strings. The symphonic stream becomes at the very end an overpowering torrent as the tonic chord—prime source and goal of all activity—is hurled forth by the orchestra over and over again.

Chronologically Beethoven's life fell in almost equal parts in the eighteenth and nineteenth centuries. His career bridged the transition from the old society to the new. The romantics, responding to the grand rhetoric and sweep of his music, claimed him as one of their own. It is a mistake to regard him thus. He was not "the man who freed music"—presumably from the shackles imposed on it by Haydn and Mozart. On the contrary, he brought the great classical forms to their ultimate development in terms of logical structure and power. However, into these forms he injected the dynamic force and expressiveness that were the essence of the new century. He was the spokesman of the rising age of individualism. The sum of his message was freedom. By freedom, though, he understood not romantic license but the Hegelian "recognition of necessity," not romantic revolt but the inner discipline that alone constitutes freedom. This exalted conception he projected with such intensity of vision and mastery of means that his shadow lengthened across the next hundred years.

Beethoven is the orator of the democratic era. His music stems from a Promethean struggle for self-realization. It is the expression of a titanic force, the affirmation of an all-conquering will.

⩓46⩓

Classical Chamber Music

"No other form of music can delight our senses with such exquisite beauty of sound, or display so clearly to our intelligence the intricacies and adventures of its design."

Henry Hadow

By *chamber music* is meant ensemble music for from two to about eight or nine instruments with one player to the part, as distinct from orchestral music in which there are several players for each part. The essential trait of chamber music is its intimacy and refinement; its natural setting is the home. In this domain we find neither the surge and thunder of the symphony nor the grand gesture of the operatic stage. The drama is of an inward kind. Each instrument represents an ideal type and is expected to assert itself to the full; but the style of playing differs from that of the solo virtuoso. The soloist is encouraged to exalt his own personality. In chamber music, on the other hand, the various instruments blend into a perfect whole. It has been said that in no other kind of music is it so difficult to create a masterpiece. Certainly in no other kind is the texture (and the composer) so exposed.

The classical era saw the golden age of chamber music. Haydn and Mozart, Beethoven and Schubert established the true chamber-music style, which is in the nature of a friendly conversation among equals. Limpid harmony and chiseled form, clarity of thought and freshness of feeling characterize their enchantingly subtle art. In their chamber music the Viennese masters addressed themselves to a limited audience of friends and connoisseurs of music. They attained thereby a degree of personal utterance not possible in the large public forms of musical communication such as the opera and oratorio, symphony and concerto. Some of their profoundest thoughts are to be discovered in their chamber works.

The central position in classical chamber music was held by the string quartet. Consisting of first and second violins, viola and 'cello, this group came to represent the ideal type of happy comradeship among instruments, lending itself to music of exquisite detail and purity of style. Other favored combinations were the duo sonata—piano and violin or piano and 'cello; the trio—piano, violin, and 'cello; and the quintet, consisting of string quartet and solo instruments such as the piano or clarinet. The age produced, too, some memorable examples of chamber music for the larger groups—sextet, septet, and octet.

HAYDN: STRING QUARTET IN F, OPUS 3, NO. 5

Haydn was in his early twenties when he wrote his first string quartet. He was past seventy when he commenced his last. His approximately eighty works in this medium testify to a half century of artistic growth.

The six quartets of Opus 3 were written some time after 1760, during his first years in the service of the Esterházys. They mark the transition from his early manner to a more mature style. The fifth of the set contains an andante cantabile that for generations has been a favorite with the public. Often heard separately and known as the Serenade, the movement is based on one of those indestructible tunes that bear the imprint of a composer's melodic genius. The first violin carries the melody against a pizzicato accompaniment by the other strings. The

movement, in 4/4 time, is a two-part form. The first part proceeds from C major to G, the second returns to C. One has but to hear it to realize how important an element of Haydn's art was Austrian popular song.

This Andante is the second movement. The first is a Presto in F in 3/8, bright, gay, and uncomplicated, with a flow of artless melody within a clear sonata form. The third movement, the Minuet, is in F. It opens with a four-bar phrase which is answered by one of six. Such a nonsymmetrical formation, we have noticed, is as closely related to the classical style as are the usual symmetries of four-bar construction. The finale is a rondo marked Scherzando (gaily, jestingly), in 2/4. Here the spirit of *opera buffa* holds sway. In a movement such as this may be discerned, fully formed, the line of thought and feeling that culminated in the great rondo finales of the master's last period.

MOZART: QUINTET FOR CLARINET AND STRINGS

The spirit of Viennese house-music pervades this celebrated quintet (K. 581). The work is based on the opposition between two protagonists—the clarinet, which because of its striking tone is the center of attention, and the string group. Mozart brings into play all the qualities of the clarinet, its capacity for broad singing melody as well as its agility in ornate virtuoso passages that run the gamut from low to high register.

The first movement is an ample sonata-allegro. The opening theme has a sweet serenity. Introduced by the strings, it is set off by arpeggios on the clarinet. The second theme displays the exquisite songfulness of the Mozartian cantabile. It is presented by the second violin and shifted into minor when the clarinet takes it over, imparting to the movement a

romantic tone. The development section lends itself to animated rivalry between clarinet and strings, after which the thematic material is restated.

The Larghetto, in D, is a broadly spun song for clarinet against a background of muted strings. Mozart here captures the spirit of his great operatic arias. The middle section contains an exciting dialogue between clarinet and first violin. Then the aria returns.

The Minuet, in the home key of A major, has two trios instead of one. After each, the Minuet is repeated da capo. The first in A minor is for strings alone. The second trio, emphasizing the clarinet, is based on one of those bouncy arpeggio themes that so vividly capture the buoyancy of Austrian popular dance. Here is the spirit of the ländler, the peasant dance from which descended the Viennese waltz.

The finale, an Allegretto in A, is a theme and variations. The melody is of utmost simplicity, to allow room for elaboration; yet it is stamped with aristocratic refinement. The variations include embellishment of the melody; a change to triplet rhythm in the accompaniment; a new melody spun over the harmonies of the old; the original theme heard against florid arabesques; and a change of pace—and character—first to adagio, finally to allegro. This is music in the great tradition.

Chamber music, because of its nature, has never commanded the wide public of symphony, opera, or oratorio. There was a time not so long ago when it was considered to be accessible only to the connoisseur. But the impact of radio and recordings upon our musical life has helped to change all this. Recognized as an ideal music for the home, it has been made familiar to the American public through frequent broadcasts of both live and recorded chamber groups, with the result that it now occupies its rightful place in our musical scene. It holds out to the listener a quite special musical experience, and offers him delights that no other branch of music can duplicate.

From Classic to Romantic: Schubert's *Unfinished*

"I am very greatly obliged by the diploma of honorary membership you so kindly sent me. May it be the reward of my devotion to the art of music to become wholly worthy of such a distinction one day. In order to give musical expression to my sincere gratitude as well, I shall take the liberty before long of presenting your honorable Society with one of my symphonies in full score."

WE DISCUSSED the songs and piano pieces of Franz Schubert in connection with the romantic movement, whose first stirrings found in them so vivid an expression. In his symphonies, however, as in his chamber music, Schubert was the heir of the classical Viennese tradition. For this reason we consider his most celebrated symphony in a section devoted to the achievements of Haydn, Mozart, and Beethoven. The work forms the natural link between their music and the romantic era.

The title *Unfinished* which attaches to Schubert's Symphony No. 8 in B minor is somewhat unfortunate, suggesting as it does that the composer was snatched away by death before he could complete it. Actually the work was written when Schubert was twenty-five years old, in 1822, and was sent to the Styrian Musical Society in the town of Graz in fulfillment of the promise made in the letter just quoted. He completed two movements and sketched the opening measures of a scherzo. Given his facility, a work was no sooner conceived than written down; if he abandoned the task in this instance it was probably because he had said all that he had to say. The Symphony in B minor is no more unfinished than those sonatas of Beethoven that contain only two movements. It is a superb artistic entity in which Schubert adapts the conventional symphonic scheme to his own purpose.

The work displays his radiant orchestral sonority, his power of making the instruments sing, his unique handling of woodwinds and brass. The wonder is all the greater when we remember that Schubert never heard his finest symphonic scores. The B-minor Symphony, for example, was never performed during his lifetime. The manuscript lay gathering dust for more than thirty-five years after his death.

The first movement, Allegro moderato, is based on three ideas. The first, in the nature of an introductory theme, establishes the home key

of B minor. It emerges out of the lower register in a mysterious pianissimo, played by 'cellos and double basses.

The second is a broadly curved melody in the home key, given out by
oboes and clarinets over the restless accompaniment of the strings. The
downward leap from the opening note imparts to the melodic line a
characteristically Schubertian poignancy.

Third is the great lyric theme in G major, sung by 'cellos against syncopated chords in the clarinets and violas. Extraordinary is the broad
arch traced by the forward surge of this melody, which circles about
and repeats itself in a way that sets at nought the accepted rules of
melody writing. The intuitions of genius transcend the rules.

A codetta derived from this theme rounds off the Exposition and establishes the contrasting key of G major.

The development section is remarkable for its architectonic force, its
dramatic intensity and momentum. With sure symphonic instinct Schubert picks what seems like the least promising of his themes—the first
—for expansion and working out. The idea reveals its latent energies
in a symphonic fabric that grows steadily in power and impetus. Now
it is presented by the lower strings and imitated in the upper. Now a
fragment flowers into new lines of thought. The violent contrasts between loud and soft, between high and low intensify a drama that is
conceived and executed in wholly symphonic terms. Characteristic is
the way that ideas are broken off abruptly, only to resume with greater
force. Altogether novel is Schubert's use of the sumptuous resonance
of the trombones, which he pits against the woodwinds, the one answering the other against a turbulent string background. The constructive logic and symphonic verve of this development bespeak the high
classical tradition.

The Recapitulation restates the material of the first section. The lyric theme of the 'cellos is transposed to D, the major key most closely related to the home key of B minor. The Coda brings back the opening idea, so that the movement ends with the germ theme out of which it flowered.

The second movement in E major is marked Andante con moto (at a going pace, with movement), in spite of which conductors persist in taking it at a drawn-out adagio that is utterly out of character. How romantic a sonority is that of the opening chords on bassoons and horns against a descending pizzicato on the double basses, out of which the principal motive emerges in the strings.

An orchestral crescendo leads to the next idea in the related key of C-sharp minor. This is a long-breathed song introduced by clarinet and answered by oboe against syncopated chords in the strings. The melody undergoes an exciting symphonic expansion. Thereafter, the two ideas are repeated, so that the movement is a four-section structure (A-B-A-B) capped by a coda. There are subtle changes of color in the repetition. This time, for example, it is the oboe that introduces the broadly curved second idea and the clarinet that answers.

Schubert's *Unfinished* reveals, in relation to the classical age, nothing less than a new world of sound. Its harmonies are poetically expressive; its delicate coloring stems from a most subtle differentiation between the different instrumental voices. Its melodic imagery is of surpassing power and breadth. The prodigal creator of this music passed his uneventful life in the city of Beethoven; too diffident to approach the great man, he worshiped from afar. He could not know that of all the composers of his time, his name alone would be linked to that of his idol. They who far surpassed him in fame and worldly success are long forgotten. Today we speak of the four masters of the classical Viennese school: Haydn, Mozart, Beethoven—and Schubert.

PART FIVE

The Older Music

❧

"Music was originally discreet, seemly, simple, masculine, and of good morals. Have not the moderns rendered it lascivious beyond measure?"

Jacob of Liége (fourteenth century)

≫48≪

Harmony and Counterpoint: Musical Texture

IN WRITINGS on music we encounter frequent references to the fabric or texture. Such comparisons between music and cloth are not as unreasonable as may at first appear. Both are composed of threads woven together in such a way as to create patterns against a background. The weave of the musical fabric may be one of several types.

MONOPHONIC TEXTURE

The simplest is *monophonic* or single-voice texture. Here the melody is heard without a harmonic accompaniment. Attention is focused on the single line. All music up to about a thousand years ago, of which we have any record, was monophonic. To this day the music of the oriental world—Chinese, Japanese, Hindu, Javanese, Balinese, and Arabic—is largely monophonic. The melody may be accompanied by a variety of rhythm and percussion instruments that embellish it, but there is no third dimension of depth or perspective such as harmony alone confers upon a melody. To make up for this lack the single line, being the sole bearer of musical meaning, takes on great complexity and finesse. The monophonic music of the Orient boasts subtleties of pitch and refinements of rhythm unknown in our music.

The great heritage of the monophonic period in Western music is *Gregorian chant* (also known as *plainchant* or *plainsong*), the age-old liturgical music of the Catholic Church, which was conceived as pure melody without a harmonic background. This was descended from the music of the Greeks and Hebrews. The task of assembling the chants into an organized liturgy spread over several generations, but is associated chiefly with Pope Gregory the Great, who reigned from 590 to 604. Gregorian chant consists of a freely flowing vocal line subtly attuned to the inflections of the Latin text. It is free from regular accent and embodies what may be called prose rhythm in music, or free-verse rhythm (as distinguished from metrical-poetry rhythm, such as we find in the regularly accented measures of two-four or three-four time). Untrammeled by regular phrase structure, the continuous, undulating vocal line of Gregorian chant is the counterpart in sound of the sinuous traceries of Romanesque art and architecture. The Gregorian melodies —there are over three thousand of them—have nourished fifteen hun-

Romanesque ivory carving.

"The undulating vocal line of Gregorian chant is the counterpart in sound
of the sinuous traceries of Romanesque art."

dred years of European folk, popular, and art music. They bring us as close as we shall ever come to the lost musical art of the Mediterranean world—the monophonic art of ancient Greece, Syria, and Palestine.

POLYPHONIC TEXTURE

When two or more melodic lines are combined we have a *polyphonic* or many-voiced texture. Here the music derives its expressive power and its interest from the interplay of the several lines. Polyphonic texture is based on counterpoint. This term comes from the Latin *punctus contra punctum*, "dot against dot" or "note against note"—that is to say, one line against the other. Counterpoint is the art and science of combining several lines or voices into a unified musical fabric. "Contrapuntal" and "polyphonic" are used in a general sense as synonyms. Strictly speaking, they are not. We have polyphonic music when several people harmonize a melody. It is only when each of the parts has a melodic and rhythmic life of its own that we have true counterpoint.

It was a little over a thousand years ago that European musicians hit upon the device of combining two or more lines simultaneously. (Folk music had known this procedure a long time before.) At this point Western art music parted company from the monophonic Orient. There ensued a magnificent flowering of polyphonic art that came to its high point in the fifteenth and sixteenth centuries. This development of contrapuntal technique was tied up with the predominance of religious choral music.

HOMOPHONIC TEXTURE

In the third type of texture a single voice takes over the melodic interest while the accompanying voices surrender their individuality and become blocks of harmony, the chords that support, color, and enhance the principal part. Here we have a single-melody-with-chords or *homophonic* texture. Again the listener's interest is directed to a single line; but this line, unlike that of oriental music, is conceived in relation to a succession of chords. Homophonic texture is familiar to all; we hear it when the pianist plays the melody with his right hand while the left sounds the chords, or when the singer or violinist carries the tune against a harmonic accompaniment on the piano.

We have said that melody is the horizontal aspect of music while harmony is the vertical. The comparison with the warp and woof of a fabric consequently has real validity. The horizontal threads, the melodies, are held together by the vertical threads, the harmonies. **Out of their interaction comes a weave that may be light or heavy, coarse or fine.**

The several types of texture are apparent from the look of the music on the page.

a) Monophonic Gregorian Chant

Do - mi - ne De - us   Rex coe -   le -   stis   De - us   Pa -

ter   om -   ni - po -   tens

b) Polyphonic - Chorus from Messiah

c) Homophonic - Chopin Waltz

Types of musical texture.

Although we draw a distinction between the contrapuntal and harmonic aspects of music, they exist side by side. Suppose a vocal quartet to be harmonizing a tune. We hear a single melody with chords underneath—that is to say, vertical blocks of sound. Yet each of the singers as he moves from one chord to the next follows his own horizontal line. Similarly in polyphonic music, no matter how intricate the interplay of the horizontal lines, at any given point they all form a vertical block or chord. The difference between the two textures is one of emphasis. When the composer centers interest on the movement of the separate voices, the texture is said to be polyphonic. When he gives precedence to the harmonic or vertical aspect, we have homophonic or chordal texture. Needless to say there are innumerable gradations between the two extremes.

A composition need not be exclusively in one texture or the other. For example, a symphonic movement may present a theme against a homophonic texture. In the development section, however, the texture is apt to become increasingly contrapuntal. So, too, in a homophonic piece the composers may enhance the effect of the principal melody through an interesting play of counterthemes and counterrhythms in the accompanying parts. This is the case in the best orchestral music of the classic-romantic period.

Texture helps to determine the overall effect of the music. On the one hand the composer avoids a fabric that will be too simple and lacking in interest. On the other he exercises caution lest the texture grow so complex that it will distract from or even overshadow the main line. The music of certain composers is noted for lightness and transparency of texture: Mozart in the eighteenth century, Mendelssohn in the nineteenth, Stravinsky in the twentieth. The music of others, such as Brahms and Sibelius, is characterized by a heavy texture. The problem of texture is related too to the general style of an era. There was a great shifting of interest from polyphonic to homophonic music around the year 1600. Contrapuntal and harmonic texture existed side by side, the one influencing the other. After 1750 and throughout the classic-romantic period, composers emphasized the harmonic aspect of music over the contrapuntal. We may sum up the various periods of music history, from the standpoint of texture, as follows.

Pre-10th-century:	monophonic
c. 1000–1600:	polyphonic
1600–1750:	polyphonic-harmonic
1750–1900:	homophonic. Contrapuntal procedures absorbed into orchestral and chamber-music style, and of course choral music
1900– :	revival of interest in contrapuntal texture

We have studied the sonata-symphony and other forms that stemmed out of the homophonic-harmonic period. In subsequent chapters we will examine the great forms of polyphonic music.

DEVICES OF COUNTERPOINT

When several independent lines are combined, composers try to give unity and shape to the texture. A basic procedure for achieving this

end is *imitation,* in which a subject or motive is presented in one voice
and then duplicated in another. While the imitating voice restates the
theme, the first voice goes on to a countersubject. This duplication of
an idea—at different times and pitches—by all the voice parts is musically most effective. It is of the essence in contrapuntal thinking. We
have spoken of the vertical and horizontal threads in musical texture.
To these imitation adds a third, the diagonal, as is apparent from the
next example.

How long is the statement that is to be imitated? This varies considerably. It may be the entire length of a voice part that runs from the

beginning to end of a piece. Or the imitation may occur intermittently.
When the whole length of a voice part is imitated, we have a strict
type of composition known as a *canon.* The name comes from the
Greek word for "law" or "order." Each phrase heard in the leading
voice is repeated almost immediately in an imitating voice throughout
the length of the work. The most popular form of canon is the round,
in which each voice enters in succession with the same melody. Composers do not often cast an entire piece or movement in the shape of a
canon. What they do is to use canonic imitation as an effect in all sorts
of pieces. The example just given of diagonal texture shows canonic
imitation as it occurs in the final movement of César Franck's Sonata
for Violin and Piano.

Contrapuntal writing is marked by a number of devices that have
flourished for centuries. *Inversion* is a species of imitation in which the
melody is turned upside down; that is, it follows the same intervals
but in the opposite direction. Where the melody originally moved up
by a third, the inversion moves down a third. Where it descended by a
fourth, it now ascends a fourth. Thus, D-E-F inverted becomes D-C-B.
Augmentation consists of imitating a theme in longer time values. A
quarter note may become a half, a half note a whole, and so on. In consequence, the theme in its new version sounds slower. *Diminution* con-

sists of imitating a theme in shorter time values. A whole note may become a half, a half note a quarter; which makes the theme in its new version sound faster. *Retrograde*, also known as *cancrizans* or *crab motion*, means to imitate the melody backwards. If the original sequence of notes reads B-D-G-F, the imitation reads F-G-D-B. Retrograde-and-inversion imitates the theme by turning it upside down and backwards. These devices of sixteenth-century counterpoint have been revived in contemporary music, especially by Arnold Schoenberg and his school.

Counterpoint has always been regarded as one of the most advanced of compositional techniques. It represents the intellectual and structural element in music. It has appealed to certain composers and listeners as the purest type of musical expression, the ultimate in abstraction and refinement of thought. Nor need it be supposed that the procedures we have outlined reduce music to a cut-and-dried manipulation of notes. True, one may build a contrapuntal structure by applying the correct technical procedures, but to fill such a construction with poetry and emotion requires an imagination of the first order and sovereign mastery of the means of musical expression.

MUSICAL TEXTURE AND THE LISTENER

The different types of texture require different kinds of listening. Homophonic music poses no special problem to the music lover. He is able to differentiate between the principal melody and its attendant harmonies, and to follow their interrelation. He is helped in this by the fact that most of the music we hear from the time of our childhood consists of melody and chords.

The case is different with polyphonic music, which is not apt to appeal to those who listen with half an ear. Here we must be aware of the independent lines as they flow alongside each other. Polyphonic music requires greater concentration on the part of the listener. Only by dint of repeated hearings do we learn to follow the individual voices and to separate each from the contrapuntal web.

As an exercise in listening contrapuntally let us take a simple example, the chorale *Christ lag in Todesbanden* (Christ lay in Death's Dark Prison) as it is presented in the third verse of Bach's cantata of that name. We shall consider this music in a later chapter. For our present purpose let us hear the chorale in Stokowski's orchestral arrangement, which assigns the three lines to different instruments, making it easier for the ear to follow their interplay. The melody is carried by the trombones, briefly by the 'cellos, and then by the trombones again, mainly in quarter notes. The lower strings play the bass line, for the most part in eighth notes. Against this the violins play a florid counterpoint in sixteenth notes. The three lines are distinct not only in rhythm and color but also in register. The bass part is low, the violin counterpoint is high in the treble, and the chorale marches resonantly in the middle distance. It is well to listen to the piece several times, concentrating first on each voice alone, then on any two, finally on all three. One becomes aware, in following the three planes of movement, of the illusion of space which it is the unique capacity of counterpoint to create; of the fascinating tensions, both musical and psychological, brought into being by the simultaneous unfolding of several lines.

Contrapuntal music does not yield its secrets as readily as do the less severe kinds. By the same token it challenges our attention and holds our interest. With each rehearing we seem to discover another of its facets.

❧ 49 ❧

The Baroque

"Nothing is beautiful but the true. The true alone is to be loved."
Boileau (1636–1711)

THE PERIOD of the Baroque stretched across a turbulent century and a half of European history. It opened shortly before the year 1600, a convenient signpost that need not be taken too literally; and may be regarded as having come to a close with the death of Bach in 1750.

The term *baroque* was probably derived from the Portuguese *barroco*, a pearl of irregular shape much used in the jewelry of the time. During the nineteenth century the word acquired a derogatory sense, indicating a style that was ornate and showy. The notion prevailed that the painting, sculpture, and architecture of the Baroque represented a debasing of the pure Renaissance style. Since then a more just estimate has been arrived at. Baroque now stands for one of the great style periods in European art.

The Baroque is of special interest to present-day music lovers, for it is the first period to be consistently represented in the concert repertory. The twentieth century has witnessed a great revival of interest in the forms of baroque music and in neglected masters such as Claudio Monteverdi (1567–1643), Jean-Baptiste Lully (1632–1687), Henry Purcell (1659–1695), and Antonio Vivaldi (1676–1741). The century and a half of baroque art divides itself into three fifty-year periods: early, middle, and late Baroque. As public interest until recently concentrated on the late phase, many came to think of Bach and Handel as the first great composers. Viewed against the total panorama of their era, these masters are seen rather to have been the heirs of an old and surpassingly rich tradition.

The period 1600–1750 bridged the transition from the Renaissance to the modern era. It was a time of change and adventure. The conquest of the New World stirred the imagination and filled the coffers of the Old. The middle classes gathered wealth and power in their struggle against the aristocracy. Empires clashed for mastery of the world. Appalling poverty and wasteful luxury, magnificent idealism and savage oppression—against contradictions such as these unfolded the pomp and splendor of baroque art: an art bold of gesture and conception; vigorous, decorative, monumental.

The transition from the classically minded Renaissance to the Baroque was foreshadowed by Michelangelo (1475–1564). His turbulent figures, their torsos twisted in struggle, reflect the baroque love of the dramatic. The dome he designed for St. Peter's in Rome embodies baroque striving for the grandiose. In like fashion the Venetian school of painters—Titian, Tintoretto, Veronese—captured the dynamic spirit of the new age. Their crowded canvases are ablaze with color and movement. They glory in the tension of opposing masses. They dramatize the diagonal. Their rows upon rows of columns open on limitless vistas.

The Baroque was the era of absolute monarchy. Princes throughout Europe took as their model the splendor of Versailles. Louis XIV's famous "I am the State!" summed up a way of life in which all art and culture served the cult of the ruler. Courts large and small maintained elaborate musical establishments including opera troupes, chapel choirs, and orchestras.

The Baroque was also an age of reason. Adventurers more bold than the conquistadors set forth upon the uncharted sea of knowledge. The findings of Kepler, Galilei, and Copernicus in physics and astronomy, of Descartes in mathematics and Spinoza in philosophy, were so many milestones in the intellectual history of Europe. Harvey discovered the circulation of the blood. Locke laid the foundation for a scientific

Claudio Monteverdi.

study of the workings of the mind. Newton's theory of gravitation revealed a universe based upon law and order. The growing towns and
cities were centers of a forward looking culture. Descartes expressed
the confidence of a brave new world when he wrote, "Provided only
that we abstain from receiving anything as true which is not so, there
can be nothing so remote that we cannot reach to it, nor so obscure that
we cannot discover it."

Excluded from the salons of the aristocracy, the middle classes created a culture of their own. Their music-making centered about the home, the church, and the university group (known as *collegium musicum*). For them came into being the comic opera, which like the prose novel was filled with keen and witty observation of life. For them painting forsook its grandiose themes and turned to intimate scenes of bourgeois life. The leaders of the Dutch school—Vermeer, Franz Hals, Ruysdael—embodied the vitality of a new burgher art that reached its high point in Rembrandt (1609–69), a master whose insights penetrated the recesses of the soul. Under the leadership of merchant princes and financiers, the culture of the city came to rival that of the palace. These new connoisseurs vied with the court in their love of splendor, responding to the opulence of baroque art, to the sensuous beauty of brocade and velvet, marble and jewels and precious metals. This aspect of the Baroque finds expression in the art of Peter Paul Rubens (1577–1640), whose canvases exude a driving energy, a reveling in life. His voluptuous nudes incarnate the seventeenth-century ideal of feminine beauty. He himself was a symbol of the rising order: rugged individualist, dreamer, and man of action; entrepreneur and conqueror all in one.

The Baroque was an intensely devout period. Religion was a rallying cry on some of the bloodiest battlefields in history. The Protestant camp included England, Scandinavia, Holland, and the north German cities, all citadels of the rising middle class. On the Catholic side were the two powerful dynasties, Hapsburg and Bourbon, who fought one another no less fiercely than they did their Protestant foes. After decades of struggle, the might of the Spanish-Hapsburg empire was broken. France emerged as the leading state on the Continent; Germany was in ruins; England rose to world power. Europe was ready to advance to the stage of modern industrial society.

Protestant culture was rooted in the Bible. Its emphasis upon the individual promoted a personal tone and strengthened the romantic tendency in the Baroque. Milton (1608–74) in *Paradise Lost* produced the poetic epic of the Protestant world view, even as Dante three and a half centuries earlier had produced that of the Catholic. Bunyan in *Pilgrim's Progress* traced the spiritual journey of the common man. The heroic hymn tunes of the Reformation nourished the profoundly spiritual art of Bach. The oratorios of Handel harnessed baroque splendor to an ethical ideal. The two composers mark the supreme musical achievement of the Protestant spirit.

The Catholic world for its part tried to retrieve the losses inflicted

Bibiena stage set.
". . . the pomp and splendor of Baroque art: an art bold of gesture and conception, vigorous, decorative, monumental."

by Luther's secession. The Counter-Reformation mobilized all the forces of the church militant. The Jesuits, recognizing faith to be a matter of the whole personality, strove to fire the hearts and minds and senses of the faithful. They made music, sculpture, architecture, painting, and even the theater arts tributary to their purpose. Jesuit art sought direct communication with the spectator by overwhelming and exalting him. The churches of Spain and Austria testify to its impact. Their crowded decorations, pictorial clouds, and floating draperies defy both the laws of gravity and of restraint. This is an art that summons the worshiper to beatific visions. The rapturous mysticism of the Counter-Reformation found expression in the canvases of El Greco (c. 1542–1614). His elongated ash-gray figures, bathed in an unearthly light, are creatures of a visionary mind that distorts the real in its search for a reality beyond. Baroque theatricalism and pathos came to fullness in the sculptor Lorenzo Bernini (1598–1680). His famous *Ecstasy of St. Teresa* captures in marble all the restlessness and drama of the Baroque.

Between the conflicting currents of absolute monarchy and rising bourgeois power, Reformation and Counter-Reformation, the Baroque fashioned its grandiose art. Alien to its spirit were restraint and detachment. Rather it achieved its ends through violent opposition of forces,

Bernini, *The Ecstasy of St. Teresa.*

". . . captures in marble all the restlessness and drama of the Baroque."

lavish creativity, and abandon. With these went the capacity to organize a thousand details into a monumental, overpowering whole.

The artist played a variety of roles in baroque society. He might be an ambassador and intimate of princes, as were Rubens and Van Dyke;

or a priest, as was Vivaldi; or a political leader, like Milton. He functioned under royal or princely patronage; or, like Bach, was in the employ of a church or free city. He might dabble in business and make a fortune, as Lully did; or launch his own enterprises and lose them, as was the case with Handel. In social status he ran the gamut from favorite at court to something just above the valet or cook. To the aristocrats whom he served he might be little more than a purveyor of elegant entertainment. Yet beneath the obsequious manner and fawning dedications demanded by the age, there was often to be found a spirit that dared to probe all existing knowledge and shape new worlds; a voice addressing itself to those who truly listened, that was indeed "the trumpet of a prophecy."

≫50≪

Main Currents in Baroque Music

"The end of all good music is to affect the soul."
Claudio Monteverdi

EMERGENCE OF THE MAJOR-MINOR SYSTEM

THE MUSIC of the Middle Ages and the Renaissance—the thousand-year period, that is, which came to an end around the year 1600—was based upon eight *modes*. Each consisted of a group of eight tones corresponding to those sounded by the white keys of the piano. One included the tones in the octave from D to D, another those from E to E, still another extended from F to F, and so on. In other words, each mode comprised another segment of what we today call the C-major scale, and provided another pattern of whole and half steps.

The adjective *modal* consequently refers to the type of melody and harmony that prevailed in the Middle Ages and Renaissance. It is frequently used in contrast to *tonal*, which denotes the harmony based on major-minor tonality. The transition from the medieval church modes to major-minor (one of the most significant changes in all music history) took place during the Baroque. As music turned from vocal polyphony to instrumental harmony, a simplification of the harmonic system was absolutely essential. The ancient church modes gave way to two standard scales: the major and the minor. These two scales had been prominent in folk and popular music for generations. They served as the basis of Western art music from around 1650 to the opening of the twentieth century. With the establishment of major-minor tonality, the thrust to the keynote or *do* became the most powerful force in music.

Now each chord could assume its function in relation to the key center. Composers of the Baroque soon learned to exploit the opposition between the chord of rest, the I (tonic), and the active chord, the V (dominant). Many a work of the period opens with a hammer-stroke announcement of the I-V-I and ends with an emphatic repetition of the two basic chords at the final cadence. So, too, the movement from home key to foreign and back became an important element in the shaping of musical structure. Composers developed larger forms of instrumental music than had ever been known before.

The "seven out of twelve" way of hearing music introduced a sharp contrast between harmonies rooted in the key (diatonic) and those based on the five foreign tones (chromatic). Moods of well-being were linked with diatonic harmony, anguish with chromatic. In similar fashion the major came to be connected with joy and the minor with sorrow, an association that persisted for more than two hundred years.

The major-minor system was the collective achievement of several generations of musicians. It expressed a new dynamic culture. By dividing the world of sound into definite areas and regulating the movement from one to the other, it enabled the composer to mirror the exciting interplay of forces in the world about him.

EQUAL TEMPERAMENT

The raw material of sound has to be adjusted to the purposes of music. If the intervals of the scale are tuned in perfect intonation, certain of them turn out to be slightly out of tune in relation to one another. This discrepancy increases the farther we move along the cycle of keys.

As long as music was mainly vocal and remained within a narrow range, the phenomenon was not too disturbing. The use of instruments complicated the situation. If the sharps and flats were in perfect tune with the *do* of one scale they might be out of tune with that of another. An F-sharp on the keyboard might sound right in the key of D, but would be off pitch in the key of B. This made it practically impossible to use keys with a large number of sharps or flats.

An overall solution was urgently needed for instruments of fixed pitch such as the harpsichord or organ. This was achieved by adjusting, or *tempering*, the intonation. Instead of having certain intervals perfectly in tune in the simple keys but distressingly off pitch in the remote ones, they were all ever so slightly mistuned. In this way the discrepancy in nature was distributed evenly throughout the whole scale. This was done by dividing the octave into twelve equal semitones. As a result, F-sharp became identical with G-flat on the harpsichord, organ, and piano. (On the string instruments this is not so. The violinist who plays F-sharp rising to G sounds it a little higher than G-flat descending to F.) The compromise, known as *equal temperament*, made it possible to use all the major and minor keys and to move freely from one to the other. The adoption of equal temperament in European music went hand in hand with the triumph of the major-minor system.

Composers of the Baroque produced cycles of pieces that used an ever greater number of the twelve major and twelve minor keys. The most important circumnavigation of the tonal globe was that by Johann Sebastian Bach in the *Well-Tempered Clavier*, in which all twenty-four major and minor keys were included. "Well-tempered" refers not to amiable disposition, but to the new adjusted, or tempered, system of tuning.

It follows that when we speak of having our piano tuned we really mean that we want it to be slightly mistuned. If the pitches were set in pure intonation we should be unable to play a good deal of the music of the past two hundred years. As it is, nature is adjusted to art and the ear is made happier thereby.

UNFLAGGING RHYTHM

The Baroque demanded a dynamic rhythm. The time was ripe for regular recurrence of accent and for clear-cut energetic movement. The bass part became the carrier of the new rhythm. Its relentless beat is one of the most arresting traits of the period. This steady pulsation, once under way, never slackens or deviates until the goal is reached. It imparts to baroque music its singleness of purpose, its unflagging drive. It produces the same effect of turbulent yet controlled motion as animates baroque painting, architecture, and sculpture.

Composers became ever more aware of the capacity of the instruments for rhythm. They found that a striking dance rhythm could serve as the basis for an extended piece, vocal or instrumental. Popular and court dances furnished an invigorating element to musical art. Nor, in that stately age, were the rhythms necessarily lively. Idealized dance rhythms served as the basis for tragic arias and great polyphonic works. In a time when courtiers listened to music primarily for entertainment, composers had to dress up a good part of their material in dance rhythms. Many a dance piece served to make palatable a profounder discourse. In effect, rhythm pervaded the musical conception of the Baroque and helped it capture the movement and drive of a vibrant era.

CONTINUOUS MELODY

The elaborate scrollwork of baroque architecture bears witness to an abundance of energy that would not leave an inch of space unornamented. Its musical counterpart is to be found in one of the main elements of baroque style—the principle of continuous expansion. A movement will start off with a striking musical figure that unfolds through a process of ceaseless spinning out. There are no seams in this fabric; none of the balanced phrases and cadences that we know from the classical style. This music moves forward by a process of spontaneous generation, relentlessly pursuing its goal as the figures and motives flower into ever fresh designs. It is constantly in motion, in the act of becoming. When its energy is spent, the work comes to an end.

In vocal music the melody of the Baroque was imbued with the desire always to heighten the impact of the words. Wide leaps and the use of chromatic tones served to emphasize the emotional content. There resulted a noble melody whose spacious curves outlined a style of grand expressiveness and pathos.

HARMONIC COUNTERPOINT

The music of the fifteenth and sixteenth centuries, we saw, was polyphonic in texture. With the rise of opera around the year 1600, composers were encouraged to explore more and more the possibilities of single-line melody over an accompaniment of chords—that is, of homophonic texture. The Baroque witnessed the reconciliation between the horizontal and vertical ways of conceiving music. Baroque counterpoint absorbed all the innovations of the age: the pull to the tonic of baroque harmony, the forward stride of baroque rhythm, the exuberance of baroque ornamentation, the continuous expansion of baroque melody. These elements were fused in a style that came to full flower during the late Baroque in the art of Bach and Handel. They and their contemporaries created a music of richly woven texture in which the counterpoint was directed by harmony and the harmony came rhythmically alive through the counterpoint. The horizontal movement of the voices and the vertical movement of the chords met in an ideal balance whose like was not encountered either before or since.

TERRACED DYNAMICS

Baroque music does not know the constant fluctuation of volume that marks the classic-romantic style. The music moves at a fairly constant level of sonority. A passage uniformly loud will be followed by one uniformly soft, creating the effect of light and shade. The shift from one level to the other has come to be known as *terraced dynamics* and is a characteristic feature of the baroque style.

The nineteenth-century composer who desired a crescendo directed each instrument to play increasingly louder. The baroque composer called instead for a larger number of players. The nineteenth-century composer used the crescendo as a means of expression within a passage. The baroque composer found his main source of expression in the contrast between a soft passage and a loud—that is, between the two terraces of sound. Each passage became an area of solid color set off against the next. This conception shapes the structure of the music, endowing it with a monumental simplicity.

It follows that baroque composers were much more sparing of expression marks than those who came after. The music of the period carries little else than an occasional forte or piano, leaving it to the player to supply whatever else may be necessary. Performers today are so accustomed to the dynamic shadings of nineteenth-century music that they are almost incapable of the grand architectural simplicity of the baroque style. Especially the music of Bach has suffered from romantic interpretation. A modern edition of the *Well-Tempered Clavier* will carry an array of expression marks on every page. The original manuscript contained not one.

INSTRUMENTAL COLOR

The Baroque was the first period in history in which instrumental music was comparable in importance to vocal. The interest in this branch of the art stimulated the development of new instruments and the perfecting of old. The spirit of the age demanded increased brilliancy of tone. The gentle lute was ousted by the less subtle guitar. The reserved viol with its "still music," as Shakespeare called it, was supplanted by the more resonant violin. Baroque music made generous use of trumpet and trombone; oboe, bassoon, and flute.

The period boasted three keyboard instruments: organ, harpsichord, and clavichord. The baroque organ had a pure transparent tone. Its stops did not blend the colors into a symphonic cloudburst, as is the case with the twentieth-century organ, but let the voices stand out clearly so that the ear could follow the counterpoint. With its steady volume of sound, which enabled it to play a uniform soft or loud, the organ was eminently suited to the terraced dynamics of the baroque era.

The same held true for the harpsichord. This instrument differs from the piano in two important respects. First, its strings instead of being struck with hammers are plucked by quills, producing a bright silvery tone. Second, the volume of tone does not vary, as on the piano, according to the pressure of the fingers on the keys. The harpsichord is therefore incapable of the crescendo and decrescendo that are so essential a feature of nineteenth-century music. Nor does it command the personal expressiveness that made the piano the favorite instrument of the romantic era. These are hardly shortcomings from the baroque point of view. Through the use of two keyboards, one above the other, and by means of stops, it is possible to achieve even levels of soft and loud. The harpsichord is an ideal medium for contrapuntal music, for it brings out the inner voices with luminous clarity. It lends itself to a grand style of playing that on the one hand is elevated and dramatic, on the other is rhythmically precise, refined, and playful. It was immensely popular during the Baroque as a solo instrument; it was the mainstay of the ensemble in chamber music and at the opera house, and even substituted for the organ in the ensemble music at church.

The clavichord was a wooden oblong box, from two to five feet long, that rested on legs or on a table. The strings were set vibrating by small brass wedges known as tangents. Dynamic gradations were possible, within a limited range, through pressure on the keys. Clavichord tone was tender, subtle, intimate. It was, however, a small tone. By the end of the eighteenth century both clavichord and harpsichord had been supplanted in public favor by the piano.

The word "clavier" was used in Germany as the general term for keyboard instruments, taking in harpsichord, clavichord, and organ. Whether a certain piece was intended for one rather than the other must often be gathered from the style rather than the title. In any event, the rendering of Bach's *Wohltemperiertes Clavier* as "Well-Tempered Clavichord" is misleading. Closer the mark is "Well-Tempered Clavier."

ORCHESTRATION

The Baroque created the concept of the organized body of players that we know as the orchestra. As a result, composers paid more attention to the blending of timbres and the balance of tone. The first permanent instrumental ensemble was established at the French court as "the twenty-four violins of the King." This ensemble, to which woodwinds and brass were added later, gained great fame in the reign of Louis XIV under the direction of Lully. He taught his men a uniform manner of bowing, developed orchestral discipline, and achieved a rhythmic precision unknown till then. His orchestra became the model for all Europe.

It was in the opera house that the most important experiments in orchestration took place. For it was there that composers were obliged to think of color in relation to mood, atmosphere, and dramatic effect. Masters of baroque opera such as Lully and Handel were pioneers in exploiting orchestral color. Born from the mating of music and drama, the art of orchestration became a potent force in the portraying of sentiment and passion.

COMPOSER AND PUBLIC

The Baroque was a period of international culture. National styles existed—without nationalism. Lully, an Italian, created the French lyric tragedy. Handel, a German, gave England the oratorio. There was free interchange among national cultures. The sensuous beauty of Italian melody, the pointed precision of French dance rhythm, the luxuriance of German counterpoint, the freshness of English choral song—these nourished an all-European art that absorbed the best of each.

The baroque composer, employed by a court, church, municipal council, or opera house, was in direct contact with his public. As like as not he was his own interpreter, which made the contact even closer. He created his music for a specific occasion—it might be a royal wedding or a religious service—and for immediate use: in a word, for communication. He was an artisan in a handicraft society. He functioned as a religious man fired by the word of God, or as a loyal subject exalting his king. He was not troubled overmuch by the problem of self-expression, but because he spoke out of passionate conviction he expressed both himself and his era. He had never heard of art for art's sake; but because he created for his fellows and was fired by their collective aspiration, he ascended the pinnacles of art. He did not discuss esthetics or the nature of inspiration; but, impelled by a lofty moral vision, he united superb mastery of his craft with profound insights into the nature of experience. He began by writing for a particular time and place; he ended by creating for the ages.

⧽51⧼

Musical Forms of the Baroque (Vocal)

"I was aware that it is contraries which greatly move our mind. Where I have been able to find no variety in the affections I have at least sought to bring variety into my music."
                                        Claudio Monteverdi

THE OPERA

THE DRAMATIC spirit of the Baroque lives for us, paradoxically, in its nontheater forms: oratorio, cantata, instrumental music. The vast literature of its music for the stage has ceased to be part of our heritage. One reason for this is that opera by its nature is more subject to the fashions of the moment than are all other forms of music. The formal or serious opera of the Baroque, the *opera seria*, is not easily adapted to the modern temper. Its conventions were attuned to the social order that ended with the French Revolution. The court opera of the Baroque, the favorite diversion of Hapsburgs, Bourbons, Medici, and the rest, embodied the world-view of a feudal caste whose gaze was directed to the past. Seeking an escape from the disintegrating order about them, they found refuge in a dream-world where heroes torn between love and honor declaimed to noble music while time stood still in an enchanted grotto out of antiquity or the medieval age. For all its lofty rhetoric, the lyric drama of the Baroque is alien to the conventions that govern the modern theater; alien, too, to present-day notions of what constitutes valid human motivation. The plots are too complicated; the characters are idealized types rather than individuals; the passions are elevated and correct.

Baroque opera was a vital force whose influence extended far beyond the theater. It created the great forms of the lyric drama—recitative and aria, ensemble and chorus—that served as models to every branch of the art. The aria *da capo* (from the beginning) in which the first part was repeated after the middle section, established A-B-A as a basic formula of musical structure. Baroque opera within its own conventions taught composers to depict the sentiments and the passions, the lyric contemplation of nature, the quintessence of love, hate, fear, jealousy, exaltation. It invigorated the stately music of the courts with popular song and dance, and established new standards of vocal and instrumental performance. In the opera house of the Baroque, music attained a dramatic-expressive power such as it had never possessed before.

THE LUTHERAN CHORALE

A *chorale* is a hymn tune, specifically one associated with German Protestantism. The chorales were the battle hymns of the Reformation. Their sturdy contours bear the stamp of a heroic age.

Martin Luther (1483–1546) established as one of his reforms that the congregation must participate in the service. To this end he inaugurated services in the vernacular. Music, he saw, could be made to play a prime role in religious experience by means of congregational singing. "I wish," he wrote, "to make German psalms for the people, that is to say sacred hymns, so that the word of God may dwell among the people also by means of song."

Luther and his aides created the first chorales. They adapted a number of tunes from Gregorian chant, from popular sources as well as from secular art music. Appropriate texts and melodies were drawn, too, from Latin hymns and psalms. In the course of generations there grew up a body of religious folk song that was in the highest sense a national heritage. Originally sung in unison, the chorales soon became familiar in four-part harmony. The melody was put in the soprano, where all could hear it as it moved in four-square rhythm to the pause at the end of the line. The chorales greatly strengthened the trend to clear-cut melody, harmony, and rhythm. As they had to be sung by the musically untutored, they assumed the elemental simplicity and universality which, as in myth and fairy tale, are the essence of folk art.

In the elaborate vocal forms that presently appeared in the Protestant church service—cantata, oratorio, and passion—the chorale served as a unifying thread. When at the close of an extended work the chorale unfolded in simple four-part harmony, its granitic strength reflected the faith of a nation. One may imagine the impact upon an audience attuned to its message. The chorale nourished centuries of German music. It came to full flower in the art of Johann Sebastian Bach, an art whose spiritual roots reach back to the Reformation.

THE CANTATA

A *cantata* (from the Italian *cantare*, "to sing"—that is, a piece to be sung) is a work for vocalists, chorus, and instrumentalists based on a poetic narrative, either religious or secular, of a lyric or dramatic nature. It generally contains several movements, such as arias, recitatives, duets, and choruses.

Originally an Italian form, the cantata took root in Germany where it developed into the most important type of Lutheran sacred music. It was enriched by all the instrumental and vocal forms of the Baroque. The various elements were cemented into a unity by the all-embracing presence of the Lutheran chorale.

The sacred cantata was an integral part of the service. It was related, along with the sermon that followed it, to the Gospel for the Day. Every Sunday of the church year required another. What with some extra works for holidays and special occasions, an annual cycle came to about sixty cantatas. Cantors of Lutheran churches were required to furnish such cycles. Bach composed five cycles—approximately three hundred cantatas, of which only about two hundred have come down to us. The rest were lost, as a result of the casual attitude toward masterpieces—and posterity—of that superabundant age.

ORATORIO AND PASSION

An *oratorio* is a large-scale musical work for solo voices, chorus, and orchestra, set to a libretto of sacred or serious character. It is longer than a cantata and, unlike the latter, is not part of a religious service, although it is often based on a biblical story and imbued with devotional feeling. It is performed in a concert hall or church without scenery, costumes, or acting; in which respect oratorio differs from opera. There is much greater emphasis on the chorus. The poem, although cast in dialogue form, is of a contemplative rather than dramatic nature. No use is made of the rapid question-and-answer that serves to build tension in the opera house. A narrator is often employed to connect the scenes and introduce the characters. He lifts the drama from the plane of action to that of reflection.

The oratorio grew out of the sacred operas of the Italian Counter-Reformation. It was introduced into Germany during the seventeenth century. There it absorbed the spirit of Lutheran church music. Out of the fusion came Bach's *Christmas* Oratorio and *Easter* Oratorio.

But it was through the genius of Handel that the baroque oratorio fulfilled its destiny. He endowed it with its massive architecture, its shattering choruses, its dramatic power. He removed it from its churchly surroundings, endowing it with a universal quality that embraced all faiths. Himself a world figure, he created in the oratorio a hymnic work of world-wide significance for generations to come.

The *passion* is a musical version of the Crucifixion set to the text of one of the four gospels. Like the oratorio, the passion featured chorales and impressive choral scenes. Both drew on the recitative and aria of the operatic theater and the dramatic force of the new orchestral style. Where they differed was in the subject matter of the libretto.

The quality of drama inseparable from the passion was emphasized during the Baroque. Composers characterized in their music the three protagonists of the tale—the narrator or Evangelist, the voice of Christ, and the crowd demanding his death. Bach occupies the same commanding position in regard to the passion as Handel does to the oratorio. The two great passions of Bach are those according to St. John and St. Matthew.

THE MASS

The Mass is the most solemn ritual of the Roman Catholic Church. It constitutes a symbolic re-enactment of the sacrifice of Christ. The name is derived from the Latin *missa*, "dismissal" (of the congregation at the end of the service).

The aggregation of prayers that make up the Mass falls into two categories: those that vary from day to day throughout the church year, the Proper; and those that remain the same in every mass, the Ordinary. The liturgy, which reached its fixed form about nine hundred years ago, provides Gregorian melodies for each item of the ceremony. With the rise of polyphony composers began to weave additional voice parts around the plainchant. They concentrated on the prayers that were an invariable part of the service rather than on the variable items that were heard only once during the liturgical year. Thus came into prominence the five sections which the public knows as the musical setting of the Mass: Kyrie, Gloria, Credo, Sanctus, and Agnus Dei. The opening section, the Kyrie, is a prayer for mercy consisting of nine invocations: three *Kyrie eleison* (Lord, have mercy upon us), three *Christe eleison* (Christ, have mercy upon us), and again three *Kyrie eleison*. There follows the *Gloria in excelsis Deo* (Glory be to God on high). The third movement is the confession of faith, *Credo in unum Deum, Patrem omnipotentem* (I believe in one God, the omnipotent Father). It includes also the *Et incarnatus est* (And is incarnate), the *Crucifixus* (He was crucified), and the *Et resurrexit* (And He arose). Fourth is *Sanctus Sanctus Sanctus* (Holy Holy Holy) which includes the *Hosanna in excelsis* (Praise in the highest) and the *Benedictus qui venit in nomine Domini* (Blessed be He who cometh in the name of the Lord). The fifth and last part, *Agnus Dei qui tollis peccata mundi* (Lamb of God who beareth the sins of the world), concludes with the prayer *Dona nobis pacem* (Give us peace).

Of the masses for special services the most important is the Mass for the Dead, which is sung at the funeral service. It is known as the Requiem, from the opening verse *Requiem aeternam dona eis* (Rest eternal grant them). Included are prayers in keeping with the solemnity of the occasion, among them the awesome depiction of the Last Judgment, *Dies irae* (Day of Wrath).

The history of the mass as an art form extends over the better part of eight hundred years. It reached great artistic heights, immediately prior to the Baroque, at the hands of Giovanni Pierluigi da Palestrina (c. 1525–94). He gave such complete expression to the religiosity of the Counter-Reformation that for posterity he has remained *the* Catholic composer. Palestrina's art incarnates the pure *a cappella* (literally, for the chapel, i.e., unaccompanied) style of religious vocal music. Within this style he created a universal type of expression ideally suited to moods of mystical exaltation. The contemplative beauty of his music does not exclude intense emotion; but this is emotion directed to an act of faith.

In the seventeenth century, the taste for overpowering effects characteristic of baroque art invaded even the musical setting of the Mass. The pure devotional style of the age of Palestrina gave way to the vogue of the "colossal Baroque." Masses were composed for quadruple choir—that is, for four choirs accompanied by orchestras that included woodwind and brass instruments and organs. With their vast dimensions and dynamic contrasts these works captured in tone all the flamboyance of baroque architecture. Never did music come closer to the monumental art of stone that has been called "frozen music."

Musicians of the Baroque did not draw the distinction between sacred and secular that is customary nowadays. They held that the composer worshiped God best by speaking the language of his time and by using all the resources of his art. Inevitably the new dynamic instrumental style and the spirit of opera found their way into this most hallowed of art forms. As in the case of baroque opera, the rich literature of the baroque mass has not survived in the repertory. The one example that has become part of our heritage, Bach's Mass in B minor, amply attests to the magnificent vitality of baroque music.

≱52≰

Musical Forms of the Baroque (Instrumental)

> "For by exactly observing this opposition or rivalry of the slow and the fast, the loud and the soft, the fullness of the great choir and the delicacy of the little trio, the ear is ravished by a singular astonishment, as is the eye by the opposition of light and shade."
>
> Georg Muffat (1701)

TWO-PART FORM

THE classic-romantic period, we saw, was partial to the three-part form based on the principle of statement-departure-return (A-B-A). The Baroque, for its part, was inclined to binary, or two-part, structure (A-B). This is the question-and-answer type of formation embodied in a tune such as *London Bridge*. The principle gave rise to a tightly knit structure in which the A part moved from home to foreign key while the B part made the corresponding move back. Both parts used closely related or even identical material. The form was made apparent to the ear by a full stop at the end of the first part. As a rule each part was repeated, giving an A-A: B-B structure.

In the three-part form, contrast is injected by the middle section. Binary form, on the other hand, is all of a piece in texture and mood. It embodies a single mood, for which reason it was favored by a musical style based on continuous expansion. Binary form prevailed in the short harpsichord pieces of dance character that were produced in quantities during the seventeenth and early eighteenth centuries. It was a standard type in the suite, one of the favorite instrumental forms of the Baroque.

THE SUITE

The *suite* consisted of a series of dance movements all in the same key. It presented an international galaxy of dance types: the German allemande, French courante, Spanish sarabande, English jig (gigue). These had been popular dances, but by the time of the late Baroque they had left the ballroom far behind and become abstract types of art music.

The harpsichord suite as cultivated by Bach consisted of four principal numbers: an allemande in moderate duple meter, a courante in moderate triple, a stately sarabande in slow three-time and a lively gigue in 6/8 or 6/4. Between sarabande and gigue might be inserted a variety of optional numbers of a graceful song or dance type—minuet or gavotte, lively bourrée or passepied. These dances, of peasant origin, introduced a refreshing earthiness into their more formal surroundings. The harpsichord suite occasionally opened with a prelude. In the suite for orchestra this was expanded into an overture. Best-known examples of the baroque orchestral suite are the four by Bach and the *Water Music* of Handel.

The essential element of the suite was dance rhythm, with its imagery of physical movement. The form met the needs of the age for elegant entertainment music. At the same time it offered composers a wealth of popular rhythms that could be transmuted into art.

BASSO OSTINATO

The principle of unity in variety was embodied in an important procedure of baroque music, the *ground bass* or *basso ostinato* (obstinate bass). This consists of a short phrase, either melodic or accompanimental, that is repeated over and over in the bass while above it the upper parts change with each repetition, weaving an ever fresh texture of melody, harmony, and counterpoint. The ostinato supplied the fixed framework within which the composer's imagination freely disported itself. Baroque musicians developed a consummate technique of variation and embellishment over the ground bass.

The upper parts were frequently improvised. This technique was especially popular in England where, as it involved breaking up or dividing the melody into quick rhythmic figures, it was known as *divisions on a ground*. The principle has reappeared in modern jazz as the basis of boogie-woogie piano playing, in which the left hand re-

peats a rhythmic ostinato while the right engages in free improvisation.
The ostinato is little short of infallible both as a unifying device and
as a means of building tension. We shall find it playing a prominent
part in twentieth-century music.

PASSACAGLIA AND CHACONNE

The principle of the ground bass was embodied in one of the most
majestic forms of baroque music, the *passacaglia*. Here a melody is
presented in the bass, generally four or eight bars long, in stately triple
meter. The theme is repeated again and again, becoming the basis for
an intricate polyphonic structure founded on continuous variation.

With each repetition the composer has to reveal the theme in a new
light. He must also see to it that the variations as a whole sustain interest
and mount cumulatively to the climax. In the building of his edifice the
composer marshals all the resources of melodic, harmonic, and rhythmic
variation and all the devices of counterpoint. The famous example of
the form is Bach's Passacaglia in C minor for Organ, a magnificent
example of the baroque art of variation.

In the *chaconne*, a related type, a fixed succession of chords in a characteristic rhythm is repeated as the basis for each variation. In other
words, the unifying element in the chaconne is the harmony rather
than melody.

Chaconne and passacaglia are by no means exclusively instrumental
forms. They figured in numerous arias in the operas and cantatas of
the period. They exemplify the baroque urge toward abundant variation and embellishment of a given musical idea—the urge to make much
out of little that is the essence of the creative act.

THE FUGUE

From the art and science of counterpoint issued one of the most
exciting types of baroque music, the *fugue*. The name is derived from
fuga, the Latin for "flight," implying a flight of fancy (possibly the
flight of the theme from one voice to the other). In a fugue, several
independent voices—generally three or four—take turns in presenting
a striking theme or subject. A fugue consequently is a type of music
based on imitative counterpoint, in which a theme of strongly marked
character pervades the entire fabric, entering now in one voice, now
in another. The subject is often rather short and constitutes the unifying idea, the focal point of interest in the contrapuntal web.

A fugue may be written for a group of instruments; for a solo instrument such as organ, harpsichord, or even violin; for several solo voices, or for full chorus. Whether the fugue is vocal or instrumental, the several lines are called voices, which indicates the origin of the type. In vocal and orchestral fugues each line is articulated by another performer or group of performers. In fugues for keyboard instruments the ten fingers—on the organ, the feet as well—manage the complex interweaving of the voices.

The subject is stated at the outset in one of the voices (soprano, alto, tenor, or bass) without accompaniment. It is then imitated in another voice—this is the answer—while the first continues with a countertheme or countersubject. It will then appear in a third voice and be answered in the fourth, if there are four, while the first two weave a free contrapuntal texture against these. When the theme has appeared in each voice once, the first section of the fugue—the exposition—is at an end. The exposition may be repeated, in which case the voices will enter in a different order. From there on the fugue alternates between exposition sections that feature the entrance of the subject, and less weighty interludes known as episodes. The latter serve as areas of relaxation.

As the fugue unfolds there must be not only a sustaining of interest but the sense of mounting urgency that is proper to an extended art work. The composer throughout strives for continuity and a sense of organic growth. Each recurrence of the theme reveals new facets of its nature. It may be presented in longer or shorter note values, turned upside down, presented backwards, or upside down and backwards. It may be combined with new subjects or with some other version of itself. It may be presented softly or vigorously. The composer manipulates the subject as pure musical material in the same way that the sculptor molds his clay. Especially effective is the *stretto* (from the Italian for "close") in which the theme is imitated in close succession, with the subject entering in one voice before it has been completed in another. The effect is one of voices crowding upon each other, creating a heightening of tension that brings the fugue to its climax. There follows the final statement of the subject, generally in triumphal mood. The mission has been accomplished, the tension released.

The fugue is based on a single mood—the subject that dominates the piece. Episodes and transitional passages are woven from its motives or from those of the countersubject. There results an astounding unity of texture and atmosphere. Another factor for unity is the unfaltering rhythmic beat (against which, however, the composer may weave a diversity of counter-rhythms). The only section of the fugue that follows a set order is the exposition. Once that is done with, the further course of the fugue is bound only by the composer's fancy. Caprice, exuberance, surprise—all receive free play within the supple framework of this form.

It is well to distinguish between fugue and sonata form. The sonata movement exploits the contrast between two themes; the fugue is a monolithic whole based on a single theme. The sonata movement depends on theme development, the fugue on theme imitation. The sonata themes undergo substantial changes as the material is developed; the fugue theme remains essentially the same, variety being supplied by the counterpoint. The sonata is the most ambitious form based on harmonic or vertical texture; the fugue is the most ambitious form based on contrapuntal or horizontal texture. The sonata form is sectional (exposition-development-recapitulation); the fugue is continuous. As someone has well said, the sonata is sewn together, the fugue woven together.

The subject of the fugue is stated in the home key. The answer is given in a contrasting key, that of the dominant which lies five tones above the tonic. There is free modulation to foreign keys in the course of the fugue, which builds up tension against the return home. The baroque fugue thus embodied the contrast between home and foreign key that was one of the basic principles of the new major-minor system. However, it did not develop this contrast to the same degree as did the later sonata form.

Composers of the Baroque found in the fugue a unique combination of qualities. The form represented a mode of thought rooted in the past, into which they poured the living substance of their own time. It mobilized the resources, on the one hand of contrapuntal skill, on the other of imagination, feeling, and exuberant ornamentation. There resulted a form of musical art that may well be accounted one of the supreme achievements of the Baroque.

THE CONCERTO GROSSO

No less important than the principle of unity in baroque music was that of contrast. This found expression in the *concerto grosso*, a form based on the opposition between two dissimilar masses of sound. (The verb *concertare* means "to fight side by side," "to vie with one another as brothers in arms.") A small group of instruments known as the *concertino* was pitted against the large group, the concerto grosso or tutti (all). The contrast was one of color and dynamics, a uniform level of soft sound being set off against loud. In other words, the orchestra here took over the terraced dynamics of organ and harpsichord.

The concertino, or solo group, might consist of a string trio such as two violins and a 'cello, or any combination that caught the composer's fancy. The large group as a rule was based on the string choir, but might be supplemented by winds. The harpsichord furnished harmonic support for both groups. The composer was able to write more difficult music for the solo group than for the full ensemble. This was a signal advantage in an age when expert players were none too plentiful.

Two Italian masters were outstanding in this field, Arcangelo Corelli and Antonio Vivaldi. Both strongly influenced the Germans, especially Bach and Handel. The fact is worth noting. Because of the pre-eminence of German orchestral music during the classic-romantic period, a popular myth has been built up that instrumental music is the exclusive achievement of German genius. As a matter of fact, the concerto grosso was one of several important instrumental forms that originated in Italy, whence they passed to France, Germany, and England for further development.

PRELUDE, TOCCATA, FANTASIA

A *prelude* is a piece in imaginative style based on the continuous expansion of a melodic or rhythmic figure. It is a free form—that is, not bound by rules. The prelude originated in improvisation on the lute and keyboard instruments. In the late Baroque it served to introduce a group of dance pieces or a fugue. In each of the two volumes of Bach's *Well-Tempered Clavier*, every one of the twenty-four major and minor keys is represented by a prelude and fugue. The prelude achieved great variety and expressiveness during the Baroque. As its texture was for the most part harmonic, it made an effective contrast with the contrapuntal texture of the fugue that followed it.

The baroque *toccata* (from the Italian toccare, "to touch," referring to the keys) was a composition for organ or harpsichord that exploited the resources of the keyboard in a glittering display of chords, arpeggios, and scale passages. It was free and rhapsodic in form, marked by passages in a harmonic style alternating with fugal sections. The toccata is specifically associated with the great Italian organist Girolamo Frescobaldi (1583–1643). In the hands of the north German organists it became a virtuoso piece of monumental proportions, either as an independent work or as companion piece to a fugue.

By *fantasia* we understand a type of composition in which the play of fancy takes precedence over regularity of structure. The term includes a variety of pieces imbued with the spirit of improvisation. In the great fantasias of Bach, massive sonorities, abrupt changes of mood, poetic expression, and luxuriant ornamentation are contained within an architecture at once grandiose and supple. Like the toccata, the fantasia may be either an independent piece or coupled with a fugue.

Church organists, in announcing the chorale to be sung by the congregation, fell into the practice of embellishing the traditional melodies. In so doing they drew upon the wealth of baroque ornamentation, harmony, and counterpoint. There grew up a magnificent body of instrumental art—chorale prelude and fantasia, chorale variations and fugue—in which organ virtuosity of the highest level was imbued with the spirit of inspired improvisation.

OTHER INSTRUMENTAL FORMS

The sonata for one or more instruments was widely cultivated throughout the Baroque. Despite the identity of name, there was a great difference between the baroque sonata and that of the classical era. This was the difference in general outlook that separated the age of Bach and Handel from the age of Haydn and Mozart. The sonata movement of the Baroque was based on the continuous expansion of a single theme in more or less contrapuntal texture, whereas the classical sonata movement was based on the development of two theme groups set forth in contrasting sections and homophonic texture. A similar distinction separates the solo concerto of the Baroque from the classical concerto.

The operatic overture was an important type of large-scale orchestral music. The French overture was a ceremonious form associated with Lully. It opened with a slow pompous introduction based on dotted rhythms, which was followed by an allegro in loosely fugal style. Sometimes the form was rounded off with a return to the stately pace of the opening, which resulted in an A-B-A form: slow-fast-slow. The Italian overture consisted of three sections too: fast-slow-fast, a scheme later adopted by the concerto grosso and the solo concerto. We have referred to the opera house as a center of experimentation that had a fruitful effect on all branches of music. The operatic overture of the Baroque was one of the ancestors of the symphony.

An *invention*—the word signifies an ingenious idea—is a short piece for the keyboard in contrapuntal style. The title is known to pianists from Bach's collection of fifteen Inventions in two voices and a like number in three. Bach called the latter group Sinfonias, which shows how flexible was musical terminology in those days. His purpose in the Inventions, he wrote, was "upright instruction wherein the lovers of the clavier, and especially those desirous of learning, are shown a clear way not alone to have good *inventiones* but to develop the same well."

The instrumental forms of the Baroque manifest great diversity and venturesomeness. In this they epitomize the spirit of the era that shaped their being.

✇ 53 ✇

Johann Sebastian Bach (1685-1750)

"The aim and final reason of all music should be nothing else but the Glory of God and the refreshment of the spirit."

JOHANN SEBASTIAN BACH was heir to the great polyphonic art of the past. This he vitalized with the passion and humanity of his own spirit. He is the culminating figure of baroque music and one of the titans in the history of art.

HIS LIFE

He was born at Eisenach of a family that had supplied musicians to the churches and town bands of Thuringia for upwards of a century and a half. Left an orphan at the age of ten, he was raised in the town of Ohrdruf by an older brother, an organist who prepared him for the family vocation. From the first he displayed inexhaustible curiosity concerning every aspect of his art. "I had to work hard," he reported in later years, adding with considerably less accuracy, "Anyone who works as hard will get just as far."

His professional career began when he was eighteen with his appointment as organist at a church in Arnstadt. The certificate of appointment admonishes the young man to be true, faithful, and obedient to "our Noble and Most Gracious Count and Master . . . to conduct yourself in all things toward God, High Authority, and your superiors as befits an honorable servant and organist." High Authority soon had cause to reprove the new organist "for having made many curious *variationes*

Johann Sebastian Bach.

in the chorale and mingled many strange tones in it, and for the fact
that the Congregation has been confused by it." The church elders were
inquiring shortly after "by what right he recently caused a strange
maiden to be invited into the choir loft and let her make music there."
The maiden was his cousin Maria Barbara, whom he married.

After a year at a church in Mülhausen, Bach—at twenty-three—
received his first important post: court organist and chamber musician
to the Duke of Weimar. His nine years at the ducal court (1708–17)
were spent in the service of a ruler whose leaning toward religious
music accorded with his own. The Weimar period saw the rise of his
fame as an organ virtuoso and the production of his most important
works for the instrument.

Disappointed because the Duke had failed to advance him, Bach decided to accept an offer from the Prince of Anhalt-Cöthen. He needed
his master's permission to take another post. This the irascible Duke

refused to give. The musician stood up for his rights; whereupon, as the court chronicle relates, "on November 6, the former Concertmeister and court organist Bach was placed under arrest in the County Judge's place of detention for too stubbornly forcing the issue of his dismissal and finally on December 2 was freed from arrest with notice of his unfavorable discharge."

At Cöthen, Bach served a prince partial to chamber music. In his five years there (1717–23) he produced suites, concertos, sonatas for various instruments, and a wealth of clavier music; also the six concerti grossi dedicated to the Margrave of Brandenburg. The Cöthen period was saddened by the death of Maria Barbara. The composer subsequently married Anna Magdalena, a young singer in whom he found a loyal and understanding mate. Of his twenty children—seven of the first marriage and thirteen of the second—half did not survive infancy. One son died in his twenties, another was mentally deficient. Four others became leading composers of the next generation: Wilhelm Friedemann and Carl Philipp Emanuel, sons of Maria Barbara; and Anna Magdalena's sons Johann Christoph and Johann Christian.

Bach was thirty-eight when he was appointed to one of the most important posts in Germany, that of Cantor of St. Thomas's in Leipzig. The cantor taught at the choir school of that name, which trained the choristers of the city's principal churches (he was responsible for non-musical subjects too); and served as music director, composer, choirmaster, and organist of St. Thomas's Church. Several candidates were considered before him, among them the then much more famous composer Georg Philipp Telemann, who declined the offer. As one member of the town council reported, "Since the best man could not be obtained, lesser ones would have to be accepted." It was in this spirit that Leipzig received the greatest of her cantors. He undertook to "set the boys a shining example of an honest, retiring manner of life . . . show all proper respect and obedience to the Honorable and Most Wise Council . . . so arrange the music that it shall not last too long, and shall be of such a nature as not to make an operatic impression but rather impel the listeners to devotion"; also to teach the boys their Latin.

Bach's twenty-seven years in Leipzig (1723–50) saw the production of stupendous works. The clue to his inner life must be sought in his music. It had no counterpart in an outwardly uneventful existence divided between the cares of a large family, the pleasures of a sober circle of friends, the chores of a busy professional life, and the endless squabbles with a host of officials of town, school, and church who never conceded that they were dealing with anything more than a competent choirmaster. The city fathers were impressed but also disquieted by the soul-shattering dramaticism of his religious music. Besides, like all officials, they were out to save money and were not averse to lopping off certain rights and fees that Bach felt belonged to him. He fought each issue doggedly, with an expenditure of time and emotion that might have gone to better things. He describes himself as living "amidst continual vexation, envy, and persecution; accordingly I shall be forced, with God's help, to seek my fortune elsewhere." Even the wind seemed to be against him. "When there are rather more funerals than usual, the fees rise in proportion; but when a healthy air blows, they fall accordingly, as for example last year when I lost fees that would ordinarily come in from funerals to an amount of more than 100 thaler." Despite his complaints he remained in Leipzig. With the years the Council learned to put up with their obstinate cantor. After all, he was the greatest organist in Germany.

The routine of his life was enlivened by frequent professional journeys, when he was asked to test and inaugurate new organs. His last and most interesting expedition was to the court of Frederick the Great at Potsdam, where his son Carl Philipp Emanuel served as accompanist to the flute-playing monarch. Frederick on the memorable evening announced to his courtiers with some excitement, "Gentlemen, old Bach has arrived." He led the composer through the palace showing him the new pianos that were beginning to replace the harpsichord. Upon Bach's invitation the King gave him a subject on which he improvised one of his astonishing fugues. After his return to Leipzig he further elaborated on the royal theme, added a sonata for flute, violin, and clavier, and dispatched *The Musical Offering* to "a Monarch whose greatness and power, as in all the sciences of war and peace, so especially in music everyone must admire and revere."

The prodigious labors of a lifetime took their toll; his eyesight failed. After an apoplectic stroke he was stricken with blindness. He persisted in his final task, the revising of eighteen Chorale Preludes for the organ. The dying master dictated to his son-in-law the last of these, *When in the Hour of Direst Need*. In the final moment faith triumphed over anguish. He renamed it *Before Thy Throne, My God, I Stand*.

HIS MUSIC

The artist in Bach was driven to conquer all realms of musical thought. His position in history is that of one who consummated existing forms rather than originate new ones. Whatever form he touched he brought to its ultimate development. He cut across boundaries, fusing the three great national traditions of his time—German, Italian, French—into a convincing unity. His sheer mastery of the technics of composition has never been equaled. With this went incomparable profundity of thought and feeling and the capacity to realize to the full all the possibilities inherent in a given musical situation.

Bach was the last of the great religious artists. He considered music to be "a harmonious euphony to the Glory of God." And the glory of God was the central issue of man's existence. It was more than convention that made him inscribe at the head of his cantatas, "Jesus, help me!" and at their close, "To God alone be the praise." Given this exalted conception of the purpose of art, grandeur and sublimity were as native to his thoughts as were charm and elegance to that of more worldly musicians. Not without reason has he been called "the greatest of preachers."

Bach's music issued in the first instance from the Lutheran chorale. The indestructible tunes of the Reformation imparted to his art its strength and universality. Through the chorale the most learned composer of the age was united to the living current of popular melody, to become the spokesman of a faith. The prime medium for Bach's poetry was the organ. His imagery was rooted in its keyboard and pedals, his inspiration molded to its majestic sonorities. He created for the instrument what is still the high point of its literature: chorale preludes, fantasias, preludes, toccatas, fugues, and the great Passacaglia. In his own lifetime he was known primarily as a virtuoso organist, only Handel being placed in his class. When complimented on his playing he would answer disarmingly, "There is nothing remarkable about it. All you have to do is hit the right notes at the right time and the instrument plays itself."

The fugue is closely associated with Bach. He transformed it into a fantasy piece in which contrapuntal art was suffused with expressive elements. What sets Bach's fugues apart is the absolutely personal stamp of his themes, those chiseled patterns of melody that engrave themselves indelibly upon mind and heart. In the field of keyboard music his most important work is the *Well-Tempered Clavier*. The forty-eight preludes and fugues in these two volumes have been called the pianist's Old Testament (the New, it will be recalled, being Beethoven's sonatas). The suites for clavier transform the conventional dance forms of the time into abstract movements as diversified as they are appealing. Here the Leipzig cantor dons the grace and elegance of the French style. Two sets of six each are known as the *French* and *English* Suites; the titles were not Bach's. Another six dating from the Leipzig period were named Partitas. The keyboard music includes a variety of preludes, toccatas, fantasias, inventions, fugues, and fughettas. Two popular works in this category are the *Italian Concerto* and *Chromatic Fantasy and Fugue.* A favorite with young pianists is the collection of little dance pieces known as *Anna Magdalena's Notebook.* At the other extreme are the *Goldberg* Variations, so called after a virtuoso of the time. Over a ground bass in triple meter Bach constructs a gigantic edifice that sums up the art of variation as his age knew it.

Of the sonatas for various instruments, a special interest attaches to the six for unaccompanied violin. The master creates for the four strings an intricate polyphonic structure—the celebrated Chaconne is an example—and wrests from the instrument forms and textures of which one would never have suspected it capable. Whether writing for instruments or voices, Bach as often as not forced his medium to transcend its natural limitations. The instrument served his ideas; the idea was never made subservient to the instrument.

The *Brandenburg Concertos* present various instrumental combinations pitted against one another. These six works, conceived within the framework of baroque social music, bring the concerto grosso to its summit. The four Suites for Orchestra contain dance forms of appealing lyricism. The introductory movements, consisting of a stately largo followed by an allegro, descend from the French overture. Theirs is the ornate charm of a vanished world.

The two hundred-odd cantatas that have come down to us form the centerpiece of Bach's religious music. They constitute a personal document of transcendent spirituality; they project his vision of life and death. Despair, exultation, the burden of sin, the hope of redemption, the wonder of heaven and earth unfold before us in a vast canvas that can be compared only to those of the great mystical painters of an older time—Albrecht Dürer, Lucas Cranach, Hieronymus Bosch. The drama of the Crucifixion inspired Bach to plenary eloquence. His two passions are epics of the Protestant faith. The earlier, that according to St. John, depicts the final events in the life of Christ with almost violent intensity. The *St. Matthew* Passion, a work of grand proportions, is more contemplative in tone. Its double choruses embody all the splendor of the Baroque. The intensity of the music laid the composer open to the inevitable charge of being operatic. "When this theatrical music began," one critic wrote, "all were thrown into the greatest bewilderment. An old widow of the nobility said, 'God save us, my children!

It's just as if one were at an Opera Comedy!'" Despite the widow—and the critic—the *St. Matthew* Passion represents the artistic pinnacle of the Lutheran oratorio-passion.

The Mass in B minor was dedicated to Friedrich Augustus, Elector of Saxony. The greatest of Protestant composers turned to the Catholic Mass because he desired to be named court composer to the Catholic Elector, whose support he solicited in his squabbles with the authorities at Leipzig. The honorary title was granted. To the Kyrie and Gloria originally sent to the monarch "as an insignificant example of that knowledge which I have achieved in musique" he added the other three movements required by Catholic usage, the Credo, Sanctus, and Agnus Dei. The dimensions of this mightiest of masses make it unfit for liturgical use. In its mingling of Catholic and Protestant elements the work symbolically unites the two factions of Christendom. It has found a home in the concert hall, a place of worship to whose creed all that come may subscribe.

In his final years the master, increasingly withdrawn from the world, fastened his gaze upon the innermost secrets of his art. *The Musical Offering*, in which he elaborated the theme of Frederick the Great, runs the gamut of fugal and canonic thinking. Bach's last opus, *The Art of the Fugue*, constitutes his final summation of the processes of musical thought. As if to emphasize the abstract nature of his inquiry he did not specify the instrument or instruments on which the music was to be played, writing it as so many independent lines in open score. He was taken ill just when he had for the first time introduced the fugal subject B-A-C-H (the German letters for B-flat, A, C, and B-natural). This encyclopedic work, "the eternal monument of polyphony," brings to a close the history of the fugue as the central musical type of an epoch. There is a symbol in the fact that he did not live to finish it: the ultimate question had still to remain unanswered.

ORGAN FUGUE IN G MINOR

The G-minor Fugue known as "the Little," to distinguish it from a longer fugue in the same key called "the Great," is one of the most popular of Bach's works in this form. It is based on a sturdy subject that begins by outlining the tonic chord and flowers into fanciful arabesques. Announced in the soprano, the subject is answered by the alto. Next it enters in the tenor and is answered by the bass. In accordance with fugal procedure these entries alternate between the home key and the foreign, D minor.

The Exposition completed, an episode appears in which a characteristic motive is heard in imitation between alto and soprano. This motive takes on increasing significance as the fugue proceeds.

Dating from the early Weimar period, the piece is marked by compactness of structure and directness of speech. The subject, as is customary in fugues in the minor mode, is presently shifted to the major. After a climactic expansion of the material the theme makes its final appearance on the pedals, fortissimo, in the home key. The work closes with a triumphant major chord.

A brilliant if overblown transcription for orchestra has made this fugue a favorite with the public. It will be instructive, in point of style, for the reader to compare the orchestral version with the original.

PRELUDE AND FUGUE IN C MINOR

The Prelude in C minor from the *Well-Tempered Clavier*, Vol. I, No. 2, is redolent of the emotional atmosphere that endeared Bach to the nineteenth-century romantics. Tumultuous harmonies outline a melody that is implied rather than expressed. The composer investigates two problems that were close to his heart: the keyboard idiom and the progression of harmonies. The overall effect is of a rhapsodic improvisation culminating in extended arpeggios. This prelude shows off the grand sonority of the harpsichord and the capacity of the instrument for dramatic expressivity. Because of the romantic character of the music it comes off well on the piano too. Admirers of Chopin will be interested to observe how strongly his Preludes were influenced by a piece such as this.

The fugue is in three voices. The subject is of Bach's mintage, bold of contour, rhythmically varied, rich in motives, and susceptible of great diversity of treatment. Announced by alto in C minor, the subject is answered by soprano in G minor and reproduced by tenor in the

home key. The episodes are woven out of motives derived from subject and countersubject. Frequent entries of the main theme sustain tension. The play of the inner voices comes out with wonderful clearness on the harpsichord. To achieve an effect at all comparable on the piano requires a crisp and precise touch. The final announcement of the theme leads to the Coda on a sustained C in the bass—the effect known as *organ point* or *pedal point*—while the voices above make their way to a strong ending on a C-major chord.

Like the Organ Fugue in G minor, this fugue has found popularity in an orchestral transcription that expands it beyond the sonority of the instrument for which it was written. Here, too, it is illuminating to listen to the fugue in its several versions—harpsichord, piano, and orchestra.

DOUBLE VIOLIN CONCERTO IN D MINOR

The two solo violins are treated as a unit that vies "in friendly rivalry" with the accompanying group. The latter consists of first and second violins, violas, and thorough-bass. The work stands midway between concerto grosso and solo concerto. Bach follows the tradition of the Italian school in exploiting the violin's capacity for melody and brillliant figuration.

The entire ensemble announces the spirited theme that generates the opening movement.

There is continuous flowering and expansion of motives. The bass maintains the relentless beat of the Baroque. The solo passages are set off
against the tutti that furnish the architectural frame. They are written
in a virtuoso style demanding nimble leaps from low to high register.
There is animated dialogue and imitation between the two solo violins.
The writing is tuneful, relaxed, and springs from the nature of the
instrument.

The Largo ma non tanto (slow and broad, but not too much) presents
the two violins as soloists against an orchestral background. The flowing 12/8 meter, traditionally associated with pastoral or idyllic moods,
lends itself to Bach's contemplative lyricism. The movement has the
quality of a lofty duet out of baroque opera, the passages in vocal style
being interspersed with others of instrumental character. We are reminded again that opera vitally influenced the evolution of modern instrumental style.

The concluding movement is an Allegro of the same motoric type as
the first. Outcroppings of melody serve to relax the forward drive without impeding it. The solo instruments are presented in animated opposition to the group. There are some tricky triplet figures and double stops
that allow fiddlers to show the stuff they're made of. The movement
exudes a sense of physical well-being. One can see why the twentieth
century, in its rebellion against the grandiose emotionalism of the late
romantics, turned to this wholesome and well-tempered music.

CHRIST LAG IN TODESBANDEN (CHRIST LAY IN DEATH'S DARK PRISON)

In this cantata for Easter Sunday Bach tapped hallowed sources. The
words were Martin Luther's. The hymn tune had been associated with
the idea of resurrection as far back as the twelfth century and was a
favorite of the great Reformer. The seven verses of the poem give rise
to as many movements preceded by a brief Sinfonia. The cantata is in
effect a grandiose set of variations on the chorale melody that pervades
the whole fabric. Steeped in medieval mysticism, the work proclaims
the triumph of faith over death, a concept to which Bach returned again
and again.

The four-part chorus is supported mainly by first and second violins

and violas. In certain movements the voices are doubled by trombones
and by the cornett, a gentle-voiced wood instrument of the sixteenth
and seventeenth centuries (not to be confused with the modern cornet). The Sinfonia, only fourteen measures long, establishes the atmosphere of sorrow. It sets forth the basic motive, the first two notes
of the hymn tune. These outline the descending interval of a half tone
from which the work germinates.

"Christ lay in death's dark prison, sent us for our sins. He is risen
again and brings us life. Let us rejoice and praise the Lord." The opening chorus presents the chorale melody in the sopranos doubled by
cornett, against an elaborate contrapuntal background. Altos, tenors,
and basses supported by trombones present fragments of the tune in
varied rhythmic patterns against the majestic stride of the chorale.
Repetition of words and phrases allows for musical expansion. The
setting of the word *fröhlich* (joyous) with its roulades of notes on a
single syllable has all the floridity of the Baroque. The movement
mounts to a jubilant hallelujah. The key of E minor that dominates this
and the following movements is a subtle example of baroque symbolism. The sameness of key represents a prison; the change to major on
the final chord—deliverance.

"Death no man may conquer. . . ." The second verse consists of a
duet between soprano and alto, the former doubled by cornett, the latter
by trombone. This scheme prevails throughout the number. The word
Tod (death) is sung repeatedly to the descending germinal motive. The
broad curve of melody is set off by short interludes in the accompaniment. Baroque symbolism manifests itself in the setting of the line
"Death came and won power over us": the melody reaches its high
point on the word *über* (over). The concept of force in the text is
vividly depicted by wide leaps and the stride of the bass.

Verse Three brings a change of mood. The chorale, vigorously in-
toned in the tenor, announces the coming of Christ to conquer death.
The tidings give rise to an exuberant counterpoint on the violins marked
by an upward leaping figure in sixteenth notes. There is drama in the
sudden adagio on the line "And Death's image was reduced to naught,"
with a spectacular fall of the melody on the key word of the cantata,
Tod. The allegro movement is resumed.

The fourth verse is a fantasia for chorus with the chorale in the alto. "There was a wondrous battle waged between Life and Death. Life won the victory . . . and Death was reduced to mockery." The titanic struggle is reflected in the hurling of tone masses against each other, with much tossing about of the crucial word *Spott* (mockery). In Verse Five, an aria for bass, the solo voice is pitted against the violin. The chorale, heard in triple meter, takes on the character of a solemn ceremonial dance. "The Slayer cannot harm us." The sustained high note on the word *Würger* (slayer) is a joy to hear, as are the exultant repetitions of *nein* (not).

The sixth verse introduces two new patterns, the pompous dotted rhythms of the French overture and the triplets that Bach handled with particular effect. "So celebrate we the high feast. Christ is risen even as the sun . . . and the hearts of the faithful rejoice. Hallelujah." In the concluding verse the chorale is heard in Bach's harmonization, revealing its primal strength—granite-like, indestructible, a song for the ages.

We ce-le-brate this Ho-ly Feast in re-ve-rence u-ni-ted

EXCERPTS FROM THE MASS IN B MINOR

The quality of sublimity that is the salient characteristic of the B-minor Mass informs the conception as a whole. Excerpts may serve as an introduction to the work. Only a hearing of it in its entirety will reveal the vast terrain that has here been subjugated to the creative will.

The first chorus of the Gloria (No. 4) is set to the text, "Glory to God in the highest and peace on earth to men of good will." The movement is in the trumpet key of D major and allows full scope to an instrument which, to the Baroque, symbolized power and glory. The three high trumpet parts wreathe the chorus in luminous sound. Wide leaps and brisk triple meter impart to the opening motive its vigor and mobility.

The chorus is in five parts: first and second sopranos, altos, tenors, and basses. Luxuriant counterpoint unfolds in flowing lines molded to the Latin. As is apparent from the example, words like *gloria* and *excelsis* (highest) are repeated and expanded until they dissolve in music. The steady beat of the triple meter provides the framework for a rich diversity of subordinate rhythms. The voices enter in rapid succession

Glo - - - - ri- a in _ ex - cel - · - - - sis

and build steadily to the abrupt change of mood and pace on the words "and peace on earth." A new motive establishes a mood of supplication. The interrupted movement begins anew, picks up momentum, and broadens into a majestic stream.

The arias and duets distributed through the mass supply areas of relaxation between the overpowering choruses. The arias embody a cardinal principle of baroque style, the voice being pitted against the same instrument throughout an entire number. This sameness of color ensures the predominance of a single mood. The vocal arabesques are not especially differentiated from the instrumental. The writing is not necessarily unvocal (although in the hands of any but a first-class singer it may sound so). Rather, as so often in Bach, is the medium made to serve the idea: in short, to surpass itself.

A characteristic aria is that for alto on the text, "Thou who sittest at the right hand of the Father, have mercy on us" (No. 9). The solo voice is contrasted with the oboe d'amore, a low oboe whose sweet tone was much prized by the Baroque. The key word *miserere* (have mercy) establishes a mood of entreaty which is admirably underlined by the dark resonance of the alto voice and the plaintive timbre of the oboe. The aria is in minor, in a gentle 6/8 that sounds the better for not being dragged. The vocal line is florid yet impregnated with feeling. The opening phrase returns at the close to round off the form in an abbreviated A-B-A.

"And He was crucified for our sake under Pontius Pilate, He suffered and was buried" (No. 16). For the most dramatic chorus of the mass, Bach ventured into the territory that lies between church and opera

Bach
Grave

house. Two symbols of grief—chromatic harmony and descending movement—dominate this choral passacaglia. The ground bass is repeated thirteen times. Minor mode and the use of dissonance reinforce the atmosphere of sorrow, as does the depersonalized sound of two flutes that stand out against the tone mass. When the nethermost point has been reached there is an abrupt modulation to G major. Despair gives way to the jubilant chorus of the Resurrection.

"And He was resurrected on the third day according to Scripture and ascended into heaven" (No. 17). Three trumpets and kettledrums help announce the joyful tidings. The movement is in the trumpet key of D major. The basic mood is established by brisk triple meter, vigorous triplets, and the bold upthrust of the theme.

The high trumpet parts give players plenty to worry about. The voices pile one upon the other in intricate imitation as the central word *resur-rexit* expands into florid arabesque. Orchestral interludes set off the spacious architecture. This is music to resound over hills and valleys: the pronouncement of one who saw God enthroned in heaven and translated the vision into an enduring memorial to the divinity in man.

The notion may be dismissed that Bach was unappreciated in his lifetime. He could not have continued to write cantatas for forty-five years if he had not reached his public. He was known and admired by his generation even if his greatness was not realized in full. It was the following generations that neglected him. The Lutheran world out of which he stemmed ceased to be a living force even while he was immortalizing its spirit. Great changes were impending, in life and art alike. In this new climate his polyphony seemed pedantic, his baroque monumentality heavy and oppressive. Rejected by fashionable taste, his music disappeared from the scene. Manuscripts of his were suffered to be lost. The plates of *The Art of Fugue* were sold for the price of the metal when the work failed to attract purchasers. For fifty years after his death no single work of his was deemed worthy of separate publication. To the musical public of the 1760s the name Bach meant his four sons, whose success as composers far exceeded his. Even they considered his music old-fashioned. One of them, with engaging lack of filial piety, referred to him as "the old Wig."

Yet the memory of him did not wholly die. It was kept alive in the decades after his death by his sons, his pupils, and by those who had heard him play. Then the revival began, tentatively at first but with increasing force until it had become a veritable renascence. Scholars, composers, and performers alike contributed to this extraordinary reinstatement. The romantic age felt akin to his fervor, his chromatic harmonies, his vaulting architecture, the thrust and splendor of his polyphony. The *St. Matthew* Passion, forgotten for more than three quarters of a century, was resurrected by the twenty-year-old Mendelssohn in an epochal performance. Chopin practiced Bach before his concerts. Liszt transcribed the organ works for the piano. Schumann was one of the founders of the Bach Society, an organization that undertook the monumental task of publishing a complete edition of the master's works. The Cantor of Leipzig at last came into his own.

His spirit animated not only the nineteenth century but, in even more fruitful manner, the twentieth. We see him today not only as a consummate artist who brought new meanings to music, but as one of the gigantic figures of Western culture.

⪢54⪡

George Frideric Handel (1685-1759)

"Milord, I should be sorry if I only entertained them. I wished to make them better."

IF BACH represents the subjective mysticism of the late Baroque, Handel incarnates its worldly pomp. Born in the same year, the two giants of the age never met. The Cantor of Leipzig had little point of contact with the redoubtable Saxon who from the first was cut out for an international career. Handel's natural habitat was the opera house. He was at home amid the intrigues of court life. A magnificent adventurer, he gambled for fame and fortune in a feverish struggle to impose his will upon the world; and he dominated the musical life of a nation for a century after his death.

HIS LIFE

He was born at Halle in Saxony, son of a prosperous barber-surgeon who did not regard music as a suitable profession for a young man of the middle class. His father's death left him free to follow his bent. After a year at the University of Halle the ambitious youth went to Hamburg, where he gravitated to the opera house and entered the orchestra as second violinist. He soon absorbed the Italian operatic style that reigned in Hamburg. His first opera, written when he was twenty, created a furore. Its full title echoes the grandiloquence of the Baroque: *The Changes of Fortune undergone by the Crown;* OR *Almira, Queen of Castille.*

Handel's thoughts turned to Italy. Only there, he felt, would he master the operatic art. He reached Rome shortly before his twenty-second birthday; the three years he spent in Italy unfolded against a splendid background peopled by music-loving princes and cardinals. His opera *Rodrigo* was produced in Florence under the patronage of Prince Ferdinand de Medici. The libretto of his opera *Agrippina* was written by the Viceroy of Naples, Cardinal Grimani. Presented at Venice, the work sent the Italians into transports of delight. The theater resounded with cries of "Long live the dear Saxon!"

At the age of twenty-five, Handel was appointed conductor to the Elector of Hanover. He received the equivalent of fifteen hundred dollars a year at a time when Bach at Weimar was paid eighty. A flying visit to London in the autumn of 1710 brought him for the first time to the city that was to be his home for well-nigh fifty turbulent years. *Rinaldo,* written in a fortnight, conquered the English public with its fresh tender melodies. A year later Handel obtained another leave and returned to London, this time for good. With the *Birthday Ode for Queen Anne* and the *Te Deum* (hymn of thanksgiving) for the Peace of Utrecht he entered upon the writing of large-scale works for great public occasions. Anne rewarded him with a pension; whereupon nothing would make him go back to his Hanoverian master. By an unforeseen turn of events his master came to him: Anne died and the Elector ascended the throne of England as George I. The monarch was vexed with his truant composer; but he loved music more than protocol, and soon restored him to favor.

Handel's opportunity came with the founding in 1720 of the Royal Academy of Music. The enterprise, launched for the purpose of presenting Italian opera, was backed by a group of wealthy peers headed by the King. Handel was appointed one of the musical directors and at thirty-five found himself occupying a key position in the artistic life of England. For the next eight years he was active in producing and directing his operas as well as writing them. His crowded life passed at a far remove from the solitude we have come to associate with the creative process. He produced his works in bursts of inspiration that kept him chained to his desk for days at a time. He would turn out an opera in from two to three weeks.

Hardly less feverish was the struggle for power inseparable from a

George Frideric Handel.

position such as his. Overbearing, obstinate when crossed, the Saxon was no mean master of the art of making enemies. His fiery temper found much to exercise it. He was at the mercy of the cliques at court, and he was subject to pressure from the peers who had invested in the enterprise. He was viewed with suspicion by the leaders of English thought who saw in his operas a threat to native music and theater.

Addison and Steele, in the pages of the *Spectator* and *Tatler*, missed no opportunity to attack his ventures. It must be said that other men of letters more justly estimated his stature. Pope in the *Dunciad* (1742) thus describes his monumental style:

> Strong in new Arms, lo! Giant HANDEL stands,
> Like bold Briareus, with a hundred hands;
> To stir, to rouze, to shake the Soul he comes,
> And Jove's own Thunders follow Mars's Drums.

Handel functioned in a theater riddled with the worst features of the star system. When the celebrated soprano Cuzzoni refused to sing an aria as he directed, Handel, a giant of a man, seized her around the waist and threatened to drop her out of a window if she would not obey. The rivalry between Cuzzoni and the great singer Faustina Bordoni culminated in a hair-pulling match on the stage, accompanied by the smashing of scenery and fist fights throughout the house. A rivalry no less fierce developed between Handel and his associate in directing the Academy, the composer Marc' Antonio Bononcini. The supposition that genius resided in one or the other, which brought to the arena of art the psychology of the prize-ring, appealed strongly to the fashionable hangers-on of the Royal Academy. Bononcini was the protégé of the Tory Duchess of Marlborough; whereupon Handel, whose interest in British politics was—to say the least—limited, became *the* Whig composer. The feud was immortalized in a jingle that made the rounds of the coffee houses.

> Some say that Signor Bononcini
> Compared to Handel is a ninny;
> Whilst others say that to him Handel
> Is hardly fit to hold a candle.
> Strange that such difference should be
> 'Twixt Tweedledum and Tweedledee.

It was amid such distractions that Handel's operas—he produced forty in a period of thirty years—came into being. Some were written too hastily, in others he obviously accommodated himself to the needs of the box office; yet all bear the imprint of a genius unfolding his powers within the frame of a dying art form. Despite his productivity the Royal Academy tottered to its ruin, its treasury depleted by the extravagance of the peers, its morale sapped by mismanagement and dissension. The final blow was administered in 1728 by the sensational success of *The Beggar's Opera*. Sung in English, its tunes and humor related to the experience of the audience, this ballad opera was the answer of middle-class England to the gods and heroes of the aristocratic *opera seria*. Ironically, even a bit of Handel's *Rinaldo* found its way into the score.

It should have been apparent to the composer-impresario that a new era had dawned; but, refusing to read the omens, he invested thousands in the New Royal Academy of Music. Again a succession of operas rolled from his pen, among them *Orlando Furioso*, "the boldest of his works." But not even Handel's colossal powers could indefinitely sustain the pace. He was fifty-two when he crashed. "This infernal flesh," as he called it, succumbed to a paralytic stroke. His mind buckled. He owed thousands of pounds, and for a space he stood in the shadow of debtors' prison. Desperate and grievously ill, he acknowledged defeat and went abroad to recover his health. His enemies gloated: the giant was finished.

They underestimated his powers of recovery. He came back to resume the battle. It needed five more expensive failures—among them *Serse* (Xerxes), whence the famous Largo—to make him realize that *opera seria* in London was finished. At this lowest point in his fortunes there opened, by chance, the road that was to lead him from opera in Italian to oratorio in English, from ruin to immortality. Admirers of his got up a private performance of *Haman and Mordecai*, a masque he had written many years before. The combination of Pope's text and Handel's music pleased so greatly that he decided to bring this "sacred opera" before the public. When the Bishop of London forbade the representation of biblical characters in a theater, Handel hit upon a way out. "There will be no acting upon the Stage," he announced, "but the house will be fitted up in a decent manner, for the audience." In this way London heard its first Handelian oratorio.

He saw at once the advantage of a type of entertainment that dispensed with costly foreign singers and lavish scenery. *Deborah* and *Athalia* were followed by two of his greatest oratorios, *Saul* and *Israel in Egypt*, both composed in the space of a little over three months. Many dark moments still lay ahead. He had to extricate himself from the debts of the past, and to find his way to his new middle-class public. That indomitable will never faltered. *Messiah, Samson, Semele, Joseph and His Brethren, Hercules, Belshazzar*, although they did not conquer at once, were received sufficiently well to encourage him to continue on his course. Finally, with *Judas Maccabeus* (1746), the tide turned. The British public responded to the imagery of the Old Testament. The suppression of the last Stuart rebellion created the proper atmosphere for Handel's heroic tone. He kept to biblical subjects in the final group of oratorios—*Alexander Balus, Joshua, Susanna, Solomon, Jeph-*

tha—an astonishing list for a man in his sixties. With these the master brought his work to a close.

There remained to face the final enemy—blindness. But even this blow did not reduce him to inactivity. Like Milton and Bach, he dictated his last works, which were mainly revisions of earlier ones. He continued to appear in public, conducting the oratorios and displaying his legendary powers on the organ. A contemporary account tells how, when *Samson* was performed, at Milton's famous lines on the blinded hero, "Total eclipse–no sun, no moon; All dark amid the blaze of noon," "the view of the blind Composer then sitting by the Organ affected the audience so forcibly that many persons present were moved to tears."

Shortly after his seventy-fourth birthday he began his usual oratorio season, conducting ten major works in little over a month to packed houses. The *Messiah* closed the series. He collapsed in the theater at the end of the performance and died some days later. The nation he had served for half a century accorded him its highest honor. "Last night about Eight O'clock the remains of the late great Mr Handel were deposited at the foot of the Duke of Argyll's Monument in Westminster Abbey. . . . There was almost the greatest Concourse of People of all Ranks ever seen upon such, or indeed upon any other Occasion."

HIS MUSIC

Himself sprung from the middle class, Handel made his career in the land where the middle class first came to power. A vast social change is symbolized in his turning from court opera to oratorio. In so doing he became one of the architects of the new bourgeois culture and a creator of the modern mass public. Like Bach, he stood in the mainstream of European music, assimilating to his art German, Italian, French, and English elements. Bach and he complement each other as the representative figures of the late Baroque. Bach's art is introspective; Handel is the man of action. Bach broods in the organ loft; Handel is the courtier. Bach is the meticulous artist who brings every form he touches to perfection; Handel, tossing off his scores for the theater, is a magnificent improviser. Bach is a master of detail; Handel works with sweeping brush strokes. Bach's mystic gaze is turned upon the world to come; Handel hymns the pomp and power of this world. Both men were inspired by an ethical ideal; but Bach was the Lutheran, while Handel was a man of the Enlightenment whose moral sense was bound to no creed or dogma.

The oratorios of Handel are choral dramas of overpowering vitality and grandeur. Vast murals, they are conceived in epic style. Their soaring arias and dramatic recitatives, stupendous fugues and double choruses consummate the splendor of the Baroque. With the instinct of the born leader he gauged the need of his adopted country (whose language, in forty-seven years of residence, he never wholly mastered). He created in the oratorio an art form replete with the blood and thunder of the Old Testament, ideally suited to the taste of England's middle class. In the command of Jehovah to the Chosen People to go forth and conquer the land of Canaan they recognized a clear mandate to go forth and secure the British Empire.

Handel made the chorus—the people—the center of the drama. Freed from the rapid pace imposed by stage action, he expanded to vast dimensions each scene and emotion. The chorus now touches off the action, now reflects upon it. As in Greek tragedy it serves both as protagonist and ideal spectator. The characters are drawn larger than life-size. Saul, Joshua, Deborah, Judas Maccabeus, Samson are archetypes of human nature; creatures of destiny, majestic in defeat as in victory, through whom is proclaimed the redemption of the strong and the rejection of the weak. The oratorios are folk dramas of monumental cast in which are fused dramatic, lyric, contemplative, and descriptive elements. Through them surges the rhetoric of a heroic age and a heroic temperament.

The Handelian oratorio emerged as England's national art form soon after the master's death. The hundredth anniversary of his birth was marked by a celebration in Westminster Abbey in which over five hundred singers and players participated. This number was enlarged in subsequent Handel festivals until a chorus of three and a half thousand drowned out an orchestra of five hundred, occasioning Horace Walpole's lovely remark: "The Oratorios thrive abundantly; for my part they give me an idea of Heaven, where everybody is to sing whether they have voices or not." Handel, be it remembered, produced his oratorios with a chorus of about thirty singers and a like number of instrumentalists. To increase the size of this group more than fiftyfold meant sacrificing many subtleties of his writing. Yet his art, with its grand outlines and sweeping effects, was able to take such treatment. It was indeed "the music for a great active people," inviting mass participation even as it demanded mass listening.

Handel's rhythm has the powerful drive of the Baroque. One must hear one of his choruses to realize what a simple 4/4 time can achieve in the way of momentum. He leaned to diatonic harmony even as

Bach's more searching idiom favored the chromatic. His melody, rich in mood and feeling, unfolds in great majestic arches. His is a basically vocal conception, whereas Bach's is instrumental. In respect to form he was conservative, his kind of communication demanding a clear elegant simplicity rather than experiment. His fluent, singing counterpoint comes from Italian rather than German sources. Nor does it seek the transcendental regions of Bach's. His thinking is based on massive pillars of sound—the chords—within which the voices interweave. His fugues are impulsive and free. They do not hesitate to abandon contrapuntal logic for the massed harmonies that fired his imagination.

Rooted in the world of the theater, Handel made use of tone color for atmosphere and dramatic expression. He was thoroughly progressive in this regard, hastening to use what were then new instruments such as the clarinet or the contrabassoon whose construction he himself suggested. In *Saul*, for example, trombones suggest the majesty of the King; two bassoons accompany the utterances of the prophet Samuel's ghost. Trumpets and horns impart a baroque opulence to his music. His wonderful sense of sound comes out in the pieces intended for outdoor performance, the *Water Music* and *Royal Fireworks Music*. In the latter work he realized the dream of many a later composer, scoring for forty trumpets, twenty horns, sixteen oboes, sixteen bassoons, and eight kettledrums; also a cannon!

The big choral pieces to celebrate occasions of national rejoicing exemplify what has been called Handel's "big bow-wow" manner. Most famous are the Coronation Anthems for the accession of George II, one of which—*Zadok the Priest*—has helped crown every subsequent ruler of England. The operas contain some of the composer's finest measures. They have not maintained themselves on the stage chiefly because they demand a kind of vocal virtuosity that no longer exists. Also, as we indicated in our discussion of baroque opera, they were conceived for a theater whose conventions are alien to our own.

Besides his dramatic works Handel produced an impressive amount of instrumental music. Best known in this category are the twelve concerti grossi, which together with Bach's *Brandenburg Concertos* represent the peak of baroque orchestral music. The concertos for organ and orchestra are brilliant showpieces that he performed between the acts of the oratorios. He wrote down only a skeletal version of what he improvised in public. His keyboard pieces are undeservedly neglected. One, a theme and variations known as *The Harmonious Blacksmith*, has achieved universal popularity. There never was a blacksmith who sang the tune as he smote the anvil, nor a thunderstorm during which Handel found shelter in the smithy and heard him sing it—another good Handel story that never happened.

Handel's music contained the elements of popular art. Several of his tunes became song hits of the time. The March from *Rinaldo* turned up in *The Beggar's Opera* as "Let's take the road." In *Polly*, the sequel to that work, a minuet from the *Water Music* became "Cheer up, my lads." The official march of England's Grenadier Guards comes from a processional in the opera *Scipione*. In a letter of the time we find: "The great Handel has told me that the hints of his very best songs have several of them been owing to the sounds in his ears of cries in the streets." Given his temperament, it was inevitable that the rhythms of life, the accents of song and dance, the inflections of living speech would nourish his warmly human art.

MESSIAH

"For the Relief of the Prisoners in the several Gaols, and for the Support of Mercer's Hospital in Stephen's-street and of the Charitable Infirmary on the Inn's Quay, on Monday the 12th of April, will be performed at the Musick Hall in Fishamble-Street, *Mr Handel's new Grand Oratorio, called the Messiah,* in which the Gentlemen of the Choirs of both Cathedrals will assist, with some Concertos on the Organ, by Mr Handel." In this fashion Dublin was apprised in the spring of 1742 of the launching of one of the world's most widely loved works.

The music was written down in twenty-four days, Handel working as one possessed. His servant found him, after the completion of the Hallelujah Chorus, with tears streaming from his eyes. "I did think I did see all Heaven before me, and the great God Himself!" Upon finishing *Messiah* the master went on without a pause to *Samson*, the first part of which was ready two weeks later. Truly it was an age of giants.

With its massive choruses, tuneful recitatives, and broadly flowing arias *Messiah* has come to represent the Handelian oratorio in the public mind. Actually it is not typical of the oratorios as a whole. Those are imbued with dramatic conflict, while *Messiah* is cast in a mood of lyric contemplation. Although it has been ranked with the religious master-pieces, *Messiah* in no way partakes of the mysticism of a Palestrina mass or of the *St. Matthew* Passion. It expresses rather the humane faith of a man of the world—the eighteenth-century world—who happened to be a great musician.

The libretto is a compilation of verses from the Bible that appeared under the name of Charles Jennens, a wealthy dabbler in the arts. (There is reason to believe that Jennens's chaplain more than took a hand in the task.) The first part treats of the prophecy of the coming of Christ and His birth; the second of His suffering, death, and the spread of His doctrine; and the third of the redemption of the world through faith. The verses are drawn from various Prophets of the Old Testament, especially Isaiah, from the Psalms and Evangelists. Upon this assorted material the music imposes a magnificent unity. The great choruses become the pillars of an architectonic structure in which the recitatives and arias serve as areas of lesser tension.

Handel's original orchestration was extraordinarily modest and clear in texture. He wrote mainly for strings with an occasional use of oboes, trumpets, and drums. The work was conceived, in terms of baroque practice, for a small group of players supplemented at the climactic moments by a larger group. The orchestration we hear in performances today was augmented to keep pace with the ever growing size of the chorus. Various musicians produced these additional accompaniments, Mozart among them.

The Overture, in the French style, opens with a *grave* (slow, solemn) in dotted rhythms, in a somber E minor, and passes over into a sturdy three-voiced fugue. The recitative *Comfort ye, my people* is a tenor arioso in E major, larghetto e piano, over one of those broadly flowing accompaniments of which Handel knew the secret. Characteristic is the majestic span of the melody. There follows the aria, *Every valley shall be exalted*, with baroque expansion of the word "exalted." In this and later arias the architecture is broadened by orchestral introductions, interludes, and postludes. The music unfolds continuously from the opening figure which imparts to each number its sovereign unity of thought and expression.

The first chorus, *And the glory of the Lord*, is an allegro in A major. The vision of Divine glory fires Handel's imagination to a spacious choral fresco in which an exciting contrapuntal texture alternates with towering chords. The vigorous triple meter assumes the character of a festal dance. From the opening motive

mf And the glo- ry, the glo-ry of the Lord shall be re - veal - ed

and those that follow is fashioned a fabric of continuous imitation and expansion, with much repetition of text. The forward stride of the bass never slackens. Highly dramatic is the grand pause before the end. In the final chords, as often happens with Handel, the choral writing is influenced by organ sound.

The bright A-major sound gives way to a somber D minor in the recitative and aria for bass, *Thus saith the Lord of Hosts: Yet once a little while, and I will shake the heav'ns and the earth.*" The florid expansion on the word "shake" is worthy of note. Handel's operatic background is revealed by the expressive accompaniment with its urgent dotted rhythm and repeated chords. The fugal chorus in G, *And He shall purify the sons of Levi,* is one of four choral numbers in *Messiah* whose themes Handel drew from an earlier work. There follows a group in a gracious D major. The recitative for alto, *Behold! a virgin shall conceive,* leads into the aria *O thou that tellest good tidings to Zion.* The expressive melody in flowing 6/8 meter is one of Handel's happiest inspirations. It is taken over, in subtly altered guise, by the chorus: the emotion projected at first through the individual is now experienced by mankind as a whole.

An affecting change from major to minor comes with the recitative for bass, *For behold, darkness shall cover the earth.* The idea of darkness is projected through a sinuously chromatic figure, both here and in the aria *The people that walked in darkness have seen a great light.* We encounter at this point a memorable example of Handel's sensitivity to key. The movement from darkness to light is marked repeatedly by a modulation from minor to major.

There follows one of the highlights of the score, the chorus *For unto us a child is born.* The theme, taken from one of the master's Italian duets, is of Handelian sturdiness.

The piece displays the unflagging rhythmic energy of the Baroque. Harmonic and contrapuntal elements are fused into a stalwart unity. There is joyously florid expansion on the word "born." Unforgettable is the pomp and glory at "Wonderful . . . Counselor." The words peal forth in earth-shaking jubilation; yet with what economy of means the effect is achieved.

The Pastoral Symphony is cast in the gently flowing, dotted 12/8 rhythm that recurs throughout the work as a unifying thread. Generally associated with bucolic moods, this is derived from an Italian folk dance—the siciliano—and sets the scene for the following recitative,

There were shepherds abiding in the field, keeping watch over their flocks by night. The celebrated arioso for soprano establishes the traditional association of *Messiah* with the Christmas season. Wonder and tenderness pervade this music. There follows the chorus *Glory to God* in the trumpet key of D major, where for the first time in the work Handel calls for trumpets. This number is usually begun in a bright fortissimo, as befits good tidings; yet Handel intended rather a mood of reverence and awe, for he wrote in the score Da lontano e un poco piano (as from afar and somewhat softly). The soprano aria *Rejoice greatly, O daughter of Zion!* is a brilliant allegro. The basic mood, an exalted joy, is established at the outset by the leaping figure in the vocal line.

There follows one of the most beautiful arias of the oratorio, *He shall feed His flock like a shepherd*, in the pastoral siciliano rhythm. An infinite quietude of spirit informs this promise of rest to the heavy laden. The chorus *His yoke is easy* is a finely wrought fugal piece marked by lively interplay of the voices. A dramatic pause interrupts the intricate polyphonic expansion, after which the voices unite in the grandiose chords that bring the first part of *Messiah* to an end.

The tone of the second part is established by the sorrowful chorus *Behold the Lamb of God*, with its slow dotted rhythm and drooping inflection. The tragic mood continues with the aria for alto, *He was despised and rejected of men*. The affective words "sorrows" and "grief" inspire chromatic harmony and modulations to dark keys such as B-flat minor and F minor. The vocal declamation takes on dramatic intensity in the part that follows, *He gave His back to the smiters*, as does the agitated orchestral accompaniment. Personal grief broadens into collective expression in a grandly pathetic chorus in F minor, *Surely He hath borne our griefs and carried our sorrows*. Plangent discords underline the thought *He was bruised for our iniquities*. The tone of anguish is carried into the chorus *And with His stripes we are healed*. The subject of this spacious fugue is marked by the downward leap of a diminished seventh—an emotionally charged interval—on the word "stripes."

This compact theme was common property in the eighteenth century: Bach used it in his *Well-Tempered Clavier* and Mozart in the *Requiem*.

A third chorus completes the majestic fresco. *All we like sheep have gone astray* is marked by characteristic rhythm, relentless contrapuntal energy, and briskly moving harmonic masses. But this is one of the spots where Handel's ear for his adopted language goes astray. "All we like sheep" would not sound right no matter who set it to music.

Concerts today are considerably shorter than they were in the leisure-class society of Handel's time. It is customary to reduce *Messiah* in length by omitting some numbers, especially from the second and third parts. A favorite among the later pieces is the chorus *Lift up your heads, O ye gates!* The question "Who is the King of Glory?" elicits a reply of Handelian grandeur. The 12/8 siciliano rhythm returns in the deeply felt soprano aria in G minor, *How beautiful are the feet of them that preach the gospel of peace.* Hardly less popular is the bass aria *Why do the nations so furiously rage together?* in which the florid expansion of the word "rage" demands some virtuoso singing.

The climax of the second part is of course the Hallelujah Chorus. The musical investiture of the key word is one of those strokes of genius

that resound through the ages. The triumphal outburst has been compared to the finale of Beethoven's Fifth Symphony. (It is significant that Beethoven, himself the orator of a heroic age, admired Handel profoundly.) A grand effect is the sustained "Kings of Kings and Lord of Lords" in the upper voices against the jubilant Hallelujahs of the lower. The drums beat, the trumpets resound. This music sings of a victorious Lord, and His host is an army with banners.

The third part opens with *I know that my Redeemer liveth*, a serene expression of faith that is one of the great Handel arias. When on the crucial words "For now is Christ risen from the dead" the soprano voice ascends stepwise to the climactic G-sharp on "risen," there is established unassailably the idea of redemption that is the ultimate message of the work. The thought triumphs with the two final choral numbers, *Worthy is the Lamb that was slain* and the Amen Chorus.

Of the latter one need only say that it meets the supreme challenge of following the Hallelujah Chorus without a sense of anticlimax. With this is consummated a work as titanic in conception as in execution.

Messiah today is popularly associated with a religious setting. Yet it was in no way written for a church service. The work was meant to be an Entertainment, as its librettist described it. That is, it was intended for the commercial concert hall by a bankrupt impresario-composer eager to recoup his losses. That so exalted a conception could take shape in such circumstances testifies to the nature of the age whence it issued—and to the stature of the master of whom Beethoven said, "He was the greatest of us all."

PART SIX

The Twentieth Century

✠

"The century of aeroplanes has a right to its own music. As there
are no precedents, I must create anew."

Claude Debussy

≥55≤

The Post-Romantic Era

"I came into a very young world in a very old time."
Erik Satie

IT BECAME clear in the final decades of the nineteenth century that the romantic impulse had exhausted itself. The grand style had run its course, to end in the overblown gestures that mark the decline of a tradition. The composers who were born in the 1860s and reached artistic maturity in the last decade of the century could not but feel, as did Satie, that they had come into the world in a "very old time." It was their historic task to bridge the gap between dying romanticism and the twentieth century.

Three leaders of German post-romanticism became international figures: Richard Strauss, Gustav Mahler, and Hugo Wolf. In Italy the operatic tradition was carried on by Giacomo Puccini. His generation included Ruggiero Leoncavallo, remembered for *I Pagliacci* (The Clowns), and Pietro Mascagni, whose reputation likewise rests on a single success, *Cavalleria Rusticana* (Rustic Chivalry). These Italians were associated with the movement known as verismo (realism), which tried to bring into the lyric theater the naturalism of Zola, Ibsen, and of the modern drama. Instead of choosing historical or mythological themes, the realists picked subjects from everyday life and treated them in down-to-earth fashion. The action was swift, ofttimes brutal, and emphasized tragedies of peasant life.

The national schools of the late romantic period ended the supremacy of German musical culture. This development came to a head with the First World War, when Germany and Austria were cut off from the rest of Europe. In the post-romantic period several newcomers appeared on the musical horizon. Besides Finland these included England, Spain, and the United States. A school of French orchestral composers came into prominence; national schools continued to flourish in Russia and Bohemia. And there emerged the movement that more than any other ushered in the twentieth century—impressionism.

The decades that framed the turn of the nineteenth century are of paramount interest to music lovers. They not only brought the art from the twilight of one epoch to the dawn of another, but also contained the seeds of much that is important to us today.

ᕗ56ᕘ
Giacomo Puccini (1858-1924)

"Almighty God touched me with his little finger and said, 'Write
for the theater—mind you, only for the theater!' And I have
obeyed the supreme command."

GIACOMO PUCCINI was the foremost composer of Italian opera at the
turn of the century. He was one of those fortunate artists who combine
a refined sensibility with the popular touch. Coming out of a great
tradition, he was able to communicate directly and easily with the
varied public that the romantic period had brought into being.

HIS LIFE

He was born in Lucca, son of a church organist in whose footsteps
he expected to follow. It was at Milan, where he went to complete his
studies, that his true bent came to the fore. He studied at the Conservatory with Amilcare Ponchielli, composer of *La Gioconda*. The ambitious young musician did not have to wait long for success. His first
opera, *Le Villi* (The Vampires), produced when he was twenty-six,
was received with enthusiasm. *Manon Lescaut*, based on the novel of
Abbé Prévost—it was the source also of Massenet's *Manon*—established
him as the most promising among the rising generation of Italian composers. In Luigi Illica and Giuseppe Giacosa he found an ideal pair of
librettists, and with this writing team he produced the three most
successful operas of the early twentieth century: *La Bohème* in 1896;
Tosca in 1900; and *Madame Butterfly*, after a play by David Belasco,
in 1904. The dates should dispel the popular notion of Puccini as a facile
melodist who tossed off one score after another. Each of his operas
represented years of detailed work involving ceaseless changes until he
was satisfied.

The *Girl of the Golden West* (1910) was based, like its predecessor,
on a play by Belasco. The world première, at the Metropolitan Opera
House, was a major event. Despite its brilliant launching the work did
not maintain itself in the repertory. A more substantial achievement
was the trio of one-act operas: *Il Tabarro* (The Cloak), *Suor Angelica*

(Sister Angelica), and the comic opera *Gianni Schicchi*. The first two are not heard frequently. The third is a masterpiece.

Handsome and magnetic, Puccini was idolized and feted wherever he went. His wife was jealous not without reason. "I am always falling in love," he confessed. "When I no longer am, make my funeral." As he entered middle age this singer of youth and love began to feel that his time was running out. "I am growing old and that disgusts me. I am burning to start work but have no libretto and am in a state of torment. I need work just as I need food." After much seeking he found a story that released the music in him and embarked on his final task—*Turandot*. He labored for four years on this fairy-tale opera about the beautiful and cruel princess of China. A work of consummate artistry, it is his most polished score. Puccini, ill with cancer, pushed ahead with increasing urgency. "If I do not succeed in finishing the opera someone will come to the front of the stage and say, 'Puccini composed as far as this, then he died.' "

He was sent to Brussels for treatment, accompanied by his son and the rough draft of the final scene. He succumbed after the operation, at the age of sixty-six. *Turandot* was completed from his sketches by his friend Franco Alfano. At the first performance at La Scala, however, the composer's wish was fulfilled. Arturo Toscanini, his greatest interpreter, laid down the baton during the lament over the body of Liu. Turning to the audience he said in a choking voice, "Here ends the master's work."

HIS MUSIC

Puccini was a practical man of the theater with a wonderful instinct for what "goes" on the stage. Like Verdi before him he functioned within the requirements of a living tradition, striving with endless ingenuity to adapt those requirements to the needs of his public. Comparisons with Verdi are dangerous, for Puccini had none of the elemental grandeur that made the older man the mouthpiece of a nation. He was quite clear as to the scope of his talent. "I am not made for heroic gestures. I love the souls that feel, that know hope and illusion, that respond to bright joy and tearful melancholy."

The problem of the libretto was crucial for Puccini. With the completion of each work began anew a frantic search for the right story. He was able to create only out of utter conviction and enthusiasm. "Without fever there is no creation. For emotional art is a kind of sickness, an abnormal mental state accompanied by over-excitement of every fiber and atom of a man's being." He shaped each detail of the drama; his letters to his librettists cajole, instruct, spur on to further effort. "There are certain fixed laws in the theater—to interest, to surprise, to move. . . . Put all your strength into it, all the resources of your hearts and heads, and create me something that will make the world weep. . . . I want a libretto that can move the world. Let it be passionate, stirring, not of vast but of varied scope." He drove his collaborators frantic; Giacosa and Illica vowed times without number that they would never work with him again. But he refused to let be, lashing them on to version after version until they had turned out librettos that remain models of achievement for all future aspirants in this impossible branch of literary composition.

Italian to the core, Puccini had the gift of melody—a flowing amorous melody molded to the curve of the voice, that pervades the entire musical fabric, recitative as well as aria. He often transforms recitative into the more tuneful arioso—that is, into a free and finely molded vocal line which makes even his dialogue and action melodious. The harmonies are pungent and rich in atmosphere. The orchestration is full of light and shade, effective without being obtrusive. Suddenly violins, violas, and 'cellos unite with the voice; and we are launched on one of those flowing sensuous tunes that Puccini's instinct rightly told him would be hummed and whistled everywhere. All this moves in rhythms animated and varied, it never lags, it never stops to teach or preach or philosophize. It is theater pure and simple. Puccini had the supreme wisdom of the operatic composer: he never permitted the music to stop the drama.

LA BOHÈME

Puccini's best-loved work is based on Henri Murger's *La Vie de Bohème* (Bohemian Life). The novel depicts the joys and sorrows of the young artists who flock to Paris in search of fame and fortune, congregating in the Latin Quarter on the left bank of the Seine. "A gay life yet a terrible one," Murger called their precarious existence woven of bold dreams and bitter realities. Puccini's characteristic vein —vivacity shot through with melancholy—was peculiarly suited to this atmosphere of "laughter through tears." Remembering his own life as a struggling young musician in Milan, he recaptured its wistfulness and its charm.

The Bohemian mood is set by the exuberantly rhythmic motive with which the opera opens.

The curtain rises at once, disclosing the attic in which live Rudolf the poet, Marcel the painter, and their two comrades-in-arms, the young philosopher Colline and the musician Schaunard. Rudolf's first arietta is associated with him throughout the work. Its mixture of ardor and dreaminess well characterizes the young poet.

Marcel and Rudolf try to work, but can think of nothing but the cold. They are presently joined, first by Colline, then by Schaunard who by a stroke of luck has come on some money. The landlord arrives with a nasty word—the rent!—and is got rid of. The young men go off to the Café Momus to celebrate Christmas Eve, Rudolf remaining behind to finish an article he is writing.

There is a knock on the door. Enter Mimi and romance. Her arrival is heralded in this act as in later ones by a poignant phrase. Her candle has gone out. Will Rudolf light it? Their dialogue—a *parlando* (speech-song) bathed by the orchestra in a current of emotion—exemplifies the spell that Puccini casts over even the homeliest sentiments. "A little wine? . . . Thank you . . . Here it is . . . Not so much . . . Like this? . . . Thank you."

Mimi returns, having missed her key. Their candles are extinguished by a gust of wind; they search for the key, on the floor, in the dark. Rudolf, finding it, has the presence of mind to slip it into his pocket. When their hands touch it is time for an aria. First Rudolf's—*Che gelida manina* (How cold your little fingers, let me warm them into life). Here is the Italian *cantabile*, the melody gliding along the scale and rising in a broad golden curve to its crest. Three centuries of operatic tradition stand behind an aria such as this.

Her reply, the aria *Mi chiamano Mimi* (I'm known as Mimi), is followed by the duet. This is based on a phrase from Rudolf's aria which now becomes the love theme of the opera.

Rudolf, smitten, invites her to the café, to phrases that have become part of the Italian folklore of flirtation. "Give me your arm, my little

lady . . . I obey you, my lord." The act ends on the word *amor*, as it should, with a high C for the soprano to bring down the curtain.

Act II—Christmas Eve in the Latin Quarter—is a festive street scene. Puccini's feeling for atmosphere is manifest in the bright brassy parallel chords with which the act opens. Rudolf, having bought his new flame a rose-colored bonnet, brings her to the table where his friends await. The appearance of Musetta causes a stir, proving especially agitating to her former love Marcel. This pert young lady is accompanied by an elderly councilor named Alcindoro, whom she persists in calling, in the tone of addressing a pet dog, Lulù. Marcel's agitation increases visibly as she sings her coquettish waltz song *Quando me'n vo'* (As through the streets I wander).

Having decided to get rid of "the old boy," she sends him on an errand. A grand reconciliation ensues between her and Marcel. The waiter brings the bill. The young men realize to their dismay that they haven't enough to pay it, whereupon the resourceful Musetta instructs the waiter to add it to Alcindoro's and present it to that gentleman upon his return. The young people disappear in the crowd as the act ends with great éclat.

In dramatic contrast the next act opens in a pallid wintry dawn. We see a tollgate outside Paris. Peasant women enter bringing butter and eggs. From the tavern sound the voices of the last carousers, including Musetta's. Mimi appears, seeking Marcel. She confides to him her difficulties with Rudolf who is insanely jealous and makes their life unbearable. In this dialogue and the next the voices move in a free *parlando* while the orchestra carries the melody. It is a favorite device with Puccini, and one that he uses with infallible effectiveness.

Rudolf awakes within. To avoid a scene Mimi hides to one side behind some trees. Rudolf pours out his heart to Marcel; he is helpless against his jealousy and fears. Mimi is ill, she is dying. He is too poor to provide her with the care she needs. Mimi's tears and coughing reveal her presence. She bids farewell to Rudolf in a touching aria.

The peak of the act is the quartet—better, double duet—at the close. Mimi and Rudolf melodiously resign themselves to the parting they dread; while Marcel and Musetta quarrel violently backstage, he accusing her of flirting, she retaliating with lively epithets. Upon this Puccinian combination of pathos and comedy the curtain descends.

Act IV is introduced by the Bohemian motive of the opening. We are back in the attic. Marcel and Rudolf try to work, as they did in the opening scene; but their thoughts revert to their lost loves. Schaunard and Colline arrive with rolls and a herring for their scanty meal. The young men indulge in horseplay that builds up to the agitated entrance of Musetta. She tells them that Mimi is below, too weak to climb the stair. They help her in.

The friends depart on various errands to lighten Mimi's last moments. Now the lovers are alone. "Ah, my lovely Mimi . . . You still think me lovely? . . . Fair as the dawn in spring . . . The comparison fits not. You meant fair as the sunset . . ." They recollect the night they met. The scene derives its impact from Puccini's masterful use of reminiscence. How better underline their blasted hopes than by quoting the music of that first encounter?

The others return, Marcel with medicine, Musetta with Mimi's muff to warm her hands. Rudolf weeps. Mimi comforts him. "Now I will sleep . . ." Musetta prays. Schaunard whispers to Marcel that Mimi is dead. Rudolf's outcry "Mimi . . . Mimi!" is heard against the brief and terrible postlude of the orchestra. Puccini wrote the final scene with tears in his eyes. It has been listened to in like fashion.

"I love small things. And the only music I can or will make is the music of small things, so long as they are true and full of passion and humanity and touch the heart." But when small things are true and full of passion and humanity they become big things. *La Bohème* has retained its freshness for more than half a century. Within its genre it is a masterpiece. Its creator, if he is not among the greatest composers, is certainly one of the most lovable.

❧57❧
Richard Strauss (1864-1949)

"I work very long on melodies. The important thing is not the beginning of the melody but its continuation, its development into a fully completed artistic form."

RICHARD STRAUSS was the spiritual offspring of Liszt, Wagner, and Berlioz. Like them he had the instinct of the world conqueror, driven with inexhaustible psychic energy to impose his image upon the world. He carried the esthetic of program music into our time, to give it its final expression. With him the romantic tone poem as the nineteenth century had known it comes to its end.

HIS LIFE

Strauss was born in Munich, son of a virtuoso horn player who was a member of the court orchestra. His mother was the daughter of Georg Pschorr, the brewer of Munich beer. The boy played the piano when he was four and wrote his first pieces at six. By the time he was sixteen he had had performed a string quartet, a number of songs, and a symphony.

His first works were in the classical forms. At twenty-one he found his true métier in the writing of vivid program music, setting himself to develop what he called "the poetic, the expressive in music." *Macbeth,* his first tone poem, was followed by *Don Juan,* an extraordinary achievement for a young man of twenty-four. Then came the series of tone poems that blazed his name throughout the civilized world. *Death and Transfiguration, Till Eulenspiegel's Merry Pranks, Thus Spake Zarathustra, Don Quixote, A Hero's Life,* and two program symphonies, the *Domestic* and the *Alpine*—these works shocked the conservatives and secured Strauss's position as the *enfant terrible* of modern music, a role he thoroughly enjoyed.

In the early years of the century Strauss conquered the operatic stage with *Salome* (1906), *Elektra* (1909), and *Der Rosenkavalier* (The Knight of the Rose, 1911). The international triumph of the last-named on the eve of the First World War marked the summit of his career. He collected unprecedented fees and royalties for his scores. Strauss had an excellent business sense. He did not approve of the fact that publishers piled up fortunes from the works of composers who had lived and died in poverty and he was active in forming an alliance of German composers that would look after their interests. He was eager to dispel the romantic notion that the artist is better off starving in a garret. On the contrary, he insisted that "worry alone is enough to kill a sensitive man, and all thoroughly artistic natures are sensitive."

Strauss's collaboration with Hugo von Hofmannsthal, the librettist of *Elektra* and *Rosenkavalier*, continued until the latter's death in 1929. They turned out opera after opera; but Strauss's later works did not take the public in nearly the same degree as had the earlier ones. New conceptions of modernism had come to the fore in the years of the Weimar Republic; the one-time bad boy of music, now entrenched as a conservative, was inevitably left behind. The coming to power of the Nazis in 1933 confronted Strauss with a challenge and an opportunity. He was a staunch social-democrat, his daughter-in-law was Jewish, and the cosmopolitan circles in which he traveled were not susceptible to Hitler's ideology. Hence the challenge to speak out against the Third Reich; or to leave Germany as Thomas Mann, Hindemith, and other intellectuals were doing. On the other hand the new regime was courting men of arts and letters. Strauss saw the road open to supreme power, and took the opportunity. In 1933, on the threshold of seventy, he was elevated to the official hierarchy as president of the Reichsmusik-kammer (Reich Chamber of Music). His reign was brief and uneasy. He declined to support the move to ban Mendelssohn's music from Teutonic ears. His opera *The Silent Woman* was withdrawn after its première because the librettist, Stefan Zweig, was non-Aryan; where-upon Strauss resigned.

The war's end found the eighty-one-year-old composer the victim of a curious irony. He was living in straitened circumstances while huge sums owing him for performances of his works in England and America were impounded as war reparations. He was permitted to return to his villa at Garmisch, in the Bavarian Alps. To his friends Strauss explained that he had remained in Nazi Germany because someone had to protect culture from Hitler's barbarians. There were speeches at the Bavarian Academy of Arts on the occasion of his eighty-fifth birthday. He died shortly after.

HIS MUSIC

Strauss carried to its extreme limit the nineteenth-century appetite for story-and-picture music. He lived in a realistic age, and his vivid imagination leaned toward action and movement. He went much farther than either Liszt or Berlioz in allowing the course of the music to be affected by the program. His tone poems are a treasury of sound effects—the clatter of pots and pans, the bleating of sheep, the gabble of geese, hoofbeats, wind, thunder, storm. Much more important, they are packed with movement and gesture, with the sound and fury of an imperious temperament.

Strauss transformed the orchestra of Berlioz, Liszt, and Wagner into a mammoth virtuoso ensemble in which all the instruments participated on an equal basis. Even those hitherto used mainly for support—double basses, trombones, tuba—were now brought into solo prominence. With *Elektra* the grandiose orchestra of the post-romantic period reached its peak. The score calls for twelve trumpets, four trombones, eight horns, six to eight kettledrums. Strauss's orchestration springs from an individual sense of sound and gives an effect of riotous color. To the sober palette of the German masters he added French verve and Italian sensuousness. His scores show the most intricate interweaving of the separate instrumental parts; page after page is strewn with notes that the ear cannot possibly unravel. When chided for his complexity he would exclaim, "The devil! I cannot express it more simply."

Strauss's tone poems dominated the international repertory up to the thirties; however, they are less in evidence today. On the operatic front he holds his own. *Salome,* to Oscar Wilde's famous play, and *Elektra,* based on Hofmannsthal's version of the Greek tragedy, are long one-act operas. In them Strauss explores the dark caverns of the soul. The princess of Judaea who dances for Herod and demands the head of John the Baptist on a silver charger is the incarnation of psychopathic lust. Elektra, demoniacal figure of revenge, bursts into an exultant dance when Orestes kills their mother Clytemnestra. Both lyric tragedies are swiftly paced, moving relentlessly to their climax. They are intimate with evil, frightening, and superb theater.

"I always wanted to write an opera like Mozart's," Strauss is reported to have said at the opening of *Rosenkavalier,* "and now I've done it." He was mistaken. *Rosenkavalier* has neither the wholeness of *Figaro* nor the grandeur of *Don Giovanni.* But it possesses attractions of its own: sensuous lyricism, sophistication, entrancing waltzes. The scene is Vienna in the reign of Maria Theresa. The theme is eternal: the fading of youth and beauty. The aging Marschallin, waging her losing battle with time; the disreputable Baron Ochs; Sophie and Octavian awaking to the wonder of young love—they ring true in the theater, they come alive through music. Strauss here summoned all his wizardry of color, his mastery of the stage, his knowledge of the human heart. There comes a time, alas, when *Rosenkavalier* seems a trifle long. It is a sign that one's youth is over.

TILL EULENSPIEGEL'S MERRY PRANKS

Till Eulenspiegel (literally, "Till Owl-Glass") was a lovable rogue of the fourteenth century who "visited all cities and plied all trades." His escapades reflect the lusty comedy of the Middle Ages, and the triumph of the eternal rebel over bourgeois respectability. Till was put into a book a century after his death and ended as a folklore figure known to every German child.

The annotations that Strauss appended to the score afford some clue to the episodes he had in mind. Till rides his horse into the midst of a crowd of market women. He joins a group of priests, disguised as one of them, and engages in theological disputation, only to horrify them with his irreverence. He declares his love to a damsel who sends him packing. His nonconforming shocks the Philistines, those staid pillars of society. He proceeds on his way singing a gay street song. But as he watches the life about him he experiences the loneliness that is the lot of the outsider. Why cannot he be like those about him—why cannot he change? But no—he realizes that Till he is and Till he must remain no matter what the cost. He discovers the cost when he is brought to trial for his misdeeds. His cockiness deserts him: this time there is no escaping. "Up the ladder! There he swings. He gasps for air. A final shudder. The mortal part of Till is no more."

Strauss's brilliant tone poem is fashioned out of two basic motives, one lyric, the other rhythmic. These, as the composer says, "pervade the whole in the most manifold disguises, moods, and situations." The first, given out by the violins, is tender and reflective. The downward leap in the melody becomes a characteristic feature of the work.

The other Till motive is the celebrated theme for horn. A subtle syncopation, achieved by shifting the accent repeatedly within the phrase, suggests the mischief-loving side of the rogue.

The two themes are subjected to a process of continuous transformation. It is their merry pranks rather than Till's, ultimately, that concern our ears.

The lyric theme is set forth at the outset, establishing a Once-upon-a-time atmosphere. Immediately the "mischief" theme sends the rascal off on his adventures. We hear the lyric theme transformed from tenderness to cocky impudence by the simple device of reducing the time values of the notes (diminution).

The commotion of the frightened market women and their wares gives Strauss an opportunity for one of those passages of orchestral hubbub so dear to his heart. The encounter with the priests is introduced by a hymn tune in popular style. Strauss's occasional ventures into the folk manner stand out sharply against his sophisticated style. A descending glissando on solo violin ushers in the section devoted to Till's amours. The music takes on an Italianate sensuousness. You would never suspect it, but this glowing serenade is a clever transformation of the "mischief" motive. To express the emotions of the rejected lover the lyric theme, with its downward leap, is transformed into a furious fortissimo. Till's rage passes quickly; he is ready for the next escapade.

The plodding rhythms of the Philistines sound deep in the bass, against which is hurled the defiance of the two Till motives in the treble. Tension sags in this episode, which is the weak link in the work. Momentum resumes with Till's cocky street song—the song of the

eternal gamin. Here too the popular style stands out against its sumptuous surroundings. Till's self-questioning imparts to the music an upward inflection. The orchestra weighs the possibility of his reforming.
But no, the horn theme returns to remind him of his destiny. His decision to remain true to himself is proclaimed by horns and trombones,
which give out the "mischief" theme in longer note values (augmentation).

The orchestra crackles with defiance. Suddenly Till is summoned to
his doom—by eight horns and six trumpets. Sentence is pronounced to
the roll of the drum and harmonies that Strauss marked "menacing" in
the score. At the climax of his tale he is a master of economy. The basic
descending interval, enlarged, becomes a grim portent given out by the
bass instruments. A trill on the flutes, woodwinds fluttering over a dark
curtain of sound—and Till has paid the penalty. There is a long pause.
We hear the Once-upon-a-time of the opening as the Epilogue bids Till
a gentle farewell. At the very end his motive flares into life. Till is gone
—but the spirit of youthful rebellion lives on.

The question arises: What would we make of the music if Strauss
had given us the piece without title or program, simply as a set of Variations on Two Themes? One thing is certain. We should never, from
the sounds, have deduced either Till or his escapades.

Strauss was just such a rebel as Till when the comet of his genius
blazed over the musical horizon. Years later a critic wrote of him, "He
was not a meteor but a falling meteorite"; yet one that gave off a daz-
zling light in its passage across the sky. A world figure, he dominated
his era as few artists have done. He may have suspected toward the
end that the world had been too much with him. "We are all of us
children of our time," he said, "and can never leap over its shadows."

Let there be no mistaking. He was one of the major artists of our
century.

❧58❧
Jan Sibelius (1865-)

"I love the mysterious sounds of the fields and forests, water and
mountains. It pleases me greatly to be called a poet of nature,
for nature has truly been the book of books for me."

FINLAND, in the final decades of the nineteenth century, was swept by
agitation for independence from tsarist Russia. Out of this ferment
flowered the art of Jan Sibelius, whose work served notice of his country's musical coming of age.

A NATIONAL ARTIST

Sibelius's identification with his people was so complete that his
music, even at its most personal, bore the stamp of their spirit. Such
nationalism goes deeper than the quotation of folk tunes. "There is a
mistaken impression among the press abroad," he wrote, "that my
themes are often folk melodies. So far I have never used a theme that
was not of my own invention." The important point is that some of
them could have been folk melodies, and at least one of them—the
Chorale from *Finlandia*—became one.

Sibelius, like Grieg before him, revealed the northern landscape. The
more fanciful of his listeners like to discover in his music the brooding
forests and lakes of his native land or the legendary heroes of its sagas.
Sibelius's rugged strength and his command of the large forms enabled
him to win and to hold the attention of the world—or at least part of it.
England and the United States became the centers of his cult, where he
was acclaimed as enthusiastically as in his homeland. Neither in Paris,
Berlin, Vienna, nor Rome has he achieved a comparable eminence.

Sibelius's reputation in serious music circles rests upon his seven symphonies. The first two are in the romantic tradition and pose no problem for the listener. Their successors show a steady development toward refinement of style, conciseness of thought, and tightness of
structure. In these works Sibelius discourses upon the great themes of
nineteenth-century music—nature, man, destiny. His idiom is sparse
and avoids sensuous brilliance. He exploits the somber colors and low
registers of the orchestra. He uses short incisive motives that lend

themselves to symphonic expansion and development. His speech is direct, abrupt, pithy.

To the vast number of music lovers who thirty years ago were bewildered by Stravinsky and other innovators, Sibelius came to represent a haven. He met the need of the big public for a contemporary who was modern enough to say something new but not so modern as to frighten people away. He had a great vogue in this country in the period between the two wars. In England as in America he was hailed by leading critics as successor to the giants of the past. His symphonies were described as "the highest point attained in this form since the death of Beethoven." He influenced several among the rising generation of American composers.

The reaction was bound to come. Those who were attracted by the modernity of his work went on to composers who more adequately represent the contemporary spirit. Those who responded to his traditionalism went back to composers who more completely represent the romantic style. If in the twenties he suffered from adulators who compared him to Beethoven, in the forties he suffered from equally extreme spirits who denied him any merit whatsoever. Needless to add, the truth lies well between the two poles.

It is in the orchestral and choral works of his first period that Sibelius is most explicitly national. The bardic *En Saga* was followed by a number of works based on the Finnish national epic, the Kalevala, among them the orchestral legends *The Swan of Tuonela* and *Lemminkainen's Homefaring* and the symphonic fantasy *Pohjola's Daughter*. These appeared during the years of tsarist oppression, when to be patriotic was tantamount to being a revolutionary. Conceived in epic mood, they accorded with the temper of the liberation movement. And they brought the national genius before the world.

This phase of the composer's activity is summed up in the symphonic poem *Finlandia*. The mood of defiance is established at the outset by the snarling of massed brass in lower register, andante sostenuto. There follows an organ-like passage in the woodwinds solemnly answered by the strings, leading to a moderate Allegro based on a persistent rhythm. The stirring trumpet calls are of a character designed to appeal to national emotion, as is the exultant phrase in the strings punctuated by the rhythmic interjection of the brass. The famous tune that appears at

first in prayerful quiet returns at the close as a triumphal chorale. The melody has become practically a national anthem in the composer's homeland, where the work occupies the same position as does *The Moldau* in Smetana's. Such music can be judged critically only by foreigners. The artist's compatriots hear it through a mist of pride and fervor. Admirers of Sibelius resent the frankly popular *Finlandia* for having obscured, with masses of listeners, the more elevated aspects of his art. Despite them the piece has established itself both in Finland and abroad as a popular classic.

Sibelius is the last survivor of the generation of Richard Strauss, a generation whose historic role it was to bridge the transition from the romantic era to the twentieth century. Although his works are not played nearly as much as they were a quarter century ago, the best among them are well established in the current repertory. In Finland he is regarded with the special reverence that a small nation lavishes on the favorite son who has become a world figure. As he approaches the end of his life this sincere and high-minded musician can look back to more than sixty years of honorable achievement. He is assured a place in the annals of his art.

❧ 59 ❧

Impressionism

For we desire above all—nuance,
Not color but half-shades!
Ah! nuance alone unites
Dream with dream and flute with horn.
                                    Paul Verlaine

In 1867 Claude Monet, rebuffed by the academic salons, exhibited under less conventional auspices a painting called *Impression: Sun Rising*. Before long impressionism had become a term of derision to describe the hazy, luminous paintings of this artist (1840–1926) and his school. A distinctly Parisian style, impressionism counted among its exponents Camille Pissarro (1830–1903), Edouard Manet (1832–83), Edgar Degas (1834–1917), and Auguste Renoir (1841–1919). Discarding those elements of the romantic tradition that had hardened into academic formulas, they strove to retain on canvas the freshness of their first impressions. They took painting out of the studio into the open air. What fascinated them was the continuous change in the appearance of things. They painted water lilies, a haystack, or clouds again and again at different hours of the day. Instead of mixing their pigments on the palette they juxtaposed brush-strokes of pure color on the canvas, leaving it to the eye of the beholder to do the mixing. An iridescent sheen bathes their painting. Outlines shimmer and melt in a luminous haze.

The impressionists abandoned the grandiose rhetoric of romanticism. The hero of their painting is not man but light. Not for them the pathos, the drama-packed themes that had inspired centuries of European art. They preferred "unimportant" material: still life, dancing girls, nudes; everyday scenes of middle-class life, picnics, boating and café scenes; nature in all her aspects, Paris in all her moods. The impressionists, it has been said, presented nature glimpsed through a keyhole; more properly, nature glimpsed through the temperament, dreams, and desires of the individual painter. Derided at first—"Whoever saw grass that's pink and yellow and blue?"—they ended by imposing their vision upon the age.

Monet, *Bridge over Pool of Pond Lilies.*

"An iridescent sheen bathes impressionist painting. Outlines shimmer and melt . . ."

Degas, *The Foyer*.

"They preferred 'unimportant' material: still life, dancing girls, boating and café scenes."

THE SYMBOLISTS

A parallel revolt against traditional modes of expression took place in poetry under the leadership of the symbolists, who strove for direct poetic experience unspoiled by intellectual elements. They sought to suggest rather than describe, to present the symbol rather than state the thing. Symbolism as a literary movement came to the fore in the work of Charles Baudelaire (1821–67); Stéphane Mallarmé (1842–98); Paul Verlaine (1844–96), and Arthur Rimbaud (1856–91). These poets used a word for its color and its music rather than its proper meaning, evoking poetic images "that sooner or later would be accessible to all the senses."

The symbolists experimented in free verse forms that opened new territories to their art. They achieved in language an indefiniteness that had hitherto been the privilege of music alone. Characteristic was Verlaine's pronouncement: "Music above all!" Like the impressionist painters, the symbolists discarded the grand pathos of romanticism. They emphasized the manner rather than the matter; they rejected the humanism—and the rhetoric—of the poetry of the early nineteenth century; they glorified the tenuous, the intimate, the subtle. "Nothing more dear," sang Verlaine, "than the gray song where the indefinite meets the precise." The symbolists discarded the story element in poetry. They avoided the moral, either expressed or implied. Nourished by art rather than life, their exquisite idiom leaned toward the precious. They expressed the moral lassitude of their time, its longing for enchantment of the senses, its need for escape.

The essentially musical approach of the symbolists was not lost upon the musicians. The composer Paul Dukas, in reminiscing about his friend Debussy and their circle, states: "Verlaine, Mallarmé, and Laforgue provided us with new sounds and sonorities. They conceived their poetry or prose like musicians. It was the writers, not the musicians, who exerted the strongest influence on Debussy."

IMPRESSIONISM IN MUSIC

When young Debussy submitted to the authorities of the Conservatory his cantata *The Blessed Damozel* they stated in their report: "It is much to be desired that he beware of this vague impressionism which is one of the most dangerous enemies of artistic truth." Therewith was transferred to the domain of music a term that was already firmly established in art criticism. Debussy himself never liked the word and expressed himself acidly concerning "what some idiots call impressionism, a term that is altogether misused, especially by the critics." But the label stuck, for it seemed to describe what most people felt about his music.

Impressionism came to the fore at a crucial moment in the history of European music. The major scale—the "seven out of twelve" way of hearing music—had served the art since the seventeenth century. Composers were beginning to feel that its possibilities had been exhausted. Debussy's highly individual tone sense was attracted to other scales, such as the medieval modes that impart an archaic flavor to his music. He was sympathetic to the novel scales introduced by Russian and Scandinavian nationalism, and lent a willing ear to the harmonies of Borodin, Musorgsky, Grieg. He responded to the Moorish strain in Spanish music. Especially he was impressed by the Javanese and Chinese orchestras that were heard in Paris during the Exposition of 1889. In their music he found a new world of sonority: rhythms, scales, and colors that offered a bewitching contrast to the stereotyped forms of Western music.

The major scale, as we saw, is based on the pull of the active tones to the tonic or rest tone. Debussy regarded this as a formula that killed spontaneity. We do not hear in his music the triumphal final cadence of the classic-romantic period, in which the active chord is punched home to the tonic. His fastidious ear explored subtle harmonic relationships; he demanded new and delicate perceptions on the part of the listener. Classical harmony looked upon dissonance as a momentary disturbance that found its resolution in the consonance. But Debussy used dissonance as a value in itself, freeing it from the need to resolve. He enriched his harmony by overlaying the consonant chords with dissonant intervals. In other words, sounds that were considered dissonant he heard as consonances. He thus taught his contemporaries to accept tone combinations that had hitherto been regarded as inadmissible, even as the impressionist painters taught them to see colors in sky, grass, and water that had never been seen there before. Obviously this expansion of musical resources was not the result of his effort alone. But he was without question the most important among the leaders of harmonic advance in the post-romantic era.

Debussy is popularly associated with the whole-tone scale. This is a pattern built entirely of whole-tone intervals, as in the sequence C-D-E-F♯-G♯-A♯-C. The whole-tone scale avoids the semitone distances 3–4 and 7–8 (*mi-fa* and *ti-do*) of the major scale. Thereby it sidesteps the thrust of *ti* to *do* that gives the traditional scale its drive and direction. The newer scale also avoids the fifth step *sol*, the dominant that represents the active harmony; for in the whole-tone scale the fifth step is G♯, whereas in the C-major scale it would be G. In this way the whole-tone scale avoids the clear-cut resolution of active harmony to rest. There results a fluid scale pattern whose elusive charm can be gauged only from hearing it played. Debussy did not invent the whole-tone scale nor did he use it as frequently as many suppose. It lent itself admirably, however, to the nuances of mood and feeling that haunt his music.

Several other procedures have come to be associated with musical impressionism. One of the most important is the use of parallel or gliding chords, in which a chord built on one tone is duplicated immediately on a higher or lower tone. Here all the voices move in parallel motion, the effect being one of blocks of sound gliding up or down. Such parallel motion was prohibited in the classical system of harmony; but it was precisely these forbidden progressions that fascinated Debussy. Also, he sustains a chord in the bass that suggests a definite key while the chords above it give the impression of having escaped to another key. Such "escaped" chords point the way to twentieth-century harmony.

As a result of these procedures, impressionist music wavered between major and minor without adhering to either. In this way was abandoned one of the basic contrasts of classical harmony. Impressionism advanced the disintegration of the major-minor system. It floated in a borderland between keys, creating elusive effects that might be compared to the misty outlines of impressionist painting.

These evanescent harmonies demanded colors no less subtle. No room here for the thunderous climaxes of the romantic orchestra. Instead there was a veiled blending of hues, an impalpable shimmer of pictorial quality: flutes and clarinets in their dark lower register, violins in their lustrous upper range, trumpets and horns discreetly muted; and over the whole a silvery gossamer of harp, celesta, and triangle; glockenspiel, muffled drum, and cymbal brushed with a drumstick.

Impressionism inclined toward the miniature. Debussy's turning away from the grand form led him to short lyric pieces: preludes, nocturnes, arabesques—the titles indicate his leaning toward intimate lyricism. The question arises: Was impressionism a revolt against the romantic tradition or simply its final manifestation? Beyond question Debussy rebelled against certain aspects of romanticism, notably the Wagnerian gesture. Yet in a number of ways impressionism continued the fundamental tendencies of the romantic movement: in its love of beautiful sound, its emphasis on program music, its tone painting and nature worship, its rejection of classical form, its addiction to lyricism; its striving to unite music, painting, and poetry; and its emphasis on mood and atmosphere. In effect, the impressionists substituted a thoroughly French brand of romanticism for the German variety.

Impressionist music enjoyed an enormous vogue in the first quarter of the twentieth century. It attained the proportions of an international school. In France a whole generation of musicians came either partly or wholly under its spell, among them Maurice Ravel, Paul Dukas, and Albert Roussel. Its influence in England is manifest in the works of Frederick Delius and Cyril Scott. Among the American impressionists may be mentioned Charles Martin Loeffler, John Alden Carpenter, and Charles Griffes. Isaac Albeniz and Manuel de Falla in Spain, Ottorino Respighi in Italy, and Karol Szymanowski in Poland testify to the extent of its orbit. Nor was it without influence on the leaders of the next generation—Stravinsky, Schoenberg, Bartók.

Yet from our vantage point impressionism turns out to have been largely a one-man movement. No one else of Debussy's stature found in it the complete expression that he did. In this respect it differed from the romantic style, which allowed room for so many diverse personalities. The procedures of impressionism worked in a limited area; they became stereotyped and soon lost their novelty. It grew to be practically impossible to write impressionist music without sounding like Debussy. Composers were consequently forced to seek other idioms.

Also, by excluding pathos and the heroic element impressionism narrowed its human appeal. It valued elegance above passion, refinement and chic above intellectual content. It was therefore unable to muster the spiritual energy which alone transforms an artistic movement into a universal force.

But on its own premises it created a finely wrought, surpassingly decorative art. It opened up to music a world of dream and enchantment. It captured a vision of fragile beauty in a twilight moment of European culture.

﹥60﹤

Claude Debussy (1862-1918)

"I love music passionately. And because I love it I try to free it from barren traditions that stifle it. It is a free art gushing forth, an open-air art boundless as the elements, the wind, the sky, the sea. It must never be shut in and become an academic art."

HIS LIFE

THE MOST important French composer of the early twentieth century was born near Paris in the town of St. Germain-en-Laye, where his parents kept a china shop. He entered the Paris Conservatory when he was eleven. Within a few years he shocked his professors with bizarre harmonies that defied the sacred rules. "What rules then do you observe?" inquired one of his teachers. "None—only my own pleasure!" "That's all very well," retorted the professor, "provided you're a genius." Although the Conservatory was a citadel of tradition, several among its faculty soon had a notion that the daring young man was.

He was twenty-two when his cantata *L'Enfant prodigue* (The Prodigal Son) won the Prix de Rome. A typical Parisian, he looked upon his stay in the Italian capital as a dreary exile from the boulevards and cafés that made up his world. Already he discerned his future bent. "I shall always prefer," he wrote a friend, "something where the action will be subordinated to a long and patient expression of feelings and states of mind. The music I desire must be supple enough to adapt itself to the lyrical effusions of the soul and the fantasy of dreams."

Back in Paris, Debussy frequented the advanced artistic circles where were discussed the latest theories in literature and painting. He was extraordinarily sensitive to the stimulus of the other arts and came to the conclusion that "perfumes, colors, and sounds correspond to one

Bettmann Archive

Claude Debussy.

another." At the home of Mallarmé—the poet's "Tuesday evenings" were famous—he met the painters and writers whose search for new avenues of expression coincided with his own. He was thus peculiarly fitted to become the leader of a movement in music that owed so much to painting and poetry.

The nineties, the most productive decade of Debussy's career, culminated in the writing of *Pelléas and Mélisande*. The work, based on the symbolist drama by the Belgian poet Maurice Maeterlinck, occupied him for the better part of ten years. He continued to revise the score up to the opening night which took place on April 3, 1902, at the Opéra-Comique. *Pelléas* was attacked as being decadent, precious, lacking in melody, form, and substance. Nevertheless, its quiet intensity and subtlety of nuance made a profound impression upon the musical intelligentsia. It caught on and embarked on an international career.

After *Pelléas* Debussy was famous. He was the acknowledged leader of a new movement in art, the hero of a cult. "The Debussyists," he complained, "are killing me." He appeared in the capitals of Europe as conductor of his works and wrote the articles that established his reputation as one of the most trenchant critics of his time. In the first years of the century he exhausted the impressionist vein and found his way to a new and tightly controlled idiom, a kind of distillation of impressionism.

His energies sapped by the ravages of cancer, he worked on with remarkable fortitude. The outbreak of war in 1914 rendered him for a time incapable of all interest in music. France, he felt, "can neither laugh nor weep while so many of our men heroically face death." After a year of silence he realized that he must contribute to the struggle in the only way he could, "by creating to the best of my ability a little of that beauty which the enemy is attacking with such fury." He was soon able to report to his publisher that he was "writing like a madman, or like one who has to die next morning." To his perturbation over the fate of France were added physical torment and, finally, the realization that he was too ill to compose any longer. His last letters speak of his "life of waiting—my waiting-room existence, I might call it—for I am a poor traveler waiting for a train that will never come any more."

He died in March 1918 during the bombardment of Paris. The funeral procession took its way through deserted streets as the shells of the Big Berthas ripped into his beloved city. It was just eight months before the victory of the nation whose culture found in him one of its most distinguished representatives.

HIS MUSIC

For Debussy, as for Monet and Verlaine, art was primarily a sensuous experience. The epic themes of romanticism were distasteful to his temperament both as man and artist. In art for art's sake he recognized the triumph of Latin grace over Teutonic "spirituality" and love of the grandiose. "French music," he declared, "is clearness, elegance, simple and natural declamation. French music aims first of all to give pleasure."

Upholding the genius of his race, he turned against the grand form that was the supreme achievement of the Germans. Exposition-development-restatement he regarded as an outmoded formula, "a legacy of clumsy, falsely interposed traditions"; thematic development was for him a species of dull "musical mathematics." At a concert he whispered to a friend, "Let's go—he's beginning to develop!" He summed up his attitude by quoting Fontenelle's famous question, "Sonata, what do you want of me?"

But the Viennese sonata-symphony was not the only form alien to the Gallic spirit. A greater threat was posed by the Wagnerian music drama which at that time attracted the intellectuals of France. "The French forget too easily the qualities of clarity and elegance peculiar to themselves and allow themselves to be influenced by the tedious and ponderous Teuton." Wagner's grandiose drama he finds false from the French point of view. "The idea of spreading one drama over four evenings! Is this admissible, especially when in these four evenings you always hear the same thing? . . . My God! how unbearable these people in skins and helmets become by the fourth night." In the end, however, he paid moving tribute to the master whose fascination he had had to shake off before he could find his own way. Wagner, he writes, "can never quite die." He calls him "a beautiful sunset that was mistaken for a dawn," and speaks with feeling of "the past greatness of this man who, had he but been a little more human, would have been great for all time."

From the romantic exuberance that left nothing unsaid Debussy sought refuge in an art of indirection, subtle and discreet. He substituted for the sonata structure those short flexible forms that he handled with such distinction. Mood pieces, they evoked the favorite images of impressionist painting: gardens in the rain, sunlight through the leaves, clouds, moonlight, sea, mist. A true nature poet, he turned from subjective brooding to the world without. Significant is his use of names borrowed from the painters: *images, estampes* (engravings), *esquisses* (sketches). Titles such as *The Snow is Dancing* or *Sounds and Per-fumes Waft in the Evening Air* create an atmosphere, a frame within which the picture takes shape. But we should not be misled by the nebulous outlines. Debussy was a master craftsman. He traced his lineage from the French masters of the past who imprinted on their material a crystalline clarity. His music has a capricious quality; yet its impulses are directed by an artistic intelligence that is conscious of its resources and calculates to the minutest detail how best to use them.

Debussy worked slowly, and his fame rests on a comparatively small output. Among the orchestral compositions the *Prelude to the After-noon of a Faun* is firmly established in public favor, as are the three Nocturnes—*Nuages* (Clouds), *Fêtes* (Festivals), *Sirènes* (Sirens)—and *La Mer* (The Sea). His handling of the orchestra has the French sensi-bility. He favors pure colors rather than mixtures, and individualizes each instrument. There are surprisingly few notes in his scores; the lines are widely spaced, the texture light and airy.

Debussy is one of the important piano composers. His manner is un-mistakably his own. The widely spaced chords with their parallel suc-cessions of seconds, fourths, and fifths create a sonorous halo. He exploits the resources of the instrument with infinite finesse—the con-trast of low and high registers, the blending of sonorities through the use of pedal, the clash of overtones. His piano pieces form an essential part of the modern repertoire.

Debussy was one of the most important among the group of com-posers who established the French song as a national art form independ-ent of the lied. In his settings of Baudelaire, Verlaine, and Mallarmé—to mention three poets for whom he had a particular affinity—the natural inflections of the French language are released in a music of exquisite refinement. Debussy's songs are poetic meditations which demand a special sensitivity on the part of the singer, the pianist, and the listener.

Finally, there is *Pelléas and Mélisande*. This "old and sad tale of the woods" captures the ebb and flow of the interior life. The characters move in a trancelike world where a whisper is eloquence: Mélisande of the golden hair and the habit of saying everything twice; Pelléas, caught in the wonder of a love he does not understand; Golaud, who marries Mélisande but never fathoms her secret, driven by jealousy to the murder of his younger half brother; and Arkel, the blind king of this shadowy land. The orchestra provides the frame, creating an atmos-phere steeped in nature poetry within which the action takes on the muted quality of a dream. "There is too much singing in music drama," wrote Debussy. "My ambition is to find poems in which the characters will not argue but live their lives and work out their destinies." Maeterlinck's drama gave him his ideal libretto. The result was a unique lyric drama that justifies Romain Rolland's description of him as "this great painter of dreams."

PRÉLUDE À L'APRÈS-MIDI D'UN FAUNE
(PRELUDE TO THE AFTERNOON OF A FAUN)

Debussy's best-known orchestral work was inspired by a pastoral of Stéphane Mallarmé that evokes the landscape of pagan antiquity. The poem centers about the mythological creature of the forest, half man, half goat. The faun, "a simple sensuous passionate being," in Edmund Gosse's phrase, awakes in the woods and tries to remember. Was he visited by three lovely nymphs or was this but a dream? He will never know. The sun is warm, the earth fragrant. He curls himself up and falls into a wine-drugged sleep.

Debussy completed the tone poem in 1894 when he was thirty-two. In it we encounter full-fledged his personal idiom. "The music of this prelude," he tells us, "is a very free illustration of the beautiful poem of Mallarmé. It makes no pretensions to being a synthesis of the poem. It projects rather a changing background for the dreams and desires of the faun in the heat of that summer afternoon." Debussy's imagination was attuned to the pagan setting, and his music invokes emotions as voluptuous as they are elusive. It unfolds what he well called his "harmonious harmony."

The piece opens with a flute solo in the velvety lower register. The melody glides along the chromatic scale, narrow in range, languorous. Glissandos on the harp usher in a brief dialogue of the horns. Of these sounds it may be said, as of the opening chords of *Tristan*, that their like had never been heard before.

Almost every fragment of melody is repeated forthwith, a trait that the composer carries to the length of mannerism. Characteristic is the relaxed rhythm which flows across the bar line in a continuous stream. By weakening and even wiping out the accent Debussy achieved that dreamlike fluidity which is a prime trait of impressionist music. The movement is marked *Très modéré—doux et expressif* (very moderate—soft and expressively; like most nationalists, Debussy gave the tempo directions in his native tongue rather than in Italian). The dynamic scheme is discreet; pianissimo and mezzo-piano predominate. There is only one fortissimo. The whole-tone scale is heard. Notable is the limpid coloring. The strings are muted and divided. Flute and oboe, clarinet and horns are used soloistically, standing out against the orchestral texture.

A contrasting motive emerges, played in unison first by woodwinds, then by the strings. It is an ardent melody that carries the composition to its emotional crest.

At the close an antique cymbal is heard, *ppp*. "Blue" chords played by muted horns and violins glide in parallel motion, infinitely remote. The work dissolves in silence. It takes nine minutes to play. Rarely has so much been said with so little.

A sensitive tone poet who was relentlessly exacting with himself, Debussy looms as the first major composer of our era. He bridges the gap between romanticism and the twentieth century. His is a domain limited in scope but replete with beauty. Every note he set down justifies the proud title he assumed in the time of his country's peril: Claude Debussy, *musicien français*.

❧ 61 ❧
Maurice Ravel (1875-1937)

"Does it never dawn on these people that I may be artificial by nature?"

MAURICE RAVEL had to make his way in a milieu dominated by Debussy. He succeeded in remaining himself. Ravel may be accounted a post-impressionist. As in the case of Cézanne, a classical streak in his make-up led him to impose form and order on what, he feared, might otherwise degenerate into amorphous fantasy.

HIS STYLE

Ravel shared with Debussy an affinity for the scales of medieval and exotic music. His sense of key is firmer, the harmonic movement more definitely outlined; he avoided the whole-tone scale. Both men were attracted by the same aspects of nature—daybreak, the play of water and light. Both exploited exotic dance rhythms, especially those of Spain. Both loved the fantastic and the antique, and the old French harpsichordists. Both were repelled by the passion of nineteenth-century music, and believed the primary purpose of art to be sensuous delight. Ravel too was inspired by the symbolist poets and had a gift for setting the French language to music. Both men in surpassing degree exemplified Gallic sensibility. And both considered themselves rebels against the nineteenth-century spirit, although it is apparent to us now that romanticism was the soil out of which their music flowered.

The differences between the pair are as pronounced as the similarities. There is an enameled brightness about Ravel's music that contrasts with the twilight softness of Debussy's. He is less visionary. His rhythms are more incisive and have a verve, a drive that Debussy rarely strives for. His mind is more precise, his humor dryer, his harmonies crisper. He goes beyond Debussy's conception of dissonance. He is more conventional in respect to form, and his melodies are broader in span, more direct. His texture is contrapuntal, often being based on the interplay of lines rather than on the vertical blocks of sound that fascinated Debussy. Ravel's orchestration derives in greater degree from the nineteenth-century masters; he stands in the line of descent from Berlioz,

Cézanne, *Mont St. Victoire.*

"Ravel may be accounted a post-impressionist. As in the case of Cézanne, a classical streak in his make-up led him to impose form and order on what, he feared, might degenerate into amorphous fantasy."

Rimsky-Korsakov and Richard Strauss. Whereas Debussy aimed to "decongest" sound, treating each instrument as a soloist, Ravel handled the huge post-romantic orchestra with brilliant virtuosity, and with special emphasis on what has well been called the confectionary department—harp glissandos, glockenspiel, celesta, triangle.

Ravel, like Debussy, has always been immensely popular in the United States. His harmonies and orchestration have exercised a particular attraction for jazz arrangers and Hollywood composers. As a result his idiom (somewhat watered down, to be sure) has become part of the daily listening experience of millions of Americans.

DAPHNIS AND CHLOË SUITE NO. 2

The second suite drawn from his ballet *Daphnis and Chloë* is generally accounted Ravel's masterpiece. The work, commissioned by

Diaghilev for his Ballet Russe, was produced in Paris in 1912. The action is derived from a pastoral of the Greek poet Longus. Chloë, beloved of the shepherd Daphnis, is abducted by a band of pirates. Daphnis, prostrate with grief, arouses the sympathy of the god Pan. Daphnis dreams that the god will come to his aid. He awakes to find Chloë restored to him. The second suite contains three excerpts from the latter part of the ballet—Daybreak, Pantomime, and General Dance. The scoring is unusually rich and displays Ravel's mastery of orchestration.

I. *Daybreak*. "Nothing is heard but the murmur of rivulets, Daphnis lies stretched in front of the grotto of the nymphs. Day breaks gradually. The song of the birds is heard. Shepherds discover Daphnis and awaken him. In anguish he looks about for Chloë. She appears, surrounded by shepherdesses. The two rush into each other's arms."

The music paints a morning mood. Woodwinds set up a flickering

sound in the upper register. A broadly arching theme emerges in the lower strings. Harp glissandos, celesta, and a violin solo soaring above the harmony create a characteristically Ravelian luminosity. At the point in the action where the lovers embrace, a rapturous outburst sweeps the orchestra. The brass enters, vividly suggesting an upsurge of light.

II. *Pantomime*. "The old shepherd Lammon explains that Pan saved Chloë in remembrance of the nymph Syrinx whom the god once loved. Daphnis and Chloë mime the story of Pan and Syrinx. Chloë represents the young nymph wandering through the fields. Daphnis represents Pan who declares his love. The nymph repulses him. In despair he plucks some reeds, fashions a flute, and plays a melancholy air."

A dialogue between oboe and flute sets the pastoral scene. The famous flute solo—Pan's melancholy air—is heard against arpeggios in the strings. This is a rhapsodic melody that Ravel marked "expressive and supple," free in rhythm and unfolding in ornate traceries. Typical of the many felicities of color is a spot where the flute sustains a high trill while piccolo, harps, and violins outline the harmonic background and are answered by parallel chords on celesta and divided strings—impressionism with a vengeance.

III. *General Dance.* "Before the altar of the nymphs Daphnis swears his fidelity. Young girls enter dressed as bacchantes and shaking tambourines. Daphnis and Chloë tenderly embrace. A group of young men appear. Joyous tumult. A general dance."

The finale abounds in never-failing effects. The frequent changes of meter and the 5/4 time (three plus two) achieve a plasticity of rhythm that is of the twentieth century. The movement is *Animé* (lively). There is an unabashed use of chromatic scales to whip up excitement. Each fragment of melody is heard twice, a Debussy-like mannerism, and the "confectionary department" is much in evidence. The hectic climax is an example of Ravel's orchestral wizardy at its calculated best.

Every movement in history engenders a reaction. Because of the enormous prestige that accrued to the music of Debussy and Ravel in the second quarter of the century, it is currently the fashion to deprecate their achievement. As we noted, their art limited the emotional-spiritual ambit of music. Yet it is important not to underestimate what they accomplished. They created an image of French music that incarnated the sensibility of their nation's genius. They held up an ideal of sonorous beauty that electrified a generation. And they opened wide the door to the twentieth century.

≥ 62 ≤

The New Music

"The entire history of modern music may be said to be a history
of the gradual pull-away from the German musical tradition of
the past century."

Aaron Copland

As WE look back over the history of art we find that one thing never
changes, and that is the element of change itself. What does vary from
age to age is the rate of change. At certain times the cultural process
moves so rapidly as to assume the character of a revolution. There were
three occasions in the history of music, as it happens at equal intervals
from one another, when the change was so abrupt that the word *new*
became a battle slogan. The year 1300 is associated with the rise of the
ars nova (new art), the year 1600 with the *nuove musiche,* and the
year 1900 with the New Music.

Each of these caused bewilderment and heated polemics, as the chronicles of the time attest. After the initial shock came a period of adjustment; the new concepts were assimilated to the old. The twentieth-
century revolution caused the greatest dislocation of all. Changes that in
former times would have been spread over generations were now telescoped into a few years. Now that half the century is over, the process
of adjustment is well under way. Composers whose first performances
thirty or forty years ago touched off riots are today accepted as masters.
Their disciples occupy key posts in our universities and critical journals.
Their works are disseminated through concerts, broadcasts, recordings.
Twentieth-century music stands revealed not as a temporary aberration
of mind and heart, but as the newest and therefore most spectacular
link in the chain that binds the present to the past.

THE REACTION AGAINST ROMANTICISM

"Epochs which immediately precede our own," writes Stravinsky,
"are temporarily farther away from us than others more remote in
time." The first quarter of the twentieth century was impelled before
all else to throw off the oppressive heritage of the nineteenth. Composers of the new generation were fighting not only the romantic past
but the romanticism within themselves.

Matisse, *Piano Lesson.*

"After the initial shock came a period of adjustment: the new concepts were assimilated to the old."

The turning away from the nineteenth-century spirit was manifest everywhere. Away from the subjective and the grandiose; from pathos and heaven-storming passion; from the romantic landscape and its picture-book loveliness; from the profound musings on man and fate; from the quest for sensuous beauty of tone—"that accursed euphony," as Richard Strauss called it. The rising generation viewed the romantic agony as Wagnerian histrionics. It considered itself to be made of sterner stuff. Its goal was a sweeping reversal of values. It aimed for nothing less than "to root out private feelings from art."

The United Nations Buildings. An example of contemporary architecture.
"Changes that in former times would have been spread over generations were now telescoped into a few years."

PRIMITIVISM

The new music came of age just before the First World War. The spiritual exhaustion of Western culture showed itself in an indefinable restlessness. European art sought to escape its overrefinement, to renew itself in a fresh and unspoiled stream of feeling. There was a desire to capture the spontaneity, the freedom from inhibition that was supposed to characterize primitive life. People idealized brute strength and the basic impulses that seemed to have been tamed by an effete civilization. Even as the fine arts discovered the splendid abstraction of African sculpture, music turned to the dynamism of African rhythm.

The twentieth century, in even greater degree than the nineteenth, was interested in the borderlands of Western culture—eastern Europe, Russia, Asia. Out of the unspoiled, vigorous folk music in these areas came primitive rhythms of an elemental fury that tapped fresh sources of feeling and imagination, as in Bartók's *Allegro Barbaro* (1911) and Stravinsky's *The Rite of Spring* (1913).

MACHINE MUSIC

With the mechanization of Western society came a widespread feeling that man had surrendered his soul to forces he neither understood nor controlled. The machine became a symbol of power, motion, energy; a symbol too of what one writer well called "the dehumanization of art."

Europe after World War I found surcease for its shattered nerves in athletics and sports. The body itself came to be viewed as a rhythmic machine. It is no accident that the ballet came to provide an important platform for the new music, and that some of the foremost musicians of the twentieth century won success in this field.

Under the influence of primitivism, machine music, sports, and ballet, romantic introspection gave way to twentieth-century physicality. Emotion was replaced by motion. Melody, the stronghold of sentiment, yielded to the irresistible propulsion of rhythm. The shift of emphasis is expressed in Stravinsky's dictum that "rhythm and motion, not the element of feeling, are the foundation of musical art."

OBJECTIVISM

Romantic art was based on the "pathetic fallacy" that the world exists in our minds. The romantic artist saw nature as the mirror of his moods; when the heroine was melancholy, it rained. The twentieth century rejected this sort of subjectivity. It glorified the scientific spirit and tried to see the world as it really is. The vivid colors of the romantic imagination were toned down to a sober detachment. Objectivism became still another means of shaking off the grip of the past.

Musicians now learned that objects exist independently of the artist's personality and feelings. They came to believe that a work of art is not simply a projection of its creator's fantasy, as the romantic period assumed, but that it is rather a self-contained organism obeying laws and purposes of its own. The artist sets it going and sees that it gets to its destination. He remains outside his creation; he respects its nature as pure art.

African sculpture.

"Even as the fine arts discovered the splendid abstraction of African sculpture, music turned to the dynamism of African rhythm."

Once this point was reached, the stage was set for the neoclassic attitude that soon took a dominant position in contemporary musical esthetics.

THE NEW CLASSICISM

One way of rejecting the nineteenth century was to return to the eighteenth. The movement "back to Bach" assumed impressive proportions in the early twenties. There was no question here of duplicating the accents of the Leipzig master; the slogan implied rather a reviving of certain principles that appeared to have been best understood in his time. Instead of worshiping at the shrine of Beethoven and Wagner, as the romantic era had done, composers began to emulate the great musicians of the eighteenth century—Handel, Scarlatti, Couperin, Vivaldi—and the detached, objective style that was supposed to characterize their music.

Basic to the new esthetic was the notion that the composer's function is not to express emotions, but to manipulate abstract combinations of sound. This view found its spokesman in Stravinsky. "I evoke neither human joy nor human sadness," he declared. "I move towards a greater abstraction." A classicist by temperament and conviction, he upheld the rule of law and order in art. Music, he maintained, "is given to us with the sole purpose of establishing an order among things." This order, to be realized, requires a construction. "Once the construction is made and the order achieved, everything is said."

The neoclassicists rid the art of the story-and-picture meanings with which the nineteenth century had endowed it. "People will always insist," Stravinsky points out, "upon looking in music for something that is not there. They never seem to understand that music has an entity of its own apart from anything it may suggest to them." Neoclassicism spelled the end of the symphonic poem and of the Wagnerian "union of the arts" which Stravinsky called "a terrible blow upon music itself." It led composers from program music back to absolute forms.

Neoclassicism focused attention on craftsmanship, elegance, taste. It concentrated on technique rather than content and elevated the *how* over the *what*, as generally happens in periods of experimentation. It strove for the ideal balance between form and emotion. It went even further, proclaiming that form *is* emotion. It pointed up the intellectual rather than emotional elements in art, rejecting the idea of passion in favor of a passion for ideas. Future generations will find it significant that in a period of social, political, and artistic upheaval there should have been affirmed so positively the classical virtues of detachment, serenity, and balance.

THE NEW NATIONALISM

Neoclassicism advocated a return to an international musical culture such as had prevailed in the eighteenth century. At the same time the impulse toward nationalism unleashed by the nineteenth century was too strong to be disregarded. The two tendencies existed side by side, now the one predominating, now the other.

Nationalism in the twentieth century pursued different aims from what it had in the nineteenth. The romantic composers had idealized the life of the people. They fastened on those elements of local color and atmosphere that were picturesque and exportable. The new nationalism went deeper. It approached folk song in the spirit of scientific research, separating authentic peasant music from the watered-down versions of the café musicians. It sought the primeval soul of the nation and encouraged the trend toward primitivism. Also a new type of nationalism came into being that emanated from the culture of cities rather than the countryside and sought to capture the pulse of modern urban life.

Twentieth-century nationalism uncovered the harsh dissonances, percussive rhythms, and archaic modes that became elements of a new tonal language. Its discoveries enriched the resources of music and encouraged the breaking away from nineteenth-century ideals.

EXPRESSIONISM

If Paris was the center of the new classicism, Vienna remained the stronghold of dying romanticism. From the city of Freud emanated the attempt to capture for art the shadowy terrain of the subconscious.

Expressionism was the German answer to French impressionism. Whereas the Latin genius rejoiced in luminous impressions of the outer world, the Germanic dug down to the subterranean regions of the soul. Expressionism set up inner experience as the only reality. It enthroned the irrational. Through the symbolism of dreams it released the primitive impulses suppressed by intellect. "There is only one greatest goal towards which the artist strives," declared Arnold Schoenberg. "*To express himself.*"

As with impressionism, the impulse for the movement came from painting. Wassily Kandinsky, Oscar Kokoschka, Paul Klee, and Franz

Marc influenced Schoenberg and his disciples even as the impressionist painters influenced Debussy. The distorted images on their canvases issued from the realm of the unconscious—hallucinated visions that defied conventional notions of beauty in order to achieve the most powerful expression of the artist's inner self. So, too, musical expressionism defied the laws of what had hitherto been accepted as beauty and gave birth to new conceptions of melody, harmony, tonality, rhythm, and form.

Like the romantic movement itself, expressionism in music triumphed

Collection, *Museum of Modern Art*

Kandinsky, *Abstraction.*

"Expressionism was the German answer to French impressionism. It set up inner experience as the only reality."

first in the central European area that lies within the orbit of Germanic culture. The movement reached its peak in the period of the Weimar Republic. It is familiar to Americans through the painting of Kandinsky and Klee, the writings of Franz Kafka, the dancing of Mary Wigman (acclimated in the United States through the art of Martha Graham), the acting of Conrad Veidt, and through such films as *The Cabinet of Dr. Caligari*. Expressionist tendencies entered European opera through Richard Strauss's *Salome* and *Elektra*. They reached their full tide in the theater works of Schoenberg and his disciple Alban Berg.

Expressionism was the suppressed, the agonized romanticism of an anti-romantic age. It offered emotional release of a more than normal intensity. Its violence was the violence of a world overwhelmed, a world in flight from reality.

✺63✺

Style Elements in Contemporary Music

"Music is now so foolish that I am amazed. Everything that is wrong is permitted, and no attention is paid to what the old generation wrote as composition."
                                                Samuel Scheidt (1651)

THE REVITALIZATION OF RHYTHM

PRIMITIVISM, machine music, ballet, the influence of sports and gymnastics, the hectic pace of city life—all these called into being rhythms more complex than had ever been known before. The new music turned away from the standard patterns of duple, triple, or quadruple meter. Composers explored the possibilities of nonsymmetrical patterns based on odd numbers: five, seven, eleven, thirteen beats to the measure.

In nineteenth-century music a single meter customarily prevailed through an entire movement or section. Now the metrical flow shifted constantly, sometimes with each bar, as in the following exerpt from Stravinsky's *The Rite of Spring*. Formerly music presented to the ear one rhythmic pattern at a time, sometimes two. Now several rhythms might unfold simultaneously (polyrhythm). As a result of these innovations, Western music achieved something of the complexity and supple-

ness of Asiatic and African rhythm. The music of Stravinsky and Bartók revealed to their contemporaries an explosive, elemental rhythm of enormous force and tension. Both men were partial to the rhythmic ostinato—the use of a striking rhythmic pattern which, by being repeated over and over again, takes on an almost hypnotic power.

Nineteenth-century rhythm was subject to the regular recurrence of accent. Twentieth-century rhythm was emancipated from the "tyranny of the bar line"—that is, from the regular beat. One might say that the new music turned from the rhythmic patterns of metrical poetry to those of free verse, or to the flexible rhythm of prose. The listener will not respond to these new rhythms as he would to a Strauss waltz or a Sousa march, by tapping his foot or waving his hand with the beat. To compensate him he will find rhythms that are plastic in the highest degree, of an almost physical power and drive. The revitalization of rhythm is one of the major achievements of twentieth-century music.

MELODY

Rhythm was not the only element that abandoned symmetrical structure. Melody followed suit. In the nineteenth century melody was often based on regular phrases of four or eight measures set off by evenly spaced cadences. This expansive rhetoric was not congenial to the contemporary style.

Composers today do not fill out a phrase to last eight measures because the phrase before was that long. Nor do they develop the neatly balanced repetitions and contrasts that prevailed formerly. Their ideal is a direct forward-driving melody from which all nonessentials have been cut away. They assume a quicker perception on the part of the hearer than did composers in the past. A thing is said once rather than in multiples of four. The result is a taut angular melody of telegraphic conciseness which bears the same relation to the rounded melody of the romantic era as does the lean hard prose of a Hemingway to the rolling cadences of Walter Scott.

Nineteenth-century melody was fundamentally vocal in character; composers tried to make the instruments "sing." Twentieth-century melody is based primarily on an instrumental conception. It is neither unvocal nor antivocal; it is simply not conceived in relation to the voice. Melody today abounds in wide leaps and dissonant intervals; it aims for expressiveness but avoids the obvious; it addresses the mind as well as the heart.

Contemporary music is often accused of being unmelodious. This is because it has departed from the romantic ideal. As the public grows familiar with the modern idiom it begins to recognize melodies in many works that at first seemed lacking in melody. Composers have in no sense abandoned melody. Now as in the past melody is the soul of music. What twentieth-century composers have done is to expand our concept of melody. In so doing they have demonstrated that a melody is a more flexible thing than had been supposed.

HARMONY: THE EMANCIPATION OF THE DISSONANCE

The history of music, we have seen, has been the history of a steadily increasing tolerance on the part of the human ear. Combinations at first rejected as dissonant were in time accepted as consonant. Throughout this long evolution one factor remained constant. A clear distinction was drawn between dissonance, the element of tension, and consonance, the element of rest. Consonance was the norm, dissonance the temporary disturbance. Twentieth-century harmony wiped out this distinction. Tension tended to become the norm—a clear case of art imitating life.

Composers emancipated the dissonance, first, by making it more familiar to the ear; second, by freeing it from the obligation to resolve to consonance. Thereby they expanded the traditional notion of what is beautiful in music. They no longer sought the "harmonious harmony" of which Debussy dreamed. They preferred percussive harmonies, of a degree of friction never known before. They set streams of chords one against the other as freely as composers in the past did single notes. To ears which only recently had heard the harmonies of Brahms and Tchaikovsky, the new procedures seemed like the most brutal cacophony and evoked sensations verging on physical pain. Human nature, however, changes more readily than we realize. Today the same music is listened to with pleasure by a rapidly growing public.

TEXTURE: DISSONANT COUNTERPOINT

The nineteenth century was preoccupied with harmony; the twentieth emphasizes counterpoint. The romantic composer thought in terms of vertical mass; the contemporary composer thinks largely in terms of horizontal line. Where the romantics exalted the magic sonority of the chord, their successors stress a neat fabric of tightly woven lines. This is part of the movement "back to Bach" and to the earlier masters of contrapuntal art.

By substituting line for mass, composers lightened the swollen sound of the post-romantic period. The new music swept away both the romantic cloudburst and the impressionist haze. In their stead was installed a well-ventilated texture of widely spaced lines from whose interplay the music derived its tension; a texture suitable for a neoclassic age.

Consonance unites, dissonance separates. Composers began to use dissonance to separate the independent lines, to set them off against one another. Thus came into being a linear texture based on dissonant counterpoint, objective, logical, powered by motor rhythms, and marked by solid workmanship as by sober sentiment.

ORCHESTRATION

Orchestral writing followed the same anti-romantic direction as prevailed in other departments of the art. The rich sonorities of nineteenth-century orchestration were alien to the modern temper. The trend was toward a smaller orchestra and a leaner sound, one that was hard, bright, sober. "One is tired," wrote Stravinsky, "of being saturated with timbres." Similarly Schoenberg: "Perhaps the art of orchestration has become too popular, and interesting-sounding pieces are often produced for no better reason than that which dictates the making of typewriters and fountain pens in different colors."

The decisive factor in the handling of the orchestra was the change to a linear texture. Color came to be used in the new music not so much for atmosphere or enchantment as for bringing out the lines of counterpoint and of form. Whereas the nineteenth-century orchestrator made his colors swim together, the neoclassicist desires each to stand out against the mass. Instruments are used in their unusual registers. The emotional crescendo and diminuendo of romantic music gives way to even levels of soft or loud. This less expressive scheme revives the solid areas of light and shade of the age of Bach. The string section loses its traditional role as the heart of the orchestra. Its tone is felt to be too personal. Attention is focused on the more objective winds. Because of improvements in construction and technique, the woodwind and brass achieve virtuoso status. Their music abounds in special effects, such as muted tubas and the trombone glissando that Schoenberg was one of the first to exploit. There is a movement away from brilliancy of sound.

The darker instruments come to the fore—viola, bassoon, trombone. The romantic horn is supplanted in favor by the more incisive trumpet. The emphasis on rhythm brings the percussion group to full equality with the other sections. Percussion sound pervades the entire orchestra. The piano, which in the romantic era was pre-eminently a solo instrument, finds a place for itself in the orchestral ensemble. Both in solo and ensemble music, composers explore the piano's capacity for percussive rhythm, in this way opening up new possibilities for the favored instrument of Chopin and Liszt.

The new music revives the eighteenth-century practice of pitting one instrument against another; that is, the *concertante* principle. Since the instruments function more and more as soloists rather than as part of a group, orchestral sound draws steadily closer to the chamber-music ideal. The chamber orchestra becomes a mainstay of the new classicism. Also, contemporary composers place great emphasis on chamber music. The most diverse ensembles are cultivated—strings, winds, or combinations of both. All in all, the new music rejects the romantic use of sonority as an end in itself. Twentieth-century musicians have restored color to its classical function, as the obedient handmaiden of idea, line, structure, and design.

REVIVAL OF ABSOLUTE FORMS

Neoclassicism led the way back to the abstract forms. Sonata, symphony, and related types took a new lease on life, as did a number of eighteenth-century forms: theme and variations, suite, toccata, fugue, passacaglia and chaconne, concerto grosso, and the social forms of the Viennese period, the divertimento and serenade.

The preoccupation with form which tends to elevate it above expressive values is known as formalism. Ours, it goes without saying, is a formalist age. Purity of line and proportion are the aim of the new classicism as they were of the old. The contemporary composer strives for the classical ideal: the unity of content and form. Stravinsky's rejection of emotional expression through music goes hand in hand with his emphasis upon formal beauty: "One could not better define the sensation produced by music than by saying that it is identical with that evoked by contemplating the interplay of architectural forms. Goethe thoroughly understood this when he called architecture frozen music."

Twentieth-century music has altered materially the sonata form of Haydn and Mozart. The contrast between home and foreign key and the careful modulations from one to the other mean far less today than they did when the major-minor system was at its height. Contemporary composers have cut away many details of the exposition-development-restatement pattern. What they retain is the impressive architecture and the flexibility of a form that enables them to present purely musical ideas in a purely musical way. They prize the sonata and symphony as a construction. They feel that it suits the abstract nature of their material. Their attitude is summed up in Prokofiev's observation, "I want nothing better than sonata form, which contains everything necessary for my purpose."

There were times during the romantic period when the grand form was in danger of being swamped by program music and the short lyric forms. Today, in an astonishing renewal of vitality, it has re-established its supremacy.

THE INFLUENCE OF JAZZ

America's specific contribution to world music invaded Europe shortly after the First World War. Immediately it claimed the attention of serious musicians. Composers through the ages vitalized their art by using popular dance forms. Now, at a time when a new rhythmic conception was taking shape, the syncopations and polyrhythms of the jazz band opened up fascinating perspectives.

The vogue of primitivism made Europeans particularly susceptible to the exotic. They were enchanted by a music whose ancestry went back to the African drums, that reflected both the restless American temperament and the Negro's genius for rhythm. The excitement of jazz seemed to echo the pulse of big-city life. Also, the chamber-music character of the jazz band appealed to the time. With its independent melody lines and rhythms, jazz music wove a contrapuntal tissue as complex as it was transparent. The linear texture of jazz, its unconventional sound, and its rhapsodic improvising made a strong impact on the European mind. Debussy and Ravel; Stravinsky, Milhaud, and Honegger; Hindemith, Křenek, Kurt Weill, and Constant Lambert were among the Europeans who fell under the lure of the importation from America. It is worthy of note that composers abroad were ahead of their American colleagues in realizing the possibilities of jazz as an art form.

It goes without saying that jazz assumed some strange shapes as soon as it left American hands. Nevertheless, the new classicism for a time advanced under the twin banners of Bach and jazz—a formidable combination.

COMPOSER AND PUBLIC

The changes we have just described swept away the landmarks that had guided listeners for decades through the maze of sound. A gap ensued between composer and public whose like had never been before. The composer found himself in a dilemma. On the one hand he was resolved to exclude from his art the rhetoric that had enabled Handel, Beethoven, and Verdi to address the multitude. On the other he found himself creating in a vacuum, writing advanced works for a coterie of musicians like himself. Lacking a mass base, the new music was soon the exclusive concern of the advance-guard. The public, excluded, found its nourishment in the music of the past.

After 1930, a reconciliation began to take shape. The battle of contemporary music had been won; a more relaxed atmosphere prevailed: one no longer had to be modern at all costs. Besides, the advances had been so breath-taking that it was necessary to pause and consolidate one's gains. A new conservatism set in, with the curious result that composers born after 1900 were markedly less radical than the earlier generation had been. It even ceased to be fashionable to sneer at the romantic period. Stravinsky announced his admiration for such nineteenth-century musicians as Gounod and Delibes, Weber and Rossini, Glinka, Verdi, Tchaikovsky. The pendulum began to swing toward a reinstatement of flowing melody, toward a simplification of means and an emphasis upon the emotional element in music; in short, toward a new romanticism.

Composers began to break through their isolation. There was a turning to mass-audience forms, such as ballet, opera, and film music. A widespread attempt took shape to bring music back into contact with life. The gap between composer and public began to close, each moving to meet the other halfway. Gradually contemporary music took its place as a rounded expression of our culture. And the creative musician affirmed anew that deep need to reach out to one's fellows which no artist, being human, can ever escape.

GEBRAUCHSMUSIK (FUNCTIONAL MUSIC)

One symptom of the new orientation was the interest in *Gebrauchsmusik* (literally, "music for use"—i. e., practical everyday music). This was music designed for the home and the amateur, as distinguished from the art-for-art's-sake variety intended for concert performance by the professional virtuoso. *Gebrauchsmusik* emerged in the Weimar Republic with its youth movement, its workers' choruses, and socialist ideals. Among its exponents were Paul Hindemith and Ernest Křenek, Kurt Weill and Hanns Eisler. "It is to be regretted," wrote Hindemith in 1927, "that in general so little relationship exists between the producers and the consumers of music." The corrective was to create a functional music that would meet the needs of a particular group and occasion. *Gebrauchsmusik* favored pieces of modest dimensions written in clear simple style. It emphasized group playing rather than the soloist: works for chorus or small orchestra, and chamber music. The parts were so designed that they could be played on whatever instruments happened to be available. Hindemith turned out music for children, students, amateur groups; music to eat to and music to play games to. Characteristic is his *Kammermusik* (Chamber Music) *No. 1* and his musical game for children, as he called it, *Wir Bauen eine Stadt* (We Build a City). The desire to bring music close to life also penetrated the opera, which turned from gods and kings to topics of the day, to scenes laid in factories, hotels, and bars.

Gebrauchsmusik was unpretentious and anti-romantic. Hindemith described it as "music which is not written solely for the composer's pleasure, the inference being that it must be practical for all concerned, both participants and auditors." The name attached itself to everything he wrote, with the result that he came to dislike it even as Debussy disliked "impressionism." In a sense the label is meaningless, as all music is written for some use or other. It survived, as did "impressionism," because it caught the essence of an attitude. *Gebrauchsmusik* was an important movement in the twenties. It represented one of the first attempts on the part of contemporary music to find its way back to the public. As such it heralded what was to become, after 1930, an increasingly important trend in the New Music.

≱64≰

New Conceptions of Tonality

> "Every tone relationship that has been used too often must finally
> be regarded as exhausted. It ceases to have power to convey a
> thought worthy of it. Therefore every composer is obliged to
> invent anew, to present new tone relations."
>
> Arnold Schoenberg

IN THE major-minor system seven tones were chosen out of the twelve
to form a key. This "seven out of twelve" way of hearing music has
been supplanted in the twentieth century by a "twelve out of twelve."
In other words, contemporary harmony has expanded our conception
of key and of what can be included in it. A piece is no longer in C major
as Mozart understood the term. It is "sort of" in C major, the composer
using all twelve tones freely around the center C. The supremacy of
the keynote is less pronounced than formerly, although the harmony
still gravitates to it. Much less pronounced, too (where it hasn't been
altogether wiped out), is the distinction between major and minor.

Expansion of tonality was encouraged by a number of factors: interest in the exotic scales of Bali, Java, and other Far Eastern cultures; use
of scales derived from the folk music of areas more or less outside the
major-minor orbit, such as those of Russia, Scandinavia, Spain, Hungary, and other Balkan countries; revival of interest in the medieval
church modes and in composers who wrote long before the major-
minor system evolved, such as the masters of fifteenth- and sixteenth-
century counterpoint. The musicians of our era have gone far afield
both in time and space in order to find new means of revitalizing
their art.

POLYTONALITY

Tonality implies the supremacy of a single key and a single tone
center. Composers in the past made the most out of the contrast between
two keys heard in succession. The next step was to heighten the contrast by presenting them simultaneously.

To confront the ear with two keys at the same time means to depart
radically from the basic principle of traditional harmony. The use of
two keys together (*bitonality*) and of several (*polytonality*) came to

the fore in the music of Stravinsky and Milhaud, whence it entered the vocabulary of the age. Toward the end of the piece one key is generally permitted to assert itself over the others. In this way the impression is restored of orderly progression toward a central point.

Polytonality is used to bring out the different levels or planes of the harmony. By putting two or more streams of chords in different keys the friction between them is immeasurably heightened. Piano music especially lends itself to this usage, right and left hands playing progressions of chords in different keys.

Since the tension comes from the clash of keys, each stream of harmony must be rooted solidly in its own key. Stravinsky's *Petrushka*, for example, despite its daring harmonic combinations has a surprisingly C-major look—that is, comparatively few sharps or flats: what is nowadays referred to as "white" music. The tendency toward "whiteness" was one of the characteristics of Parisian neoclassicism.

By the same token Vienna, the center of expressionism, inherited the fondness for chromatic harmony that was at the heart of German romanticism.

ATONALITY

Although the principle of key was flexible enough in adjusting to the needs of the new music, there was bound to appear a musician who questioned whether such adjustment was at all possible. This was Arnold Schoenberg, who proclaimed that the concept of key had outlived its usefulness.

Schoenberg rebelled against the tyranny of the tonic. He maintained that as long as the tones of the key, whether seven or twelve, were kept subordinate to a central tone, it was impossible to utilize all the resources of the chromatic scale. He advocated doing away with the tonic—in other words, treating the twelve tones as of equal importance. In this way, he maintained, music would be freed from a number of procedures that had ceased to be fruitful.

To do away with the tonic means abandoning a principle as fundamental in the musical universe as gravitation is in the physical. How fundamental is evident in the upward pull of the seventh step of the major scale, *ti*, to the *do*. Schoenberg pointed out that since the major-minor system had not existed longer ago than three centuries, there was no reason to suppose that it could not be superseded. "Tonality is not an eternal law of music," he asserted, "but simply a means toward the achievement of musical form." The time had come, according to him, to seek new means.

To the music of Schoenberg and his school there attached itself the label *atonality*. He disliked the term as strongly as Hindemith did *Gebrauchsmusik*. "I regard the expression atonal as meaningless. Atonal can only signify something that does not correspond to the nature of tone." However, the name persisted.

Atonal music is much more of an innovation than is polytonal, for it rejects the framework of key. It excludes consonance which, according to Schoenberg, is no longer capable of making an impression. Its starting point is dissonance; it moves from one level of dissonance to another. There results a music that functions always at maximum tension, without areas of relaxation. This circumstance imparts to it its furious restlessness, what Schoenberg's biographer Dika Newlin calls "its well-nigh hysterical emotionality." Dissonance resolving to consonance was, symbolically, an optimistic act. It affirmed the triumph of rest over tension, of order over chaos. Atonal music, significantly, appeared at a time in European culture when belief in that triumph was sorely shaken.

Having accepted the necessity of moving beyond the existing tonal system, Schoenberg sought a unifying principle that would take the place of the key. He found this in a strict technique which he had worked out by the early twenties. He named it "the method of composing with twelve tones."

TWELVE-TONE MUSIC

"I was always occupied," he wrote, "with the desire to base the structure of my music *consciously* on a unifying idea." The unifying idea in twelve-tone music is the *tone row*. This is an arrangement of the twelve tones in a fixed sequence which serves as the basic material for a given composition.

By including all the twelve tones, the total resources of the chromatic scale are utilized. The twelve tones are considered to be related to each other but to no one central tone. In other words, they are all of equal importance. No tone appears more than once in the row lest it take on the prominence of a tonic. When the basic set of twelve has unfolded, it is repeated—always in its fixed order. The principle is somewhat related to the passacaglia and the theme with variations. Twelve-tone composition may be said to be a highly integrated species of variation form; indeed, the most highly integrated that ever was.

Schoenberg desired the unifying idea to produce not only all the other ideas but also the accompanying lines and chords. The tone row pervades the entire fabric of the piece. It may be turned upside down (inversion). It may be presented backwards (retrograde) or upside down and backwards. Each of these four versions—the original row and its three variants—may begin on any one of the twelve tones of the scale, giving forty-eight possibilities. The tones of the row may be duplicated in any octave. They may be distributed among various instruments, combined vertically into chords, varied rhythmically in an endless number of ways. Even as the constant repetition of the row safeguards the unity of the work, its constant transformation furnishes the element of variety. In this process are called into play all the resources of imagination and technique at the composer's disposal.

All this, you will object, is quite arbitrary. To which your Schoenbergian will retort that all art is arbitrary. Precisely its artifice makes it art. Musical composition has always had its rules of the game. If they seem to be more in evidence here it is only because they are as yet unfamiliar. The only valid criterion is: Are the rules such as to enable a creative musician to express himself and his time? Schoenberg's followers would answer with an emphatic yes.

Twelve-tone thinking is contrapuntal thinking. It does away with the repetitions and sequences, the balanced phrases and cadences of traditional harmonic music. It represents a horizontal, a linear conception of music. This is implemented by the devices of sixteenth-century counterpoint—canonic imitation, augmentation, diminution, inversion, and the like. Through these procedures it aims to achieve a continuous texture of maximum concentration, abstraction, and expressiveness.

To its opponents twelve-tone music is a tortured idiom that signals the death agony of German romanticism. To its adherents it is the language of the future, the one way out for an art which—but for it—would be at a standstill. They see in it a conception of truth and beauty to which they are dedicated with an almost religious fervor. In a few decades, they are persuaded, twelve-tone music will be the only music; for it alone makes possible further advance. "Indeed," writes Schoenberg, "tonal is perhaps nothing else than what is understood *today* and atonal what will be understood in the *future*."

The tendencies we have summarized in the past few chapters were part of a ferment over the whole of Europe. They filled the opening decades of our century with a vast excitement. When the battles of cliques and isms had subsided, when the booings and the hissings had cleared away, it transpired that the contemporary school of composers had brought into being a new grammar and syntax of music—in effect, a new world of sound.

❧65❧
Igor Stravinsky (1882-)

"I hold that it was a mistake to consider me a revolutionary. If one only need break habit in order to be labeled a revolutionary, then every artist who has something to say and who in order to say it steps outside the bounds of established convention could be considered revolutionary."

IGOR STRAVINSKY is the most celebrated of present-day composers. Boundlessly admired in some quarters and as roundly denounced in others, he has for forty years been a major force on the contemporary scene.

HIS LIFE

He was born in a suburb of what was then St. Petersburg, son of a leading bass at the Imperial Opera. He was intended by his family for the law, but soon realized his vocation for music. Largely self-taught up to the time he studied with Rimsky-Korsakov, he began his creative career within the tradition of the Russian national school.

His First Symphony was performed when he was twenty-six. Shortly thereafter he met Serge Diaghilev, impresario of the Ballet Russe, who played a decisive part in bringing his name before the world. Diaghilev, sensing the potentialities of the as yet unknown musician, commissioned a work for his company. *L'Oiseau de feu* (The Firebird), produced in Paris with Nijinsky and Karsavina in the main roles, established Stravinsky's reputation. His success brought him into contact with such leaders of the modern movement in art as Picasso and Cocteau. *Petrushka*, given in 1911, caused a sensation. Two years later came the most daring of the three ballets of his first period, *Le Sacre de printemps* (The Rite of Spring). The opening night witnessed one of the "scandals" of modern musical history. Part of the audience was persuaded that the work, as one critic put it, constituted "a blasphemous attempt to destroy music as an art." They jeered and hissed. A fracas broke out, in the course of which several score persons were extricated from their clothes and wound up in the police station. Presented a year later at a symphony concert under Pierre Monteux, the *Sacre* was received enthusiastically and established itself as a masterpiece of the new music.

Bettmann Archive

Igor Stravinsky, by Picasso.

With the outbreak of war in 1914 Stravinsky found a haven in Switzerland, where he remained for six years. He drew steadily closer to the new classicism whose most important spokesman he was to become. The revolution in Russia caused the composer, who was descended from the landed gentry, to accept his exile as permanent. He became a French citizen in 1920. The next decade saw Stravinsky concertizing extensively throughout Europe as pianist and conductor of his works.

He paid two visits to the United States, where he was very much admired; and in 1939 was invited to deliver the Charles Eliot Norton lectures at Harvard. He was there when the Second World War broke out and decided to remain in this country. He settled in California, outside Los Angeles, and in 1945 became an American citizen.

HIS MUSIC

Stravinsky has shown a continuous development throughout his career. With inexhaustible avidity he has tackled new problems and pressed for new solutions. It happened several times that a certain phase of his development pointed in the opposite direction from what had come before. Seen in retrospect, however, the various periods reveal themselves to have been stages in a steady growth toward greater abstraction of style and refinement of thought.

This evolution led from the post-impressionism of *The Firebird* and the audacities of *The Rite of Spring* to the austerely controlled classicism of his maturity. In the course of it he has laid ever greater emphasis upon tradition and discipline. "The more art is controlled, limited, worked over, the more it is free." He consistently extolls the element of construction as a safeguard against excess of feeling. "Composing for me is putting into an order a certain number of sounds according to certain interval relationships." A piece of music is for him first and foremost a problem. "I cannot compose until I have decided what problem I must solve." The problem is esthetic, not personal. As one of his biographers points out, "We find his musical personality in his works but not his personal joys or sorrows."

Stravinsky, we noted, was a leader in the revitalization of European rhythm. His first success was won as a composer of ballet, where rhythm is allied with body movement and expressive gesture. His is a rhythm of unparalleled dynamic power, furious yet controlled. It has the elemental force that creates forms and ideas. In harmony Stravinsky has reacted against the restless chromaticism of the romantic period. No matter how daring his harmony, he retains a robust sense of key. He achieves excitement by superposing streams of chords in different keys. For all its explosive force his harmony, like his rhythm, is immensely refined. Stravinsky's subtle sense of sound makes him one of the great orchestrators. Unmistakably his is that enameled brightness of sonority and a texture so clear that, as Diaghilev remarked, "One could see through it with one's ears." Stravinsky was one of those who led contemporary music to purity of color. The classicist in him demands that color serve form and design. He achieves his effects with astonishing economy of means. Whereas a Richard Strauss puts down as many notes as possible, Stravinsky writes as few.

The national element predominates in his early works; as in *Petrushka*, in which he found his personal style. *Le Sacre de printemps* re-creates the rites of pagan Russia. To the fashionable audience that frequented Diaghilev's dance entertainments, this savage score came as an electrifying shock. Its primitive force, set forth by a powerful creative imagination, brought to the fore what was practically a new tonal language.

The war decade saw the turn toward simplification of means. To this period belong the smaller ballets, *Renard* (The Fox), *Les Noces* (Village Wedding) and *L'Histoire du Soldat* (The Soldier's Tale, 1918). The "return to Bach" took shape in the Octet for Woodwinds (1923), the Sonata and the Concerto for Piano. There followed a return to the nineteenth century, in which Stravinsky paid homage both by word and music to leading figures of the romantic era. In his late period Greek antiquity supplants Russian folklore as a source of inspiration. *Oedipus Rex* (1927) was followed by *Apollo Musagetes* (Apollo, Leader of the Muses), *Persephone*, and *Orpheus*. The last-named works display his continuing preoccupation with the classical ballet, whose "aristocratic austerity," as he calls it, corresponds so closely to his conception of art. "In classical dancing I see the triumph of studied conception over vagueness, of the rule over the arbitrary, of order over the haphazard."

Among the late works the undoubted masterpiece is the *Symphony of Psalms* for chorus and orchestra. Few things of our century compare, for sheer grandeur and inwardness of spirit, with its closing pages. In 1950 Stravinsky completed *The Rake's Progress*, an opera on a libretto by W. H. Auden and Chester Kallman after Hogarth's celebrated set of engravings. Written as the composer was approaching seventy, this is a radiant score, although it lacks effectiveness in the theater. The eighteenth-century setting proved thoroughly congenial to the composer. As he put it, "I will lace each aria with a tight corset."

Stravinsky's aphorisms display his gift for trenchant expression. "We have a duty to music, namely, to invent it . . . Instinct is infallible. If it leads us astray it is no longer instinct . . . It is not simply inspiration that counts. It is the result of inspiration—that is, the composition." Speaking of his Mass: "The Credo is the longest movement. There is much to believe." When asked to define the difference between *The Rite of Spring* and *Symphony of Psalms:* "The difference is twenty years." Of the innumerable anecdotes to which his ready tongue has given rise it will suffice to quote one. After the out-of-town opening of Billy Rose's revue *Seven Lively Arts,* for which he wrote a ballet, the producers of the show became apprehensive as to how his music would be received on Broadway. They wired him: "Great success. Could be sensational if you authorize arranger Mr. X to add some details to orchestration. Mr. X arranges even the works of Cole Porter." To which Stravinsky wired back: "Am satisfied with great success."

PETRUSHKA

One of the most widely enjoyed of contemporary ballets, *Petrushka,* a burlesque in four scenes, is a legitimate offspring of the Russian national school. The setting—a street fair during carnival week in St. Petersburg about 1830—enabled the composer lovingly to evoke the colorful atmosphere of his native city. Although manifesting all the sharp gesture and movement of the ballet, the music leads its independent lyrical life and has found as important a place in the concert hall as in the theater.

The opening scene shows the crowds milling about the booths and stalls of the fair ground. A troop of drunken men pass by. An Italian organ grinder accompanies a dancer, while near by a rival dancer performs to the strains of a music box. The crowd is summoned by a drum roll to the marionette theater. The Charlatan, a shrewd showman if ever there was one, plays his flute. The curtain of his diminutive theater rises, disclosing three puppets—Petrushka, the Ballerina, and the Moor. The Charlatan touches the dolls with his flute; whereupon, to the delight of the crowd, they spring to life and perform a Russian dance.

The second tableau takes place inside the marionette theater, in Petrushka's room. Petrushka is kicked unceremoniously into the room. On the wall hangs a portrait of his heartless master; he curses it. "Although the Showman's magic has imbued all three puppets with human feelings and emotions, it is Petrushka who feels and suffers most." He is only too aware of his unprepossessing appearance; he resents his dependence on his master. At thought of the Ballerina he is filled with tenderness; a love song takes shape in his heart. When she appears, Petrushka, overwhelmed by emotion, declares his love. The Ballerina flees, leaving Petrushka in despair.

Third is the scene in the Moor's room. Stretched on the divan, the sumptuously attired Moor toys with a coconut. "Although he is brutal and stupid, his magnificent appearance charms the Ballerina." She enters; they dance together. Petrushka appears, mad with jealousy. The Moor throws him out; the Ballerina swoons.

The fourth tableau returns us to the fair ground. It is evening. Nursemaids dance. A peasant plays his pipe and leads a dancing bear. A merchant in jovial mood, accompanied by two Gypsy girls, throws bank notes to the crowd. Coachmen and grooms dance and are joined by the nursemaids. A group of masked figures appear. Their antics amuse the crowd, which joins in a frenzied dance led by a masked devil. Suddenly there is a commotion in the puppet theater. Petrushka rushes out from behind the curtain, followed by the Moor whom the Ballerina vainly tries to hold back. The Moor overtakes the luckless Petrushka and strikes him with his sword. Petrushka falls, mortally hurt. To the consternation of the crowd, he dies.

A policeman fetches the Charlatan who, to reassure the bystanders, picks up and shakes the little body, showing them that it is only a doll stuffed with sawdust. The crowd disperses. The Charlatan begins to drag the puppet to his room. Above the little theater, however, he catches sight of Petrushka's ghost, grimacing and menacing. He had not foreseen that his creation, through suffering, would achieve a soul. Stricken with fear the Charlatan drops the doll and steals away. . . .

The opening measures evoke the "big accordion" sound of the folk music that surrounded Stravinsky in his childhood. The orchestra teems with movement and animation. A solo flute, etched precisely against a background of clarinet and horn tone, presents a theme that recurs as a unifying element throughout the score.

At the rise of the curtain we encounter Stravinsky's rhythmic subtlety. The meter at this point changes with each measure: 7/8, 5/8, 7/8, 5/8, 8/8, 7/8, 5/8. Suddenly we hear the percussive harmonies, imbued with rhythmic élan, that are the hallmark of this composer. The motive of the drunkards is typical of the melodies in *Petrushka:* it is compact, strong, rooted in the key. It moves stepwise along the scale, with an occasional narrow leap, and remains within a narrow range, outlining the basic interval of a fifth and repeating fragments of itself. It bears the imprint of the folk, yet is thoroughly assimilated to Stravinsky's personal style.

The hurdy-gurdy sound is well simulated by flute and piccolo, clarinet and bass clarinet. A triangle marks the beat for the dancer and casts a tinsel charm over her wistful little melody. The Charlatan's flute solo sets the scene for miraculous doings. After he animates the dolls the orchestra breaks into the Russian Dance, another compact, scalewise tune of primitive strength whose repeated fragments stress the interval of a fifth. The C-major sound of this music announced to the

world that the turning away from post-Wagnerian chromaticism had begun, while the closely bunched dissonant chords on the piano point up the new percussive style of writing for that instrument.

The second scene presents the famous Petrushka chord, the harmonic kernel out of which the work grew: a C-major arpeggio superposed upon one in F-sharp major that serves it as a kind of "double."

It is a strikingly original sonority, and pointed the way to the polyharmony and polytonality that were to play so important a part in the new music. Petrushka's love song, whimsical and tender, makes a fine contrast to his despair after the Ballerina's departure.

The third tableau, *At the Moor's,* contains a series of charming numbers. The percussive harmonies that introduce this vain and brutal character are followed by the Moor's languid dance, an exotic theme pre-

sented by the clarinet against tricky syncopated rhythms on drums and
cymbals. The entrance of the Ballerina makes for a gay bit on cornet
and snare drum. Her dance with the Moor starts out, according to
Stravinsky's direction, sentimentalmente: a staid duet for flute and
cornet that veers into a Viennese waltz, grazioso e poco grotesco. The
familiar fanfare on the trumpet announces the appearance of Petrushka.
The quarrel between him and the Moor turns on agitated harmonies
and colors that stem out of the romantic heritage—but with a difference!

The final tableau brings back the "big accordion" sound of the opening scene. Out of the swarming orchestral voices emerges the Dance
of the Nursemaids, a memorable tune out of the heart of the Russian
national school. It moves through the two fundamental intervals—
octave and fifth—a circumstance that imparts to the melody its quality
of simplicity and strength.

The peasant and his bear are characterized by clarinet and tuba against
heavy chords in the lower strings. The dance of the coachmen and
grooms gives the composer opportunity for those dark percussive harmonies that he was to exploit so brilliantly in *The Rite of Spring*. When
the nursemaids join the dance, their theme is given a sumptuous orchestral garb. The appearance of Petrushka pursued by the Moor is
accompanied by provocative sonorities, including chromatic scales on
cornet, xylophone, and strings. The death of Petrushka is given with
wonderful economy of means: harmonics on the violas, a flicker of
piccolo sound, tremolo on muted violins, with the melody line traced
in turn by clarinet, violin solo, and bassoon. The C-major chord appears against its F-sharp major "double"; and the work ends with a
suggestion of the bitonal harmony from which it sprang.

Petrushka is characteristic of Stravinsky in its rhythmic and orchestral virtuosity, its harmonic imaginativeness and compactness of form,
its diatonic melody and strong tonal feeling. Above all, the music is

objective; it brings us not Stravinsky's emotions but those of his characters.

It was Stravinsky's historic role to incarnate a phase of the contemporary temper. In upholding the Apollonian discipline in art he revealed the age to itself. His spirit was one with the spirit of our time. This is made plain in the closing lines of his *Autobiography:* "I live neither in the past nor in the future. I am in the present. I cannot know what tomorrow may bring forth. I can only know what the truth is for me today. This is what I am called upon to serve, and I serve it in all lucidity."

≥ 66 ≤
Arnold Schoenberg (1874-1950)

"I personally hate to be called a revolutionist, which I am not. What I did was neither revolution nor anarchy."

IT IS worthy of note that, like Stravinsky, the other great innovator of our time disclaims revolutionary intent. Quite the contrary, his disciples regard him as having brought to its culmination the thousand-year-old tradition of European polyphony. He was at various times branded a charlatan and a madman. But he imposed his vision, if not on the musical world as a whole, at least on an important segment of it. And he continues to be, as he was during his lifetime, one of the most discussed figures in contemporary art.

HIS LIFE

Arnold Schoenberg was born in Vienna. He left school while in his teens in order to devote himself to music. In the last year of the nineteenth century he wrote the string sextet *Verklärte Nacht* (Transfigured Night). Conceived in the idiom of post-Wagnerian romanticism, this is the work by which he is best known to the public. There followed the *Gurrelieder*, a work for voices and orchestra that called for extraordinarily huge forces. Richard Strauss reported to his friends: "There is a young man from Vienna who leaves us all behind. He needs sixty-five staves for his score, for which he has his music paper specially printed. I told him I could make neither head nor tail of it."

To earn a living Schoenberg orchestrated popular operettas and did some conducting. The symphonic poem *Pelleas und Melisande*, after the same drama that inspired Debussy's opera, belongs to this period. When it was performed some years later in Vienna, one critic pronounced it to be "a fifty-minute-long wrong note." Schoenberg now became active as a teacher in Vienna. A band of enthusiastic young disciples gathered about him—the most gifted were Alban Berg and Anton von Webern—who sustained their master in the fierce struggle for recognition that lay ahead.

Despite the hostility of the public, Schoenberg's music and ideas slowly made their way. The tide turned with the first performance in Vienna, in 1913, of the enormously difficult *Gurrelieder*. The composer's creative activity was interrupted by military service during the First World War. Behind him were two decades during which he had moved to the outermost bounds of the traditional key system. There followed a silence of seven years (1915–23) during which he clarified his position in his own mind. He was preparing for as bold a step as artist ever took: the abandonment of tonality. This meant nothing less than to create a new grammar of musical speech. "I suspect," he wrote, "that even those who have believed in me hitherto will refuse to accept the necessity for this development. It is not lack of invention or technical skill, or ignorance of the demands of contemporary esthetics that has urged me in this direction. I am obeying a law that is natural to me and therefore stronger than my artistic training."

The goal once set, it was pursued with the tenacity of a temperament that brooked no obstacles. His "method of composing with twelve tones" aroused even greater opposition than had his early works. But his position as a leader of contemporary musical thought was firmly established. Recognition came when he was appointed Professor of Composition at the Berlin Academy of Arts. The uniquely favorable attitude of the Weimar Republic toward experimental art had made it possible for one of the most iconoclastic musicians in history to carry on his work in a high academic post.

With the coming to power of Hitler in 1933 Schoenberg was dismissed from the Academy. He arrived in the United States in the fall of 1933 and became Professor of Composition at the University of California in Los Angeles. He taught there until his retirement at the age of seventy, and remained active in music till his death six years later.

HIS MUSIC

In turning from Stravinskyan neoclassicism to Schoenberg, we traverse much more than the distance from Paris to Vienna. We cross over into another cultural tradition, another way of life: from Latin elegance to Germanic emotionalism. Whereas Stravinsky rejected the concept of art as personal expression, Schoenberg adhered to it with romantic fervor. "I write what I feel in my heart—and what finally comes on paper is what first coursed through every fibre of my body." And to the same point: "A work of art can achieve no finer effect than when it transmits to the beholder the emotions that raged in the creator, in such a way that they rage and storm also in him."

Schoenberg indicates his natural bent when he says, "The composer of today without some trace of romanticism in his heart must be lacking in something fundamentally human." Romantic too is his desire for unflagging intensity, his aim "to say the most important things in the most concentrated way in every fraction" of time. The new classicism recoils from any attempt to attach metaphysical meanings to music. For Schoenberg—some consider him typically German in this, others typically Hebraic—the mystical approach to sound is highly congenial. "My personal feeling is that music conveys a prophetic message revealing a higher form of life towards which mankind evolves."

Like Stravinsky, Schoenberg is an explorer of new musical frontiers. "The secret of the tone must always be pursued anew." We have said that his music combines the two extremes in the German character—soulfulness and the need for a rigid orderliness. On the one hand his art embodies an expressive content descended from the turbulent world of *Tristan;* on the other, a system of structural devices as rigidly intellectual as any artist ever imposed on himself. We encounter here what psychologists recognize as compensation: precisely because the content is so turbulent, the form must be nothing less than a severely logical chain of cause and effect.

To his first period belong, besides the works already mentioned, the String Quartet No. 1 in D minor and the Chamber Symphony for Fifteen Instruments, Op. 9. It was in his middle period that Schoenberg moved beyond the major-minor system. Best-known work of these years is *Pierrot Lunaire* (Pierrot of the Moon, Op. 21, 1912) for female reciter and five instruments—flute, clarinet, violin, 'cello, and piano—with three alternating instruments—piccolo, bass clarinet, viola. The work is written in free rhythms and unequal measures, what

Anton von Webern called "the prose of music"; and in an eerily expressive kind of declamation between song and speech, known as *Sprechstimme* (speaking voice). This was the first composition to carry Schoenberg's name beyond his immediate circle. Its moonstruck hero, a Pierrot very far removed from his Russian counterpart Petrushka, remains one of the signal creations of German expressionism.

The Five Piano Pieces, Op. 23, herald the transition to the twelve-tone method, which is in evidence in the Serenade, Op. 24. Of the compositions that immediately followed, the most important are the Suite for Piano, Op. 25, the Wind Quintet, and the Variations for Orchestra. Schoenberg's years in America produced a number of major works. Among these are the Fourth String Quartet, his final utterance in this medium; the Violin Concerto, a severely classicistic work that is fantastically difficult to play—Schoenberg used to say that it needed a "six-fingered violinist"; the Piano Concerto, one of the more accessible works in the twelve-tone idiom; and *A Survivor of Warsaw* for reciter, male chorus, and orchestra, the master's tribute to his coreligionists who perished at the hands of the Nazis. These works embody the conviction that sustained him to the last: "I believe composition with twelve tones is not the end of an old period but the beginning of a new one."

VERKLÄRTE NACHT (TRANSFIGURED NIGHT)

Originally written for string sextet, this impassioned tone poem (Op. 4) was later arranged by the composer for string orchestra. The work was inspired by a romantic poem of Richard Dehmel which tells of two who wander through a moonlit grove. The woman confesses that she is with child by another man. Now that she has found love, she is tormented by guilt. The man bids her cast away despair. He will raise the child as his own, for their love has made him even as a child. Through his forgiveness he is transfigured. They embrace in the moon-drenched night.

The music sets forth passages of poetic landscape painting. Thoroughly romantic are the chromatic harmonies, the evocative quality of the pure string tone, the restless modulations, the frenzied climaxes. Schoenberg subtly exploits the possibilities of the medium, the piercing sweetness of strings in their high register, the dark resonance of the low, and the rich palette of hues between. The material is overexpanded, an interesting circumstance in view of Schoenberg's later striving for the utmost conciseness of speech. Although the emotional atmosphere of this music derives from Wagner, its sensibility is Viennese. Certain turns of the harmony remind one of a composer who is never mentioned in connection with Schoenberg—Franz Liszt. *Verklärte Nacht* became something of a hit as the score for Antony Tudor's ballet *Pillar of Fire*, bringing Schoenberg a measure of the popular approval that his later works were denied.

The descending figure in D minor with which the work opens, played by violas and 'cellos, evokes a brooding terrain.

In evidence are certain devices dear to the romantics, such as the tremolo in dark lower register and a solo violin soaring high above the harmony. The piece proceeds through a continuous unfolding of themes and motives, achieving admirable unity of idea and mood. There is much imitation between one instrument and another, in a manner which to the romantic age suggested tender dialogue. The seven interweaving lines—two groups each of violins, violas, and 'cellos supported by double bass—create a finely spun texture. Despite its sensuous harmony, Schoenberg's music even at this early stage leans toward counterpoint. After restless wandering the music reaches its resolution and a Lisztian cadence in D major.

The piece is sweet and tender and warm; also vastly adroit. It forcefully refutes those who maintain that the master turned to the iron logic of his twelve-tone method because he lacked the lyric gift.

SERENADE FOR SEVEN INSTRUMENTS

The Serenade (Op. 24) belongs to the period when the tone-row technique was taking shape. To offset the revolutionary implications of his rejection of key, Schoenberg in this work turned back to the classical serenade associated with the age of Haydn and Mozart. The seven instruments are clarinet, bass clarinet, mandolin, guitar, violin, viola, and 'cello. Mandolin and guitar contribute a plucked-string timbre that pervades the ensemble; they also take the role of percussion instruments. Their presence emphasizes the nature of the serenade as a type of popular entertainment music.

The sonorities are such as to point up and contrast the lines of the texture. This combination of counterpoint and chamber style is the basis of Schoenberg's mature manner. The twelve-tone technique is not used strictly, being still in its formative stage. Sections are repeated in their entirety. There are symmetrical eight-bar formations. (Neither repetition nor symmetry is permitted in later twelve-tone works.) So, too, the tone row omits or repeats one or more of the twelve tones, a license that was discarded when the method was fully developed.

1. *March.* The tone row appears after an eight-bar introduction.

It is inverted at the interval of a fifth above. Both versions are repeated. The middle section is heard twice. The melody displays the wide leaps characteristic of this style. Violin and clarinet are used as melody instruments while the rest of the ensemble provides a bright percussive background.

2. *Minuet.* This is a minuet and trio, after which the first part is repeated da capo. Despite the dance character, the first part is lyric in mood. Free cadenzas appear in the high register of the muted violins, in the nature of songful declamation. The lively trio opens with an eight-bar introduction based on a rhythmic ostinato. A brief coda is woven out of a four-note figure that is basic to the piece.

3. *Variations.* The theme is played by clarinet alone. It consists of a succession of fourteen tones—eleven different ones—which is immedi-

ately presented backwards (beginning with the fermata or ⌢, which indicates a pause or that a note is to be held). There are five variations and a coda. The theme is subjected to rhythmic alteration and to the more intricate devices of counterpoint. The orchestration is sparse, exemplifying the rarefied texture characteristic of many twelve-tone works.

4. *Sonnet No. 217 of Petrarch*, for bass-baritone. "Ah! that I might soon wreak vengeance, On her who has destroyed me with sweet glances. . . ." The voice part is fashioned out of a twelve-tone row which also furnishes the motives and chords of the accompaniment. Schoenberg does not hesitate to distort the normal accentuation of the words for the sake of expressiveness. The vocal line unfolds in a kind of free declamation. The music underlines the structure of the sonnet through interludes. These divide in half the larger and smaller sections of the fourteen-line scheme, enclosing the poem in a formal frame.

5. *Dance Scene*. This movement is based on the rhythm and character of the ländler, the lively ancestor of the Viennese waltz. Eight-bar periods and the repetition of sections create the symmetry inseparable from popular dance. The ear is caught by a plaintive tune on the clarinet that returns in a varied version. The Coda grows steadily louder and faster and brings the movement to a climactic close. In short, unfamiliar content is presented in a thoroughly familiar form.

6. *Song without Words*. In free style and in a vein of contemplative lyricism. A muted violin sings an expansive melody which is then taken over by the 'cello. There is a brief dialogue between the two. As in the old dance suite, this air constitutes an area of repose between two active movements.

7. *Finale*. The work is rounded off with a movement that repeats the main material of the opening March. Introduction and Coda make passing allusion to earlier movements. Brisk syncopation and a lilting pace strike a festive note. Schoenberg thereby affirms the kinship of this serenade with the classical Viennese tradition of social music.

A lot of people can make neither head nor tail of this music. They may find comfort in the statements of its chief practitioners that it is intended for the audience of the future rather than for the generality of music lovers today. As to how posterity will take to Schoenberg, we can leave it to posterity to decide. It is clear already, however, that he has profoundly affected the musicians of our time. His doctrine has focused attention on basic problems of composition. It has raised key issues in musical esthesis and technique. And it has stimulated many even among those who violently disagree with the method, the man, and the music.

✎67✎

Béla Bartók (1881-1945)

"What is the best way for a composer to reap the full benefits of his studies in peasant music? It is to assimilate the idiom of peasant music so completely that he is able to forget all about it and use it as his musical mother tongue."

It was the mission of Béla Bartók to reconcile the folk melody of his native Hungary with the main currents of European music. In the process he created an entirely personal language and revealed himself as one of the major prophets of our age.

HIS LIFE

Bartók was born in a small Hungarian town where his father was director of an agricultural school. He studied at the Royal Academy in Budapest, where he came in contact with the nationalist movement that aimed to shake off the domination of German musical culture. His interest in folklore led him to realize that what passed for Hungarian in the eyes of the world—the idiom romanticized by Liszt and Brahms and kept alive by café musicians—was really the music of the Gypsies. The true Hungarian folk idiom, he decided, was to be found only among the peasants. In company with his fellow composer Zoltán Kodály he toured the remote villages of the country, determined to collect the native songs before they died out forever. Bartók's folklore studies are models of scientific research and scholarship. He became an authority on the songs of the Danubian basin—Slovakian, Rumanian, and Bulgarian—and subsequently extended his investigations to include Turkish and Arab folk song.

Personal contact with peasant life brought to the surface the profound humanity that is the essential element of Bartók's art. "Those days I spent in the villages among the peasants were the happiest of my life. In order really to feel the vitality of this music one must, so to speak, have lived it. And this is possible only when one comes to know it by direct contact with the peasants."

In 1907 Bartók was appointed Professor of Piano at the Royal Academy in Budapest. Together with Kodály he founded a society for the presentation of contemporary music. The project was defeated by the apathy of a public that refused to be weaned from the traditional German repertoire. Bartók was sufficiently embittered to give up composing for a time. He resumed his folklore studies and during the First World War devoted himself to a collection of soldier songs.

With the performance at the Budapest Opera of his ballet *The Wooden Prince*, Bartók came into his own. The fall of the Hapsburg monarchy in 1918 released a surge of national fervor that created a favorable climate for his music. In the ensuing decade Bartók became a leading figure in the musical life of his country.

The alliance between Admiral Horthy's regime and Nazi Germany on the eve of the Second World War confronted the composer with issues that he faced squarely. He protested the performances of his music on the Berlin radio and at every opportunity took an anti-Fascist stand. To go into exile meant surrendering the position he enjoyed in Hungary. But he would not compromise. "He who stays on when he could leave may be said to acquiesce tacitly in everything that is happening here." Bartók's friends, fearing for his safety, prevailed upon him to leave the country while there was still time. He came to the United States in 1940 and settled in New York City.

The last five years of his life yielded little in the way of happiness. Sensitive and retiring, he felt uprooted, isolated in his new surroundings. He made some public appearances, playing his music for two pianos with his onetime pupil and wife Ditta Pásztory-Bartók. These did not suffice to relieve his financial straits. To his son he wrote in the fall of 1941, "Concerts are few and far between. If we had to live on those we would really be at the end of our tether."

In his last years he suffered from leukemia and was no longer able to appear in public. Friends appealed for aid to ASCAP (American Society of Composers, Authors, and Publishers). Funds were made available that provided the composer with proper care in nursing homes and enabled him to continue writing to the end. He worked feverishly to complete the Third Piano Concerto and a concerto for viola and orchestra that had been commissioned by William Primrose. When he realized that he was dying he concentrated on the piano concerto in order to leave his wife "the only inheritance within his power." In his race against time he wishfully wrote *vége*—The End—on his working sketch a few days before he actually finished the piece. The Viola Concerto, left unfinished, was brought to completion from his sketches by his friend and disciple Tibor Serly.

The tale of the composer who spends his last days in poverty and embitterment only to be acclaimed after his death would seem to belong to the romantic past, to the legend of Mozart, Schubert, Musorgsky.

Yet it happened in our time. Bartók had to die in order to make his success in the United States. Almost immediately there took place an upswing of interest in his music that rapidly assumed the proportions of a boom. With one accord conductors, performers, record companies, and broadcasting stations rushed to pay him the homage that might have brought him comfort had it come a little sooner.

HIS MUSIC

Like Stravinsky and Schoenberg, Bartók disclaimed the role of revolutionary. "In art there are only fast or slow developments. Essentially it is a matter of evolution, not revolution." Despite the newness of his language he was rooted in the classical heritage. "In my youth my ideal was not so much the art of Bach or Mozart as that of Beethoven." He adhered to the logic and beauty of classical form, and to Beethoven's vision of music as an embodiment of human emotion.

Bartók found authentic Hungarian folk music to be based on ancient modes, five-tone scales, and nonsymmetrical rhythms—elements, he pointed out, "almost unknown to so-called romantic music." His investigations brought him to new conceptions of harmony and rhythm and freed him from what he called "the tyrannical rule of the major and minor keys." Folk music taught him "to cultivate the utmost excision of all that is nonessential." The time had passed for embedding folk songs in large-scale movements according to the Austro-German formula. "What we had to do was to divine the spirit of this unknown music and to make this spirit, so difficult to describe in words, the basis of our works."

Classic and romantic elements intermingle in Bartók's art. His classicism shows itself in his emphasis on construction. His idiom is concentrated, reticent, austere. The powerful melodic line flowers into rhapsodic curves. It can also be angular and taut. Characteristic is a type of melody which, like Stravinsky's, moves in a narrow range and creates an effect of primitive force. His harmony can be bitingly dissonant. In the popular *Allegro Barbaro*, written in 1911, we find the percussive treatment of dissonant chords that was to come into vogue with Stravinsky's *The Rite of Spring*. Polytonality abounds in his work; his *Bear Dance* has four keys going at once. Despite a tendency toward atonalism, he never wholly abandoned the principle of key.

Bartók's is one of the great rhythmic imaginations of modern times. His pounding, stabbing rhythms constitute the primitive aspect of his art. Passages in his scores have a Stravinskyan look, the meter changing almost at every bar. Like the Russian master, he is fond of syncopation and repeated patterns (ostinato). Bartók played a major role in the revitalization of European rhythm, infusing it with earthy vitality, with kinetic force and tension.

He was more traditional in respect to form. His model was the sonata of Beethoven even as Stravinsky adopted the continuous expansion of Bach. In his middle years he came under the influence of pre-Bach music and turned increasingly from harmony to linear thinking. His complex texture is a masterly example of modern dissonant counterpoint. It sets forth his development toward greater abstraction, tightness of structure, and purity of thought.

In orchestration Bartók exemplifies the contemporary tendency to make color serve idea. From the orchestra of Richard Strauss and Debussy he found his way to a palette all his own. He ranges from brilliant mixtures to threads of pure color that bring out the intertwining melody lines; from a hard bright glitter to a luminous haze. A virtuoso pianist himself, Bartók is one of the masters of modern piano writing. He typifies the twentieth-century use of the piano as an instrument of percussion and rhythm. The most important work for piano of his later years is *Mikrokosmos,* a collection of one hundred and fifty-three pieces ranging from simplest grade to virtuoso playing.

The six string quartets may very well rank among the major achievements of our century. These are uncompromising and extraordinarily expressive works, certain of them impregnated with the brooding pessimism that was the aftermath of the First World War. Bartók is best known to the public by the three major works of his last period. The Music for Strings, Percussion, and Celesta, written in 1936, is regarded by many as his masterpiece. Tonal opulence and warmth characterize the Concerto for Orchestra, a favorite with American audiences. The master's final statement, the Third Piano Concerto, is an impassioned and broadly conceived work, its three movements by turn dramatic, contemplative, satanic.

CONCERTO FOR ORCHESTRA

In the summer of 1943 Bartók was confined in Doctors Hospital in New York City. One day he received a visit from Serge Koussevitzky, who came offering a thousand-dollar commission and a first performance by the Boston Symphony Orchestra for any piece he would write. The knowledge that his music was wanted and that a major orchestra was waiting to perform the as yet unwritten score had a beneficent effect on the incurably ill composer. He was able to quit the hospital and left for Asheville, North Carolina. Here he set to work on the Concerto for Orchestra, which was completed the year before he died. "The general mood of the work," he wrote, "represents, apart from the jesting second movement, a gradual transition from the sternness of the first movement and the lugubrious death-song of the third to the life-assertion of the last."

Of symphonic dimension, the work is called a concerto because of its tendency, as Bartók explained, "to treat the single instruments in a *concertante* or soloistic manner." In other words, he used the term as the early eighteenth century did. The element of virtuosity prevails, but the virtuoso is the entire orchestra. The work exemplifies Bartók's wonderful sense of sound, his mastery of the grand form, and his passion for folklore. Written in his most communicative mood, the concerto was the first of his compositions to establish itself with the American public.

I. *Andante non troppo—Allegro vivace.* The Introduction is spacious of gesture. It prepares the listener for a large work. In the composer's best vein are the sonorities of the opening passage, a solemn statement by 'cellos and basses set off by tremolos on upper strings and flute. The theme is based on the interval of the fourth (indicated by brackets), which occupies a prominent position in the melody image of this composer.

The first subject of the Allegro consists of a vigorously syncopated figure that ascends to a climax and as briskly subsides. Here too the

fourth is prominent. A contrasting idea in folklore style consists mainly of two notes. The Development builds up tension through contrapuntal imitation. The Restatement is abbreviated, as is customary in twentieth-century works. The movement has the quality of inevitable progression that is the essence of symphonic style.

II. *Game of Pairs.* So called because the wind instruments are paired at specific intervals, bassoons in sixths, oboes in thirds, clarinets in sevenths, flutes in fifths, muted trumpets in seconds. This "jesting second movement," as Bartók called it, is marked Allegretto scherzando. Bass drum and bassoons usher in music of a processional nature that is filled with teasing ideas. In evidence is the element of the bizarre that appealed to Berlioz and Mahler no less than to Bartók. The form is a "chain" of five little sections, each featuring another pair of instruments. There is a chorale for brass. The five sections are then restated with more elaborate instrumentation.

III. *Elegy.* The "lugubrious death song" is marked Andante non troppo. An oboe traces a long line of lamentation against Bartókian flickerings of clarinet, flute, and harp tone. The music is rhapsodic, visionary; it rises to a tragic climax. This is a heroic canvas in the great line of the hymnic adagios of Beethoven.

IV. *Interrupted Intermezzo.* A plaintive tune in folk-song style is introduced by the oboe and continued by the flute. The nonsymmetrical rhythm, an alternation of 2/4 and 5/8, imparts to the movement a wayward charm. There follows a broadly songful theme on the strings. The mood is interrupted as the music turns from folk lyricism to the sophisticated tone of the cafés. The return of the lyric theme on muted strings makes a grandly poetic effect. The movement is replete with capriciousness and tender sentiment.

Copyright 1946 by Hawkes & Son (London), Ltd. Used by permission.

V. *Finale.* Presto. There is an introduction of a few bars marked pesante (heavily), in which the horns outline the germinal theme. The movement of "life-assertion" gets off to a whirlwind perpetuum mobile (perpetual motion) on the strings. The fugue that follows parades intricate devices of counterpoint; yet so lightly does Bartók wear his learning that there is nothing here to tax the untutored ear. The fugue subject is presented by the trumpet. Notice again the decisive role played by the interval of a fourth.

The folk tune as Bartók uses it here has nothing in common with the prettified peasant dances of the nineteenth century. Its harmonies are acrid, its rhythms imbued with primitive strength. The movement rises to a mood of heroic affirmation.

The work follows the progression "through suffering to the stars" that formed the epic theme of Beethoven's symphony-dramas. Like those, the Concerto for Orchestra moves from a sense of the tragic to indomitable optimism. Like those, too, it seeks to "embrace the millions." The composer's intention was realized. At the first international Bartók festival held in Budapest in the fall of 1948 his works were applauded by tens of thousands of his countrymen. The mass sale of Bartók recordings in England and America testifies similarly to the wide appeal and profoundly human quality of his art.

Bartók's prime characteristic both as musician and man was the uncompromising integrity that informed his every act—what a compatriot of his has called "the proud morality of the mind." He was one of the great spirits of our time.

PART SEVEN

The American Scene

❧

"What we must arrive at is the youthful optimistic vitality and the undaunted tenacity of spirit that characterizes the American man. That is what I hope to see echoed in American music."

Edward MacDowell

✑68✑

The Past

"Music . . . the favorite passion of my soul."
Thomas Jefferson

THE FIRST book to be printed in the New World was an almanac. Second was the Bay Psalm Book which was published in Cambridge in 1640. Its appearance underlines what was the chief function of music in early New England: the singing of psalms and hymns.

In Virginia, on the other hand, there evolved a society of planters who adhered to the social amenities of Cavalier England. As in the aristocratic circles of Europe, music served for polite and elegant entertainment. Jefferson was an amateur violinist, played string quartets at the weekly musicales of Governor Fauquier, and invented an ingenious violin stand which when folded did duty as an end table. Years later, in planning Monticello, he inquired of a friend in France whether there might not be found a gardener, weaver, cabinetmaker, and stone cutter who could double on French horn, clarinet, oboe, and bassoon. "The bounds of an American fortune," he writes, "will not admit the indulgence of a domestic band of musicians, yet I have thought that a passion for music might be reconciled with that economy which we are obliged to observe."

In the absence of an aristocracy to act as patrons, music in colonial America had to find other outlets, one of which was the public concert. The first of which there is record took place in Boston in 1731. Ballad opera was given in Charleston as early as 1735. The ordinance against theater in Boston stated that such entertainments discouraged industry, frugality, and piety (in that order). To get around the law, stage shows masquerade as "moral lectures" and "readings." By the end of the century the Bostonians had succumbed to several dozen ballad operas.

The honor of being the first American-born composer belongs to an aristocratic amateur. Francis Hopkinson (1737–91) came from the same stratum of society in Philadelphia as did his friend Jefferson in Virginia. Composing was but one of the many interests of this jurist, writer, statesman, signer of the Declaration of Independence, and framer of the Constitution.

Hopkinson's best-known song is *My Days Have Been So Wondrous Free*. A collection of songs "in an easy, familiar style, intended for young practitioners on the harpsichord or forte piano"—he was responsible also for the texts—appeared in Philadelphia in 1788. The work was dedicated to Washington, to whom he wrote, "However small the Reputation may be that I shall derive from this work, I cannot, I believe, be refused the Credit of being the first Native of the United States who has produced a Musical Composition." To which Washington replied, "I can neither sing one of the songs, nor raise a single note on any instrument to convince the unbelieving. But I have, however, one argument which will prevail with persons of true estate (at least in America)—I can tell them that *it is the production of Mr. Hopkinson*."

A more substantial composer was William Billings (1746–1800). A tanner by trade, this exuberant figure was the product of a pioneer culture. The little knowledge he had was gleaned from the rudimentary treatises contained in the hymn books of the time. Billings is specifically associated with the lively "fuguing pieces" in which he treated psalm and hymn tunes contrapuntally. The fugal treatment—actually, merely a sort of simple imitation—produced a music that was, he claimed, "twenty times as powerful as the old slow tunes. Each part striving for mastery and victory. The audience entertained and delighted. Now the solemn bass demands their attention; next the manly tenor. Now here, now there, now here again! O ecstatic! Rush on, you sons of harmony." Such ebullience was not to be resisted. Billings's psalms, anthems, humorous pieces, and patriotic songs were widely performed in the late eighteenth century. He was rewarded for his efforts with a pauper's grave near Boston Common. His memory lived on, however, to inspire some twentieth-century Americans. William Schuman's *A Billings Overture* and Henry Cowell's *Hymn and Fuguing Tunes* pay homage to this extraordinary American primitive.

THE NINETEENTH CENTURY

The young republic attracted an influx of musicians from England, France, and Germany, who brought with them a tradition and a level of technique beyond any that existed here. In consequence, the new generation of American musicians was better equipped than their predecessors. A typical figure was Lowell Mason (1792–1872), who wrote *Nearer, My God, to Thee* and other standard hymns. It was Mason's great achievement to establish music in the public-school curriculum. His son William Mason (1829–1908) studied with Liszt at

Weimar and became one of the foremost pianists and teachers of his day. The circle was now complete—Europeans had come to the New World to live, Americans were returning to Europe to study.

The vogue of the visiting virtuoso began. The Norwegian violinist Ole Bull was followed, in 1850, by Jenny Lind. What with her gift for song and P. T. Barnum's genius for publicity, Jenny was a sensation.

Jenny Lind at Castle Garden.
"The vogue of the visiting virtuoso began."

Toward the middle of the century, America produced its own virtuoso in Louis Moreau Gottschalk. Born in New Orleans in 1829, the son of an English Jew and a Creole, Gottschalk was one of the adored pianists of the romantic period. Handsome and magnetic, he was a Lisztian figure who left his white gloves on the piano to be torn to shreds by overwrought ladies in need of a little something to press between the pages of a book. Gottschalk left behind some salon pieces such as *The Last Hope* and *The Dying Poet* that nourished several generations of pupils and parents. More important were the exotic bits—*Bamboula, Le Bananier, The Banjo*—which, by exploiting the New Orleans locale, pointed the way to an awakening nationalism.

The revolutions of 1848 caused thousands of liberals to emigrate from central Europe. German musicians came over in large numbers. They formed the backbone of the symphony orchestras, singing societies, and chamber-music groups. In this way the traditions of Weimar and Leipzig, Munich and Vienna were established in our midst and became a decisive factor in shaping our musical taste.

But the great American composer of the pre-Civil War period did not issue from the tradition of Haydn and Mozart. He came out of the humbler realm of the minstrel show. Stephen Foster (1826–64) was born in Lawrenceville, Pennsylvania. His was a substantial middle-class environment in which music was not even remotely considered to be a suitable career for a man. His parents took note of his talent but did nothing to encourage or train it. Foster's lyric gift, unassimilated to any musical culture, found its natural outlet in the sphere of popular song.

Foster's was a temperament unable to accommodate itself to the bourgeois ideal of success. He was, as his biographer John Tasker Howard has written, "a dreamer, thoroughly impractical and . . . never businessman enough to realize the commercial value of his best songs." His course led with tragic inevitability from the initial flurries of good fortune, through the failure of his marriage, to the hall bedroom on the Bowery and the alcoholic's lonely death at the age of thirty-eight. In that time he managed to write some two hundred songs, a half dozen of which have imprinted themselves on the American soul.

Seen in the perspective of history this lovable weakling, the despair of his parents, his wife, and his brothers, emerges as one of our great artists. He stands among the very few musicians whose personal vision created the songs of a nation.

THE POST-ROMANTIC PERIOD

The decades following the Civil War witnessed an impressive expansion of musical life throughout the country. Most important, there appeared a native school of trained composers. First to achieve more than ephemeral fame was John Knowles Paine (1839–1906), who for thirty years was Professor of Music at Harvard, and mentor of the so-called Boston or New England group that included leading American composers at the turn of the century. Among these was George W. Chadwick (1854–1931), Horatio Parker (1863–1919), Mrs. H. H. A. Beach (1867–1945), and Edgar Stilman Kelley (1857–1944). The Boston group issued from a cultural environment that since the days of Emerson was rooted in German philosophy and culture. They finished their studies in Leipzig, Weimar, or Berlin and worked within the German tradition. It was their historic role to raise the technical level of American music to that obtaining in Europe.

A more striking physiognomy was that of Edward MacDowell (1861–1908), the first American composer to achieve a reputation abroad. He studied composition in Germany and came to the notice of Liszt, who secured performances of his works. MacDowell settled in Germany and taught there for several years. After Liszt's death he returned to the United States.

The four piano sonatas and two concertos for piano and orchestra reveal MacDowell to have been at home in the large forms. He was at his best, however, in the small lyric pieces that are still favorites with young pianists. The *Woodland Sketches*, whence the perennial *To a Wild Rose*, the *Fireside Tales* and *New England Idyls* are the work of a miniaturist of great charm and sensibility.

The composers just mentioned were really belated romanticists. The post-romantic label is more properly applied to the Alsatian-born Charles Martin Loeffler (1861–1935), who came to this country when he was twenty. He is remembered chiefly for *A Pagan Poem*, a work for thirteen instruments he later rewrote for piano and orchestra. Loeffler was a recluse and a mystic. His was a music of shadowy visions, betraying an affinity for Gregorian chant, medieval modes, and impressionist harmonies. His style resembles that which came to be associated with Debussy; yet he found his way to it in the 1890s, before he could have heard much of the Frenchman's music. Loeffler anticipated what was to become the most important development in American music of the twentieth century: the turning from German to French influence.

The American composers of the late nineteenth century ill deserve the oblivion we have permitted to overtake them. Our present-day musicians feel little kinship with these disciples of Liszt, Schumann, and Mendelssohn. And in the world arena they have been overshadowed by their European contemporaries, compared to whom they appear to take second place. Yet comparisons are hardly in order. The European post-romantics were heirs to a rich past. The Americans were building for a rich future. They were pioneers dedicated to a noble vision. We have every reason to remember them with pride.

≫69≪

The Present

"The way to write American music is simple. All you have to
do is to be an American and then write any kind of music you
wish."

Virgil Thomson

THE POPULARITY of impressionism in America broke the grip of the
German conservatory. The new generation of composers went to Paris,
even as their predecessors had gone to Leipzig or Weimar. This trend,
strengthened by the boycott of all things German during the First
World War, occasioned a major change of orientation during the
twenties.

THE NEW NATIONALISM

As our composers became more sure of themselves they aspired in
ever greater measure to give expression to the life about them. They
sought in their music a quality specifically American. At first they concentrated on those features of the home scene that were not to be found
in Europe: the lore of the Indian, the Negro, and cowboy. An impetus
in this direction was furnished by Dvořák's *New World* Symphony.
Composers became aware of a wealth of native material they could use:
the songs of the southern mountaineers that preserved intact melodies
brought over from England hundreds of years ago; the patriotic songs
of the Revolution and the Civil War, several of which had become
folk songs; hymns and religious tunes. There were the work songs from
various parts of the country: songs of sharecroppers, lumberjacks,
miners, river men; songs of prairie and railroad, chain gang and frontier.
And then there was the folklore of the city dwellers, the commercial-
ized ballads, songs of musical comedy and jazz. All these offered stimulus to the composer's imagination and released deep-lying emotions
associated with the American scene.

Some composers, on the other hand, were not sympathetic to what
they considered a species of provincialism. They preferred the international idioms of twentieth-century music that were denatured of folk
elements: Parisian neoclassicism, Viennese atonality, and the new ro-

manticism. Their hand was strengthened by the arrival in America, on the eve of the Second World War, of leading European figures: Stravinsky, Schoenberg, Bartók, Hindemith, Milhaud, and others. In certain cases composers revealed themselves as internationally minded in some works and attracted by folklore in others. It was gradually realized

Metropolitan Museum of Art

Benton, *The Cotton Pickers.*

"As our artists became more sure of themselves they aspired in ever greater measure to give expression to the life about them."

that American music could not but be as many-faceted as America itself; and that a work did not have to quote a Negro spiritual, an Indian harvest song, or a dirge of the prairie in order to qualify for citizenship.

The music of the contemporary American school follows no single formula. Rather it reflects the contradictory tendencies in our national character: our jaunty humor and our sentimentality, our idealism and our worship of material success, our rugged individualism and our wish to look and think like everybody else, our reverence for culture and our philistinism, our daring and our practicality, our ready emotionalism and our capacity for intellectual pursuits. All these are present in a music that has bigness of gesture, astonishing vitality, and the exuberance of youth.

≥70≤

The Senior Group

THE ASCENDANCY of French musical culture in this country produced one figure of lasting interest. Charles Tomlinson Griffes (1884–1920) was born in Elmira, New York. He studied abroad, and from the Parisian school he carried away a decided interest in exotic music. Upon his return from Europe he accepted a teaching post at a boys' school in Tarrytown, New York. His health, never robust, was undermined by years of protracted work at night after the hours of teaching. His death at thirty-six robbed our music of a major talent.

Griffes's best-known piano piece, *The White Peacock*, is widely played in the composer's orchestral version. The work stems from the years when the Debussyan influence was strongest. The music is languid, capricious; it discourses of strange and lovely things. It wears the jeweled raiment of the impressionist orchestra: oboes and flutes gliding along the chromatic scale, the shimmer of harps, the flash of trumpet tone at the single climax, the whispered ending. Debussy's disciples never found it easy to retain their own individuality. Griffes succeeded. His music displays a fastidious lyricism not devoid of melancholy. It bears the promise of important things to come, a promise cheated of fulfillment by a turn of fate.

Charles Ives (1874–1954) presents the unusual spectacle of an artist who was content to go his own way without any desire to impinge his work on the world. For more than a quarter century his compositions accumulated unnoticed. Then in the thirties he was discovered by the younger men and acclaimed a master of the contemporary American school.

Ives was born in Danbury, Connecticut, son of a band master who was a remarkably progressive musician. The boy absorbed the sights and sounds of a New England village—the scraping of fiddlers at the Saturday night dance; the wheezing harmonium at church; the blaring of brass bands at the parade, each playing its own piece but close enough to one another to create that gay conflict of sound. All this music was just a little off pitch, a little off rhythm. It attuned the ear to formations that lay outside the traditional rules. When Ives came to use folk material as the stuff of his art, he realized that to iron out its idiosyncrasies would be to rob it of its flavor. He was thus led to novel concepts in harmony and rhythm, and began to experiment with the advanced procedures that are commonly supposed to have originated in Europe about a decade later—polytonality, dissonant counterpoint, atonality, polyrhythms, cluster chords, unusual leaps in the melody line, and the song-speech that came to be known as *Sprechstimme*. All this at the turn of the century!

Ives's music is marked by complexity of thought and inwardness of spirit. It has tenderness, folk humor, and a gaunt power peculiarly its own. It stems from a musical temperament at once sophisticated and naïve. Ives evoked images and associations that are rooted deep in the American consciousness. For all his command of twentieth-century procedures he was a romantic; also an original—one of the most arresting that our country has produced.

Edgar Varèse, born in Paris in 1885, came to the United States when he was thirty-one. He settled in New York City and became an ardent propagator of the new music. Varèse was one of the extreme radicals of his generation. Music for him was an organization of pure sound, a material to be molded, rather than a state of soul. "The world of sound is infinite," he stated, "and only a small and arbitrary portion has been used by composers." He set himself the task of expanding this portion with all the wit, clarity, and elegance of his French heritage.

Like Stravinsky, Varèse was interested in sound for sound's sake. But he went even further in rejecting traditional concepts. As he put it, "I refuse to submit myself only to sounds that have already been heard." Melody, harmony, and thematic development were subordinate, for him, to primal rhythm and timbre. His attention focused on that group in the orchestra which stands closest to sheer sonority, the percussion. Varèse's is music for a machine age. It has the hard tensile quality of steel, the rasp of pistons and turbines. It stems out of the climate of disillusionment in the twenties when intellectuals found themselves facing a mechanistic world seemingly driven by forces beyond human control. Romantic emotion is alien to this music. But its naked clarity arouses another kind of emotion, as compelling as that which the nineteenth century fed on. Varèse gave his works fanciful titles that smack of the foundry or the laboratory: *Ionisation, Hyperprism, Metal, Density 21.5*. The best known of these, *Ionisation*, is a study in percussion sound. It is written for thirteen players who handle thirty-five instruments, most of which are of indefinite pitch. Tubular gongs and piano represent those of fixed pitch. There are also two sirens that slide across and between the degrees of the scale. The freshness of the rhythmic patterns, the projection of dynamic tension, and the illusion of space created by the several planes of sound attest to a musical imagination of the first order.

To a public accustomed to Wagner and Brahms, Varèse's music seemed to prophesy the end of the world. However, a younger generation of Americans, accustomed to the audacious combining of rhythms and timbres of modern swing, may prove to be altogether receptive to his art. Now that Varèse's chief works are available on records, a full measure of recognition promises finally to be accorded this intrepid explorer of uncharted realms.

Of the other members of this generation mention should be made of John Alden Carpenter (Illinois, 1876–1951), who found a stimulus in French impressionism; Carl Ruggles, "The Cape Cod composer" (Massachusetts, 1876–), whose nobility of style and meticulous craftsmanship have won the admiration of the musical fraternity; and Wallingford Riegger (Georgia, 1885–), a dedicated atonalist whose symphonies and string quartets have made a deep impression.

The rise of a national school in the United States had its parallel in Latin America. This movement united contemporary trends with folk elements drawn from Indian, Negro, and Spanish-Portuguese sources. The first South American composer to command the attention of the world was the Brazilian nationalist Heitor Villa-Lobos (1881–), an exuberant musician who turns out music with a tropical abundance. He has produced more than fourteen hundred compositions. In an artist of this type, for whom creating is as natural as breathing, a raft of indifferent works paves the way for the few that represent his top level. Villa-Lobos has written six symphonies, five operas, eighteen ballets, ten symphonic poems, to mention but a few items. A form specifically associated with him is the *choros,* a type of serenade or fantasy for diverse instrumental combinations that reflects, according to the composer, "the rhythms and characteristic melodies of the people." Villa-Lobos has the faults and virtues of a young culture. He is spontaneous, uninhibited, and not self-critical. His collected works, whenever that project is put through by a grateful nation, will cover a wall in the library at Rio de Janeiro. Out of that mass of notes enough will survive to keep his memory green.

The members of the 1880 generation fulfilled the task of bringing American music into the orbit of the twentieth century. In so doing they prepared the way for a group of composers born in the final decade of the nineteenth century who became the core of the contemporary American school.

≫ 71 ≪

The Middle Generation

WALTER PISTON (1894–)

"The self-conscious striving for nationalism gets in the way of the establishment of a strong school of composition and even of significant individual expression. . . . The composer cannot afford the wild-goose chase of trying to be more American than he is."

WALTER PISTON is a leading representative of the international outlook among American composers. Art limits itself, he believes, through exclusive preoccupation with native themes. "Is the Dust Bowl more American," he asks, "than, say, a corner in the Boston Athenaeum?" An intellectual by temperament, a humanist by profession, he leans rather to those values in art that transcend the local. This does not mean that American elements are wholly absent from Piston's style; but they are there only as part of a larger, a universal conception.

Piston speaks the current language of neoclassicism which is understood with equal readiness in Paris, London, or Berlin. Such art, from the nationalist point of view, lacks the raciness that comes from contact with the soil. By the same token it gains, in the eyes of its devotees, dignity and universality of outlook. Piston's music is urbane, polished, witty, controlled. It is to be admired no less for the distinction of its ideas than for the perfection of its workmanship. "Piston's music, if considered only from a technical viewpoint, constitutes a challenge to every other American composer. It sets a level of craftsmanship that is absolutely first-rate in itself and provides a standard of reference by which every other American's work may be judged." This is praise indeed, coming from a fellow composer—Aaron Copland.

Walter Piston was born in Rockland, Maine, where his grandfather, an Italian sailor named Antonio Pistone, settled, married an American girl, and dropped the *e* from the family name in token of his acclimatization. The composer's first ambition was to become a painter. While at art school he learned the piano and supported himself by playing in dance bands, restaurants, and theaters. He enlisted in the navy band at the outbreak of the First World War and acquired some knowledge of the saxophone. Subsequently he went to Harvard, where he soon made up for his late start as a composer. A fellowship enabled him to continue his studies in Paris, where he came under the influence of Nadia Boulanger, a remarkable teacher who played an important role in training the post-war generation of young Americans in Paris. Upon his return home he was appointed to the music faculty of Harvard, where he is now Professor of Composition.

Producing slowly but steadily over the space of a quarter century, Piston has turned out a body of works that exemplify his fondness for the absolute instrumental forms. His natural habitat is a music free from "pictorial, narrative, political, or philosophical intent": symphony and suite, sonata, concerto grosso, string quartet. He describes his Concertino for Piano and Chamber Orchestra as "an adventure of a musical idea." The description applies to almost his entire output. His symphonies, string quartets, and such works as the Quintet for Flute and Strings form an addition of prime importance to the contemporary repertoire. Piston's art is based on linear counterpoint. Although he adheres to tonality, he has been intrigued by certain aspects of Schoenbergian thinking. He favors fugal forms and is not averse to the intricate, even scholastic, devices, which to many contemporary musicians represent the ultimate refinement of thought and feeling. In his use of these we glimpse the craftsman's joy in the shaping of his material.

THE INCREDIBLE FLUTIST

The work by which Piston is best known to the American public is the gay and tuneful concert suite drawn from his ballet *The Incredible Flutist*, which was written for Hans Wiener's dance group and first performed in Boston in 1938. The suite contains about half the music of the ballet.

The scene is laid in a Spanish village in carnival time. The siesta hour is over, the shop reopens. The merchant's daughters display their father's wares to the customers. Various village characters appear. Suddenly a march is heard announcing the arrival of the circus. The grand parade files past, led by the circus band—barker, jugglers, snake charmer, monkey trainer, and the star attraction of the show, the Incredible Flutist, whose playing charms even the circus animals. He charms also one of the merchant's daughters who meets him that evening in the village square. They are not alone; other couples have been lured out by the romantic night. The merchant courts a rich widow who has resisted his suit for years. Love is in the air: she suddenly yields and grants him a kiss. They are discovered by their prying neighbors. The lady from sheer embarrassment swoons, but is revived by a little music from the Incredible Flutist. The enchanted moment is over, the circus must be on its way. The band strikes up. The Incredible Flutist, so gallant and debonair, is off for new adventures.

The introductory melody establishes the Spanish atmosphere, its languid arabesques suggesting the siesta hour in the market place. The Dance of the Vendors, with its tart dissonances, has a Stravinskyan flavor: the Stravinsky of *Petrushka*. The Tango of the Four Daughters (moderato, espressivo) is a suave tune in 5/8 that displays Piston's hitherto unsuspected flair for popular melody. The villagers greet the

circus with shouts of joy. These noisy measures well give the expectancy of the crowd. The Circus March is followed by the solo of the Flutist, who weaves his spell with trills and roulades that derive their character and shape from the instrument's sound. The Widow and the Merchant mark their rendezvous with a brief minuet, which is followed by a gay Spanish waltz. The Flutist and the Merchant's Daughter have their romantic moment to the tender measures of a siciliano. In the brilliant polka finale, Piston has recourse to a device that is always effective: a catchy tune repeated over and over, each time a bit faster.

This music is tender and gracious. It has the feel of the theater, the balletic suggestion of body movement and gesture. Its gay measures offer a charming introduction to Walter Piston's more serious works.

ROY HARRIS (1898–)

"I am trying to write a music which expresses our time and period in America. What I am trying to say in music is related principally to the region of the West where I was born and where I understand life best."

In the early thirties Roy Harris was hailed as the white hope of American music, a young genius come out of the West to reveal to us our soul. For a decade he was the most played and most publicized composer in America. Then, quite suddenly, he dropped from the limelight. Such vagaries of fortune make the hazards of a public career among us. They in no way affect the ultimate value of Harris's contribution to his art.

He was born in a log cabin in Lincoln County, Oklahoma, of Scotch-Irish stock. His parents moved shortly afterwards to less rigorous surroundings near Los Angeles; but the log cabin remained part and parcel of the Harris legend. The youth was torn between his artistic leanings and an environment that had little room for art. At eighteen he was working his own farm. After two years in the army during the First World War he enrolled at the University of California. He drove a truck, delivering butter and eggs; worked as usher in the Los Angeles Auditorium so that he could hear music; and wandered about the country doing odd jobs, on one occasion acting as gatekeeper at a rodeo. When he was twenty-four his musical impulse was no more to be denied. He began to study with the composer Arthur Farwell in Los Angeles. The young man's passionate eagerness made a deep impression on the teacher. Years later, when writing about his astonishing pupil, Farwell remembered Schumann's famous tribute to the young Chopin: "Hats off, gentlemen—a genius!" He began his own article with "Gentlemen, a genius—but keep your hats on!"

Harris's rise to fame was as spectacular as his start was halting. The performance by Howard Hanson and the Rochester Symphony of his *Andante for Orchestra* launched his public career. There followed a period of study in Paris. Harris returned after three years to find himself *the* American composer. With his spare frame and soft drawl, looking "like a midwestern farmer in city clothes," he captured the imagination of his contemporaries as no American musician had done. He saw himself as a national artist, a kind of Walt Whitman who was the voice, whether for exhortation or prophecy, of a young and vital civilization. As Virgil Thomson quipped, "One would think, to read his prefaces, that he had been awarded by God, or at least by popular vote, a monopolistic privilege of expressing our nation's deepest ideas and highest aspirations."

Harris's music is American in its buoyancy and momentum, its expansiveness and manly strength. Its epic quality suggests to some the vastness and loneliness of the prairie. Others are attracted by its intimate lyricism. Harris belongs to the spontaneous type of artist who is apt to appear during the youth of a culture. Such artists yield without inhibition to the creative impulse within; and even their awkwardness, as in the case of Theodore Dreiser's prose, imparts to their style an element of strength. They are likely to do their most arresting work fairly early in their career; for their gift, being essentially lyric, loses in freshness by as much as it gains in technique.

Harris's seven symphonies form the core of his output. Of the shorter pieces for orchestra the most popular are the overture *When Johnny Comes Marching Home* and the *Time* Suite. Chamber music occupies a prominent place in Harris's work, revealing his melodious polyphony at its best. The early Piano Sonata and the *Children's* Suite have been recorded by the composer's wife, the pianist Johanna Harris. There is a quantity of choral music, including two major works: the *Symphony for Voices* and *A Song for Occupations*, both on texts of Walt Whitman. Although he wrote music for the documentary film *One-Tenth of a Nation* and several ballets, Harris's gift is not for the theater. His dramatic powers are at their best in the abstract instrumental forms.

THIRD SYMPHONY

Harris's most frequently performed work reveals the composer at the peak of his "singing strength." The symphony is in one movement made up of contrasting sections. The composer's description indicates its content and scope. "Section I: *Tragic*—low string sonorities. Section II: *Lyric*—strings, horns, woodwinds. Section III: *Pastoral*—emphasizing woodwind color. Section IV: *Fugue*—dramatic. A. Brass, percussion predominating. B. Canonic development of Section II material, constituting background for further development of fugue. C. Brass climax. Rhythmic motif derived from fugue subject. Section V: *Dramatic-Tragic*. Restatement of violin theme of Section I."

The opening motive expands into one of those vaulting lines that accord with the composer's goal of a continuous, self-generating melody.

Con moto

etc.

This mood spills over into the section identified by Harris as the second. The word "section" is used loosely here. For the symmetrical, sectional structure of the classical symphony he substitutes a seamless, steadily evolving texture. The lyricism is of that rugged, contemplative cast which has affinity with such symphonists as Brahms and Sibelius. The dark orchestral resonance is also related to those two masters.

In the pastoral section Harris reveals himself as a poet of nature. Here is the tender "morning mood" of the romantic era translated into a twentieth-century setting. The music abounds in the free flexible rhythm that is one of Harris's marked characteristics. His harmonic idiom, for all its tensions, is diatonic.

The fugue subject is one of sharp melodic profile, rhythmic bite, and dramatic gesture.

The elaborate fugal development broadens into a spacious passage based on the steady beat of the drum. This processional strikes the epic tone. It justifies those of Harris's admirers who find in the Third Symphony echoes of "the dark fastness of the American soul, of its despair and its courage, its defeat and its triumph."

Opinion is divided over Harris's ultimate place in our music. Time will decide that. It is well to remember, however, that the Third Symphony is still one of the finest works yet produced by an American in the grand form; and that its creator has been one of the vital personalities in our musical coming of age.

AARON COPLAND (1900–)

"I no longer feel the need of seeking out conscious Americanisms. Because we live here and work here, we can be certain that when our music is mature it will also be American in quality."

Aaron Copland is generally recognized as the representative figure among present-day American composers. He manifests the serenity, clarity, and sense of balance that we regard as the essence of the classical temper. He is describing his own point of view when he writes, "The typical contemporary composer prefers an objective, impersonal approach; a complex, contrapuntal texture; a concentration on perfection of line and beauty of proportion." Yet, as he makes clear, the new classicism implies the disciplining rather than the rejection of emotion. "Every artist's work," he states, "is of course an expression of himself, but none so direct as that of the creative musician. He gives us, without relation to exterior 'events,' the quintessential part of himself."

Copland was born of Russian-Jewish parentage "on a street in Brooklyn that can only be described as drab. . . . Music was the last thing anyone would have connected with it." He studied in Paris with Nadia Boulanger, whose first full-time American pupil he was. When Boulanger was invited to give concerts in America, she asked Copland to write a work for her. This was the Symphony for Organ and Orchestra. Contemporary American music was still an exotic dish to New York audiences. After the first performance Walter Damrosch found it necessary to assuage the feelings of his subscribers. "If a young man at the age of twenty-three," he announced from the stage of Carnegie Hall, "can write a symphony like that, in five years he will be ready to commit murder." Damrosch's prophecy, as far as is known, was not fulfilled.

Copland was soon active as propagandist for the new American music. He organized concerts, festivals, and composers' organizations. He lectured, turned out magazine articles, and wrote several eminently readable books. His prose has the qualities of his music. It is simple, lucid, spare, direct; it avoids rhetorical effect; it is personal.

In his growth as a composer Copland has mirrored the dominant trends of his time. After his return from Paris he turned to the jazz idiom, a phase that culminated in his Piano Concerto. Leaving behind him the opulent sonorities of his early works, he moved toward a manner he has well described as "more spare in sonority, more lean in texture." There followed a period during which the neoclassicist experimented with the abstract materials of his art; he produced his *Piano Variations, Short Symphony*, and *Statements for Orchestra*. "During these years I began to feel an increasing dissatisfaction with the relations of the music-loving public and the living composer. It seemed to me that we composers were in danger of working in a vacuum." He realized that a new public for contemporary music was being created by the radio, phonograph, and film scores. "It made no sense to ignore them and to continue writing as if they did not exist. I felt that it was worth the effort to see if I couldn't say what I had to say in the simplest possible terms." In this fashion Copland was led to what became a most significant development after the thirties: the attempt to simplify the new music so that it would communicate to a large public.

The decade that followed saw the production of the scores that established Copland's popularity. *El Salón México*, an orchestral piece based on Latin-American tunes and rhythms. The ballets *Billy the Kid*, *Rodeo*, and *Appalachian Spring*. Two works for high-school students —*Outdoor Overture* and the opera *Second Hurricane*. The film scores for *The City*, *Of Mice and Men*, *Our Town*, *The Heiress* (which won him an "Oscar"), and *The Red Pony*. Two works written in time of war: *Letter from Home* and *A Lincoln Portrait*. And the Third Symphony (1946), in which he achieved a fusion of the personal and the universal, the emotional and the intellectual that makes this one of the most notable productions by an American in the grand form.

BILLY THE KID

For the ballet based on the saga of Billy the Kid Copland produced one of his freshest scores. In it are embedded either in whole or in part such cowboy classics as *The Old Chisholm Trail*, *The Dying Cowboy*, and *Git Along Little Doggy*. These are not used literally. They are assimilated to the composer's style and flavor the work without subjugating it.

Billy the Kid—the Brooklyn-born William Bonney—had a brief but intense career as desperado and lover, in the course of which he became one of the legends of the Southwest. The ballet touches on the chief episodes of his life. We see him first as a boy of twelve when, his mother having been killed by a stray bullet in a street brawl, he stabs the man responsible for her death. Later, during a card game with his cronies, he is accused of cheating and kills the accuser. Captured after a running gun battle, he is put in jail. He murders his jailer and gets away. A romantic interlude ensues when he rejoins his Mexican sweetheart in the desert. But the menacing shadows close in on him. This time there is no escaping. At the close we hear a lament for the death of the dashing outlaw.

The concert suite contains about two thirds of the music of the ballet. *The Open Prairie*, which serves as Prologue, evokes a spacious landscape. The mingling of tenderness and strength is typical Copland, as is the climax of blocklike masses of tone with emphasis on the winds. *Street Scene* conjures up the square of a frontier town. The tune in cowboy style blends with Copland's sophisticated harmony and strutting syncopations.

Card Game has the quality of wistful lyricism that marks Copland's later works. The setting is a starry night in the desert. The music projects a mood of gentle contemplation. In violent contrast is *Fight*, with its overtones of brutality. The literal imitation of gunfire, legitimate in the theater, is less effective in the concert hall, for the more vividly music depicts, the less it suggests. The *Celebration* that follows Billy's capture is properly brassy and gay. Altogether lovely is the Epilogue

in which the prairie music of the opening returns. The physical landscape is transformed into a poetic symbol, a brooding expanse that is incalculably vast, changeless, remote.

It is in passages such as these that Aaron Copland shows himself to be, as he has often been described, the most American of our composers. What is local or regional is dissolved in personal lyricism, thereby assuming a value that extends beyond the particular time or place. At work here is the unconscious nationalism referred to in the quotation at the head of this section—an inevitable nationalism that comes about when the artist has achieved oneness with his environment and its people.

We have named only a handful out of the well over one hundred active composers of this generation. To give anywhere near an adequate account of their work would carry us far beyond the scope of the present volume. Yet it is clear, even from this brief description, that the composers of the middle generation represent all the main trends in contemporary music. They acclimated those to our temperament and our needs. In so doing they freed American music from all traces of provincialism and brought it into the mainstream of twentieth-century art.

≥72≤

The Younger Men

SAMUEL BARBER (1910–)

COMPOSERS in the past two centuries, if performers at all, as a rule were instrumentalists. Samuel Barber is that comparatively rare phenomenon, a singer-composer. For a time he considered a concert career. The fact that his contact with music came through vocal lyricism has played its part in shaping his melodic imagery.

Barber is one of the best known among the younger generation of American composers. He owes his popularity in equal measure to innate musicality and to the circumstance that he is a conservative. Barber is an avowed romantic; his music is poetic and suffused with feeling. Nor is it averse to the grand rhetoric of the nineteenth-century tradition. Its gentle melancholy alternates with passages that have brilliancy and dramatic impact. Barber's music avoids the knotty problems of contemporary musical thought, seeking rather a relationship to the past. It is elegant music which, despite a certain reserve, makes a wide appeal.

Barber was born in West Chester, Pennsylvania. A nephew of the singer Louise Homer, he grew up in a musical environment. He attended the Curtis Institute in Philadelphia, where he distinguished himself in composition. Recognition came to him early with such works as *Dover Beach* for baritone and string quartet, set to the verses of Matthew Arnold, and *The School for Scandal,* a sunny overture inspired by Sheridan's comedy. At twenty-five Barber won both the Prix de Rome and the Pulitzer Award. He spent several years in Europe. Besides composing he gave a number of recitals at which, along with the traditional lieder, he performed his own songs. He also appeared as a conductor. Two romantic pieces, the *Adagio for Strings* and *Essay for Orchestra,* have achieved great popularity abroad; in England they have been performed more than any other modern American works. During the war Barber served in the Army Air Corps. His Second Symphony was commissioned by and is dedicated to the United States Army Air Forces.

KNOXVILLE: SUMMER OF 1915

Barber's commitment to lyricism and the avowal of personal emotion is well exemplified in *Knoxville: Summer of 1915,* a work for soprano and orchestra. (A later version with chamber orchestra has been re-corded.) *Knoxville* is set to the final section of an autobiographical fragment by James Agee that appeared in the magazine *Partisan Review*. Agee's lyric prose, with its Proustian remembrance of childhood things, releases a flow of music in the composer. Barber is of a more expansive temperament than the author. Where the prose poem is marked by subtlety and reserve, Barber's vocal line is exuberant and sweeping at the high points. But then, as we have seen, in any musical setting the tones subjugate the words to their own purpose.

"It has become that time of evening when people sit on their porches, rocking gently and talking gently and watching the street." There is longing in Barber's evocation of the landscape of the past: the nostal-gia that is in all men for the lost paradise of childhood. The "little phrase" (as Proust might have called it) of the opening section finely captures the mood of tender reminiscence. The relaxed movement is

interrupted by vivid flashes of color. "A streetcar raising its iron moan; stopping; belling and starting, stertorous . . . swimming its gold win-dows and straw seats on past and past and past." The lyric mood re-sumes. The broad arch of the soprano line and the rich orchestral sound invest the words with a radiance that is perhaps alien to them. "On the rough wet grass of the back yard my father and mother have spread quilts. We all lie there. . . ." The climax mounts steadily to higher register, with that peculiar vibrance which characterizes Barber's han-dling of string tone. "May God bless my people, my uncle, my aunt, my mother, my good father, oh remember them kindly in their time of trouble." And now the "little phrase" returns in the gentle subsiding of the final passage. "After a little I am taken in and put to bed. Sleep, soft smiling, draws me unto her: and those receive me, who quietly treat me as one familiar and well-beloved in that home: but will not, oh, will not, not now, not ever; but will not ever tell me who I am."

This is an American work in the larger sense. Its music is wedded to the subtle music of American speech. It beautifies the memory of child-hood in an American town. At the same time both words and music reach beyond the national to take their place in the European tradition. For they deal with things seen and felt and communicated in ways that are not peculiar to any one land.

GIAN-CARLO MENOTTI (1911–)

"My goal is to say something simple and clear in as simple and clear a way as possible."

We have had occasion to point out the recent tendency of contemporary music to find its way back to the public. None has given greater impetus to this trend than the most popular opera composer of our day, Gian-Carlo Menotti.

Menotti's flair for the lyric theater stems out of the Italian tradition; he is the natural heir of Puccini and Mascagni. Like them he knows how to put in just enough music to further the drama, and no more. He is most at home in the intimate frame of the chamber opera: his niceties of characterization project in an intimate theater rather than across the vast space of the grand opera house. Menotti writes his own librettos. As a result he is able to shape the dramatic action to the musical line from the very beginning, an inestimable advantage. The music and the script, if examined separately, do not seem to be particularly potent. Put them together—and you have enchantment! For Menotti is no less a magician than the memorable one he created in the second act of *The Consul;* a magician at whose bidding the phantom shapes of the theater spring to life, its hoariest devices made fresh and invested with poetry.

Menotti was born in Italy and began to compose as a child. He reversed the familiar pattern of the young American who goes to Europe to study: he came here at the age of seventeen and attended the Curtis Institute in Philadelphia. His first works acclimated the tradition of Italian *opera buffa* to the American theater. *Amelia Goes to the Ball, The Old Maid and the Thief,* and *The Telephone* were remarkably deft works for a man in his twenties. They display lightness and sureness of touch and an engaging admixture of sentiment.

Menotti's first success in serious vein came with *The Medium,* an opera about a fake spiritualist who falls victim to her own myth. The work combines the Italian love of strong situations with the spice of French *grand-guignol.* In *The Consul* the humanity of Menotti's art attains its full dimension. Granted, the dramatic treatment is at times more arresting than the musical, but the composer's fantasy and his uncanny sense of timing are nowhere used to greater effect. In *The Consul* Menotti created believable human beings who are both individuals and poetic symbols. Within the operatic medium—probably the most artificial in all art—he succeeded in capturing the accents of our tragic time. In 1951 the composer produced *Amahl and the Night Visitors*, a fantasy for Christmas Eve and television. The work bids fair to become a classic. In *The Saint of Bleecker Street*, Menotti makes an important advance in terms of the musical material, although the subject of the opera is less effective than those of his previous works. The second act is stunning in its impact and contains two memorable arias.

NBC

A scene from the television production of *Amahl and the Night Visitors*
". . . a fantasy for Christmas Eve."

Menotti's is not an epic gift. Rather it is sweet and tender and heartwarming. The composer is well represented on records. A hearing of either *The Medium* or *The Consul* will introduce the listener to the exciting art of this born man of the theater.

NORMAN DELLO JOIO (1913–)

"To know music is to become greater in knowledge and insight and to know many other things than music. It is to develop a sense of values about art and to learn about another dimension of reality previously hidden."

A variety of influences have molded the music of Norman Dello Joio. Gregorian chant and liturgical music were a natural part of his background as the son of an Italian church organist. Jazz and motoric rhythm belonged to the environment of his native New York City. Hardly less important were the Verdi arias gleaned from the singers who frequented the Dello Joio home. Finally there was the German tradition absorbed from his teacher Hindemith. Each of these might have been encountered in a number of places; the combination could have taken place only in this country and in this generation. It is this circumstance that roots Dello Joio's music in the contemporary American scene.

Descended from a long line of Italian musicians, he received his first training from his father. He led his own jazz band and was tempted for a time by a professional career in baseball. He studied at the Julliard School in New York City and came under the influence of Hindemith in the summer school of the Berkshire Music Center at Tanglewood. Hindemith's dedication and constant endeavor to plumb the deepest levels of artistic awareness left an indelible mark upon the pupil. Recognition was not slow in coming to Dello Joio. In 1949 his *Variations, Chaconne and Finale* received the New York Music Critics Circle Award. He was one of three composers (Copland and Barber were the others) invited by the Polish government to appear in a series of concerts in that country. After having taught at Sarah Lawrence College for six years, he resigned in 1950 in order to devote himself to composition.

Dello Joio is a natural musician who mistrusts an overly intellectual approach to art. He represents the type of craftsman-composer who would rather make music than theorize about it; who produces work after work out of an abundance of creative energy. The art forms to which he has most directly responded—Catholic plainchant, Italian opera, American jazz, and the modern ballet—have one significant feature in common. They all communicate to a mass audience. This goes hand in hand with his conviction that "music is an expression of something real in human life. It is not a retreat from life." Dello Joio consequently stands with those who are trying to de-intellectualize their art, to return music to its wellspring of emotion and thereby re-establish its power over a broad base of listeners.

He is essentially a lyricist, for whom melody constitutes the direct embodiment of feeling. His admiration for the great Italians derives from their pre-eminence in this regard. "What I strive for most of all is the complete confidence, the lyric quality, the feeling for line we find in Verdi." Given this heritage, he belongs to the internationally minded wing among our composers. For him an Italian neighborhood in Manhattan is no less a part of America than the prairies and mountains of the West. In effect, his music stems out of the European tradition as practiced in the United States today rather than out of any attempt to recreate images that we have come to regard as specifically American.

His music is marked by elegance of workmanship and fineness of texture. The harmony is based on the free use of twelve tones around a center; the orchestral tone is bright and limpid. His rhythms are resilient, animated; his forms supple and compact. But the vital element of this music is its melody, which achieves the long line. It is personal, distinctive, and bears the stamp of a strong lyric imagination.

NEW YORK PROFILES

Dello Joio's orchestral suite consists of four tone sketches of his native city. *Prelude—The Cloisters* evokes the monastery-like museum of medieval art overlooking the Hudson. The horns outline the interval of a fifth which is basic to the work, after which the oboes intone the Gregorian melody which in one guise or another serves as source ma-

Copyright 1952 by Carl Fischer, Inc., New York. By permission.

terial for all the movements. Motives drawn from this theme flower into a continuous fabric. Modal harmonies strike the properly archaic note. A sense of remoteness pervades the movement, a tranquil melancholy.

Second is a caprice, *The Park*. The basic interval of a fifth is filled in, rhythmically and melodically, to create a colorful image of children at play. The orchestral mass is handled with admirable lightness of touch, as are the ostinato rhythms in the bass. This balletic movement wears its contrapuntal learning lightly.

There follows a chorale fantasy that conjures up the atmosphere of Grant's Tomb. The basic thematic material is transformed anew in a movement that is remarkably homogeneous in mood and facture. The melodic curve, noble of gesture, leads to an eruption of trumpet tone at the climax. The composer moves in the orbit of the grand tradition, whose romantic pathos carries conviction in our day only when handled, as here, unself-consciously. The piece closes with a moving reference by muted trumpets to the *Battle Hymn of the Republic*.

Last is *Little Italy*, a festal dance finale. The Gregorian phrase is transformed into the underlying motive of an exuberant tarantella. The basic interval of a fifth frames a melody imbued with rhythmic élan and dance imagery. Despite the folkish tone, the movement never loses its refinement of style. Lyricism enters in the middle section, on the woodwinds. The formal unity of the suite becomes apparent at the jubilant finale when the horns chant the Gregorian melody against the tarantella background.

Dello Joio has produced an extensive list of orchestral and choral works, chamber and piano music, ballets and songs. He is now directing his efforts to opera. His melodic gift, felicitous setting of English text, vivid dramatic sense, and forthright communication of emotion lead one to expect much of him in that domain.

Once again we have named only a handful out of a generation of musicians that abounds in sturdy talent. But our purpose is only to introduce a subject that would need many pages to cover adequately. The young composers of this group are no less rich in achievement than in promise, and in the next years their works will come more and more to the attention of the general public.

A musical culture depends not on the foreign performers and composers whom a nation attracts to its shores but on what it brings forth by its own efforts. Our present situation indicates that we have established in this country all the preconditions for a flourishing musical culture. Our conservatories and colleges turn out musicians who in point of technical equipment are second to none in the world. *Composers in America*, a compilation by Claire Reis, lists the works of approximately three hundred active composers, with a supplementary list of about two hundred more. The point is not whether each of these is a Beethoven. History shows that a Beethoven emerges only out of a tradition that is fruitful and a climate that is receptive. Such a tradition and climate we are well on the way toward achieving.

Postscript

WE HAVE included in these pages a variety of facts, historical, biographical, and technical, that have entered into the making of music and that must enter into an intelligent listening to music. For those who desire to explore the subject further we include in Appendix II a brief list of books that will guide the music lover in his reading. But books belong to the domain of words, and words have no power over the domain of sound. They are helpful only insofar as they lead us to the music.

The enjoyment of music depends upon perceptive listening. And perceptive listening (like perceptive anything) is something that we achieve gradually, with practice and some effort. By acquiring a knowledge of the circumstances out of which a musical work issued, we prepare ourselves for its multiple meanings; we lay ourselves open to that exercise of mind and heart, sensibility and imagination that makes listening to music so unique an experience. But in the building up of our musical perceptions—that is, of our listening enjoyment—let us always remember that the ultimate wisdom resides neither in dates nor in facts. It is to be found in one place only—the sounds themselves.

✄ APPENDIX I ✄
A List of Records

THE FOLLOWING discography lists the basic works discussed in the text as well as supplementary titles for those readers interested in further study. These will be found in the standard catalogues of records (78, 45, and 33⅓ r.p.m.). Because new recordings are constantly being issued, it was not found expedient to list specific recordings here. For guidance in choosing among the several recordings of a work the reader is referred to David Hall's *Records: 1950 Edition* (New York, Alfred A. Knopf, 1950) or to Irving Kolodin's *The New Guide to Recorded Music* (New York, Doubleday & Co., 1950).

Chapter 2. Music and Life: the Sources of Musical Imagery
I. SONG

FOLK SONG:

Greensleeves
Black Is the Color of My True Love's Hair
Lord Randall
Barbara Allen
I Gave My Love a Cherry
Water Boy

ART SONG:

Schubert, *Serenade*
Schumann, *Die Beiden Grenadiere* (The Two Grenadiers)
Brahms, *Lullaby*
Grieg, *Ich Liebe Dich* (I Love Thee)

"SONG" FOR PIANO:

Schubert, Impromptu in A-flat, Op. 142
Chopin, Nocturne in F-sharp
Schumann, *Träumerei* (Dreams)
Mendelssohn, *Venetian Boat Song in F-sharp minor* (Song Without Words)

"SONG" FOR ORCHESTRA:

Schubert, Symphony in C, second movement
Brahms, Symphony No. 3, third movement
Tchaikovsky, Symphony No. 5, second movement

II. THE DANCE

Bach, J. S., Suite No. 3 in D, Gavotte
Haydn, Symphony No. 104 (*London*), Minuet and Finale
Mozart, Symphony No. 39, Minuet
Beethoven, Country Dance in E-flat
Chopin, Waltz in C-sharp Minor
Johann Strauss, *Emperor* Waltz
Brahms, Hungarian Dances
Dvořák, Slavonic Dances
Ravel, *Pavane for a Dead Princess*
Stravinsky, *Circus Polka*

III. THE MARCH

Schubert, *Marche Militaire*
Chopin, *Polonaise Militaire*
Verdi, Triumphal March from *Aïda*
Elgar, *Pomp and Circumstance*
Ippolitov-Ivanov, Procession of the Sardar from *Caucasian Sketches*
Prokofiev, March from *Love for Three Oranges*

IV. OF RELIGIOUS INSPIRATION

Palestrina, Kyrie from the Mass for Pope Marcellus
Bach, J. S., Chorale, *Jesu, Joy of Man's Desiring*
Handel, Hallelujah Chorus from *Messiah*
————, *I Know that My Redeemer Liveth* from *Messiah*
Go Down, Moses
Deep River
Schubert, *Ave Maria*
Wagner, Prelude to *Lohengrin*
Gruenberg, *Standin' in the Need of Prayer* from *The Emperor Jones*

Chapter 3. Melody: Musical Line

CONTRAST IN DEGREE OF ACTIVITY OF MELODY LINE:

Schubert, *Ave Maria*
Brahms, Hungarian Dance No. 5
Ravel, *Pavane for a Dead Princess*
Verdi, Triumphal March from *Aïda*

CLIMAX IN MELODY LINE:

Schumann, *Träumerei* (final phrase)
Chopin, Nocturne in E-flat (final section)
Londonderry Air

MELODY PERVADED BY A RHYTHMIC FIGURE:

Handel, Hallelujah Chorus from *Messiah*

Chapter 4. Harmony: Musical Space

DEGREES OF HARMONIC DISSONANCE:

Mozart, Sonata No. 15 in C Major for Piano, first movement
Wagner, Liebestod from *Tristan und Isolde*
Debussy, *La Soirée dans Granade*
Bartók, *Allegro barbaro*

Chapter 5. Rhythm and Meter: Musical Time

2/4 TIME:

Schubert, *Marche Militaire*

3/4 TIME:

Mozart, Symphony No. 39, Minuet
Strauss, Johann, *Emperor* Waltz

4/4 TIME:

Verdi, Triumphal March from *Aïda*

6/8 TIME:

Grieg, *Morning* from *Peer Gynt* Suite No. 1

5/4 TIME:

Tchaikovsky, Symphony No. 6 (*Pathétique*), second movement

Chapter 6. Tempo: Musical Pace

LARGO:

Handel, Largo from *Xerxes*
Dvořák, Symphony No. 5 (*New World*), second movement

ADAGIO:

Beethoven, Piano Sonata in C Minor, Op. 13 (*Pathétique*), second movement
————, Piano Sonata in C-sharp Minor, Op. 27, No. 2 (*Moonlight*), first movement

ANDANTE:

Haydn, Symphony No. 94 (*Surprise*), second movement

ANDANTINO:

Rimsky-Korsakov, *Scheherazade*, second movement (*Kalendar Prince*)

ALLEGRETTO:

Franck, Symphony in D Minor, second movement

ALLEGRO:

Beethoven, Symphony No. 5, fourth movement

ALLEGRO MOLTO:

Mozart, Symphony No. 40, first movement

VIVACE:

Mendelssohn, Scherzo from *A Midsummer Night's Dream*

PRESTO:

Haydn, Symphony No. 104 (*London*), *Finale*

Chapter 7. Timbre: Musical Color—Chapter 8. The Instruments—Chapter 9. The Orchestra

Victor Album, *Instruments of the Orchestra*
Columbia Album, *Instruments of the Orchestra*
Tchaikovsky, *Nutcracker* Suite
Saint-Saëns, *Carnival of Animals*
Prokofiev, *Peter and the Wolf*
Britten, *The Young Person's Guide to the Orchestra*

Chapter 10. Dynamics: Musical Volume

CRESCENDO-DIMINUENDO (from *pp* to *ff* and back):

Wagner, Prelude to *Lohengrin*
Debussy, *Fêtes* from Three Nocturnes for Orchestra

CLIMAX THROUGH STEADY CRESCENDO AND RISE IN PITCH:

Ravel, *Bolero*

INTENSIFICATION (CLIMAX) THROUGH CRESCENDO, ACCELERANDO, AND RISE IN PITCH:

Rossini, Overture to *The Barber of Seville* (final section)
Tchaikovsky, Waltz of the Flowers from the *Nutcracker* Suite (final section)
Grieg, *In the Hall of the Mountain King* from *Peer Gynt* Suite No. 1
Honegger, *Pacific 231*

Chapter 11. Form: Musical Structure and Design

TWO-PART OR BINARY FORM (A-B):

Bach, J. S., Suite No. 2 in B Minor for Flute and Strings, Saraband, Minuet, Badinerie

THREE-PART OR TERNARY FORM (A-B-A):

Mozart, Symphony No. 40 in G Minor, Minuet
Schubert, *Marche Militaire*
Beethoven, Country Dance in E-flat

Chapter 16. Franz Schubert

Der Erlkönig
Heidenröslein
Impromptu in A-flat, Op. 90, No. 4
Moment Musical in F-sharp Major
Die Forelle (The Trout)
Der Tod und das Mädchen (Death and the Maiden)
Hark, Hark, the Lark
Moment Musical in A-flat

Chapter 17. Robert Schumann

Die Beiden Grenadiere (The Two Grenadiers)
Ich Grolle Nicht (I'll Not Complain)
Aufschwung (Soaring)
Romance in F-sharp Major
Im Wunderschönen Monat Mai (In the Lovely Month of May)
Warum? (Why?), Op. 12, No. 3

Supplementary List of Romantic Piano Pieces and Songs

Brahms, *Die Mainacht* (May Night)
———, *Vergebliches Ständchen* (Futile Serenade)
———, Intermezzo in B-flat Minor, Op. 117, No. 2
———, Six Clavierstücke (Intermezzi and Rhapsody), Op. 118
Grieg, *Ich Liebe Dich* (I Love Thee)
———, *Ein Traum* (A Dream)
Tchaikovsky, *None But the Lonely Heart*
Dvořák, *Songs My Mother Taught Me*
Musorgsky, *The Flea*

Chapter 19. Felix Mendelssohn

Overture and Incidental Music, *A Midsummer Night's Dream*
Overture, *Hebrides* (*Fingal's Cave*)

Symphony No. 4 in A (*Italian*)
Songs without Words (for piano)
Octet in E-flat, Op. 20

Chapter 20. Franz Liszt

Les Préludes
Faust Symphony
Sonata in B Minor
Hungarian Rhapsody No. 12
Mephisto Valse
Valse Oubliée
Waldesrauschen (Forest Murmurs)
Etude in F Minor (caprice poétique, "*La Leggerezza*")

Chapter 21. Nationalism and the Romantic Movement

Tchaikovsky, *Overture 1812*
Dvořák, Slavonic Dances
Chopin, Polonaises and Mazurkas
Grieg, Norwegian Dances
EXOTICISM:

Ippolitov-Ivanov, *Caucasian Sketches*
Rimsky-Korsakov, *Capriccio Espagnol*
Chabrier, *España*

Chapter 22. Bedřich Smetana

The Moldau
From Bohemia's Meadows and Forests
Overture to *The Bartered Bride*

Chapter 28. Nicholas Rimsky-Korsakov

Scheherazade
Russian Easter Overture
Antar Symphony
The Snow Maiden Suite

Chapter 25. Peter Ilyich Tchaikovsky (see below, Ch. 31, for further works)

Overture-Fantasy, *Romeo and Juliet*
Symphonic Fantasy, *Francesca da Rimini*
Caprice Italien

Chapter 27. A Romantic Concerto

Mendelssohn, Concerto in E Minor for Violin and Orchestra

Chapter 28. Johannes Brahms

Symphony No. 3
Concerto No. 2 in B-flat for Piano
Symphony No. 1
Variations on a Theme by Haydn
A German Requiem
Academic Festival Overture
Concerto No. 1 in D Minor for Piano

Chapter 29. Antonin Dvořák

Symphony No. 5, *From the New World*
Symphony No. 4
Concerto in B Minor for 'Cello and Orchestra

Chapter 30. Edvard Grieg

Concerto in A Minor for Piano and Orchestra
Peer Gynt Suites Nos. 1 and 2

Chapter 31. A Late Romantic Symphony

Tchaikovsky, Symphony No. 6 (*Pathétique*)
———, Symphony No. 4
———, Symphony No. 5
———, Concerto No. 1 in B-flat Minor for Piano and Orchestra
———, Concerto in D for Violin

Chapter 33. Opera in the Romantic Period

Meyerbeer, *Les Huguenots*
Offenbach, *La Belle Hélène*
Rossini, *The Barber of Seville*
Donizetti, *Lucia di Lammermoor*
Bellini, *Norma*
Weber, *Der Freischütz*
———, Overture to *Oberon*
———, Overture to *Euryanthe*

Chapter 34. Richard Wagner

Tannhäuser
Tristan und Isolde—Prelude, Love Duet, Liebestod
Overture to *The Flying Dutchman*
Die Meistersinger: Prelude, Prize Song, Closing Scene
Die Walküre: Act I and Closing Scene
Götterdämmerung: Siegfried's Rhine Journey, Siegfried's Funeral March, Immolation Scene

Chapter 38. The Major-Minor System

DIATONIC AS AGAINST CHROMATIC HARMONY:

Mozart, Sonata in A Major for Piano
Wagner, Prelude to *Tristan und Isolde*

Chapter 43. Joseph Haydn

Symphony No. 94 in G Major (*Surprise*)
Symphony No. 92 in G (*Oxford*)
Symphony No. 101 in D (*Clock*)
Symphony No. 104 in D (*London*)
Toy Symphony
Oratorio, *The Creation*
Divertimento No. 1 in A Major

Chapter 44. Wolfgang Amadeus Mozart

Don Giovanni
Symphony No. 40 in G Minor
Eine Kleine Nachtmusik
Symphony No. 39 in E-flat
Symphony No. 41 in C (*Jupiter*)
Concerto No. 20 in D Minor for Piano and Orchestra
Sonata in A for Piano
The Marriage of Figaro

Chapter 45. Ludwig van Beethoven

Symphony No. 5 in C Minor
Piano Sonata in F Minor, Op. 57 (*Appassionata*)
Overture to *Coriolanus*
Symphony No. 6 in F (*Pastorale*)
Symphony No. 7 in A
Concerto No. 4 in G Major for Piano and Orchestra
Overture, *Egmont*
Overture, *Leonore* No. 3
Piano Sonata in C Minor, Op. 13 (*Pathétique*)
Piano Sonata in C-sharp Minor, Op. 27 No. 2 (*Moonlight*)

Chapter 46. Classical Chamber Music

Haydn, Quartet in F, Op. 3, No. 5
——, Quartet in C Major, Op. 76, No. 5 (*Emperor*)
Mozart, Quintet in A for Clarinet and Strings (K. 581)
——, Quintet in G Minor (K. 516)
Beethoven, Quartet in C Minor, Op. 18, No. 1

——, Quartet in F Major, Op. 59, No. 1 (*Razumovsky*)
——, Septet in E-flat Major, Op. 20
Schubert, Quintet in A for Piano and Strings (*Trout*)
Schubert, Trio No. 1 in B-flat Major, Op. 99
——, Quintet in C Major, Op. 163

Chapter 47. From Classic to Romantic

Schubert, Symphony No. 8 in B Minor (*Unfinished*)
——, Symphony No. 7 in C Major (also listed as No. 9)

Chapter 48. Harmony and Counterpoint: Musical Texture

MONOPHONIC:

Gregorian Chant: Alleluia, *Assumpta est Maria*

POLYPHONIC:

Bach, Chorale from *Christ lag in Todesbanden* (Stokowski's orchestral version)

HOMOPHONIC:

Chopin, Waltz in B Minor

CANONIC IMITATION:

Franck, Sonata in A for Violin and Piano, third movement

Chapter 53. Johann Sebastian Bach

Fugue in G Minor (*Little*)
Prelude and Fugue in C Minor from the *Well-Tempered Clavier*, Vol. 1
Concerto in D Minor for Two Violins
Cantata No. 4, *Christ lag in Todesbanden*
Mass in B Minor
Toccata and Fugue in D Minor
Fantasia and Fugue in G Minor
Chorale, *Jesu, Joy of Man's Desiring*
Brandenburg Concerto No. 2 in F Major
Suite No. 3 in D Major for Orchestra
Passacaglia in C Minor
Chaconne in D Minor

Chapter 54. George Frideric Handel

Messiah
Water Music
Concerto in D Minor for Organ

Concerto Grosso in G Major, Op. 6, No. 1
Judas Maccabaeus

Chapter 56. Giacomo Puccini

La Bohème
Tosca
Madame Butterfly

Chapter 57. Richard Strauss

Till Eulenspiegel
Don Juan
Death and Transfiguration
Der Rosenkavalier

Chapter 58. Jan Sibelius

Finlandia
The Swan of Tuonela
Symphony No. 1

Chapter 60. Claude Debussy

The Afternoon of a Faun
Fêtes
La Mer
Mandoline
La Soirée dans Granade

Chapter 61. Maurice Ravel

Daphnis and Chloë Suite No. 2
Bolero
Jeux d'Eau
Ma Mère l'Oye
Rhapsodie Espagnole
Le Tombeau de Couperin
La Valse

Chapter 65. Igor Stravinsky

Petrushka
The Firebird
The Rite of Spring
L'Histoire du Soldat (The Soldier's Tale)
Symphony of Psalms

Chapter 66. Arnold Schoenberg

Verklärte Nacht (Transfigured Night)
Serenade, Op. 24
Gurrelieder

Chapter 67. Béla Bartók

Concerto for Orchestra
Music for Strings, Percussion, and Celesta
Concerto No. 3 for Piano

Chapter 68. The (American) Past

MacDowell, *Woodland Sketches*
———, *New England Idyls*
———, *Indian Suite*
Loeffler, *A Pagan Poem*

Chapter 70. The Senior Group

Griffes, *The White Peacock*
Ives, *Three Places in New England*
Varèse, *Ionisation*
Carpenter, *Adventures in a Perambulator*
Riegger, *New Dance*
Villa-Lobos, *Seréstas*

Chapter 71. The Middle Generation

Moore, Symphony in A
Piston, *The Incredible Flutist*
———, Symphony No. 2
Thomson, Virgil, *Louisiana Story*
———, *Four Saints in Three Acts*
Sessions, *The Black Maskers*
Hanson, Symphony No. 2 (*Romantic*)
Gershwin, *An American in Paris*
———, *Porgy and Bess*
———, Concerto in F
———, *Rhapsody in Blue*
Copland, *Billy the Kid*
———, *Appalachian Spring*
———, *El Salón México*
Thompson, Randall, *The Testament of Freedom*
Cowell, Symphony No. 4

Chapter 72. The Younger Men

Blitzstein, *Airborne Symphony*
———, *The Cradle Will Rock*

Barber, *Knoxville, Summer of 1915*
———, Overture, *School for Scandal*
———, Adagio for Strings
———, *Music for a Scene from Shelley*
Schuman, *Undertow*
———, *Judith*
Menotti, *The Medium*
———, *The Consul*
———, *The Telephone*
Dello Joio, *New York Profiles*
———, *Triumph of St. Joan Symphony*
Gould, *Spirituals for Orchestra*
———, *Fall River Legend*
Diamond, *Music for Shakespeare's Romeo and Juliet*
———, Rounds for String Orchestra
Bernstein, *Jeremiah Symphony*
———, *Fancy Free*

❧APPENDIX II❧
A List of Books

IT IS neither possible nor desirable to append a detailed bibliography. Any list selected from so vast a literature as that on music would appear to represent an arbitrary choice. The following list includes reference works in which those who wish to pursue the subject further will find comprehensive bibliographies to guide them, as well as a small selection of books of general interest to the music lover.

ON THE NATURE OF ART

Dewey, John. *Art as Experience.* New York: G. P. Putnam's Sons, 1934.
Read, Herbert. *Art and Society.* New York: Pantheon Books, 1945.
Sachs, Curt. *The Commonwealth of Art.* New York: W. W. Norton & Company, 1946.

DICTIONARIES

Apel, Willi. *Harvard Dictionary of Music.* Cambridge: Harvard University Press, 1944.
Grove, George. *Grove's Dictionary of Music and Musicians.* New York: The Macmillan Company, 1954.
Thompson, Oscar, and Slonimsky, Nicolas. *International Encyclopedia of Music and Musicians.* New York: Dodd, Mead & Company, 1953.

THE ELEMENTS OF MUSIC

Boatwright, Howard. *Introduction to the Theory of Music.* New York: W. W. Norton & Company, 1956.

Copland, Aaron. *What to Listen for in Music.* New York: Whittlesey House, 1939.

Moore, Douglas. *Listening to Music.* New York: W. W. Norton & Company, 1937.

Grove's Dictionary of Music and *Harvard Dictionary of Music:* articles on melody, harmony, rhythm, meter, tempo, timbre, etc.

MUSIC HISTORY (single-volume works)

Einstein, Alfred. *A Short History of Music.* New York: Alfred A. Knopf, 1947.

Lang, Paul Henry. *Music in Western Civilization.* New York: W. W. Norton & Company, 1941.

Leichtentritt, Hugo. *Music, History and Ideas.* Cambridge: Harvard University Press, 1938.

Sachs, Curt. *Our Musical Heritage: A Short History of Music.* New York: Prentice Hall, 1948.

COMPOSERS AND MUSICAL PERIODS

Abraham, Gerald. *This Modern Music.* New York: W. W. Norton & Company, 1952.

Anderson, Emily (ed. and tr.). *The Letters of Mozart and His Family.* New York: The Macmillan Company, 1938.

Bauer, Marion. *Twentieth Century Music.* New York: G. P. Putnam's Sons, 1947.

Berlioz, Hector. *Memoirs.* New York: Alfred A. Knopf, 1948.

Copland, Aaron. *Our New Music.* New York: Whittlesey House, 1941.

————. *Music and Imagination.* Cambridge: Harvard University Press, 1952.

Demuth, Norman. *César Franck.* New York: Philosophical Library, 1949.

Einstein, Alfred. *Gluck.* London: J. M. Dent & Sons, 1936.

————. *Mozart: His Character, His Work.* New York: Oxford University Press, 1945.

————. *Music in the Romantic Era.* New York: W. W. Norton & Company, 1947.

————. *Schubert: A Musical Portrait.* New York: Oxford University Press, 1951.

Geiringer, Karl. *Brahms: His Life and Work.* New York: Oxford University Press, 1947.

————. *Haydn: A Creative Life in Music.* New York: W. W. Norton & Company, 1946.

Gray, Cecil. *Sibelius.* New York: Oxford University Press, 1934.

Grove, George. *Beethoven, Schubert, Mendelssohn.* New York: The Macmillan Company, 1951.

Hindemith, Paul. *A Composer's World.* Cambridge: Harvard University Press, 1952.

Kirkpatrick, Ralph. *Domenico Scarlatti.* New York: Alfred A. Knopf, 1953.

Leyda, Jay, and Bertensson, S. *The Musorgsky Reader: A Life of Modeste Petrovich Musorgsky in Letters and Documents.* New York: W. W. Norton & Company, 1947.

Locke, Arthur W. *Music and the Romantic Movement in France.* New York: E. P. Dutton & Company, 1920.

Mahler, Alma Maria. *Gustav Mahler: Memories and Letters.* New York: The Viking Press, 1946.

Marek, George. *Puccini: A Biography.* New York: Simon & Schuster, 1951.

Myers, Rollo H. *Erik Satie.* London: Dennis Dobson, 1948.

Newman, Ernest. *The Life of Richard Wagner.* 4 vols. New York: Alfred A. Knopf, 1933–46.

———. *Wagner as Man and Artist.* New York: Alfred A. Knopf, 1924.

Panassie, Hugues. *The Real Jazz.* New York: Crown Publishers, 1950.

Praz, Mario. *The Romantic Agony.* New York: Oxford University Press, 1951.

Puccini, Giacomo. *Letters.* Philadelphia: J. F. Lippincott Company, 1931.

Reich, Willi. *Alban Berg.* London: Dennis Dobson.

Reis, Claire R. *Composers in America.* New York: The Macmillan Company, 1947.

Rimsky-Korsakov, Nicholas. *My Musical Life.* New York: Alfred A. Knopf, 1942.

Sargeant, Winthrop. *Jazz: Hot and Hybrid.* New York: E. P. Dutton & Company, 1946.

Schoenberg, Arnold. *Style and Idea.* New York: Philosophical Library, 1950.

Schrade, Leo. *Monteverdi: Creator of Modern Music.* New York: W. W. Norton & Company, 1950.

Schumann, Robert. *On Music and Musicians.* New York: Pantheon Books, 1946.

Seroff, Victor I. *Rachmaninov.* New York: Simon and Schuster, 1950.

Sessions, Roger. *The Musical Experience of Composer, Performer, Listener.* Princeton: Princeton University Press, 1950.

Sitwell, Sacheverell. *Liszt.* Boston: Houghton Mifflin Company, 1934.

Slonimsky, Nicolas. *Music Since 1900.* New York: Coleman-Ross Company, 1949.

Stevens, Halsey. *Béla Bartók.* New York: Oxford University Press, 1953.

Strauss, Richard. *Correspondence with Hugo von Hofmannsthal.* New York: Alfred A. Knopf, 1927.

Stravinsky, Igor. *Autobiography.* New York: Simon and Schuster, 1936.

———. *Poetics of Music.* Cambridge: Harvard University Press, 1947.

Sullivan, J. W. N. *Beethoven: His Spiritual Development.* New York: Alfred A. Knopf, 1947.

Terry, Charles Sanford. *Bach: A Biography.* New York: Oxford University Press, 1933.

Thompson, Oscar. *Debussy: Man and Artist.* New York: Dodd, Mead & Company, 1937.

———. *Great Modern Composers.* New York: Dodd, Mead & Company, 1941.

Thomson, Virgil. *The Art of Judging Music.* New York: Alfred A. Knopf, 1948.

Toye, Francis. *Giuseppe Verdi: His Life and Works.* New York: Alfred A. Knopf, 1946.

Turner, W. J. *Beethoven: The Search for Reality.* London: J. M. Dent & Sons, 1933.

Weinstock, Herbert. *Chopin: The Man and His Music.* New York: Alfred A. Knopf, 1949.

———. *Tchaikovsky.* New York: Alfred A. Knopf, 1943.

APPENDIX III

Comparative Range of the Instruments

THE HUMAN VOICE

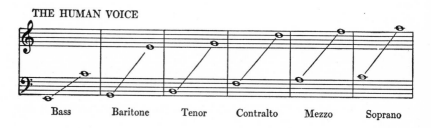

| Bass | Baritone | Tenor | Contralto | Mezzo | Soprano |

STRINGED INSTRUMENTS

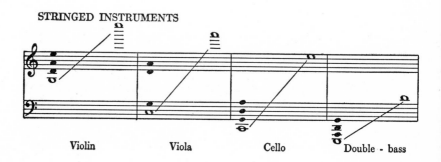

| Violin | Viola | Cello | Double - bass |

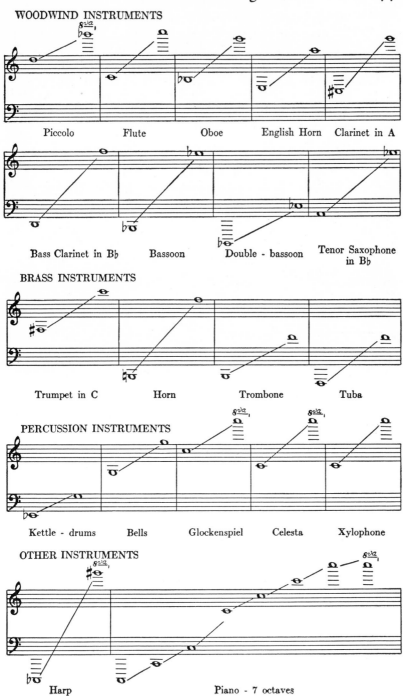

❧APPENDIX IV❧
Complete List of Major and Minor Scales

≫APPENDIX V≪

A Chronological List of Composers, 1600-1900 with Parallel Tables of World Events and Principal Figures in Literature and the Arts

(The list of composers does not presume to be complete. It includes those mentioned in the text born prior to 1900 and some additional names.)

BAROQUE (1600–1750) AND ROCOCO (1700–1775)		

Claudio Monteverdi (1567–1643)

1607 Jamestown settled.
1609 Henry Hudson explores Hudson River.
1618–48 Thirty Years' War.
1620 Mayflower Compact. Plymouth settled. Francis Bacon's *Novum Organum.*
1626 Manhattan Island purchased from Indians.
1628 Harvey discovers circulation of blood.
1637 Descartes, *Discourse on Method.*

Jean-Baptiste Lully (1632–87)

Dietrich Buxtehude (1637–1707)

1640–49 Puritan Revolution in England.
1649–60 Commonwealth and Protectorate in England.

Arcangelo Corelli (1653–1713)

1651 Hobbes' *Leviathan*
1661–1715 Reign of Louis XIV. Absolutism.
1664 New Amsterdam becomes New York

Henry Purcell (1659–95)

1666 Newton discovers Law of Gravity.

John Donne (1573–1631)

Ben Jonson (1573–1637)

Peter Paul Rubens (1577–1640)

Franz Hals (1580?–1666)

Giovanni Lorenzo Bernini (1598–1680)

Anthony Van Dyck (1599–1641)

Diego Velázquez (1599–1660)

Rembrandt van Ryn (1606–69)

Pierre Corneille (1606–84)

John Milton (1608–74)

Molière (1622–73)

François Couperin (1668–1733)

Antonio Vivaldi (1676–1741)

Georg Telemann (1681–1767)

Jean-Philippe Rameau (1683–1764)

Johann Sebastian Bach (1685–1750)

Domenico Scarlatti (1685–1757)

George Frideric Handel (1685–1759)

Giovanni Battista Pergolesi (1710–36)

PRE-CLASSICAL

(C. 1740–75)

Christoph Willibald Gluck (1714–75)

Carl Philipp Emanuel Bach (1714–88)

Johann Stamitz (1717–57)

1667 Spinoza's *Ethics*.
1669 Academy of Music (Paris Opera) founded.
1682–1725 Reign of Peter the Great.
1690 Locke's *Two Treatises on Civil Government*.
1702–14 War of the Spanish Succession.
1712 Queen Anne succeeded by George I, Handel's Patron.
1715 First Opéra Comique founded.
1715–74 Reign of Louis XV.
1719 Herculaneum and Pompeii rediscovered. Classical Revival.
1732 Linnaeus's *System of Nature*.
1732–99 George Washington.
1737 San Carlo Opera, Naples, opened.
1740–96 Age of Enlightened Despots.
1743–1826 Thomas Jefferson.
1751–72 Great Encyclopedia. Age of Enlightenment. Sensibility.

1752 Franklin's discoveries in electricity.

1756–63 Seven Years' War (in America, the French and Indian War).

1759 Wolfe captures Quebec.

1763 Canada ceded to England.

1765 Watt's steam engine.

1767 Hargreaves' spinning jenny.

c. 1770 Beginning of the factory system.

1771 First edition, *Encyclopedia Britannica*.

John Bunyan (1628–88)

John Dryden (1631–1700)

Jan Vermeer (1632–75)

Sir Christopher Wren (1632–1723)

Jean Baptiste Racine (1639–99)

Daniel Defoe (1659?–1731)

Jonathan Swift (1667–1745)

Joseph Addison (1672–1719)

Richard Steele (1672–1729)

Jean Antoine Watteau (1684–1721)

Alexander Pope (1688–1744)

Voltaire (1694–1778)

Giovanni Battista Tiepolo (1696–1770)

William Hogarth (1697–1764)

François Boucher (1703–70)

Henry Fielding (1707–54)

Samuel Johnson (1709–84)

Jean Jacques Rousseau (1712–78)

Laurence Sterne (1713–68)

Thomas Gray (1716–71)

Sir Joshua Reynolds (1723–92)

Thomas Gainsborough (1727–88)

Oliver Goldsmith (1728–74)

Pierre Augustin Caron Beaumarchais (1732–99)

Jean Honoré Fragonard (1732–1809)

Edward Gibbon (1737–94)

Johann Christian Bach (1735–82)

Domenico Cimarosa (1749–1801)

THE CLASSIC
PERIOD
(1775–1825)

Joseph Haydn (1732–1809)

Wolfgang Amadeus Mozart (1756–91)

Maria Luigi Cherubini (1760–1842)

Ludwig van Beethoven (1770–1827)

Gasparo Spontini (1774–1851)

THE ROMANTIC
PERIOD
c. 1820–1900)

*1. From Classic
to Romantic
(1800–c. 1830)*

Carl Maria von Weber (1786–1826)

Franz Schubert (1797–1828)

1774 Priestley discovers oxygen.

1775–83 American Revolution.

1776 Declaration of Independence.
1776 Adam Smith's *The Wealth of Nations.*

1778 La Scala Opera opened in Milan.

1781 Kant's *Critique of Pure Reason.*

1787 Constitutional Convention.

1788 Fitch's steamboat.

1789–94 French Revolution.

1791 Bill of Rights. Second Opéra Comique opened.

1793 Eli Whitney's cotton gin.

1796 Jenner begins vaccination.

1798 Malthus's *Essay on Population.*

1800 Laplace's mechanistic view of universe. Volta invents voltaic pile.

1803 Louisiana Purchase.

1807 Hegel's *Phenomenology of the Mind.*

1808 Fulton's steamboat.

1812 Napoleon invades Russia.

Jean Antoine Houdon (1741–1828)
Francisco José de Goya (1746–1828)
Jacques Louis David (1748–1825)
Johann Wolfgang von Goethe (1749–1832)
William Blake (1757–1827)
Robert Burns (1759–96)
Johann Christoph Friedrich von Schiller (1759–1805)
Charles Bulfinch (1763–1844)
William Wordsworth (1770–1850)
Sir Walter Scott (1771–1832)
Samuel Taylor Coleridge (1772–1834)
J. M. W. Turner (1775–1851)
John Constable (1776–1837)
Jean Auguste Dominique Ingres (1780–1867)
George Gordon Byron (1788–1824)
Alphonse Lamartine (1790–1869)
Jean Louis Géricault (1791–1824)
Percy Bysshe Shelley (1792–1822)
John Keats (1795–1821)
Thomas Carlyle (1795–1881)
John Baptiste Camille Corot (1796–1875)
Alexander Pushkin (1799–1837)
Honoré de Balzac (1799–1850)
Ferdinand Victor Eugène Delacroix (1799–1863)
Alexander Dumas (1802–70)
Victor Hugo (1802–85)

2. Romanticism, First Phase (c. 1830–c. 1850)

Niccolo Paganini (1782–1840)

Giacomo Meyerbeer (1791–1864)
Gioacchino Rossini (1792–1868)

Gaetano Donizetti (1797–1848)

Vincenzo Bellini (1801–35)

Johann Strauss (the father: 1804–49)

Michael Glinka (1804–57)

Felix Mendelssohn (1809–47)

Frédéric François Chopin (1810–49)

Robert Schumann (1810–56)

3. Romanticism, Mid-Nineteenth Century (c. 1840–c. 1880)

Hector Berlioz (1803–69)

Franz Liszt (1811–86)

Richard Wagner (1813–83)

1815 Battle of Waterloo. Congress of Vienna.

1817 Ricardo's *Political Economy and Taxation.*

1819 First steamship to cross Atlantic.

1823 Monroe Doctrine.
1824 Bolivar liberates South America. Stephenson's locomotive.

1829 Independence of Greece.

1830 First railroad, Liverpool-Manchester. July Revolution in France.

1832 Morse invents telegraph.

1833 Slavery outlawed in British Empire.

1834 McCormick patents mechanical reaper.

1837–1901 Victoria's reign.

1839 Daguerreotype invented, beginnings of photography. N. Y. Philharmonic Society founded. Vienna Philharmonic founded.

1842 Long uses ether as anaesthetic.

1843 Leipzig Conservatory founded.

1846 Repeal of Corn laws. Famine in Ireland.

1848 Revolution throughout Europe.

Ralph Waldo Emerson (1803–82)
Nathaniel Hawthorne (1804–64)
George Sand (1804–76)
Honoré Daumier (1808–79)
Edgar Allan Poe (1809–49)
Nikolai Gogol (1809–52)
Alfred Tennyson (1809–92)
William Makepeace Thackeray (1811–63)
Charles Dickens (1812–70)
Robert Browning (1812–89)
Charlotte Brontë (1816–55)
Henry David Thoreau (1817–62)
Emily Brontë (1818–48)
Ivan Sergeevich Turgeniev (1818–83)
George Eliot (1819–80)
Herman Melville (1819–91)
Walt Whitman (1819–92)
John Ruskin (1819–1900)
Pierre Charles Baudelaire (1821–67)
Gustave Flaubert (1821–80)
Feodor Mikhailovich Dostoievsky (1821–81)
Dante Gabriel Rossetti (1828–82)
Henrik Ibsen (1828–1906)
George Meredith (1828–1909)
Leo Nikolaevich Tolstoi (1828–1910)
Emily Dickinson (1830–86)

Giuseppe Verdi
(1813–1901)

4. Late Romanticism
(c. 1870–c. 1900)

Charles Gounod
(1818–93)

Jacques Offenbach
(1819–80)

César Franck (1822–90)

Édouard Lalo (1823–92)

Bedřich Smetana
(1824–84)

Anton Bruckner
(1824–96)

Johann Strauss (the son: 1825–99)

Stephen Collins Foster
(1826–64)

Johannes Brahms
(1833–97)

Alexander Borodin
(1834–87)

Camille Saint-Saëns
(1835–1921)

Léo Delibes (1836–91)

Mily Balakirev (1836–1910)

Georges Bizet (1838–75)

Modest Musorgsky
(1839–81)

Peter Ilyich Tchaikovsky (1840–93)

Alexis Emmanuel Chabrier (1841–94)

Antonin Dvořák
(1841–1904)

Sir Arthur Sullivan
(1841–1900)

Jules Massenet (1842–1908)

Edvard Grieg (1843–1907)

1848 Gold Rush in California. Mill's *Political Economy*. Marx's *Communist Manifesto*.

1852 Second Empire under Napoleon III. *Uncle Tom's Cabin* appears.

1853 Commodore Perry opens Japan to West. Crimean War.

1855 Charge of the Light Brigade.

1857 Dred Scott Decision.

1858 Covent Garden opened as opera house.

1859 Darwin's *Origin of Species*. John Brown raids Harper's Ferry.

1861 Serfs emancipated in Russia.

1861–65 Civil War in America.

1863 Emancipation Proclamation.

1865 Lincoln assassinated.

1866 Transatlantic cable completed.

1867 Marx's *Das Kapital* (first vol.). Alaska purchased.

1870 Franco-Prussian War. William I of Hohenzollern becomes German Emperor. Vatican Council proclaims papal infallibility.

1871 Paris Commune. Unification of Italy complete; Rome becomes capital. Stanley and Livingston in Africa.

1873 Dynamo developed.

1875 New Paris Opera House opened.

1876 Telephone invented. Internal-combustion engine. Bayreuth theater opened.

1877 Phonograph invented.

1880 Irish Insurrection.

1881 Tsar Alexander II assassinated. President Garfield shot.

Camille Pissarro
(1830–1903)

Édouard Manet (1832–83)

Pedro Antonio de Alarcón (1833–91)

James McNeill Whistler (1834–1903)

Hilaire Germain René Degas (1834–1917)

Mark Twain (1835–1910)

Winslow Homer
(1836–1910)

Algernon Charles Swinburne (1837–1909)

William Dean Howells (1837–1920)

H. H. Richardson
(1838–86)

Henry Adams (1838–1918)

Paul Cézanne (1839–1906)

Alphonse Daudet
(1840–97)

Émile Zola (1840–1902)

Auguste Rodin (1840–1917)

Claude Monet (1840–1926)

Thomas Hardy (1840–1928)

Pierre Auguste Renoir
(1841–1919)

Stéphane Mallarmé
(1842–98)

Henry James (1843–1916)

Paul Verlaine (1844–96)

Friedrich Wilhelm Nietzsche (1844–1900)

Anatole France (1844–1924)

Eugène Henri Paul Gauguin (1848–1903)

Augustus St. Gaudens
(1848–1907)

Nicholas Rimsky-Korsakov (1844–1908)

POST-
ROMANTICISM
(c. 1890–c. 1910)

Gabriel Fauré (1845–1924)

Henri Duparc (1848–1933)

Vincent d'Indy (1851–1931)

Engelbert Humperdinck (1854-1921)

Leoš Janáček (1854–1928)

Ernest Chausson (1855–99)

Sir Edward Elgar (1857–1934)

Ruggiero Leoncavallo (1858–1919)

Giacomo Puccini (1858–1924)

Hugo Wolf (1860–1903)

Isaac Albéniz (1860–1909)

Gustav Mahler (1860–1911)

Edward MacDowell (1861–1908)

Charles Martin Loeffler (1861–1935)

Claude Debussy (1862–1918)

Frederick Delius (1862–1934)

1881–1914 Panama Canal built. Boston Symphony founded.

1882 Koch discovers tuberculosis germ. Berlin Philharmonic founded.

1883 Brooklyn Bridge opened. Nietzsche's *Thus Spake Zarathustra*. Metropolitan Opera opened. Amsterdam Concertgebouw founded.

1884 Pasteur discovers inoculation against rabies.

1885 First electric street railway in U. S., in Baltimore.

1886 Statue of Liberty unveiled in New York Harbor.

1887 Daimler patents high-speed internal-combustion engine.

1889 Eiffel Tower, Paris World's Fair opened. Brazil expels emperor, becomes republic.

1890 Journey around world completed in 72 days.

1892 Duryea makes first American gas buggy.

1893 World's Columbian Exposition, Chicago.

1894 Nicholas II, last Tsar, ascends throne.

1894–1905 Dreyfus affair.

1895 Roentgen discovers X-rays. Pavlov discovers conditioned reflex. Marconi's wireless telegraphy.

1896 Becquerel finds radioactivity in uranium. Olympic games revived. Gold rush in Alaska.

1897 Queen Victoria's Diamond Jubilee.

Joris Karl Huysmans (1848–1907)

Guy de Maupassant (1850–93)

Robert Louis Stevenson (1850–94)

Vincent Van Gogh (1853–90)

Arthur Rimbaud (1854–91)

Oscar Wilde (1856–1900)

Louis H. Sullivan (1856–1924)

John Singer Sargent (1856–1925)

George Bernard Shaw (1856–1950)

Joseph Conrad (1857–1924)

Georges Seurat (1859–91)

A. E. Housman (1859–1936)

Anton Chekov (1860–1904)

James M. Barrie (1860–1937)

Aristide Maillol (1861–1945)

Edith Wharton (1862–1937)

Gerhart Hauptmann (1862–1946)

Maurice Maeterlinck (1862–1949)

Paul Signac (1863–1935)

Gabriele D'Annunzio (1863–1938)

George Gray Barnard (1863–1938)

Henri de Toulouse-Lautrec (1864–1901)

Rudyard Kipling (1865–1936)

William Butler Yeats (1865–1939)

Romain Rolland (1866–1943)

Wassily Kandinsky (1866–1944)

H. G. Wells (1866–1946)

Pietro Mascagni
(1863–1945)

Richard Strauss
(1864–1949)
Alexander Grechani-
nov (1864–1956)

Paul Dukas (1865–
1935)

Alexander Glazunov
(1865–1936)

Jan Sibelius (1865–)

Ferrucio Busoni
(1866–1924)

Erik Satie (1866–
1925)

Enrique Granados
(1867–1916)

Albert Roussel (1869–
1937)

1898 Pierre and Marie Curie discover radium. Empress Eliza-
beth of Austria-Hungary assassinated. Spanish-American
War.

1899 Boer War. First International Peace Conference at the
Hague.
1900 Boxer Insurrection in
China. Count Zeppelin tests
dirigible balloon. Philadelphia
Symphony founded.

1901 Queen Victoria dies, Edward VII succeeds. De Vries'
mutation theory.
1903 Wrights' first successful
airplane flight. Ford organizes
motor company.

1904–05 Russo-Japanese War.
London Symphony founded.

1905 Sigmund Freud founds psy-
choanalysis. Norway separates
from Sweden. First Russian
Revolution.

1905–10 Einstein's theories.

1906 San Francisco earthquake
and fire.

1907 Second Hague Conference.
Triple Entente. William
James's *Pragmatism.*

1908 Model T Ford produced.

1909 Peary reaches North Pole.

Arnold Bennett (1867–
1931)
John Galsworthy
(1867–1933)
Luigi Pirandello
(1867–1936)
Edmond Rostand
(1868–1918)
Stefan Georg (1868–
1933)
Maxim Gorky (1868–
1936)
Edward Arlington
Robinson (1869–
1935)
Henri Matisse (1869–
1954)
Frank Lloyd Wright
(1869–)
Stephen Crane (1870–
1900)
Ignacio Zuloaga
(1870–1945)
André Gide (1870–
1951)
John Marin (1870–
1953)
John M. Synge (1871–
1909)
Marcel Proust (1871–
1922)
Theodore Dreiser
(1871–1945)
Georges Rouault
(1871–)
Sergei Diaghilev
(1872–1929)
Piet Mondrian (1872–
1946)
Willa Cather (1873–
1947)
Hugo von Hofmanns-
thal (1874–1929)
G. K. Chesterton
(1874–1936)
Gertrude Stein (1874–
1946)
W. Somerset
Maugham (1874–)
Rainer Maria Rilke
(1875–1926)
Thomas Mann (1875–
1955)

CONTEMPORARY
MUSIC
1910–

Alexander Scriabin (1871–1915)

Ralph Vaughan Williams (1872–)

Max Reger (1873–1916)

Sergei Rachmaninov (1873–1943)

Arnold Schoenberg (1874–1950)

Charles Ives (1874–1954)

Gustav Holst (1874–1934)

Maurice Ravel (1875–1937)

Manuel de Falla (1876–1946)

John Alden Carpenter (1876–1951)

Carl Ruggles (1876–)

Ottorino Respighi (1879–1936)

Cyril Scott (1879–)

Ernest Bloch (1880–)

Ildebrando Pizzetti (1880–)

Béla Bartók (1881–1945)

Georges Enesco (1881–1955)

Heitor Villa-Lobos (1881–)

Igor Stravinsky (1882–)

Zoltán Kodály (1882–)

Francesco Malipiero (1882–)

Karol Szymanowski (1883–1937)

Anton von Webern (1883–1945)

Alfredo Cassella (1883–1947)

Arnold Bax (1883–)

Charles T. Griffes (1884–1920)

Alban Berg (1885–1935)

1910 Discovery of protons and electrons. Edward VII dies, George V succeeds.

1911 Amundsen reaches South Pole.

1912 China becomes republic. *Titanic* sinks.

1912–13 Balkan Wars.
1914–18 World War I.

1915 *Lusitania* sunk.

1916 Battle of Verdun.

1917 U. S. enters World War I. Russian Revolution. Prohibition Amendment.

1918 Kaiser abdicates. End of World War I.

1919 Treaty of Versailles. League of Nations formed.

1920 Nineteenth Amendment (women's suffrage).

1922 Discovery of insulin. Fascist revolution in Italy. John Dewey's *Human Nature and Conduct*.

1924 Lenin dies.

1927 Lindbergh's solo flight across Atlantic.

1928 First all-talking film. *Graf Zeppelin* crosses Atlantic. First radio broadcast N. Y. Philharmonic Orchestra.

1930 Penicillin discovered.

1931 Japan invades Manchuria. Empire State Building completed.

1933 Franklin D. Roosevelt inaugurated. Hitler takes over German government.

Robert Frost (1875–)

O. E. Rolvaag (1876–)

Constantine Brancusi (1876–)

Maurice Vlaminck (1876–)

Isadora Duncan (1877–1927)

Marsden Hartley (1877–1943)

John Masefield (1878–)

Vachel Lindsay (1879–1940)

Paul Klee (1879–1940)

E. M. Forster (1879–)

Raoul Dufy (1879–1953)

Jacob Epstein (1880–)

Fernand Léger (1881–1955)

Pablo Picasso (1881–)

Martinez Sierra (1881–)

Georges Braque (1881–)

James Joyce (1882–1941)

Jean Giraudoux (1882–1944)

Virginia Woolf (1882–1945)

Franz Kafka (1883–1924)

Kahlil Gibran (1883–1931)

José Clemente Orozco (1883–)

Maurice Utrillo (1883–1955)

José Ortega y Gasset (1883–1954)

Amadeo Modigliani (1884–1920)

Georges Duhamel (1884–)

D. H. Lawrence (1885–1950)

Edgar Varèse
(1885–)
Wallingford Riegger
(1885–)
Jaromir Weinberger
(1886–)
Ernest Toch
(1887–)
Bohuslav Martinu
(1890–)

Jacques Ibert
(1890–)
Sergei Prokofiev
(1891–1952)
Arthur Bliss (1891–)
Darius Milhaud
(1892–)
Arthur Honegger
(1892–1955)
Douglas Moore
(1893–)
Walter Piston
(1894–)
Karol Rathaus
(1895–1954)
Paul Hindemith
(1895–)
Leo Sowerby
(1895–)
William Grant Still
(1895–)
Virgil Thomson
(1896–)
Howard Hanson
(1896–)
Roger Sessions
(1896–)
Henry Cowell
(1897–)
Quincy Porter
(1897–)
George Gershwin
(1898–1937)
Ernst Bacon (1898–)
Roy Harris (1898–)
Carlos Chavez
(1899–)
Randall Thompson
(1899–)
Francis Poulenc
(1899–)
Kurt Weill (1900–
1950)
Aaron Copland
(1900–)

1935 Italy invades Ethiopia.

1936 Sit-down strike first used.
Sulfa drugs introduced into
U. S.

1937 Japan invades China. Spanish Civil War. Nylon introduced.
1938 Munich appeasement.

1939 World War II starts: Germany invades Poland. Britain
and France declare war on
Germany. Russia invades Finland. U. S. revises neutrality
stand.

1940 Roosevelt elected to third
term. First radio broadcast of
Metropolitan Opera performance.

1941 U. S. attacked by Japan,
declares war on Japan, Germany, Italy.

1942 United Nations Alliance.
Allied North African cam-
paign successful.

1943 Italy surrenders.

1944 Allies invade Germany.
Roosevelt elected to fourth
term.

1945 Germany surrenders. Atom
bomb used against Japan, Japan surrenders. New York becomes seat of United Nations.
Franklin D. Roosevelt dies.

1946 First assembly of United
Nations.

1947 Marshall Plan implemented.

1948 State of Israel proclaimed.

1949 North Atlantic Defense
Pact. China passes to Commu-
nism.

Sinclair Lewis
(1885–1951)
François Mauriac
(1885–)
André Maurois
(1885–)
Diego Rivera
(1886–)
William Zorach
(1887–)
Mary Ellen Chase
(1887–)
Georgia O'Keeffe
(1887–)
Alexander Archipenko
(1887–)
Marc Chagall
(1887–)
T. E. Lawrence
(1888–1935)
Giorgio de Chirico
(1888–)
Thomas Hart Benton
(1889–)
Karel Čapek (1890–
1938)
Grant Wood (1892–
1944)
John P. Marquand
(1893–)
Carlos Merida
(1893–)
Joan Miro (1893–)
E. E. Cummings
(1894–)
Aldous Huxley
(1894–)
F. Scott Fitzgerald
(1896–1940)
William Faulkner
(1897–)
Sergei Eisenstein
(1898–1948)
Ernest Hemingway
(1898–)
Alexander Calder
(1898–)
Stephen Vincent Benét
(1899–1943)
C. S. Forester
(1899–)
Hart Crane (1899–
1932)
Eugene Berman
(1899–)

George Antheil
(1900–)
Otto Luening
(1900–)
Ernst Křenek
(1900–)

1950 Korean War starts. Atomic Energy Commission plans hydrogen bomb.

Rufino Tamayo
(1899–)
Thomas Wolfe
(1900–1938)

Index

Definitions or illustrations will be found on pages indicated by boldface numbers.

453

Index